THE
KENNEDY
BROTHERS

THE RISE AND FALL OF JACK AND BOBBY

RICHARD D. MAHONEY

Kennedy Scholar Emeritus of the University of Massachusetts

ARCADE PUBLISHING • NEW YORK

Arcade Publishing books may be purchased in bulk at special discounts for sales promotion, corporate gifts, fund-raising, or educational purposes. Special editions can also be created to specifications. For details, contact the Special Sales Department, Arcade Publishing, 307 West 36th Street, 11th Floor, New York, NY 10018 or info@skyhorsepublishing.com.

Arcade Publishing® is a registered trademark of Skyhorse Publishing, Inc.®, a Delaware corporation.

Visit our website at www.arcadepub.com.

10 9 8 7 6 5 4 3 2 1

Library of Congress Cataloging-in-Publication Data

Mahoney, Richard D.
 [Sons & brothers]
 The Kennedy brothers : the rise and fall of Jack and Bobby / Richard D. Mahoney.
    p. cm.
 Originally published as: Sons & brothers, c1999.
 Includes bibliographical references and index.
 ISBN 978-1-61145-048-4 (alk. paper)
 1. Kennedy, John F. (John Fitzgerald), 1917-1963. 2. Kennedy, Robert F., 1925-1968. 3. Presidents--United States--Biography. 4. Legislators--United States--Biography. 5. Brothers--United States--Biography. 6. United States. Congress. Senate--Biography. 7. United States--Politics and government--1961-1963. 8. United States--Politics and government--1963-1969. 9. Kennedy family. I. Title.
 E842.1.M34 2011
 973.922092'2--dc22
 [B]
                          2011004231

Printed in the United States of America

For
William P. Mahoney Jr.,
father and friend

"But sometimes in the middle of the night, their wound would open afresh. And suddenly awakened, they would finger its painful edges, they would recover their suffering anew and with it the stricken face of their love."

—Albert Camus, found in RFK's
commonplace book of quotes, entry circa 1966

CONTENTS

Acknowledgments

M y association and friendship with the exceptional staff, past and present, of the John F. Kennedy Library have made this book possible. Megan F. Desnoyers, William Johnson, Suzanne K. Forbes, Jo August, Sheldon Stern, John Stewart, Alan Goodrich, Jim Cedrone, Dan Fenn, and William W. Moss made the going bearable and, at points, even easy. They of course bear no responsibility for the result. My selection in 1987 as the John F. Kennedy Scholar by the Kennedy Library and the University of Massachusetts at Boston enabled me to do much of my research for this book.

I should also thank the staffs of the National Archives and Records Services, the Library of Congress, the FBI records office in Washington, D.C., the Adlai E. Stevenson Papers at Princeton University, the Chicago Crime Commission, and the Centro de Estudios Sobre América in Havana.

Among those who read portions of the manuscript along the way, made useful suggestions, and always encouraged to me to push on: Donavon Ostrom, Paul Erickson, Stanley Sheinbaum, Bill Gilliam, Chenoweth Moffat, Grant W. Johnson, Mary Jo West, and my sisters Noel Shambayati, Eileen Mahoney, and Mary Mahoney. My mother, Alice D. Mahoney, as always, provided criticism, insight, and the indispensable service of taking care of my daughter, Molly.

I should recognize others who went out of their way to assist me: Oliver Stone, Mayra I. Alvarado, Blas Casares, Andrew and Teresa Molander, Jorge Recarey, Eric J. Farber, Robert Scheer, Samuel E. Belk III, Ricardo Alarcón de Quesada, Peter McClennen, Samuel G. Vagenas, Kenneth and Katrina Carlsen, Paul Rosenfeld, Gene Fisher, and my teaching assistants at The American Graduate School of International Management, Thunderbird: Nozar Afkhami, Laura Wente, Elka Popova, Marilyn Edelman, and

Mark A. Staehle. Each semester my foreign policy seminar students at Thunderbird gladly read portions of the manuscript, and they deserve recognition for what improvements they made.

Among Kennedy friends and lieutenants who were especially helpful: Dolores Huerta, Harris Wofford, Angela Novello, the late W. Averell Harriman, the late George W. Ball, the late Kenneth P. O'Donnell, the late David F. Powers, the late Lord Harlech, the late Edmund A. Gullion, and the late Cesar Chavez. There are those in Havana and Miami for whom printed recognition would imperil their persons, but who provided information and guidance in this project. I thank them as well.

Without my father's friendship with the Kennedys and his attentive support for each of his nine children, including myself, I would not have attempted this journey. Without the unusual skill and grace in execution of my editor, Timothy Bent, I would not have completed it.

Introduction

My father was a friend of Robert F. Kennedy and an ambassadorial appointee of John F. Kennedy. He, and consequently the rest of our large Irish-American family, admired the Kennedys uncritically, a sentiment that was reinforced by the nature of their deaths. One of the last things Robert Kennedy did on June 5, 1968, in his suite at the Ambassador Hotel in Los Angeles before going downstairs to accept victory in the California primary was to make a list of friends he wanted to call when he got back to his room later that night. Among them was my father.

In March 1974, when I first went to the Federal Records Center in Waltham, Massachusetts, which then housed the Kennedy papers, I did so more in the manner of a pilgrim than a scholar. I was a member of the faithful, looking for evidence, even relics, of the blessed era. I would sit for hours in the poorly heated research room reading JFK's office files and the oral histories of RFK's brief run for the presidency six years earlier. I became friends with the late Dave Powers, then curator of the Kennedy Library, who had been Jack Kennedy's best friend. I would often drop by his office in the late afternoon and listen to him tell stories about the Kennedy brothers, Jack in particular. The figures Powers evoked fit my family's conception of them — men full of wit, charm, and purpose who, in those Watergate years, seemed nothing less than heroic.

Yet scholarship was beginning to offer a second, far harsher evaluation of the Kennedys. President Kennedy, some scholars charged, was responsible for bringing America into the nightmare of Vietnam. Other scholars claimed that Attorney General Robert Kennedy had, for reasons of political expedience, done the minimum on civil rights. I decided that I would take a look for myself at an area of the Kennedy record that had not yet been analyzed — the Kennedy administration's policy in Africa, where I had spent part of my youth.

Over the years, I became a familiar figure to the staff of the Kennedy Library. Much of my first book, *JFK: Ordeal in African*, published by Oxford University Press in 1983, was based on what I found in the National Security Files, which the library staff had effectively declassified. Between 1974 and 1980, I also did 223 oral history interviews. These encounters opened doors that led to unexpected places. I remember a winter day in 1976 in Princeton, New Jersey. At the conclusion of an interview with the late George Ball, undersecretary of state during the Kennedy years, he invited me to have a look at his transcribed telephone conversations, about ten thousand in number. For three weeks, I read through those telephone conversations in Ball's home, often leaving at daybreak and then returning a few hours later.

I was stunned by what they revealed. The picture they painted of the Kennedys was very different from the treasured anecdotes, those memorable and canonized speeches, or the top-secret memos covering "policy options." What emerged first were traits common to powerful men — expediency, calculation, and manipulation. But the transcriptions also revealed other qualities that were, I came to believe, unique to the Kennedys — an icy wit, an awareness that they were players on a stage, and a capacity for growth nurtured by their constant collaboration. Depending on the conversation, they could be idealistic or Machiavellian, utterly conventional or suddenly imaginative, hot or cold. The Kennedy brothers seemed neither as grand and omniscient as the "court histories" that sprang up after the president's assassination portrayed them, nor as cunning and shameless as later books, such as Seymour Hersh's *The Dark Side of Camelot,* argued. They were both self-creative and self-destructive.

I began to question the standard portrait of the male Kennedys as a perfectly functioning juggernaut. That Jack, Bobby, and their father, Joseph P. Kennedy, worked as seamlessly and relentlessly as a combat unit on their path to power seemed true. That Bobby, as executor of his father's fearsome will and facilitator of Jack's ambition, was the key actor in the triumvirate seemed obvious. But I heard accounts of tensions among them. Former Arizona senator Barry Goldwater, another friend of my father, told me that Bobby, in his crusade to destroy the American Mafia in the McClellan Committee investigation in the late 1950s (a committee on which Goldwater served), had stumbled over evidence of his father's dealings with the underworld. "It just killed him," Goldwater recalled. I wondered what other kinds of combustion Bobby's moral ambitions had touched off, both within and without the family.

In 1987 I was appointed the John F. Kennedy Scholar at the University of Massachusetts and the Kennedy Library. I spent a year lecturing, writing, and organizing symposia at the Kennedy Library. Revisionary analysis of the Kennedy years had shifted once again, this time to "character issues." Private sins were said to be revealing of the Kennedys' deficient public character. I gave a lecture in which I suggested that the Kennedy story might simply be a projection of America's own unresolved self-concept, its continuing pretense of politics as redemption. The Kennedys had become, I argued, "caricatures of our unsettled national psyche." They were "warped mirror-images of our own hopes, doubts, and indulgences." Thus they could only be saints or scoundrels, disinterred on occasion to reflect some current need to moralize to the body politic. I believed then and believe today that at the base of this tendency is America's inability to see its history as tragedy: to recognize, even embrace, the incompleteness of its ideals and its own struggle against doubt and violence. Perhaps by facing this we could come to a cathartic and settled view of ourselves and the Kennedys. "Tragedy," Bobby Kennedy said during his run for the presidency in 1968, "is a tool for the living." But we have found no such tool, and our literalness has rendered the Kennedys unrecognizable, even ahistoric. Something in their story was missing.

JFK's assassination was not a subject I ever thought I would research. Practically every frame of the Zapruder film has occasioned its own book. There seemed to be enough of them. But in my twenty-year journey as a Kennedy scholar, first on Africa, then on Vietnam, I had gotten glimpses of spectral linkages between that event and the administration itself. Ralph Dungan, a White House aide during the Johnson administration, once related to me how LBJ had told him, only days after the assassination, that JFK had died because of "divine retribution." And then there was Bobby's strange phone call only hours after Jack's assassination to a Cuban safe house in Washington. "One of your guys did it," he said, apparently referring to the anti-Castro Cubans living there. He asked director of the CIA John McCone whether the agency was involved in the murder. This was, to say the least, an extraordinary question. Another spectral link was Joe Kennedy's lunch with senior members of the Chicago Mafia in February 1960, when he tried to talk them into giving money to his son's presidential campaign. These were the same people his other son had vowed to bring to justice.

In the late 1970s, the House Select Committee on Assassinations dug deeply into the motives and the roles of everyone from the anti-Castro Cubans to renegade CIA operatives and the Mafia. In so doing, it built a formidable record. But one critical question remained unanswered: what was the relationship between the Kennedy administration and the Kennedy assassination?

In 1995, having completed a term as Arizona's secretary of state, I decided to try to answer that question. I reread transcripts of the interviews I'd done in the light of new scholarship published while I was in public office. I began traveling to Florida to interview Cuban exiles, to Chicago to look at the fading traces of the Kennedy-Mafia connection, and to Havana to search through Cuban records and gather recollections of the murderous contest between the Kennedy administration and the Castro regime. I also waded through FBI and CIA files, and spoke again to some of the principals I had once interviewed about other matters.

The story that emerged from the swirl of events and characters permitted no detached discourse; it was, rather, a narrative journey into the trackless wood through which Joe, Jack, and Bobby Kennedy had made their way. History as the Kennedys lived it was neither orderly nor obvious in its unfolding; it was a struggle in which the characters of the three men, and their interaction with one another, led to their fate — a struggle in which pride and avarice, fear and strength, and, above all, ignorance of what lay ahead provided them with an ill-fitting armature of engagement.

Armed with their ambition and their money, agnostic to their enemies, they moved onto the public stage as no family had before in American history, trying to understand and somehow master the terrain of their time. "Always the next hill, always the next hill," was the way one Kennedy lieutenant described Bobby's relentless drive. They moved beyond the normal boundaries of political power, crossing into a murderous frontier where their enemies, whose faces they knew, were waiting for them.

At the moment he received the news from Dallas on November 22, 1963, Bobby Kennedy sensed a terrible thing — that he himself had somehow contributed to his brother's murder. That is what this story is about.

THE
KENNEDY
BROTHERS

Summer 1929

Nantucket Sound

The story became a JFK favorite. One summer day when Bobby Kennedy was three and a half he went sailing with some of his brothers and sisters in a yawl in Nantucket Sound. Suddenly, he jumped into the chilly water and vainly struggled to swim. His brother Joe pulled him out before he went under and hauled him back into the boat. But Bobby jumped in again, intent on learning how to swim or drowning in the attempt. Jack would later observe: "It either showed a lot of guts, or no sense at all, depending on how you looked at it."

Crusades

1951 – 1959

October 19, 1951

Saigon, Vietnam

When thirty-four-year-old congressman John F. Kennedy landed at the French air base near Saigon, he and his brother Bobby and sister Pat were met by what appeared to be "half the French army" in full regalia.[1] The fact that the Americans were now providing about 50 percent of the French munitions and supplies in France's war against the communist Vietminh lent a certain cachet to the congressman's visit. It also made him a target for Vietminh terror.

For reasons of security, the State Department had recommended that Congressman Kennedy exclude Vietnam from his seven-nation itinerary in October 1951.[2] Saigon was a city under siege, the scene of anonymous grenade throwing during the day and nightly bombings by the Vietminh. Some of the terror was random, some targeted.[3] In April, American diplomat Edmund Gullion had witnessed the assassination of the head of the French Sûreté. In July, a Vietminh sapper had succeeded in getting close enough to French general Chanson to blow them both up, along with a provincial governor.[4] Pro-French agents roamed the city at night, detaining and sometimes executing suspected communists. The morning brought scenes of bodies, sometimes headless, drifting down the Saigon River. Despite this spectacle of tension and atrocity, Saigon, which in Vietnamese means "gift to the foreigner," still extended its languorous allure. Outside the wire netting around hotels like the Majestic, and beyond heavily armed troop cordons that protected government buildings, slender Vietnamese girls in white *ao dais* still plied their trade on the wide, tree-lined boulevards under the yellow glow of gaslights.

In addition to Vietnam, Kennedy planned to visit other countries in the throes of violent insurgency or civil war, such as Korea and Malaysia, as well as the newly independent states of Israel and India. The conviction in Washington was that the contest between the United States and the Soviet Union would be won or lost in the outcome of the nationalist upheavals attempting to shake off Europe's colonial grasp. Kennedy had joined the Republican right in its assault on President Harry Truman for having done nothing to stop the "onrushing tide of communism from engulfing all of Asia."[5] This was the prevailing view of the day. The "loss" of China to communism in 1949 and the catastrophic stalemate in Korea had produced a paroxysm of anger and self-doubt in Washington. Senator Joseph McCarthy charged that the reason Americans had "died for a tie" was that within the United States government itself existed "a [communist] conspiracy so immense, an infamy so black as to dwarf any in the history of man."

Kennedy was not the only American politician — Congressman Richard M. Nixon was another — to sense that there was critical ground to be gained or lost on this issue. By touring the anticommunist front personally, Congressman Kennedy could return as an authoritative voice on containment in Asia.[6] After four desultory years in the House, he was preparing to run in 1952 statewide in Massachusetts for either governor or senator.

If there was one distinguishing trait about Jack Kennedy among his peers outside the House chamber (where he was sometimes referred to as "Mattress Jack" for his sexual truancy), it was his flair for foreign policy. His first book, *Why England Slept,* stimulated in part by a two-month sojourn in Europe between his freshman and sophomore years at Harvard, had delineated the reasons for Great Britain's somnolence in the late 1930s in the face of Nazi rearmament and aggression. (One critic thought a more apt title might be *While Daddy Slept,* in reference to his father's accommodating attitude toward the Nazi onslaught while serving as the American ambassador in London.)[7] The book revealed Jack Kennedy to be a decided internationalist. More important, perhaps, it also showed a willingness to challenge the patriarch's exacting will. Whatever the old man's reservations about Jack's thinking, he suspended his beliefs in order to prime the national press about his son's trip. He also made sure Jack saw all the right people en route — Generals Dwight Eisenhower and Matthew Ridgway, Prime Minister Jawaharlal Nehru, the Indian nationalist and leader of the so-called nonaligned world.

The risk of a Vietminh attack notwithstanding, the most immediate danger to Congressman Kennedy, who gingerly made his way down the gangway of the military transport plane, was his own shattered health. He had only recently gotten off crutches following seven weeks of therapy designed to ease the pressure on his chronically painful back. A botched operation at the end of World War II had resulted in a metal plate being placed against his spine and had left an open eight-inch wound that had suppurated off and on for months. "Is any stuff running out of it?" his friend Charles Spalding remembered Jack asking as he hobbled along the beach in Hyannis Port.[8] For all the pain, Jack's humor survived. He wrote a friend that he wished "the doc had just read one more book before picking up the saw." To another, he sardonically described his own future as being moved to "the Old Sailors' Home probably to be issued a rocking chair, a sunny place on the lawn — with the thanks of a grateful Republic ringing in my ears."[9]

He was dying, he admitted to journalist Joseph Alsop, not because of his back but rather from Addison's disease, an insufficiency in adrenal production that left its victims fatally vulnerable to infection. "The doctors say I've got a sort of slow-motion leukemia, but they tell me I'll probably last until I'm forty-five."[10] What slowed Jack's decline was dexacortisone, which was injected daily into his thighs. Later he started taking 25 milligrams of cortisone orally each day, and received boosters of pain-killing novocaine directly into his back. All of these treatments became a carefully guarded family secret, attributed in news releases when Kennedy was intermittently hospitalized to "recurrent malaria and war-related injuries."

Perhaps this was why Joe Kennedy Sr. had recommended that third son Bobby, recently graduated from the University of Virginia law school, and sister Patricia accompany Jack on the seven-week trip. Jack had not previously traveled on international fact-finding trips with family members and there had been health problems out of the range of his specialists, their drugs, and the protective cover of his family. On a trip to England in 1948, Jack had become gravely ill, and word of his disease had nearly gotten into the press. (Lord Beaverbrook's physician, Daniel Davis, told Pamela Churchill, "That young American friend of yours, he hasn't got a year to live.")[11] But he somehow recovered. Once back in the United States, off his supposed deathbed, Jack soon rediscovered his life-long delight in pursuing pretty women between political appearances. This was a tricky practice in a puritanical age, one that had nearly gotten him cashiered out of the navy in 1942, for romantically consorting with Danish ingenue Inga Arvad, whom the FBI believed was a Nazi agent. Then — and later — Jack seemed oblivious to the risks in it all, despite his father's furious intercession. He eventually shipped out to the South Pacific and became a decorated hero, a status he later preferred to dismiss: "It was involuntary. They sank my boat."

Jack moved through his life both afflicted and charmed, shadowed and romanced by the possibility of death. Toward the end of World War Two, he kept a loose-leafed notebook that contained official and personal accounts of the deaths of his brother Joe and brother-in-law Billy Hartington, who were both killed in the European theater in 1944. Jack jotted down a quotation from British novelist and diplomat John Buchan: "He loved his youth, and his youth has become eternal. Debonair and brilliant and brave, he is now part of that immortal England which knows not age or weariness or defeat."[12] He admired courage above all other traits and, in the poetry he could recite by heart, felt death beckoning. This preoccupation had a paradoxical effect on Jack. It made him fatalistic about the human prospect, but coldly resolved once engaged in the fight. For all of this, his political ambition during the late '40s and early '50s seemed fitful, and it wasn't clear whether Kennedy had the drive to become president or merely to remain a playboy. His father and younger brother were the ones who bridged that difference.

Until his death in an experimental bombing mission over France in August 1944, Joe Jr. had carried the grail of his father's ambition to make a Kennedy president. Joe was an athletic and winning young man with matinee-idol looks. So deep was the wound left by Joe Jr.'s death that his father could not even open *As We Remember Joe*, the book of remembrances Jack had given his father for

Christmas. Jack wrote: "I think that if the Kennedy children amount to anything now or ever, it will be due more to Joe's behavior and his constant example than to any other factor."[13] The melancholy conclusion was that the best among them was dead and gone. What was left, in the unwanted phrase of the Kennedys, was the second string.

World War Two had breached the family like a wrecking ball. Joe Kennedy had traversed the golden salient during the 1920s and 1930s — making millions on the stock market, millions from Hollywood through the buying and selling of three studios, millions during Prohibition and afterward from bootlegging and cornering control over key liquor imports, and finally being appointed as the U.S. ambassador to the Court of St. James in 1938. By the middle 1940s, this had all crumbled. Joe Jr. was killed, as was son-in-law Billy Hartington, Kathleen's husband. Kathleen herself died in an air crash in 1948. Jack was a near-invalid. The war had left the Kennedy patriarch himself a reviled man who could neither admit nor expiate his disgrace as a World War Two defeatist and anti-Semite. There was something dark, even Faustian, about the old man's effect on others. As penetrating a judge of human character as Franklin Roosevelt had told Treasury secretary Henry Morgenthau on more than one occasion his reason for sending Kennedy to London: "He's too dangerous to allow around here."[14] Joe Kennedy's solace — the one thing he lived for other than making more money — was his sons. He told people that he himself was a caterpillar. His sons would be his butterflies.

In the late '40s and early '50s, at least, there was little evidence of such a metamorphosis. Jack was struggling terribly with his illnesses and Bobby, bottled-up and pathologically shy, was maladroit beyond measure. Having grown up in a family of male stars, of which he simply wasn't one, Bobby's duty had been to step aside for those who were. He had nothing of Joe's good looks or robust physique, or Jack's self-possessed bookishness. The family photos of Bobby as an adolescent during the '40s show an overcast, almost embarrassed, gaze. He was small, and in the first test of the Kennedy male — athletic achievement — he was a failure. "I dropped everything," he later recalled. "I always fell down. I always bumped my nose or head." Once at a party at the Kennedy home in Bronxville,

New York, Bobby picked up a glass of tomato juice with such force that he shattered it, sending the juice and shards of glass everywhere.[15] With brother Joe (ten years older) and brother Jack (eight years older) away at college or later in the war — and with his father as yet unable to detect anything worth advancing in his third son — he grew up in the company of his mother and three sisters (Eunice, Pat, and Jean), attending no fewer than ten different schools. He performed indifferently. For all of this, journalist and family friend Arthur Krock saw something unusual in the third son when he was fifteen, "a kind of savage individuality" born of compensation and struggle.[16]

The constant element in Bobby's life outside his family became the Catholic Church. He was an avid altar boy throughout high school. If Joe Jr. could tell you all about FDR's cabinet and brain trust, and Jack about Marlborough and Sir Walter Raleigh, Bobby knew the lives of the saints and their feast days. "Bobby has taken his religion seriously," his mother Rose commented, suggesting perhaps that her husband and the two older boys treated it more as a family ritual than as a system of personal belief.

Everything seemed to come hard to Bobby. When his father sent him up to Boston in 1946 to help out with Jack's campaign for Congress, the candidate didn't quite know what to do with his younger brother. "I can't see that sober, silent face breathing new vigor in the ranks," Jack observed to a friend, suggesting that Bobby be sent to the movies.[17] The friend, Paul Fay, found Bobby monosyllabic and mournful: "Words came out of his mouth as if each one spoken depleted an already severely limited supply. . . . From his expression he might have been paying his last respects to his closest friend."[18]

But if all detectable forms of political bonhomie were lacking, what was not was the steely drive to execute. Dave Powers, the unemployed World War Two veteran and Charlestown politico whom Jack befriended one evening in January 1946, remembered advising Bobby not to knock on people's doors before 8 A.M. or after 10 P.M. — "that way they might vote for Jack."[19] Powers estimated that Bobby was hitting around three hundred homes and apartments per day. "He looked like he was about sixteen but the effect he had was very positive. When he asked people to vote for Jack, you would have thought he was inviting them to enter the kingdom of heaven."

Bobby wasn't smooth but he was tough, very tough. After Jack's election, Bobby went back to Harvard, where his central ambition was to make the football team. As with the '46 campaign, his talent was sheer will. With unremitting practice and wild aggression, he won a letter in 1947, accomplishing the feat in the Harvard-Yale game with a fractured leg in a cast. "The major difference between Bobby and his brothers," said Ethel Skakel, whom he married in 1950 after nearly six years of courtship, "is that Bobby always had to fight for everything."[20] Marriage to Ethel confirmed him in the way his upbringing had not; she was his anima, his other self in the Jungian sense — giggly, outrageous, and deeply nurturing. A few months before his trip with Jack and Pat to the Middle East and Asia in October 1951, a daughter was born to Bobby and Ethel. They named her Kathleen Hartington, in memory of Bobby's deceased sister and her husband. Joe Kennedy Sr. saw and appreciated what Jack may have not — that in Bobby the family had a soldier who could work long hours in the shadows and ask nothing for it.

Along the way of their 25,000-mile trip in the fall of 1951, Bobby dutifully kept a journal in his cramped handwriting. The conclusion he and his brother reached was that nationalism was the determinant force of the age, stronger than either communism or capitalism, and that the United States was aligning itself with reactionary forces through second-rate diplomatic representation. They felt that the bipolar approach to containing communism wouldn't work because it usually meant association with discredited local despots or the embattled colonial powers. In country after country they visited, terrorism, putsches, full-scale civil warfare, seemed hours or even a few city blocks away. Two days after their meeting with Pakistani leader Liaquat Ali Khan, he was murdered. In India, Prime Minister Nehru warned them over dinner, between longing glances at their sister Pat, that the French and their Western supporters were, as Bobby wrote, "pouring money & arms down a bottomless hole." "We have only status quo to offer these people. Commies can offer a change."[21]

As Bobby explained it in 1967, the trip made a "very, very major impression" on his brother — and nowhere more so than

Vietnam.[22] After arriving and viewing the French *défilade* at the air base with General Jean De Lattre de Tassigny, the Kennedys were taken to the palace of South Vietnam's so-called strongman Bao Dai, who looked, Jack thought, as if he had been "fried in Crisco." They were "wined and dined" and housed in a single room, the only one in the palace that had air conditioning. His back giving him problems, Jack spent the night on the floor with Bobby and Pat alongside in the beds. General De Lattre personally took command of their tour from that point on, flying them over an area where the French Foreign Legion was doing battle with the Vietminh and presenting the Kennedys to the people of Hanoi in a flag-waving parade. ("Ironic," Bobby later said.)[23] The Kennedys came away deeply impressed by the redoubtable De Lattre — a brave man who had borne his own son's death before succumbing himself to cancer in 1952 — but did not buy the French line one bit. Back in Saigon, Jack and Bobby found out the names and addresses of the best reporters and showed up at their lodgings to get the real story. What they heard was that the French cause, for which the United States was now airlifting weaponry, was doomed. Were a plebiscite held throughout Vietnam, the communist Ho Chi Minh would get 70 percent of the vote, Bobby noted in his journal.

From Vietnam, the Kennedys traveled to Singapore, then to war-torn Malaysia, where they toured Kuala Lumpur, surrounded and under siege, in a tank. From there they flew to Japan, their last stop before Korea. Jack, having struggled throughout the trip with his bad back, was suddenly hit with a high fever, the result again of his failing immune system. Bobby and Pat had him airlifted to a military hospital in Okinawa where, during the first night, his fever rose to 106 degrees. Bobby later said, "Everybody there just expected that he'd die."[24] But slowly Jack's fever subsided and he was flown back to the United States. The family and its trusted retainers went into their denial routine, secreting Jack somewhere in Virginia, pending his improvement, and telling the press that his malaria had flared up again during the trip. During his convalescence, Jack drafted a radio address about his trip that he read on the Mutual Broadcasting Network on November 14. For its time, it was a farsighted exegesis about the defining power of Third World nationalism, which, Kennedy felt, was the proper bulwark against communism. It was also Kennedy's first enunciation of the doctrine of counterinsurgency, a policy that would bedevil his presidency in Vietnam and Cuba.

In his radio address, Jack blasted United States diplomats in insurgent Asia for "toadying" to the wishes of the European powers "with no eagerness to understand the real hopes and desires of the people to which they are accredited." He was also harsh in his criticism of American policy in Vietnam. "For the U.S. to have aligned itself with the desperate effort of a French regime to hang on to the remnants of empire" without exacting in exchange political reform in Indochina was a serious mistake. The war could only be won if France conceded independence to the Vietnamese. "To check the southern drive of Communism makes sense but not only through reliance on force of arms. The task is rather to build strong native non-Communist sentiment within these areas and rely on that as a spearhead of defense."[25] This sounded right, but hadn't Bobby written in his journal that Ho Chi Minh would win if there were elections? So which was it — Ho Chi Minh or the French? In statements during that fall of 1951 in New York and Massachusetts, Jack set forth the idea of a "third force" — both anti-French and anti-communist — that could satisfy nationalist aspirations as well as stymie the Vietminh. This, in fact, emerged as America's covert policy in Vietnam in 1952–1953, as the French war effort headed toward bloody defeat.

One witness to the Americanization of France's war in Vietnam was the English novelist Graham Greene, who had arrived for his second visit in October 1951. (As Jack lay at the edge of death in the military hospital in Okinawa on the night of October 31, Greene lay, awake but dreaming, in an opium den gazing at the lovely, sprawled figure of a woman as he recited Baudelaire's "Invitation au Voyage.")[26] Greene is thought to have patterned the hero of his novel *The Quiet American* on Edward Lansdale, an American counterinsurgency expert whom he met in Vietnam in 1954. In the novel, the earnest, enthusiastic CIA station chief Alden Pyle is doggedly determined to fight the communist Vietnamese the *American* way.[27] In theory, as Kennedy had advocated, this meant finding and arming that "third force." In practice, it meant giving the pretender, Colonel Thé, the newest generation of *plastique,* which produced in one sanguinary afternoon on la Rue Catinat in Saigon a sudden hurricane of human limbs. It was the perfect hell of good, anticommunist intentions — the old story of the ends justifying the means. It was also the prologue of the peculiar tragedy of the Kennedys, one in which Bobby, the moralist like Pyle, touched off a lethal chain reaction in his vendetta against Fidel Castro.

But this was to come later. The most important outcome of the trip was that in the course of 25,000 miles together — through palaces, military parades, states of siege, war zones, and the long hours of travel in between — these two sons became brothers. Jack, who had avoided what he thought was the leaden company of his dour younger brother, saw what Bobby's Harvard buddy Kenny O'Donnell valued so much — the wry humor, the hawklike power of observation, as well as his indefatigable determination to do his duty.[28] And Bobby, for the first time, enjoyed his older brother's encompassing curiosity and piquant humor. In Okinawa at the hospital, in the quiet hours when he thought Jack was going to die, Bobby must have also reflected on his brother's vulnerability.

Once home, Jack turned his energies toward running statewide in Massachusetts. Bobby joined the Justice Department and went to work in New York in the tax division. In April 1952, Jack got the break he'd been looking for: an open shot at the United States Senate when Governor Paul Dever decided to run for reelection. But the campaign was soon a complete mess due to Joe Kennedy's insistence on controlling everything and his habit of overriding campaign manager Mark Dalton. Jack seemed unwilling to or incapable of reining in his father, so Kenny O'Donnell, who was working on the Senate campaign, called his old Harvard football teammate Bobby Kennedy for help. But Bobby brushed him off: "Don't drag me into it," he told O'Donnell.[29] O'Donnell called him back twice the next day. "Jack's going to lose," he said. There was a long pause at the other end of the line.

"OK. OK." Then another pause. "Goddamnit." About a week later, Bobby called O'Donnell back to confirm his decision. "I've thought it over and I suppose I have to do it."

With his total level of sacrifice, legion hours, and precision of execution, Bobby transformed Jack's campaign for the Senate into a winner. Ambassador Kennedy meanwhile did what he was best at, putting money into the right hands. This two-track approach to political persuasion that the Kennedys perfected in 1952 — Bobby moving the machine and Joe moving the money — foreshadowed their run for the presidency in 1960. Jack was able to overcome a 300,000-vote plurality for Eisenhower in Massachusetts to beat popular Senate incumbent Henry Cabot Lodge by 70,000 votes. Jack later observed that there wasn't a politician in Massachusetts who could stand Bobby after the '52 campaign was over, but "we had the best organization in the state." Among the family's male stars now, nobody was now regarded as tougher. Lest Bobby rest for a month or so on his laurels, his father was there to remind him within days of Jack's victory: "Are you going to sit on your tail end and do nothing now for the rest of your life? You'd better go out and get a *job*." [30]

Their father told them it was a stupid idea. If Adlai Stevenson chose Jack as his running mate at the Democratic convention in Chicago, he would do it to get the Catholic vote. When Stevenson lost, which Joe Kennedy thought he would, Jack would be blamed — and he would be finished politically. Right before he left the country in June for his French Riviera home in Cap d'Antibes, he again warned his sons about the idea. Jack and Bobby would probably have heeded their father's advice had Joe accompanied them to the convention. But with their father out of touch, Jack and Bobby, in battle mode with a nucleus of tough young men like Kenny O'Donnell and Torbert McDonald around them, went for a long shot. They had no particular strategy in mind and no experience in the arcane maneuvers of political conventions. But no sooner had they arrived in Chicago than they began plotting in their rooms at the Ambassador East and the Conrad Hilton, and on the first day of the convention began making the rounds in the Amphitheater where the conclave was being held. Then the unexpected took place.

Governor Stevenson's campaign committee had selected Senator Kennedy to narrate a film produced by Dore Schary, titled *The Pursuit of Happiness.* On the opening night of the convention, eleven thousand delegates (and millions more on television) watched and listened as Kennedy narrated an emotional depiction of Franklin Roosevelt, Harry Truman, and the ideals of the party. Kennedy, tanned and fit, a low and conversational timbre in his voice, performed exceptionally. There was applause throughout the film and the crowd roared its approval at its conclusion. When Jack walked out onto the podium to take a bow, nodding and smiling in his contained way, he was met by a floor demonstration led by the Massachusetts delegation. Jack Kennedy, a complete unknown outside the Eastern seaboard, had suddenly been discovered by a national audience. The Kennedy brothers learned something about their candidate that night: Jack was good in person, but he was far better on film. The *New York Times* reported the next morning that "Kennedy came before the convention tonight as a movie star."[31]

The Stevenson leadership now had a problem: they didn't really want Kennedy as Adlai's running mate, but they didn't know quite how to dispose of him. The governor offered him the nominating speech and the text to go with it. Jack accepted the offer and threw away the speech. He and Theodore Sorensen, his twenty-eight-year-old aide, worked all night on his remarks, and the next day wowed the convention delegates a second time. Dave Powers and Kenny O'Donnell later wrote that "it was a little like the story of the Irish girl who worked so hard at converting her Jewish boyfriend to Catholicism that he became a priest."[32] Jack was now pressuring Stevenson to select him as his running mate, whether Stevenson wanted him or not. In messages to his father, Jack characterized his activity as merely getting his name out and testing future waters, not angling for the spot of running mate.[33] If Joe found out what was really going on, he could without warning call Richard Daley, mayor of Chicago, or Robert Wagner, mayor of New York, both of whom periodically received briefcases full of campaign money from him, and cut his errant boys off at the knees.

Eleanor Roosevelt, the widow of the Democratic party's great deliverer and a close friend of Stevenson, was thought to be key to the vice-presidential selection. A Kennedy aide hastily arranged a meeting. It went disastrously. Kenny O'Donnell remembered that about twenty people, including members of the press, watched as she bored into Jack about his association with communist-hunter Senator Joseph McCarthy. Why hadn't he supported the censure of McCarthy, she asked? Jack's answer did not satisfy her and she eyed him coldly. After twenty more minutes of tense exchange, Mrs. Roosevelt broke off the encounter. The reason why she had so humbled Jack had more to do with Joe Kennedy, whom she detested, than with Jack's unwillingness to take on McCarthy. She later told Gore Vidal that in his final disgraceful weeks as her late husband's ambassador in London, Joe Sr. had insisted on visiting the president in Hyde Park. Kennedy had spent no more than ten minutes with FDR when an aide rushed up to Mrs. Roosevelt to tell her the president urgently wanted to see her. She walked in the room to find the president white-faced and furious. He invited Kennedy to step outside. "I never want to see that man as long as I live," he told her. Her uncle David Gray, the wartime American ambassador to Ireland, was sure that Kennedy had proposed that Roosevelt make a deal with Hitler.[34] Before and during the convention, "Mrs. FDR," as she came to be known, communicated her pronounced disregard for the Kennedys to Stevenson. It was a problem for Jack, then and later.

Nothing, however, could discourage Bobby, who prowled the convention floor, yellow pad in hand, cornering floor leaders and asking them to commit to Jack. Bobby was now back in his assault mode. When there were no taxis to be found outside the convention hall, Bobby simply stepped out in front of a car, which screeched to a halt. He opened the driver's door and informed the man that he needed the car. The driver seemed to understand that there was no point in arguing and agreed to take the Kennedy group downtown. En route he asked Bobby for his autograph, to which Kennedy replied, "We'll do that later."[35]

There were other discoveries during those hectic days. Jacqueline Bouvier Kennedy, whom Jack had married in September 1953, had come to the convention initially excited to be part of her first Kennedy campaign. She was eight months pregnant. A touching picture shows her beautiful and open-faced, standing on her seat with a Stevenson sign cheering at Jack's nominating speech.[36] She followed Jack around, shook hands with everyone she could, sat in on the late-night meetings, and was soon exhausted. Their room at the Conrad Hilton was choked with cigar smoke. No one slept, tempers were short, and Jack's back was killing him. Between hurried meetings with his lieutenants, Jack received an unending train of fixers, reporters, and well-wishers. He ultimately persuaded Jackie to move in with his sister Eunice. This was her first bitter dose of being Jack Kennedy's political wife — and she hated it. When Jack moved down to the Stockyards Inn, which was closer to the convention hall, she didn't accompany him, nor did she visit him until the convention was over.

Democratic nominee Stevenson was probably leaning toward Minnesota senator Hubert Humphrey as his choice for running mate, or possibly Senator Albert Gore of Tennessee, but didn't have the nerve to ignore the claim of Tennessee's other senator, Estes Kefauver, who had won several primaries and had a block of loyal delegates at the convention. On August 17 at 11 P.M., Stevenson went to the convention hall and formally threw open the vice-presidential nomination. The delegates themselves would choose. What had begun as something of a beauty contest for Jack was shaping up into a floor fight — and Kefauver, after months of campaigning for the party's top spot, had a singular advantage. Rather than beat a strategic retreat, the Kennedy brothers decided to make a fight of it.

Back at the Stockyards Inn at around midnight, Jack asked Bobby to call their father in France. "Tell him I'm going for it." Having referred this unenviable task to Bobby, Jack walked out of the room. O'Donnell watched as Bobby dialed the number and got his father on the phone. The old man exploded at the news and shouted, "Jack's a total fucking idiot and you're worse!" After several more seconds of obscene invective, the line went dead. Bobby put the phone down. "Whew. Is he mad!"[37]

The vice-presidential campaign turned into a frenzied circus, with Humphrey volunteers visiting lakefront bars and taverns at 2:30 A.M. in search of delegates and Kefauver holding a press conference at 4 A.M. The Kennedys worked through the night trying to get speakers to nominate Jack later that day and desperately calling key delegations to round up votes before the balloting began. At noon the convention was called to order. As the delegates listened to Connecticut governor Abraham Ribicoff nominate Jack, Bobby was trying to find someone to give the seconding speech for his brother. He ran into Massachusetts congressman and House majority leader John McCormack and "practically carried him to the platform."[38] McCormack, who was nursing ambitions of his own after having been nominated by his delegation for president, felt as if he was being suborned. With Bobby standing behind him, he gave a seconding speech that was so weak he scarcely mentioned Jack's name.

To no one's surprise, Senator Kefauver achieved a large lead on the first ballot, but fell short of the required majority. Kennedy was a distant though impressive second. On the second ballot, Jack's sterling convention performances and early-morning deals with other aspirants, such as New York City mayor Robert Wagner, who now had dropped out, began to pay off. Suddenly there was a Kennedy stampede and Jack stared unbelievingly at his TV set in his hotel room as he surged ahead of Kefauver, 618 to 551. He was soon within 38 votes of winning. As he hurriedly dressed to go over to the hall to accept the vice-presidential nomination, a cordon of Chicago police arrived at the hotel to serve as an escort. On the convention floor as delegations demanded to be recognized, there was pandemonium. Unexpectedly, Senator Gore, who was thought to be a Kennedy supporter, withdrew in favor of his fellow Tennessean Kefauver. This touched off a new stampede away from Kennedy toward Kefauver. Minutes later it was over. The vice-presidential nomination went to Kefauver.

Jack was angry and very disappointed but had the good judgment to hurry over to the convention, mount the rostrum, and, with a sad smile on his face, congratulate Kefauver. Bobby, bitter at a list of people including Stevenson, put on a brave face for his brother and later consoled him that he was better off to have lost. Jack responded to this sarcastically, "This morning all of you were telling me to get into this thing, and now you're telling me I should feel happy because I lost it."

The Kennedy achievement at the 1956 convention had been extraordinary, in fact, the product of Jack's grace and Bobby's pure aggression along with a large quotient of luck. Jack was now seen as someone with star appeal who in defeat was a good sport. And he had done this without actually joining the doomed Democratic ticket. Bobby, O'Donnell, and the rest had gotten an indispensable insight into the mechanics of the convention as well into the loyalties of several key bosses. It would serve them well in Los Angeles at the 1960 Democratic convention. They had catapulted their man onto the national stage.

It was revealing of his sense of the order of things that after the convention Jack left his ailing and exhausted wife with her mother in Newport and headed off to confer with his father in southern France. He and his younger brother Teddy then boarded a 40-foot yacht with several unattached female guests for a two-week cruise in the Mediterranean. Jackie was meanwhile struggling with her pregnancy. On August 23, she was rushed to the hospital due to internal bleeding. Doctors performed an emergency cesarean delivery, but the infant, a girl, was stillborn. Jack, unaware of all of this, remained at sea and did not learn of it until the yacht docked at Genoa. His rather extraordinary absence made the national press.[39]

When Bobby, who was then in Hyannis Port, heard the news, he rushed to Newport to be with Jackie, now in critical condition. He got there in time to be at her bedside when she regained consciousness and gave her the sad news about the child whose burial he had already arranged. When Jackie finally did speak to Jack, he told her that he wasn't going to cut his cruise short. Bobby and his father soon straightened Jack out on this score and he flew home. But Jackie, embittered and depressed, wanted nothing to do with him. She refused to go back to Hickory Hill, the home in northern Virginia Joe Kennedy had bought for her and Jack. She told Bobby that she could not bear to see its empty nursery. (Bobby and Ethel moved in to Hickory Hill after Jack and Jackie chose not to live there.) Both *Time* and nationally syndicated columnist Drew Pearson reported that a divorce might be in the offing. The press also alleged that Joe Kennedy had offered Jackie a million dollars to stay with Jack. Whatever deal was struck — and the precise nature of it is not clear — it involved money and the emotional allegiance of Jackie's father-in-law, Joe, and her brother-in-law, Bobby. Henceforth, they would be her protectors.[40]

December 20, 1956

Chicago, Illinois

Bobby's role in protecting Jackie was emblematic of the place he had carved out in the family firmament — the stoic, dutiful third son who would do his father's bidding. After graduating from law school in 1951, Bobby had spent the next six years shuttling among government jobs and political assignments arranged by his father. Joe Kennedy was a political friend of Senator Joseph Mc-Carthy, the chair of the Senate Government Operations Commit-tee, and arranged for Bobby to get a position as legal counsel. Shortly after Bobby joined the Senate's Permanent Subcommittee on Investigations as an assistant counsel in the fall of 1952, the sub-committee counsel, Francis D. "Frip" Flanigan, got a call from the elder Kennedy: "You'll have no problem with Bobby. But if you do, call me and I'll fly up and kick him right in the ass."[41] He would have, too. The patriarchal order of the Kennedys combined Joe's constant and heartfelt encouragement of his children, his funding of their trusts (and other forms of emoluments), and his unbend-ing insistence that father knows best. Jack's independent status as a senator combined with his natural evasive ability gave him some au-tonomy from his father, but this was not the case for Bobby.

Jack had warned Bobby away from taking the job as counsel to McCarthy, but to no avail.[42] With his work ethic and Catholic sense of communist Armageddon, Bobby threw himself into McCarthy's investigation, successfully revealing that the British merchant ma-rine had done business with communist North Korea. But he soon broke with fellow committee counsels, Roy M. Cohn and G. David Schine, whose draconian tactics and homosexual attachment ap-palled Kennedy.[43] He quit the drunken McCarthy and his power-drunk camp followers in July 1953, but he took his fervent anti-communism with him.

After serving for several months as his father's assistant on the Hoover Commission, a job he found frustrating in the extreme, Bobby applied for the job of (the Democrats') minority counsel to McCarthy's investigations subcommittee. After he got it, he was soon engaged in pitched warfare against Roy Cohn. When the Democrats took control of the Senate after the midterm elections in 1954, Bobby became chief counsel to the Permanent Subcommittee for Investigations chaired by Arkansas senator John McClellan. It was here that the twenty-nine-year-old Bobby found his true métier as a crusading investigator. It was also from this position that he began to challenge his father. In 1955, Bobby launched an investigation of Eisenhower's self-interested secretary of the air force, Harold Talbott. Soon there was commentary that Kennedy's own father had engaged in similar behavior with his Haig & Haig distributorship when he served in Roosevelt's first administration. Father Joe sent his son a stinging denial of the charge but it was a sign of things to come.[44] Bobby, with his bulldog style of locking onto every fact and mechanically dismembering his witness in cross-examination, routed Talbott out of office. It was as if his own wealth as well as his reservations about the ethics of his father impelled him to a public form of expiation. In summing up the difference between the two Kennedy brothers, Massachusetts governor Paul Dever remarked that Jack was "the first Irish Brahmin" and Bobby "the last Irish Puritan."

Throughout 1956, Bobby received informal reports that organized crime had infiltrated American labor unions and that many of these unions were deeply corrupt. The worst was said to be the largest union in the country, the Teamsters.[45] Earlier attempts by Congress to investigate the Teamsters Union had gotten nowhere because Teamsters president Dave Beck and his lieutenants had fronted hundreds of thousands of dollars in campaign donations to key members. But Kennedy's boss, Senator McClellan, couldn't be bought or otherwise neutralized. He gave Kennedy and Carmine Bellino, the Kennedy family's accountant and an aide to both Jack and Bobby, the go-ahead to make a fact-finding trip about union corruption to the West Coast and Chicago.

In late November, they set off for Los Angeles, Portland, and Seattle, traveling under assumed names and seeking out reporters, police officers, and criminal informants. In Los Angeles Kennedy first learned about the Mafia system for taking over unions — threats, beatings, payoffs, and the occasional hit — and then the diversion of union funds through captive leadership. The terror tactics were usually both well calibrated and brutal. In L.A., a union organizer who had encroached on mob turf was beaten senseless. He awoke in enormous pain and was taken to the emergency room of a hospital, where doctors removed a large cucumber that had been crammed up his anus. Next time, he had been told, it would be a watermelon.[46]

Kennedy's investigation led him to believe that Mafia penetration went far deeper than the usual criminal rackets. He and Bellino found its tentacles everywhere — in unions, police forces, corporations, law firms, political parties, foundations, and even government itself. In Chicago, with subpoenas in hand, they got back on the trail of Dave Beck. On December 20 in a blinding snowstorm, Kennedy and his chief investigator, arms burdened with bundles of documents, hurried out of the Boulevard National Bank Building on Michigan Avenue into a waiting taxi and drove back to the Palmer House, where they were staying. After poring through the documents, they concluded that Beck was a "crook" and that they had the evidence to convict him.

It was an epiphany of sorts for the thirty-one-year-old Kennedy. In *The Enemy Within,* his subsequent best-selling book about his investigation of labor and mob racketeering, he would recount the snowswept scene on Michigan Avenue as Act I of his own awakening to the crisis at hand. Beck, the "respected national figure" who had just been photographed with President Eisenhower outside the White House, was instead a corrupt, self-serving pretender who was amassing a fortune at his union's expense. The political danger, even the physical danger, of exposing Beck was something to which Robert Kennedy was drawn. He would man the investigative front himself, peruse thousands of documents, subpoena hitmen to his office, and then personally confront them to see how tough they were. He would even pick up a shovel to unearth the remains of a witness who had known too much.

24

The next morning he and Bellino checked out of the Palmer House and went to the airport only to learn that all flights had been canceled due to the snow and fog. They took a taxi instead to Chicago's main train station. Bellino boarded a train for Washington. Kennedy boarded one for Boston to attend his family's holiday reunion in Hyannis Port. During his long train ride to Boston, Bobby resolved to launch a national investigation of the Teamsters and their connections to organized crime. He was clearly excited by the prospect of breaking out of the shadows and distinguishing himself on his own. But when he told Joe Kennedy about his plan, his father responded that it was a terrible idea. What followed, in the recollection of Bobby's sister Jean, was "an unprecedentedly furious argument" between the two. The old man was "deeply, emotionally opposed."[47]

Joe Kennedy knew and feared the Mafia. Jack's boyhood friend Lemoyne Billings, who was at Hyannis Port that Christmas, also witnessed the blow-up: "The old man saw this as dangerous, not the sort of thing or the sort of people to mess around with," Billings said later.[48] When the elder Kennedy got nowhere with his son, he asked Supreme Court Justice William O. Douglas, a close and trusted mentor to Bobby, to intercede. Douglas did, but also got nowhere. Part of the makeup of the three and one-half–year-old boy who had jumped off the yawl that long-ago summer day was the drive to do or die. It tended to make him emotionally immune to the normal quotient of human fear, and it led him directly into the danger zone.

Two days after Christmas, Bobby left Hyannis Port for Washington, where he called on Senator McClellan to alert him to his findings. Kennedy asked for and got McClellan's go-ahead to take on the Teamsters. On December 27, Kennedy called the Teamsters' "marble palace" headquarters on Louisiana Avenue, a stone's throw from the Capitol, to inform Dave Beck that he was going to subpoena him. The war was on. Later that day, two Teamster officials phoned Kennedy and told him he was "out of his mind." [49] By early January, the McClellan Committee was formed and Bobby, over his father's objections, prevailed on Jack to become a member.[50]

The Kennedy clan had a new leader, one who could openly challenge what no other member dared question — the total authority of Joe Kennedy. Despite periodic clashes, Jack preferred to finesse, ignore, or otherwise evade his father's orders if he chose not to follow them. "I guess Dad has decided that he's going to be a ventriloquist," Jack told LeMoyne Billings, "so I guess that leaves me in the role of dummy."[51] Daughter-in-law Jackie, with her telling knack for nicknames, caught the lonely, questing persona of the third son — "Saint Bobby."

In mustering his crusade, Bobby turned to old friends like Kenny O'Donnell and Carmine Bellino, as well as new acquaintances like San Francisco investigative reporter Pierre Salinger and former FBI agent Walter Sheridan. No single person proved so critical to Bobby Kennedy's career as the indefatigable Angela Novello, who became his secretary. (The total number of investigators and support personnel for the McClellan Committee was to rise to over a hundred by 1959.) Initial press reports were mixed. One headline read: MILLIONAIRE TO RUN SENATE RACKET PROBE.[52]

Many years later, Arizona senator Barry Goldwater, also on the McClellan Committee, remembered the initial meeting in the old Senate Chambers. "Bobby struck me as a mean little asshole, with his high voice and his uncombed hair. He informed us about the mandate of the Committee as if he were reading a prescription off a bottle of medicine. Karl Mundt [of South Dakota] and I felt like resigning on the spot."[53] But within weeks, Goldwater had revised that first impression of Kennedy: "Then we learned that he and Bellino and O'Donnell . . . never left the staff offices — I mean, *never* — before midnight, subpoenaing hundreds of witnesses and chasing down thousands of documents. . . . When the committee was formed, we thought it was just a vehicle for Jack's campaign for president, but I can tell you it turned into a forced march and Bobby was like a Marine platoon leader."

Within weeks, through documents, subpoenas, and testimony, Kennedy had cornered Beck, a man whose bald, domed skull made him look like "an evil Easter egg." Kennedy later recounted, "Now he was dead, although still standing. All that was needed was someone to push him over and make him lie down as dead men should. The man to do that was available. His name was James Riddle Hoffa."[54]

Jimmy Hoffa, at this time vice president of the Teamsters

Union, was a sawed-off cannon of a man who had charmed, threatened, assaulted, and shot his way from local to national power. He was only five feet five inches tall but in every way that counted in his cruel habitat, Hoffa was a titan. Ever since his coal-miner father had died of silicosis when Hoffa was four, he had never stopped fighting. He was intelligent, completely fearless, and spoke openly of an arrest record "about as long as your arm." The fact that he had nearly been whipped to death with chains by antiunion goons in 1933 gave him cachet as a street warrior as well as an understanding of the ultimate manner of things. His will to power was complete; he neither smoked nor drank, was indifferent to dress (preferring to wear white gym socks with his dark suits), and remained loyal to his wife, Josephine. In his primal way, he regarded politics as war by other means. He ordered up physical violence against opponents the way a lawyer might file a particular motion against the opposing party — for precise effect. He was said to have attacked other men and beat them unconscious with his own hands. When Hoffa aide Robert Scott came to check on his boss one night in a Chicago hotel, he found the door unlocked and decided to look in: "I didn't get inside the door before Jimmy had rolled out of bed over to a table and came up standing on the other side of the room with a gun in his hand."[55]

Hoffa's central ambition was to unite the disparate and sometimes fiercely independent locals into a national front that could negotiate a single contract for the Teamsters. In this effort, he frequently used gangsters to break locals by threats, payoffs, and violence and to install pliant local leaders. The mob also was effective at extorting money from corporations via strikes and selected violence. The payoff for the Mafia was access to hundreds of millions of dollars of the Teamsters' pension funds to invest in land, or gambling resorts in Las Vegas or Havana. The Mafia fit into Hoffa's Manichaean view of the unions against the corporations. In the Sicilian, Italian, Jewish, and Irish mafiosi, he saw ethnics like himself from dirt-poor families who with their fists and street cunning had battled their way to the top. In this struggle, legitimacy necessarily came out of the barrel of the gun. Of his association with the Mafia, Hoffa told one interviewer: "Twenty years ago, the employers had all the hoodlums working for them as strikebreakers. Now we've got a few and everybody's screaming."[56] By 1957, Hoffa had been in active partnership with the Mafia in Detroit and Chicago for over twenty years. His collaboration with the New York families was a more recent development.

In 1957, at age forty-four, Hoffa knew all the tricks, and in Bobby Kennedy he saw a thirty-one-year-old spoiled Harvard busybody who could clear the way for his takeover of the Teamsters. Accordingly, Hoffa provided Kennedy with information about Beck that contributed to his rival's downfall. By March 1957, under Kennedy's pounding, the once-supercilious Beck had become a broken man looking for a place to hide. Meanwhile, two Teamsters front men who knew Kennedy set about to work out some sort of modus vivendi between Hoffa and the young prosecutor. In the Washington bestiary, as always, the scavenger is central to the disposition of old carcasses and to the discovery of new ones.

Eddie Cheyfitz, the partner of Teamsters attorney Edward Bennett Williams, arranged a private dinner to work out the right measure of peaceful coexistence. At Cheyfitz's invitation, Kennedy drove out to his elaborate home in Chevy Chase on February 19, 1957, for a private dinner with Hoffa. He found him "personable, polite and friendly," if a little boorish: "I do to others what they do to me," Hoffa boasted to Kennedy, "only worse." Kennedy must have chuckled to himself at this, for he knew Hoffa was walking into a trap of his own device. Six days earlier, a New York attorney named John Cye Cheasty had visited Kennedy's office to inform him that Hoffa had offered him a bribe to sign on with the chief counsel as an investigator and then to provide the Teamsters with purloined inside information. After he learned this, Kennedy contacted FBI director J. Edgar Hoover, who arranged a sting. The day of the dinner, at the corner of 17th and I Streets, Cheasty delivered the names of four sources to Hoffa. An FBI camera recorded the transaction. As they conversed that evening at Cheyfitz's home, Bobby felt confident that he was on the verge of taking out another Teamsters criminal. According to Hoffa, after dinner Kennedy challenged him to Indian-wrestle. Hoffa supposedly accepted and pinned Kennedy twice.[57]

Three weeks later, on March 13, Hoffa was arrested by the FBI at the Dupont Plaza Hotel for violating the federal bribery statute.

Kennedy waited around until midnight in a Washington courtroom to witness Hoffa's arraignment. When Hoffa arrived, the two began a spirited exchange over who could do the most push-ups. [58] The encounter testified to a peculiar quality in Bobby's pathology of political power. Everything was *personal*. As Ethel said, "For him the world is divided into black and white hats. The white hats are for us and the black hats are against us. Bobby can only distinguish good men and bad. Good things, in his eyes, are virility, courage, movement, and anger." Moreover, the division was not just moral but tribal. The question was not just who was better, but who was tougher.

The press later asked Kennedy whether he was sure the FBI had the evidence. "If Hoffa isn't convicted, I'll jump off the Capitol Dome," Bobby replied, smiling. But Hoffa beat the rap through a dazzling array of extralegal endeavors. The eight black jurors empaneled in the case somehow received copies of Washington's black newspaper, *Afro-American,* describing Hoffa as a champion of civil rights and pictorially showing him with an African-American attorney, Martha Jefferson. Former heavyweight champion Joe Louis attended the trial for two days and at one point, in full view of the jury, embraced Hoffa. Hoffa himself took the stand and proved a brazen prevaricator; he had merely hired Cheasty as his attorney, he said. At the conclusion of the three-week trial, Hoffa was acquitted, and suggested on the way out of the courtroom that it was time for the junior Kennedy to take a jump. Williams offered to provide a parachute.[59] Seven days later, Jimmy Hoffa announced his candidacy for the general presidency of the Teamsters. In September 1957, he clawed, bribed, and bullied his way into the job.

Given the setback in court and Hoffa's accession to the Teamsters presidency, it seemed advisable for Bobby to beat a tactical retreat. Additionally, the McClellan Committee's investigation was now moving into the mainstream of the AFL-CIO, thereby jeopardizing Jack Kennedy's bid for labor support in the 1960 presidential contest. But instead Bobby turned the assault against Hoffa into a siege. Perhaps it was Bobby's youth or his wealth, or perhaps his headstrong temperament. Whatever the source, he was a man who, as his aide Joe Dolan said, "would give no quarter."

To get Hoffa, Kennedy resorted to a full range of tactics, some outside the range of civil liberties. He blistered witnesses with invective for taking the Fifth, leading Alexander Bickel of Yale Law School to liken Kennedy's breaching of the right not to self-incriminate to Senator Joseph McCarthy's hectoring style.[60] Joey Glimco, the president of a Chicago Teamsters local, was one of those on the receiving end of Kennedy's (and Senator McClellan's) leading, ad hominem commentary:

> KENNEDY [to Glimco]: And you defraud the union?
> GLIMCO: I respectfully decline to answer because I honestly believe my answer might tend to incriminate me.
> KENNEDY: I would agree with you.
> MCCLELLAN: I believe it would.
> KENNEDY: You haven't got the guts to answer, have you, Mr. Glimco?
> GLIMCO: I respectfully decline.
> MCCLELLAN: Morally, you are kind of yellow inside, are you not?
> GLIMCO: I respectfully decline.

When Kennedy surmised that subpoenas for documents wouldn't do the trick, he resorted to extralegal means. He told the press that one of his investigators had gotten a look at a stack of Teamsters documents underneath the bed of a Teamsters employee by dating the maid who cleaned the house. But beyond the Perry Mason cat-and-mouse tactics, there was electronic penetration — the wiretap — and Kennedy grew fond of it.

With wiretapped conversations (legally derived) between Hoffa and New York gangster Johnny Dioguardi in hand, Kennedy summoned Hoffa back to the McClellan Committee. This round went to Kennedy, with Hoffa (who resolutely refused to take the Fifth) stumbling all over himself trying to keep some distance between himself and the New York mob. *Newsweek* likened Kennedy to a "Boston terrier [that] barks and bites"— altogether darting, high-pitched, and energetic in pursuit.[61] In news footage from the period, Hoffa looks ursine, glowering at Kennedy with a snarl on his lip as the chief counsel would walk into the hearing room to start the questioning. Then came the flinty stare — a "shriveling look," as Kennedy described it. Hoffa would give his answers in a slow, meaty monotone until Kennedy would corner him. Then the veins in the squat, powerful neck would begin pulsing, the brow would lower slightly, and the eyes would flash. "Sometimes his façade of bluster and bluff would crack," Kennedy later wrote, "and for an hour during a hearing he would appear morose, discouraged, and beaten. But the man has great stamina, and he would bounce back as forceful as ever."[62]

Barry Goldwater witnessed a confrontation between Kennedy and Hoffa in the hallway of the old Senate building. The characterization he used to describe it was "animal anger." Beyond the sharp exchange of words, there was a violent, physical tension between the two. But through the long months, the fury Kennedy felt toward Hoffa congealed into a respect for the latter's implacable will to fight. Bobby's own account includes descriptions of encounters with Hoffa that border on the convivial. He describes running into Hoffa one day in 1958 at the United States Courthouse Building in New York.

"Hello, Jimmy."

"Hello, Bobby."

Kennedy asked him about the Teamsters presidency. "Greatest job in the world," Hoffa replied. Then Bobby asked him about the wiretap charge Hoffa was fighting.

"You can never tell with a jury," Hoffa replied. "Like shooting fish in a barrel."[63] Thanks to the old mob practice of jury-tampering, Hoffa again beat the rap and kept his presidency. The war would go on.

Eventually, the pathology of the hunter and hunted changed. Kennedy was soon regularly referring to Hoffa as "Jimmy" and Hoffa, at first polite, turned violently derisive, referring to Kennedy as a "sadistic little monster." Going home late at night, Kennedy would stare out at the Teamsters' headquarters on Louisiana Avenue. "My first love is Jimmy Hoffa," he said sardonically one evening to John Bartlow Martin, a Kennedy friend and journalist. Perhaps to be a saint, it is necessary to find a devil. Perhaps in this particular devil, Kennedy found someone as to-the-death as he himself was. In *The Enemy Within*, Kennedy ran a photograph of "the expressive eyes and hands of Jimmy Hoffa" that made him look demonic. Over time, the devil became something of an incubus, invading Kennedy's consciousness (it was said that the first word out of one of Kennedy's toddlers' mouths was "Hoffa") and utterly exhausting him. By the end of 1957, Kennedy and his investigators had a hollow look about them. At around one o'clock one morning, Kennedy, on his way home, saw the lights in Hoffa's office on and told Pierre Salinger to turn around and head back to the office: "If he's still at work, we ought to be."[64] Martin, for one, thought there were remarkable parallels between Kennedy and Hoffa. To Bobby's shock, Martin put them in print. They both were "aggressive, competitive, hard-driving, authoritarian, suspicious, temperate, at times congenial and at others curt."

The McClellan Committee hearings made first-rate theater, with anywhere from 80 to 120 reporters in attendance. National radio and TV coverage was constant. The committee averaged about a thousand letters a week, some fan mail, some frightened appeals from trade unionists caught in the vice of racketeering. Beginning in March 1957, there was the first of a succession of stories in the major news magazines of the day. *Look, Life, Time,* and *U.S. News and World Report* all did spreads. The matrix of the stories was usually about Bobby versus Hoffa, but the bounce was the photographs of the telegenic Kennedy brothers. *Look,* which took eight thousand pictures of Jack and Bobby, gushed: "Two boyish men from Boston, with healthy shocks of hair, a father rich and benevolent, and minds honed at Harvard and by foreign travel, have become hot tourist attractions in Washington."[65] (Consistent with her total distaste for the political maelstrom into which she was now being pulled, Jackie is seen in the photos unsmiling and wearing dark glasses.) Jack may have put himself on the political map in his week-long run for the vice-presidential nomination in 1956, but Bobby's investigation kept them on the air and the front page for months. Toward the end of 1957, Joe Kennedy slipped in to see one of the hearings himself in a kind of grudging benediction of his disobedient son.

In the two and a half years of the McClellan Committee hearings, of which each day, Bobby said proudly, was "like game day against Notre Dame," 1,366 witnesses were interrogated. The final report ran to 20,432 pages of colloquy, analysis, and documents. For every hour a witness spent before the full committee, he was interrogated for five behind closed doors by the chief counsel. Through it all, there sat Ethel in the hearing chamber with her open, upturned face listening as Bobby, in his inelegant staccato, bulldozed his way through the witnesses. Only the birth of their son Michael caused her to miss two weeks, but then she was back cradling the infant in her arms, rapt, constant, and unquestioning in her devotion. And he was the same. The death of her parents in a plane crash in 1955, like the death of Bobby's beloved sister Kick in 1948, only seemed to make each moment together more essential. The growing stampede of children, dogs, and horses at Hickory Hill seemed to represent not simply the proliferation of life but some warm and breathing hedge against the mortal precipice ahead. In many ways, these were the happiest days of their lives.

A seemingly obscure event took Bobby's frontal attack against Hoffa and transformed it into the beginning of a long war against an even greater enemy. In November 1957, local law enforcement officials stumbled upon a national conclave of Mafia *capi di tutti capi* in upstate New York. The meeting, which had been called to stop the murderous infighting touched off by the execution of New York godfather Albert Anastasia, revealed the national infrastructure of La Cosa Nostra. The McClellan Committee now threw its net wider, subpoenaing Mafia overlords Anthony Accardo and Sam Giancana of Chicago, Joseph Profaci of New York, Santos Trafficante of Havana, and Carlos Marcello of New Orleans. What was unprecedented about the encounters that followed was not the appearance of these men (the Kefauver Committee had subpoenaed most of them in 1951), but the encyclopedic preparation Kennedy brought to his interrogation. He exposed them.

On March 24, 1959, Kennedy dragged Carlos Marcello, for the first time in his criminal life, through every suspected racket, payoff, and murder plot the chief counsel was able to dig up.[66] With his opaque sunglasses reflecting the klieg lights and his defiant scowl never changing, Marcello took the Fifth sixty-six times. He left the hearing room with his brother Joe and Harvard-trained attorney Jack Wasserman deeply angered by Kennedy. Sam Giancana was similarly galled. After taking the Fifth over forty times as Kennedy asked him about "bodies in trunks," Giancana began to snicker.

Kennedy stopped his questioning and looked at him: "I thought only little girls giggled, Mr. Giancana."

As he delved into their world, Kennedy was both horrified and fascinated by what he found. He would later describe their clothes ("black shirt, black pants, black coat"), their hair ("greased down" in the case of Johnny Dio, "long curls down the back of the neck" in the case of Joey Gallo) even their smell of "sickly-sweet cologne." "They are sleek, often bilious and fat, or lean and cold and hard. They have smooth faces and the cruel eyes of gangsters."[67] Everywhere he looked, he saw violence and vengeance. The six-foot six-inch, three-hundred-pound Barney Baker, whom Kennedy described as Hoffa's "roving emissary of violence," calmly described the succession of dead men he had come to know in his line of work. (Baker would be in contact with Jack Ruby in the days before President Kennedy's visit to Dallas in November 1963, according to Warren Report documents.) Bobby was actually amused by the "Academy Award performance" of New York's serial executioner Joey Gallo, who looked at Kennedy's rug and said it would be good for a crap game. "Crazy Joe" later claimed that he had called friends from Kennedy's office to make commitments for Jack for president in 1960, and once stopped a man who had walked into Bobby's reception area, frisked him for a weapon, and sent him packing. "No one is going to see Mr. Kennedy with a gun on him. If Kennedy gets killed now everybody will say I did it."[68]

Bobby himself brushed off all offers of a security detail. He also evinced no hesitation to proceed with the investigations when Hoffa threatened to murder witnesses. After Kennedy unearthed evidence that Hoffa had "literally stolen" a Detroit local of the International Union of Retail Clerks, Hoffa told the man who had squealed to Kennedy: "Don't you know I could have you killed? Don't you know I could have you pushed out this window? I got friends who would shoot you in your tracks." The man, Sol Lippmann, came to Kennedy "white and shaken," and so scared he could hardly speak. He told Kennedy he would not testify against Hoffa.[69]

After two and a half years of investigation, tens of thousands of man-hours of investigation, and months of testimony, however, Hoffa remained unindicted. He actually seemed to feed off the pressure. Invited on the Jack Paar show, Bobby spent several minutes tearing into Hoffa, describing him as "completely evil." Hoffa filed a $2.5 million libel suit against NBC. As he crisscrossed the country, consolidating control over the locals and raising the Teamsters banner in job actions, Hoffa dared Kennedy to keep after him: "If it is a question, as Kennedy has said, that he will break Hoffa, then I say to him, he should live so long."[70]

Aside from Hoffa, the casualty list of crooked unionists exposed by the McClellan Committee was impressive: James G. Cross, president of the Bakery and Confectionery Workers, whose union was thrown out of the AFL-CIO; Maurice Hutcheson, president of the Carpenters Union, who was indicted; William E. Maloney, president of the Operating Engineers, who resigned; Anthony Valente, president of the United Textile Workers, who resigned; Max and Louis Block of the Meat Cutters Union, who were ousted; and seven Teamsters officials indicted and another sixteen either dismissed or resigned.

What came to be known as the "Bobby style" was developed during his days on the McClellan Committee. The investigation was a thirty-two-month marathon marked by ruthless focus and breakneck pace. Kennedy did not just work long, he worked fast. And he expected everyone else to do the same. He was tenacious. Once he locked onto something or someone, he didn't stop grinding. Another distinguishing trait of the McClellan days was the absence of a command structure. Job descriptions and hierarchy meant little. The staff rallied to deal with emergencies as they came up. Given the low salaries, the staff might not have sustained the pace were it not for Bobby's profound devotion to those with whom he worked. Jack always impressed people, but Bobby bound them to himself. In the long hours of work, in the occasional parties he would throw at Hickory Hill, Bobby would express, often through teasing, his recognition and admiration of their work. On Good Friday, Bobby ordered orchids for every woman on his staff. When Senator McClellan's son was killed in an accident in 1958, Bobby flew back to Arkansas with him and stayed with the family. Back in Washington, Bobby would often drive the senator back to his apartment in the evening and sometimes spend the night with him. McClellan, a gruff, remote man, likened Bobby to a son.

In two comments, Joe Kennedy caught the strange duality

within his third son. "Bobby," he said, "feels more strongly for and against people than Jack — just as I do. . . . He hates the same way I do." And later the old man described the other side. "Bobby is soft — soft on people . . . he has the capacity to be emotionally involved, to feel things deeply, as compared with Jack and that amazing detachment of his."[71]

The detached Jack usually sat alongside his younger brother in the hearings, listening, taking notes, and occasionally joining in the interrogation of the witnesses. Except for their collaboration in Jack's Senate race in 1952, the two brothers had never really worked together until the McClellan Committee. There a crucial pattern emerged — Bobby blazing the path in his assault style and Jack, in his urbane, measured way, bringing up the rear. In 1958, Jack became the chair of the Senate Labor Subcommittee and developed legislation to implement the findings of the McClellan Committee. Though the Kennedy-Ives bill, as it was called, never made it into law, it was Jack's most significant achievement in the Senate.[72]

Senator Kennedy was now traveling all over the country, giving speeches and laying the groundwork for his 1960 run. He continued to struggle with his health but somehow found time for his long-standing sport of chasing (and usually securing the favor of) glamorous women. Detached he might be, but Jack's drive, sexual and political, was relentless; on the road he kept his crutches out of sight but close at hand. His father purchased a twin-engined, ten-seat DC-3 for Jack's campaign trips, enabling him to receive injections, massages, and medicated rest between appearances. On one trip, he scrawled a note to himself: "Have got to stop pooning around."[73] But it was not to be.

His marriage to Jackie alternated between skirmish and cease-fire; their attachment was deep but troubled by his habits and her moods. The birth of their daughter, Caroline, however, provided the couple a delight that brought them closer. Jackie continued to forswear any politicking herself but helped Jack in his research into the Vietnam and Algerian wars, translating books from French and writing summaries of their conclusions. In July 1957, before an empty Senate chamber, Jack stood up and rhetorically committed a form of foreign policy blasphemy. He called on France to "face facts" and abandon its bloody war against Algerian guerrillas. The speech sent shock waves through Washington and the capitals of Europe, but it won Kennedy lasting gratitude from African nationalists.[74] Critics then and later had a point in saying that aside from his looks and wealth, Jack was a conventional politician. But he was also one with an unexpected capacity for growth and insight.

For all of the propaganda and posturing necessary to his advancement, Jack was a fatalist who had traversed, in his sister Eunice's phrase, "regions of doubt." The deaths of Joe in the war and Kathleen in 1948, as well as his own brushes with death, confirmed his skeptical view of life. Perhaps because of this, he squeezed from each moment what stimulation there was, defining happiness, as he sometimes said, the way the Greeks had — "the full use of one's faculties along the lines of excellence." Jack viewed power as a worthy aesthetic pursuit. Bobby, on the other hand, saw it in terms of moral possibilities and tribal exigencies.

When Jack was on the road, Goldwater later recalled, Bobby was very protective of his brother's interests, but back in the Senate, "he pushed Jack, was tough with him." The difference between the two, Murray Kempton thought, was "the difference of those who are only properly oriented and those who are truly involved."[75] But, even in the late 1950s, Bobby was already reorienting Jack. As later on civil rights, his older brother watched and listened from the rear as Bobby scouted the moral frontier and urged them on nearly every occasion to seize the high ground. Crisis by crisis, decision by decision, he was thus transforming his brother from a charming, somewhat dilatory, character into a political leader of moral dimensions.[76] "Bobby is easily the most impressive man I've ever seen," Jack said in 1961, implicitly measuring himself and his father secondarily.[77]

Murray Kempton saw beyond the image of Bobby as the ruthless prosecutor and brother-keeper and recognized that his philosophical core was that of a "Catholic radical." The crusade against the Mafia was a struggle between good and evil. The same went for Soviet communism. In both these battles, thought Bobby, America was weak because America was materialist, undone by the greed of the "respectables," as he called them, the money-changers and their inevitable attorneys whose concept of justice was soiled by profit. "The paramount interest in self," Kennedy wrote in *The Enemy*

Within, "in material wealth, in security must be replaced by an actual, not just vocal, interest in our country, by spirit of adventure, a will to fight what is evil, and a desire to serve."[78] He detested "America the Crass," an antimaterialism essentially drawn from his Franciscan view of Catholicism. The problem is that politics is the art of the possible, not the impossible. The feast days of the saints, more often than not, commemorate the price of the radical's attempt to reorder society — martyrdom. Alice Roosevelt Longworth, that durable seer of the Washington scene, thought Bobby was miscast in the political trade; he should have been a "revolutionary priest."[79]

Within the hellish bunkers of organized crime, Bobby discovered thousands of prominent Americans trafficking with gangsters, to their moral peril. But what about Kennedy's own father, whose business dealings had skirted the dark territory of the underworld? Did Bobby see his father for what he was? Hoffa for one was quick to point the finger: "I'm no damn angel . . . I don't apologize. You take any industry and look at the problems they ran into while they were building up — how they did it, who they associated with, how they cut corners. The best example is Kennedy's old man."[80]

On several occasions in the course of his investigation, Bobby Kennedy heard allegations about his father's collusion with members of organized crime. Shortly before he was to testify before the committee, Al Capone's former attorney, Abraham Teitelbaum, reportedly told the chief counsel that he might reference his father in testimony if he, Teitelbaum, was not dismissed. Teitelbaum was called but said nothing about Ambassador Kennedy. (In *The Enemy Within*, Bobby refers to Teitelbaum's offer to help Senator Kennedy as ransom Teitelbaum was willing to pay if it would get him released from testimony.)[81] Senator Goldwater remembered "rumors flying" about Joe Kennedy, but said that Bobby "played it smart." After a speech in Milwaukee in early 1959, in which Bobby, in response to a question as to whether the Kennedys had been subjected to any "threats or promises of political support," responded affirmatively, adding that he did not take them seriously. Why had he not reported these to the committee? Senator Mundt asked. Kennedy replied that he had not since "they had never affected the work of the staff." Bobby's reply, in his own words, "caused considerable furor" and the McClellan Committee convened to decide what to do. It was decided that henceforth all such approaches be disclosed.[82]

We do not know precisely what Bobby knew about his father's relations with the likes of Frank Costello, the so-called Prime Minister of the Underworld, Sam Giancana, the godfather of the "Chicago Outfit," or Morris (Moe) Dalitz of the Mayfield Road Gang.[83] He undoubtedly knew that there had been contact — not a surprising thing — and that the gangsters were intent on making the most of it, if necessary, behind the scenes. As would later become manifest in the case of Frank Sinatra, Bobby sought to cauterize this ulcerous association. Jack, on the other hand, took a more casual view, possibly because he did not view the underworld as the embodiment of evil, or perhaps because he tended to appraise individuals without presentiment. Beginning in 1959, the senator was spotted by the Las Vegas office of the FBI in the company of Sinatra and certain mafiosi. In Tucson, Arizona, he went to mass with Smiling Gus Battaglia, an underboss in one of the New York families. Battaglia later attended a fund-raiser for Jack in Phoenix in 1959.[84]

Contact and even political communion between the Mafia and national politicians were widespread in the 1950s and afterward. Lyndon Johnson benefited from Mafia payoffs while he was a senator, according to Jack Halfen, a convicted tax evader, who claimed the mob gave LBJ $500,000. Vice President Richard Nixon had a deep relationship with the Mafia, as Carl Oglesby charges: "He began as a Syndicate person in direct connection with Syndicate people."[85] But neither Johnson nor Nixon had a brother on a Mafia search-and-destroy mission. Or a father who continued to traffic with the underworld. The compartmentalized way in which Jack and Bobby worked with their father made any resolution of this cross-purpose unlikely. The old man was still the senior partner in the triumvirate and he acted unilaterally. The implicit understanding was that he would put money where it counted, pull the strings, and do the deals. The less Jack and Bobby knew about this, the less they would have to answer for. The two-track approach had worked well up to this point. But it depended on Joe Sr.'s ability to contain the deals and Bobby's willingness not to challenge them.

"I have found it always true," Machiavelli observed, "that men do seldom or never advance themselves from a small beginning to any great height except by fraud or force." Certainly Joe Kennedy understood this. The price of power was not merely financial, it was moral — and you paid it. For Bobby, however, this was wrong. His crusade against the Mafia was not only dedicated to ridding the country of its pernicious influence, but also to severing its connection to the Kennedy family. In August 1959, he quit the crusade and returned to his role as the lesser brother to lead Jack's campaign for the White House. Jimmy Hoffa predicted that Bobby's assault had ended, but he was wrong. It had only begun.

The Campaign

1960

February 29, 1960

New York City

Of the small group of Mafia overlords in America — the so-called *capi di tutti capi* — only Sam Giancana, the rat-faced former wheelman for Al Capone, had accepted Joseph P. Kennedy's invitation to lunch. The two were well acquainted. In 1959, Kennedy had invested in the syndicate-developed Cal-Neva Lodge near Reno, which opened two years later. (Kennedy's son-in-law, Peter Lawford, would be the partner of record.)[1] What transformed their relationship into a secret alliance, however, was Giancana's steel-smooth mob compatriot, Johnny Rosselli, who had known Joe Kennedy since the early '30s in Hollywood. It was Rosselli, at Joe Kennedy's request, who organized the New York lunch.

By 1960, most Mafia chieftains had no use for Joe Kennedy. First he had competed against them during Prohibition in the smuggling and sale of illicit liquor, and afterward, on occasion, he had ignored their territorial imperative on the sensitive matter of liquor distribution. In 1944, without sufficient clearance, Kennedy had sent one of his agents, Miami Beach gangster Tom Cassara, to Chicago to arrange a Haig & Haig distributorship.[2] The man was shot dead within hours of arriving. In the middle 1950s, Kennedy reportedly cheated his sometime partner Frank Costello in a business deal in which Kennedy had fronted the purchase of a piece of Manhattan property and then pocketed the entire profit on its sale.[3] Rosselli, a trusted confederate of Costello (informing for the FBI during this period, Mafia capo Edward Cannizziro described Rosselli as a "Costello man"), had smoothed over bruised relations.[4]

As Senator John F. Kennedy's campaign for the presidency moved into high gear in the first months of 1960, his father sought

43

out Rosselli to help him arrange a summit meeting with Mafia leaders. But the best Rosselli could do was to get the Chicago Outfit to attend and, interestingly enough, the attorney Mario Brod, a friend of James J. Angleton, chief of counterintelligence for the CIA. Brod's practice combined top-secret work for the CIA's counterintelligence wing with legal troubleshooting for friends in the syndicate.[5]

According to Brod, Joe Kennedy's lunch at Felix Young's restaurant in Manhattan on February 29 started badly. The New York and Boston families didn't show.[6] Those attending were asked to make their bodyguards wait outside the restaurant, which in the murderous world of the mob was a troubling request. Kennedy himself arrived fifteen minutes late. Finally, inevitably, the subject of Robert Kennedy's investigative attack on the Mafia arose.

Under the circumstances, no one but Joe Kennedy would have attempted such an encounter. But the Ambassador (as he was known), a man of epic will who had bluffed and bulled his way to enormous wealth and political power, was not to be dissuaded from seizing any opportunity to put his son in the White House. In the 1930s, he had harbored that ambition for himself, but with the shipwreck of his diplomatic career the objective had shifted to his sons.[7]

The fact that Senator Lyndon Johnson and Vice President Richard Nixon (the other two leading presidential candidates that year) were also lining up bosses like Joe Civello and Carlos Marcello probably contributed to Kennedy's interest in approaching them. LBJ and Nixon, moreover, could make a far better claim to blocking anti-racketeering laws than the Kennedys could.[8] The difference was, Joe reportedly told his son-in-law Steve Smith, they didn't have the balls to go straight to the mob themselves. He would.[9]

It was precisely this grasping style of Kennedy's that had weakened and ultimately denatured the alliance he had initially enjoyed with Franklin Roosevelt.[10] In later years, Kennedy often spoke to friends, in anger tinged with bitter admiration, of FDR's immense cunning — how he had fleeced Kennedy for nearly a million dollars in the '36 presidential campaign, then given him the ambassadorship to get him out of the country, and then, when it got tough, set him up as a Nazi sympathizer and ruined him. As the years went by, the obsession with Roosevelt grew more grotesque and exaggerated. Kennedy claimed, for example, that FDR had personally reviewed the order to send his son on the high-risk bombing mission over France in which Joe Jr. had died. During the 1944 presidential campaign, Kennedy asked Senator Harry S Truman, Roosevelt's running mate, "Harry, what the hell are you doing campaigning for that crippled son of a bitch that killed my son Joe?"[11] Within the Kennedy family, there became such a thing as "Joe time," when their father would sit for hours on the cushioned rocker, alone in the house in Hyannis Port, looking out across the lawn past the dunes to the heaving Atlantic, a Beethoven symphony playing on the record player and filling the empty house.[12] He would sit there and cry until he fell asleep in the chair.

As deep as his grief over Joe Jr. may have been, the elder Kennedy did not let go of his ambition to make a Kennedy president. Nor did the fact that Jack's health was shattered seem to count. Early in 1945 Jack wrote his friend Paul "Red" Fay how much he envied his life in sunny California. "I'll be back here with Dad trying to parlay a lost PT boat and a bad back into a political advantage. I tell you, Dad is ready right now and can't understand why Johnny boy isn't 'all engines full ahead.'"[13] When asked by Merle Miller whether he had misgivings about having the Catholic Jack Kennedy in the White House, former president Truman replied, "It's not the Pope I fear. It's the Pop."[14]

The dilemma for the plucky but often indolent Jack Kennedy in 1960 was that without his father's money and range of relationships with the likes of *Time-Life* publisher Henry Luce and J. Edgar Hoover, he could not win. With them, however, it became increasingly hard to deny the charge that the fix was in. Jack bridged the bargain with his nimble grace. He informed the press that he had just received a telegram from "Dad." "Dear Jack," he read with mock solemnity, "Don't spend one more dime than you have to. I'll be damned if I'm going to pay for a landslide." When he heard about this, the old man exploded. The joke was unbelievably stupid, he told Kenny O'Donnell. "Jack is too loose. . . . Fortunately for all of us, we have Bobby."[15] When journalist Fletcher Knebel checked with Jack about a rumor that his father had made a substantial personal loan to *Boston Post* publisher John Fox during the 1952 Senate campaign to shut him up, Jack turned Knebel over to

Steve Smith, who read the reporter an official denial. After Knebel told Kennedy he found the explanation acceptable, Jack put a friendly hand on the journalist's shoulder: "You know, we had to buy that fucking paper or I'd have been licked."[16] Jack may have been "loose" in his father's view, but his charm and calculated insouciance did much to allay the fear and loathing of his unscrupulous father.

Brod later recalled that he was the first person to greet Joe Kennedy that February day in Manhattan. Brod, who died in 1980, was a short barrel of a man, dark-complected with thick eyebrows. He had been an OSS captain in World War Two and his former commanding officer in Italy had been the CIA's Jim Angleton. The alliance between the Agency and the Mafia was in many ways a natural: the mob offered muscle, money, and quicker ways to do things; the government offered protection and a measure of legitimacy. The matter of the CIA's protection of Brod arose in 1963 when Attorney General Robert Kennedy, learning of Brod's intimate relations with the Teamsters, sought to question him. Only a call from Angleton to Kennedy kept Brod out of the clutches of the Justice Department. Again in 1975, Angleton phoned Senate staff attorneys Walt Elder and Matt Aaron, then working for the Church Committee investigating assassination attempts by the United States government, to warn them off, claiming Brod faced Mafia retribution if it was discovered that he had worked for the CIA.[17]

Also at the table that day was Tony Accardo or "Joe Batters," the sleepy-eyed former Capone bodyguard and reported participant in the St. Valentine's Day massacre. He had earned his moniker by beating men to death with a baseball bat. Accardo stepped aside in 1956 as leader of the Chicago syndicate in favor of Giancana. Subpoenaed by the McClellan Committee in 1957, Accardo had opted to take the Fifth Amendment no fewer than 144 times under an onslaught of questioning by Bobby Kennedy and other committee members. Another silent witness before the committee and a guest that day at lunch was Murray Humphreys, a tall, gray-haired man of Welsh origin with all-American looks. He was the Chicago mob's financial wizard and specialized in giving criminal operations legitimate storefronts. Humphreys, who in the 1920s had been one of Capone's enforcers, had by the 1950s become one of the "connection guys" who studiously and effectively corrupted judges and elected officials.[18] Humphreys, according to his widow Jeanne, disliked Joe Kennedy, considering him a "a four-flusher and a double-crosser."[19]

Johnny Rosselli himself was an ex officio member of the Chicago Outfit, having gotten his start in crime as a contract killer for Capone. In 1924, he had moved to Los Angeles for health reasons. There was something undeniably magnetic and dashing about Rosselli — the low, liquid voice, the coiffed silver hair, the high humor, the expensive dark suits with always a touch of bright plumage in his tie or handkerchief.

After twenty years of both muscling and financing the studios in Hollywood, coproducing some films himself, and romancing starlets like Lana Turner, June Lang, and Donna Reed, Rosselli had orchestrated the Chicago mob's expansion into Las Vegas in the mid-'50s. In addition to his polished look and confident style, so different from the usual mode of most syndicate leaders, Rosselli was unique in another way. Although his primary allegiance was to Giancana and the old Capone outfit, he now operated as an independent player, maneuvering among the snarling, paranoid mob clans as they moved into new sunlit pastures such as San Diego, Denver, and Phoenix. Despite his grade-school education, Rosselli was well read and sophisticated. His approach was to take careful measure of a man before ruthlessly moving on him. It was Rosselli who quietly engineered the introduction of the blue-eyed brunette Judy Campbell (a young woman he himself had once dated) to Senator Kennedy in February 1960 in Las Vegas after her affair with Rosselli's protégé, Frank Sinatra. For all of this, Rosselli was a devout Catholic.[20]

Like F. Scott Fitzgerald's glossy, self-invented Jay Gatsby, Johnny Rosselli remade himself when he moved west — severing ties with his family, the Saccos, in Boston, taking the name of the Renaissance artist who had painted the walls of the Sistine Chapel, producing movies like *G Man* that belied his criminal profession, and living in opulent lodgings at the Beverly Hills Garden of Allah (at the corner of Sunset Boulevard and Crescent Heights), where Fitzgerald, Ernest Hemingway, and a host of Hollywood's top stars came and went. Beginning in 1958, as part of their Top Hoodlum

Project, the FBI put Rosselli under surveillance. But the FBI telexes revealed little more than descriptions of beautiful women, expensive clothes, and occasional drunken afternoons at the Friars Club in the company of entertainment types. During this time, as he scripted a new life for himself in the city of make-believe, Rosselli slipped in and out of Los Angeles for criminal work in Havana, Las Vegas, and Chicago. When he flew to New York (for the meeting with Joe Kennedy), the Los Angeles FBI office reasoned that it was probably to arrange for the purchase of film rights to Broadway plays.[21]

The precise circumstances under which Rosselli became acquainted with Senator Kennedy are not known but probably date to the middle 1950s, when Kennedy's relationship with Sinatra became more constant. All three were assiduous pursuers of glamorous women; Rosselli (whom the FBI office in L.A. described during this period as "sex crazy") was a purveyor of women as well. Jeanne Carmen, Marilyn Monroe's neighbor and friend, remembered that Monroe met Rosselli "through the Kennedys."[22]

Bobby Kennedy would have known little, if anything, about this. What little time he took off from work, either as a Senate counsel or later as his brother's campaign manager, he tended to spend with his family. He must have at least heard rumors of his brother's (and possibly his father's) wide-ranging sexual adventures, particularly in Hollywood. But as a junior member of the male dynasty he did not question these philanderings.[23] Bobby no doubt knew of Rosselli's reputation but had not succeeded in subpoenaing him to testify before the McClellan Committee. On a trip to Las Vegas in 1958, Kennedy learned that Rosselli had attempted to take over the garbage union by buying off its leadership and then muscling the Las Vegas city manager.[24]

Finally at the lunch that day was Giancana himself, an ugly little man with a large wedge of nose rising out of his scowling face and a sloping and balding pate to which he constantly and fruitlessly administered. Unlike his rivals and sometime partners among the five balkanized New York families, Giancana enjoyed total power in Chicago. The Chicago Outfit was more disciplined, vicious, and politically savvy than its counterparts across the country. In the West, for example, its power was greater than that of all of the other Mafia families combined; in Las Vegas, the Chicago Outfit had control-ling interests in no fewer than four casinos, which together threw off about $10 million in skim a year. When other mobsters such as New York's Bugsy Siegel got out of line, Chicago exacted execu-tion. Even the powerful Meyer Lansky, who had organized the na-tional syndicate, could not save his old partner Siegel, who was gunned down in Beverly Hills on June 20, 1947. "I had no choice," Lansky laconically commented after Siegel's murder. In 1955, when another Lansky confederate, Louis Strauss, tried to extort cash from Las Vegas casino owner Benny Binion, Rosselli and the Chicago sluggers were called in. "Russian Louie" was garroted outside Up-land, California. Lansky again waxed philosophical in conversation with Chicago mobster Marshall Caifano. "That's the last time a Jew will cheat a Sicilian in this town," he told him.[25] Within the hood-lum community, the Chicago mob was known for using torture be-fore the execution of its victims as well as for its capacity, in a business where murder was the highest art, to conceal the source of the hit after the fact.

But by far the most distinctive trait of the Chicago Outfit — and one Joe Kennedy knew well — was its huge political machine, which controlled roughly one-third of the Chicago vote and could deliver margins of over 90 percent in key wards, if required. Gian-cana and his lieutenants had a working relationship with Chicago mayor Richard Daley, who rarely opposed their will, as well as with two U.S. congressmen, Roland Libonati and Thomas O'Brien, who were completely in their pocket. One of Giancana's mob colleagues, Marshall Korshak, was then serving as Illinois State director of rev-enue. The Outfit even managed in 1962 to place one of its capos, Richard Cain (né Scalzetti), as the chief investigator in the Cook County Sheriff's Office.[26]

Joe Kennedy's pitch, Brod later reported, was direct: he wanted $500,000 for Jack's presidential campaign. For Joe Kennedy, the money itself was not the critical issue. He was worth hundreds of millions of dollars. What was critical was the support that followed the money, particularly the Chicago Outfit's vote-getting strength. There was little discussion of the merits of Jack Kennedy's candi-dacy until Giancano's lieutenant Murray Humphreys, evidently under instruction, took Joe Kennedy to task about his other son,

Bobby. Humphreys pointed out the abuse that each had suffered before the McClellan Committee. Robert Kennedy had even called Sam Giancana "a sissy" before the reporters and television cameras.[27]

The elder Kennedy replied that it was Jack who was running for president, not Bobby, and that this was "business, not politics." The argument was not exactly persuasive, as Kennedy shortly thereafter got up and excused himself from the lunch, leaving Rosselli with some explaining to do. Brod remembered that Rosselli emphasized that it was Kennedy who had come to them, and that this was significant.[28] The pitch worked. One week later Paul "Skinny" D'Amato delivered $500,000 to 230 Park Avenue, Kennedy's Manhattan office.[29]

May 10, 1960

Charleston, West Virginia

In the weeks that followed Joe Kennedy's lunch in New York the Kennedy campaign for president foundered. In the Wisconsin primary on April 5, Senator Hubert Humphrey from neighboring Minnesota put up a spirited fight against Kennedy's phalanx of paid professionals and nonstop barrage of mailings and advertisements. Kennedy's strategy was to defeat the "Catholic issue" in a Protestant state, but from the start Protestant Wisconsonians seemed resistant to his appeal.[30]

Campaign manager Bobby Kennedy, frequently bareheaded and coatless in the frozen March weather, drove desperately from town to town, personally recruiting volunteers and remorselessly pushing his staff round the clock. Family friend Charles Spalding later remembered being on a train with Bobby when it broke down several miles outside of town one night. Bobby simply jumped off and walked the rest of the way. On another occasion, Kennedy advance man Jerry Bruno got a late-night call from Bobby, who was lost and did not know what town he was in. Bruno asked him to describe some landmarks. "I'm looking out the window of a phone booth," he told Bruno. "I see one bar, another bar, and on my side of the road a huge cow pasture with a bunch of cows staring at me, wondering who the hell is this jerk in the phone booth at midnight, in the middle of winter, in the middle of Wisconsin! I can't ask someone, because there is nobody up at midnight to ask."[31] In the end, Kennedy won by 8 percent over Humphrey (probably due to a Republican crossover in the open primary) but, in both a media and political sense, it was a defeat. The vote had broken on strictly religious grounds.

According to campaign lieutenant Larry O'Brien, there was "a terrible sense of gloom" in the Kennedy camp. In an interview with the dispirited Jack, CBS anchor Walter Cronkite raised the obvious question of whether a Catholic could be elected president and Kennedy fumbled the answer. At the end of the interview, Bobby stormed over to Cronkite and berated him in front of the producers for having violated "an agreement," saying he would never again be allowed to interview Senator Kennedy.[32] Back in Washington, Lyndon Johnson huddled with senior aides in anticipation of Kennedy's defeat in the May 10 primary in solidly Protestant West Virginia.

"West Virginians for Kennedy" had been working the state for a good fifteen months before the primary, but polling in early April 1960 showed Kennedy facing defeat by better than a 60–40 margin. Interviews with voters showed widespread antipathy to Catholics. After a brief rest in Montego Bay, Jamaica, in the wake of the Wisconsin primary, Senator Kennedy flew into West Virginia and began to work the small town cafes, hollows, and coal-mine entrances at shift change in brutal daily schedules. As Theodore White described it, "Up and down the roads roved Kennedy names, brothers and sisters all available for speeches and appearances; to the family names was added the lustrous name of Franklin D. Roosevelt, Jr."[33] Roosevelt's father had brought dirt-poor West Virginia back from the economic dead during the Depression. Another West Virginia celebrity, New York Giant all-pro linebacker Sam Huff, was also pressed into doing campaign duty for Kennedy, who went on TV and explained his stand on the separation of church and state with exceptional force.

But it was not going to be easy, and Jack Kennedy, privately admitting that he expected defeat, flew to Washington on primary day morning to escape the press. What he did not know was that his father had mounted a massive vote-buying operation during the last week of the campaign, the likes of which West Virginia had never seen before.

The key element in the West Virginia primary was the printed "slate card" of approved candidates that Democratic unions, clubs, and a multitude of factions distributed to their followers in the days before the election. At the top of the slate card was the preference for president. The names of the candidates were chosen by a variety of union, party, and faction bosses, many of whom were given money, usually in the hundreds of dollars, in exchange for their exercise of preference.

In the final days of the campaign, using both planes and cars, Ambassador Kennedy's office moved in hundreds of thousands of dollars (possibly over $1 million) in suitcases into the state. In Logan County, Democratic county chairman Raymond Chafin was approached by a man who had flown into the town of Logan that morning. He asked Chafin to support Kennedy and to put Kennedy's name on the top of the slate card. Chafin replied he would need "thirty-five" to do this, meaning $3,500. He was given $35,000. Years later, in an interview with the author, Chafin pointed out that this payment only covered his own "Okie Justice" faction; that another payment was made to the larger "Ray Watts" faction in Logan County.[34] And this described the vote-buying operation in only one of West Virginia's fifty-five counties.

Lesser amounts, usually in the $2,000 to $10,000 dollar range, were given to the county sheriffs. The late House Speaker Thomas P. O'Neill described the pitch of one of Joe Kennedy's real estate partners, Eddie Ford, as he did the family business by car: "Sheriff, I'm from Chicago. I'm on my way south. I love this young Kennedy boy. He can help the nation, by God. He's got the feeling for it, you know. He'll do things for West Virginia. . . . Here's $3,000. Or here's $5,000. You carry your county for him and I'll give you a little reward on my way back."[35] And they did. The payoff scheme may well have extended to Protestant churches as well, if one believes Hubert Humphrey's published account of a conversation he later had with Richard Cardinal Cushing, the Catholic archbishop of Boston and Kennedy family prelate. Cushing told Humphrey that he and Joe Kennedy had chosen which West Virginia churches, particularly the black ones, to contribute to.[36] It stands to reason that Bobby Kennedy, as the campaign manager who was monitoring every possible vestige of the primary operation, knew about the vote-buying scheme, but we have no confirmation of this.

On May 10, 1960, by a margin of 61 percent to 39 percent, Kennedy defeated Humphrey in West Virginia, a state the national press had said a Catholic could never win. The size of the victory, in the words of Theodore White, wrote "its message for every politician in the nation to see."[37] Kennedy lieutenants Dave Powers and Kenny O'Donnell expressed the significance of West Virginia even more emphatically: "Kennedy won the Democratic presidential nomination in West Virginia, rather than at the national convention in Los Angeles two months later . . . giving him that opportunity to lick the religious issue in a showdown test that certainly must be a monument in American political history."[38] There was, in fact, no monument to be found in the West Virginia primary, only another ugly illustration of the power of money in American politics.

As FBI tapes would later reveal, certain mafiosi such as Giancana, Rosselli, and bagman Skinny D'Amato believed that it was their money that had won the Kennedy victory in West Virginia.[39] Whether this was true did not matter. What mattered was the expectation it created.

March 4, 1960

Havana, Cuba

Fidel Castro had just gotten back from a trip to the Cienaga de Zapata, a vast, uninhabited marshland on the south of the island that thirteen months later would be the site of the Bay of Pigs.[40] He had spent much of the trip hanging out at military encampments, playing dominoes, telling the troops about Cuban history over rum and cigars, testing some of their new grenade-launchers himself. After getting back to Havana, it is probable that he spent the night, as he consistently did during this period, at the Eleventh Street apartment of his lover and revolutionary collaborator, Celia Sanchez.

That morning, as usual, he moved according to mood and impression, drawing energy and insight from the people he met, and literally making it up as he went.[41] In March 1960, Cuba's turn toward the Soviet Union was taking on increasing force; there were discussions about trade deals and even arms shipments.

After sixty years as a de facto colony of the United States, Cuba's shift of allegiance and Castro's hostility toward the United States were causing mounting anger among a powerful phalanx of the American ruling class — Mafia overlords such as Meyer Lansky, for whom Havana gaming had been the crown jewel of an illicit empire; corporate chieftains of Standard Oil, United Fruit, and two dozen other multinational corporations; and the Eisenhower administration, whose CIA was already contemplating Castro's demise.

Castro was also facing internal challenges. Almost every week brought reports of defections and plots within Cuba, including some by his own Sierra Maestra comrades-in-arms. Such rumors and episodic outbreaks kept the so-called *lider maximo* in a state of armed alert. Castro was seen on one occasion standing in his open jeep, M-1 in hand, speeding through the Havana neighborhood of Miramar at the head of a convoy to attack a group of insurrectionists. In keeping with his multiple obligations and also possibly to confound those plotting against him, Castro shuttled between four different offices — the military command post in the Vedado residential district, Sanchez's apartment, a house he frequented near the Chaplin theater in Miramar, and the National Institute of Agrarian Reform, the organizational locus of the mass seizure of American and large-scale properties, including those of Castro's own family.

During Castro's first months in power in 1959, the American embassy in Havana reported to Washington that Castro's exuberant style and slapdash schedule, which included raidlike stops for ice cream at Carmelo's terrace cafe, were evidence of his youth (thirty-three) and Latin self-indulgence. By 1960, however, the embassy was communicating darker pathologies, which it characterized as involving "delusions of grandeur" and "tendencies toward paranoid violence." Never did it detect Castro's sure skill in framing and destroying his enemies. Nor did the embassy recognize that after twelve years in the murderous warren of Cuban revolutionary politics — the years in exile, in prisons, hiding out in the mountains, wading across the Rio Grande for secret meetings in the United States — Castro was a cunning man with a rat's sense of when to strike first. Despite the tension that grew between the two countries, neither side was prepared to break off the relationship — that is, until March 4, 1960, when an incident occurred that converted Castro into an avowed enemy of the United States and sent both countries into a dark spiral of hatred.

At 5 P.M. that day there was an explosion on *La Coubre,* a French freighter that had docked in Havana's inner harbor to unload seventy tons of military material Cuba had purchased from Belgium the previous year. Castro himself was dockside in minutes to direct the rescue operation of the burned and dismembered stevedores and crew members. At about 6 P.M., there was another explosion, this one killing Cuban soldiers and firemen and nearly injuring Castro as well. Castro, weeping and screaming orders to bring in trucks and medical personnel, remained on the scene until the dead, eighty-one in all, and wounded were attended to.

Castro immediately concluded that the United States was behind the disaster. Although the evidence was unclear, the effect on Cuba was like that on the United States when the *Maine* blew up in Havana harbor in 1898, burning the apparition of Spanish infamy into the American consciousness. The *La Coubre* incident left Castro and the mass of Cubans enraged at the apparition of such wanton murder and cowardice.[42] For Cuba, this coming to anger was its coming to power.

The next day, in a ceremony at the cemetery in Colon, Castro raged against the act, tears streaming down his face, at one point seizing his M-1 and shaking it over his head before the immense crowd. "Today I saw our nation stronger than ever. Today I saw our revolution more solid and invincible than ever. Cuba will never become cowardly. Cuba will not step back. The Revolution will not be detained. The Revolution will march ahead victoriously." He ended by using for the first time the slogan that would be repeated thereafter: *Patria o Muerte. Venceremos* (Fatherland or Death. We will triumph).[43]

Five days later, in a meeting of the National Security Council, President Dwight Eisenhower listened as Admiral Arleigh Burke proposed a coup d'état, noting that "any plan for the removal of Cuban leaders should be a package deal, since many of the leaders around Castro were even worse than Castro." Less than two weeks later, on March 17, President Eisenhower secretly approved a policy titled "A Program of Covert Action Against the Castro Regime." In July Eisenhower announced that the United States would stop purchasing Cuban sugar. Castro responded by seizing American oil-refining factories, sugar mills, and other assets whose total value came to $850 million. The Soviet Union promptly pledged to buy the balance of Cuba's sugar quota, and Castro's brother Raul flew to Moscow to negotiate the shipment of Soviet armaments.

The American leadership in Washington considered all of this, in Secretary of State John Foster Dulles's term, as "harrowing." For a superpower with fleets in every ocean, armies on three continents, and a martial ideology, namely anticommunism, to justify the Pax

Americana to its own as well as other peoples, armed insurgency in our own hemisphere was profoundly unsettling. To add to this, 1960 was of course an election year. The leading Democrat, Senator Kennedy, was using Cuba as an illustration of Republican weakness against communism. In campaign speeches Kennedy would charge that the threat of communism was now only "ninety miles from our shore."

To be sure, Senator Kennedy had heard countervailing opinions about the wisdom of a showdown with Castro. One such, at least in the realm of spoof, came from spy novelist (and James Bond creator) Ian Fleming, who told Kennedy over dinner in Georgetown:

> The United States should send some planes over Cuba dropping pamphlets, with the compliments of the Soviet Union, to the effect that owing to American atom-bomb tests the atmosphere over the island had become radioactive; and that radioactivity is held longest in beards; and that radioactivity makes men impotent. As a consequence, the Cubans would shave off their beards, and without bearded Cubans, there would be no revolution.[44]

The Republican nominee, Vice President Nixon, was meanwhile pushing hard in secret councils for Castro to be forcibly removed, either by invasion or "executive action." He was eagerly supported (and financially underwritten in his campaign for the presidency) by Miami multimillionaire William Pawley, former ambassador to Peru and Brazil and organizer (along with Claire Chennault) of the Flying Tigers during World War Two. Pawley was a trusted member of Eisenhower's kitchen cabinet and later claimed that the president had wanted to give him command of the secret war against Castro.[45] By midsummer 1960 the drive to eliminate Castro countenanced assassination.

It was for this reason that Johnny Rosselli was approached in Los Angeles in August 1960 and asked to fly to New York for a meeting with CIA officials in September. The morning of Rosselli's meeting with CIA officials at the Plaza Hotel, the *New York Times* reported that Castro too would be flying to New York. His osten-

sible purpose was to attend the opening of the UN General Assembly, but the real reason for entering what he called *la cueva del
lobo* (the wolf's den) was to attack the Americans on their own turf,
to ambush them diplomatically in the manner of a *guerrillero*.[46] His
plan was bold and dangerous — and, at least initially, successful.

July 16, 1960

Santa Monica, California

Democratic presidential nominee John F. Kennedy was stretched out on a lounge chair on the deck of Peter and Pat Lawford's 50-yard pool at their huge, rambling beachfront home at 625 Ocean Front Avenue in Santa Monica. He was wearing navy blue trunks and sporting square dark glasses as he angled his body and face toward the murky, tawny-colored sun. Presently, he rose stiffly and walked out the back gate of the compound and onto the long, flat Santa Monica beach.[47]

For a forty-three-year-old who had spent most of his adult life in a state of pain, Kennedy seemed unusually fit. But his appearance was misleading. The fact that Jack could even swim — much less run for president — was nothing less than remarkable. For all of his pain and multiple infirmities, his high intake of cortisone had at least the secondary effects of a heightened sense of well-being and an enhanced appetite for sex.[48] During the 1960 campaign, rumors about Jack's health abounded, as they had before. But Joe and Bobby Kennedy threw up a barrier between the press and Jack's battery of physicians, and publicly sourced his difficulties to "war-related injuries." The truth was that he was living on borrowed time. In the weeks before the Democratic convention in Los Angeles, the offices of two of Jack's doctors, Eugene Cohen and Janet Travell, were broken into and ransacked for records. Bobby was convinced it was the work of Lyndon Johnson, who, along with his lieutenant, John Connally, was spreading the rumor that Kennedy had an incurable disease.[49] But the story never quite took in the press, which in that era tended to give politicians the benefit of the doubt in matters considered to be private. As Jack stood to address the crowd of eighty thousand in the Los Angeles Coliseum to accept his party's nomination the previous day, few there knew that he had just received a heavy booster shot of novocaine in his lower back and was wearing an aluminum back brace. Those who knew only admired him more for his debonair stoicism.

As it had for Franklin Roosevelt, the daily struggle against infirmities somehow imparted a certain intensity of being and sparkle to Jack. He crossed the Santa Monica beach, nodding in his contained way at those who recognized him. He waded and then lowered himself into the surf and began to swim freestyle through the brownish water to a point two hundred yards away, where the sludgy coastal band turned a deep dark blue. From there, Kennedy began swimming parallel to the beach in a slow-cadenced stroke. By the time he swam back to his point of entry, a crowd of people had gathered to watch him emerge. When he did, with a broad grin on his darkly tanned face (due as much to a side effect of Addison's disease as to any sustained exposure to the sun), the small crowd began to cheer. Jack resembled not so much a politician as a Hollywood leading man.

But there was more to Kennedy than matinee idol at the dawn of the age of mass political merchandising. Beyond his looks — the recently disciplined shock of chestnut hair, the smiling stand of teeth, the gray, calculating eyes — the matrix of the man was unusual. He had an open, inquiring mind, a passion for ideas that was largely undulled by the neurotic and atomized practice of politics, and an experiencing nature that bordered on the Dionysian. Despite the chaos and exposure of the previous week, he had found the time and motivation to consort sexually with Judy Campbell, Marilyn Monroe, and the former wife of a diplomat.

Norman Mailer, who covered the Los Angeles convention and was to interview Kennedy in Hyannis Port three weeks later, did not know all this but he sensed that Jack had "the wisdom of a man who senses death within him and gambles that he can cure it by risking his life." It was fitting, Mailer wrote, that Kennedy should secure the nomination in a place such as Los Angeles, which combined "packaged commodities and ranch homes, interchangeable, geographically unrecognizable" with the cinematic dream factory of

Hollywood. The title of the *Esquire* article, "Superman Comes to the Supermarket," suggested that Jack Kennedy could bridge cultural and political opposites and satisfy a deep yearning in the body politic.[50] He could be Nietzsche's superman *(ubermensch)*, a "world historical individual" who would enter the undifferentiated commercial uniformity of the supermarket and impart heroic meaning to national, and even individual, life:

> It was a hero America needed, a hero central to his time, a man whose personality might suggest contradictions and mysteries, which could reach into the alienated circuits of the underground, because only a hero can capture the secret imagination of a people, and so be good for the vitality of his nation; a hero embodied the fantasy and so allows each private mind the liberty to consider its fantasy and find a way to grow.[51]

Peter Lawford remembered that by the time Kennedy had walked through the back gate of the Ocean Front Avenue compound, his partying pal and chief supporter in Hollywood, Frank Sinatra, was sitting poolside making some last-minute calls for the reception that evening. Toweling off, Kennedy heard Sinatra close a deal with another associate for a $10,000 contribution. Sinatra would later repeat to anyone who was listening what Kennedy had said when he hung up the phone:

"Frank, I'm going to tell my Dad that you're better at raising money than he is."[52]

The truth was that Sinatra, perhaps Hollywood's hottest star in 1960, had personally raised several hundred thousand dollars from the entertainment community, not counting whatever he had gotten from his friends in the mob. The person who had delivered the $500,000 to Joe Kennedy's office after that famous lunch was his boyhood friend from Hoboken, Skinny D'Amato.[53] In addition to appreciating Sinatra's role of rainmaker, Kennedy liked the man's style. There was a will there, a cunning that most of the kept, soft-edged leading men in Hollywood lacked. There was also a temper that, so Jack had heard, manifested itself in incendiary tantrums in which Sinatra broke things and attacked people. Sinatra was also unusually gifted, having remade himself from a choirboy crooner who ignited several hundred thousand bobby soxers in the late '40s, to an Academy Award–winning actor by the mid-'50s. For all his talent, at nearly every critical juncture in his meteoric rise to stardom he had depended on the ruthless intercession of his syndicate friends, chiefly Johnny Rosselli.

One such intercession occurred in May 1952. Sinatra, desperate to revive his declining career, asked Rosselli to go directly to movie mogul Harry Cohn to get him the role Cohn had already turned him down for in *From Here to Eternity*. Rosselli was able to get Cohn alone for a little chat. "Harry. I need your help. Either give Frank the role or I will have you killed."[54] Sinatra got the role and won an Academy Award.

By 1960, Sinatra was starting to call his own shots in Hollywood as a producer and actor. He had also created a hip, roguish cult of pals called the Rat Pack, who hung out in Las Vegas, making films like *Ocean's 11* and chasing women with brash aplomb. Through it all, the thing that didn't change for the skinny son of immigrants with pop-out ears and pool-water-blue eyes was that he continued to be the mob's best man in Hollywood and Las Vegas. He lent them glamour and legitimacy as well as access to the loftiest places in the entertainment industry.

By the time Peter Lawford joined Jack and Frank out near the pool that Saturday afternoon, Sinatra was cautiously, almost apologetically, explaining that among his guests tonight might be "some friends from Chicago."

"Well, Frank," Kennedy with mock sobriety, "just make sure they leave their shades in the car."

"Jack grinned," Lawford later said, "and Frank looked tremendously relieved."[55]

Sinatra proposed that Kennedy ask the stars at the reception that evening to barnstorm on his behalf. "What if Juliet Prowse or Angie Dickinson, or Judy Garland or Janet Leigh were to fly to Kennedy events around the country?" Sinatra asked.

Kennedy beamed and said it was a great idea. "I might even attend myself and do an overnight."

They subsequently talked about the wisdom of putting Lyndon Johnson on the ticket as vice president, a choice Bobby had at first angrily opposed. (Johnson later communicated to Clare Booth

Luce his own justification for taking the number two spot: "I looked it up. One out of every four presidents has died in office. I'm a gamblin' man, darlin', and this is the only chance I got.")[56]

A half-hour later, Kennedy retired to one of Lawford's five bedrooms to read and take a nap while Sinatra and Lawford continued to talk about the evening's guests. Built by Louis B. Mayer in 1926, the house was the crown jewel of the so-called Gold Coast. Its two-story, ocher-tiled rotunda rose out of a glistening white Spanish Riviera structure. The huge round living room, with a fifteen-foot-high ceiling with exposed dark beams, had a full stage under the floorboards that could be made to rise with a push of the button. During the 1940s, according to Meredith Harless, who then served as Mayer's chief assistant, it was the most important residence in Hollywood and became a mecca for the leading stars, directors, and producers associated with MGM.[57] Lawford bought the house in 1956 after marrying Patricia Kennedy. It was thereafter converted into a rambling, lavish getaway for his Kennedy in-laws as well as his Hollywood pals and gals.[58]

Sinatra was as nervous as a bridegroom that evening. In his usual prepossessing style, he advised Lawford to dress in a dark suit with Washington in mind. When Lawford walked into the living room in a cerise bow tie and a silk shirt, Sinatra, who was wearing a dark suit and a thin black tie, ordered him to change. Lawford refused and Sinatra erupted. Only the shoeless entry of Jack Kennedy, who emerged from his nap at around five, calmed matters. "I like the way Peter dresses, Frank, even though my life's ambition is to be like you."[59]

The ambition of the Kennedys for a good thirty years had been to exploit Hollywood. In the late '20s and early '30s, Joe Kennedy had invested in and at certain points managed three studios. He thereby established lifelong relationships with most of the established power brokers and studio heads. Jack's association with Hollywood, which had begun in the late '40s, was largely social, with Sinatra serving as his conduit to new stars and entertainment players. That evening at the Lawford home both generations were represented among the fifty or so guests, who included comedian Milton Berle, studio head Arthur Krim, filmmakers Otto Preminger and Darryl F. Zanuck, actors Tony Curtis and Pat O'Brien. Meredith Harless concluded that of all the actresses assembled, the leggy Angie Dickinson won the prize (as well as the attention of Jack Kennedy, who thereafter began a year-long affair with her).

As the sun went down, Sinatra asked the guests to gather in the garden near the children's playground for a short introduction of the presidential nominee. He didn't get very far. After Milton Berle interjected a wisecrack, the introduction turned into repartee between Sinatra and some of the more irreverent in the group. Someone suggested Sinatra sing instead of trying to talk.[60]

Kennedy's own remarks were brief. He thanked his brother-in-law for "lending us your house. I can assure you it will not be the last time." He then turned to Sinatra and, after a jocular aside about having the leadership of "someone who drives women wild," he plaintively thanked him for all his enthusiasm and energy. The guests' response was heartfelt and enthusiastic. As the party broke up, Kennedy and Sinatra stood near the front door to thank those attending. The next day Kennedy flew home to Hyannis Port to rest up for the long run ahead.[61]

Despite Sinatra's invitation, no Mafia chieftain attended the party that evening, according to those interviewed for this history. But the Mafia — and possibly others — was intent on covering its bets. Blackmail along with payoffs were the companion techniques that produced compliant politicians. Fred Otash, a private investigator in Los Angeles who performed jobs for a wide range of clients — including the mob — was called in to bug the Lawford home.[62] For the Kennedy brothers, their father's Faustian bargain with the Chicago mob was turning into something more — a Faustian embrace.[63]

September 24, 1960

Miami Beach, Florida

The United States government had never before in its 180-year history attempted, in a time of peace, to murder a foreign leader. But in the summer of 1960, off-balance from real and perceived defeats in foreign affairs, the Eisenhower administration authorized "wet operations" against two of the most incendiary detractors of the United States — Fidel Castro and Congolese premier Patrice Lumumba.

The world in 1960, one journalist put it, had the look of a "barroom on the verge of a brawl." There were insurgencies in Africa, Asia, and Latin America that American leaders thought might be epidemic. On May 1, the Russians shot down an American U-2 spy plane flying over Soviet territory, after Eisenhower had publicly denied any such overflight. At a Paris summit meeting of the leaders of the two superpowers, Nikita Khrushchev, whose porcine visage and podium-pounding truculence were cause enough for fright, called the president a liar and a hypocrite. The Japanese government withdrew its invitation to Eisenhower for a state visit because it could not guarantee his security in the light of anti-American demonstrations. In July, the recently decolonized Belgian Congo exploded into antiwhite insurgency. When Belgium intervened with troops, Lumumba asked Khrushchev for military help. The fatigue and near-panic of the Eisenhower administration that summer as well as the ascendancy of personalities like Richard Bissell, J. C. King, and E. Howard Hunt in Allen Dulles's CIA conduced to create a murderous expedient.

In a legal sense, President Eisenhower himself never formally authorized the attempts to murder; he rather ordered "all possible measures" to retain, in the favored phrase, "plausible deniability."

This gave the green light to Dulles and Bissell while providing them, in the event that such plotting ever came to light, the same defense as Adolf Eichmann: acting under superior orders. Hannah Arendt had termed this earlier iteration of impersonal, bureaucratic homicide "the banality of evil." The national security state itself, with its huge budgets, its institutionalized paranoia, its contending departments and agencies all armed with the imperative of anticommunist survival, swept away any sense of restraint. At least in the case of Lumumba, there also may have been a racial factor in the decision to kill him. In the course of his visit to segregated Washington that summer of 1960, he had demanded the sexual favor of *une blanche blonde* (a blonde white woman).[64]

The Mafia was already hard at work on plans to take out Castro, who had shut down its casinos and rackets and had jailed mafioso Santos Trafficante Jr., among others; Meyer Lansky had reportedly put a $1 million bounty on Castro's head. The CIA's purpose in creating a joint venture with the Mafia was to accelerate and assist in the effort to murder Castro. With Agency authorization, Robert A. Maheu, a former FBI agent who had become a freelance covert operator, approached Johnny Rosselli in early September 1960 to discuss the idea of collaboration. The two met at the Brown Derby restaurant in Beverly Hills and Maheu laid out the CIA's proposal to give Rosselli $150,000 to hit the Cuban premier. Rosselli was at first stunned, then doubtful about the idea, but after Maheu assured him that it was serious, he agreed to show up in New York on September 14 for a meeting with CIA officials.[65] From Rosselli's standpoint, there were advantages in a joint venture with the "G," as the hoodlums called the government. Beyond ridding Cuba of Castro and restoring the mob's biggest profit center east of Las Vegas, collaboration with the CIA could neutralize the federal government's nascent war against the Mafia. But could Rosselli get the job done? His experience in Mafia hits was extensive, probably numbering over thirty in the course of his career. None had involved a head of state, however. He knew Havana reasonably well, but he knew nothing of the habits and security status of Castro.[66]

The meeting at the Plaza between Rosselli, Maheu, and CIA division chief Jim O'Connell went smoothly. Rosselli agreed to go to Miami to put together a plan for the hit, but refused any payment of money for himself. If the government wanted a partner, he would sign up; if it wanted just a hit job, that was another thing. Above all, this was terra incognita for both parties.

From the start, Castro sensed that if he did not feint and move, he would be destroyed. His visit to New York was a brilliant ambuscade that both baited and bemused Washington, and gave him some breathing space to prepare to defend his island. Four days after Rosselli and the CIA men had arranged their business, Castro and his entourage of fifty arrived in the city. In almost comedic fashion, they first refused to pay their deposits at the Shelburne Hotel, then took their case in a streaming convoy of police, press, and pedestrians to Secretary General of the UN Dag Hammarskjold. Dressed in his olive-green fatigues and declaiming in a voice designed for the Plaza de la Revolucion in Havana, Castro informed the amazed Hammarskjold that if he could not find them lodging, the Cubans would march to Central Park. "We are mountain people," he boasted. "We are used to sleeping in the open air."[67]

But there was method to his madness. Although Hammarskjold found the Cubans alternative lodging, Castro, in a flamboyant motorcade up Seventh Avenue at midnight, moved into the Theresa Hotel in Harlem. Over the following week, Castro and his bearded and youthful confreres ate, drank, danced, and otherwise held court at all hours of the day and night. After receiving heads of state from the nonaligned world and Americans such as Malcolm X, Castro pulled off his coup de theatre — and the real reason for the trip — when he greeted Khrushchev at the entrance to the hotel before several hundred press and African Americans, in what the *New York Times* dryly described as "the biggest event on 125th Street since the funeral in 1958 of W. C. Handy, who wrote 'St. Louis Blues.' "

Castro had come to cement an alliance that would save revolutionary Cuba and have the additional effect of both changing the world's balance of power and bringing it to the brink of nuclear war. "He made a deep impression on me," Khrushchev wrote in his memoirs. Twenty years later, Khrushchev could still remember the embrace: "He bent down and enveloped me with his whole body."

The coupling confirmed Washington's worst fears. At a hospitality suite in the Waldorf Astoria that the CIA set up, incredibly enough, to entertain the huge detail of New York police protecting Castro, Inspector Michael J. Murphy was approached by a CIA agent who had a plan: the Agency would like to plant a special box of cigars at a place where Castro would smoke one. When he did so, the agent explained, the cigar would explode and blow his head off. Murphy was appalled.[68]

Rosselli meanwhile had boarded a plane for Miami to make his own murderous arrangements. He brought to this effort — and all his far-flung criminal pursuits — a verve that, if one accepts his FBI profile, was partly based on his devout Catholicism. There was a crusading, almost medieval, element to his use of diplomacy and terror in the cause of Mafia enterprise as well as a surprising concern about social justice. During this period, Rosselli retained Father Albert Foley, S. J., a professor at Springhill College in Mobile, Alabama, to script the true-life story, ironically enough, of a priest who traveled from New England to the South during the Civil War.[69] And so Rosselli, the criminal missionary who had traversed the Sun Belt for a decade from Los Angeles to Las Vegas to Phoenix to Dallas, providing juice and bringing in muscle, now prepared for his most ambitious mission in a city that was rapidly coming to a boil.

Miami was a city divided: the Beach, so familiar to Rosselli and his mob associates, with its pastel necklace of resorts three miles out to sea on a thin strip of coral; the opulent Miami of Coconut Grove and Coral Gables, with its verdant groves and tethered yachts; and the other Miami, a shabby freckling of stucco and clapboard, dredged and drained out of the dark green swamp and sprawling ever inward under the migrant-driven pressure of impoverished blacks and dispossessed Cubans. Nothing in any economic or cultural sense united these places except the blue apparition of sea, the heavy heat, and the vast, oozy Everglades that lay to the west and south. There was something at once glossy and seamy, growing and rotting about the place. Beneath it all lay the ulcerating swamp that continued to swell and collapse under the jerry-built development, as if to communicate the extent of the ecological imposition at hand.

Beginning in the middle of 1959, Miami turned at first slowly, then rapidly, into a war zone, altering the uneasy balance among poor blacks, south Florida rednecks, and Rotarians, and the millionaire boom-and-bust developers who ran the place. For a good twenty-five years, that balance had, strangely enough, depended on Havana. For the Cuban rich, Miami had served as a Switzerland of sorts. It was where they shopped, put their money, or boarded midnight flights to escape yet another round of Cuban political bloodletting. For the mob, flush with cash from the Havana casinos and rackets, Miami served as a pecuniary laundromat and a place where they could frolic free of any molestation from law enforcement. Accordingly, every member of the Chicago Outfit's high command had a home in Miami. Many of the Beach resorts, like the enormous Fontainebleau (where Capone's cousin, Joe Fischetti, served as social director) were mob-financed.

By September 1960, when Rosselli arrived to put the Castro conspiracy into operation, the great inundation of Cuban refugees, about two thousand per month, was cresting. In addition to the usual racial and economic frictions immigration causes, *Newsweek* detected something else, calling Miami "America's Casablanca," an enclave of the bitter and the brutalized, a place of spies and guns-for-hire, floating in a treacherous demimonde based on the dream of violently reclaiming Cuba. Miami, along with Dallas and Phoenix, had always been one of the most right-wing cities in the United States, but the Cuban dislocation gave that predilection violent cause.

With the arrival of the CIA in the summer and fall of 1960, anticommunism became south Florida's growth industry. Miami was suddenly transformed into a vast staging ground for the war against Castro. The CIA leased a 1,500-acre tract south of Miami that soon became the largest CIA base in the world. Exile recruitment centers run by Agency staff began popping up at the Opa-Locka Air Force Base, downtown Miami, Virginia Garden, and a half-dozen other places. Dozens of transport planes and de-mothballed bombers were flown into Opa-Locka and Homestead Air Force Base for use in the secret war. CIA officers began purchasing the first of some hundred safe houses to harbor exile agents and assets, as well as creating front companies — detective agencies, real estate companies, boat-repair businesses, etc. — to help conceal their vast enterprise and nominally employ thousands of exiles.

Operational sites and arms caches were scattered throughout the region, particularly in the Keys facing the Windward Passage to Cuba. The CIA navy in south Florida grew to two hundred vessels — supply ships, subchasers, high-speed patrol boats, airboats, and rubber landing craft. Meanwhile, scores, perhaps hundreds, of pro-Castro agents monitored the extraordinary buildup.

On September 24, 1960, the CIA's Jim O'Connell arrived in Miami to work out the assassination plot against Castro. He met Rosselli and Maheu at the executive suite they were sharing at the Kenilworth Hotel. It was decided beforehand that everyone at the meeting would use aliases, to maintain a deniable distance. Rosselli got O'Connell's agreement on two key concerns: that Giancana ("Sam Gold") and Trafficante ("Joe") would be looped into the plot (Rosselli simply included them in the meeting), and that the hit would be something "nice and clean," not the gangland-style ambush the CIA originally wanted. Poison was the preferred means. The next day, O'Connell and Maheu flew back to Washington and ordered up a slow-acting poison from the CIA's Technical Services Division, which CIA Director Dulles preferred to call the "Health Alteration Committee."[70]

October 21, 1960

South Florida

Jorge L. Recarey García-Vieta, a handsome, green-eyed Cuban of seventeen, looked back at the boiling wake of the Swift V-20 as it pulled out of the Miami River and accelerated into the harbor on a midnight ride across the Windward Passage. In five hours, operating under the name Julio Cesar Blanco, Recarey would be back in Cuba to join the underground fight against the regime of Fidel Castro. Concealed in his coat were sealed instructions to be given to the underground leader of the anti-Castro movement. Recarey's specialty was demolitions, a dangerous business for a rich man's son; those caught were either executed on the spot or brutally broken down by Castro's police interrogators.[71]

Recarey's odyssey from a life of privilege in Cuba to resistance training by the CIA in south Florida was fueled by several motivations. Castro's revolution had initially fascinated him and thousands of other young Cubans. By the first months of 1960, however, it had become a threat to his family and to his class. He had been revolted first by the sight of officially tolerated looting of the elegant homes in his Havana neighborhood of Vedado; then by the mass seizures of property by the state; and finally by the arrest of friends at the University of Havana, where Recarey was studying for a law degree. The fact that the Americans, with all their power and resources, had turned against Castro was a critical factor in the young Cuban's change of mind. As Manuel Artime, one of the leaders of the Cuban exiles, later commented: "The United States was great and powerful, the master not only of the hemisphere but perhaps of the world.... And the mysterious, anonymous, ubiquitous American agents who dealt with the Cubans managed to strengthen that belief."[72] Recarey dropped out of school and headed for Miami over the objections of his mother and father, who were trying to keep the family and its holdings together in Cuba.

In February 1960 Recarey signed on, and was flown to Panama with twenty other Cubans for special training in underground resistance, chiefly demolition, recruitment, and communications. The CIA case officers found that, owing to their level of education and motivation, the Cubans learned quickly and were, in the words of one of those officers, "filled with fight." Three months later, Recarey and the others were flown back to Homestead Air Force Base south of Miami, where for more than a month, under the tight supervision of three CIA officers, they exercised, passed the time in the barracks, and waited for an order to reinfiltrate. The Agency officers, known only by pseudonyms like "Carl," scrupulously excluded the young Cubans from any briefing about the covert plan. From an intelligence standpoint, keeping covert assets in the dark was sound strategy, but it reflected a basic problem in the relationship: the Americans did not trust the Cubans; they understood almost nothing of the Cuban political culture; and they did not speak Spanish. To the Americans, Cuba had no other meaning than the destruction of Castro. Put bluntly, the exiles were expendable. The full expression of this attitude would be revealed on the reefs and beaches of the Bay of Pigs and in the dangerous phenomenon that would bedevil the Kennedy administration afterward — the "disposal" of the exiled Cubans.

But these issues did not concern either Jorge Recarey or his CIA handlers that October night. As the V-20 headed out into the open ocean, the challenge was to steer through the submerged shoals off the Cuban coast, dodge any Cuban patrol boats, and rendezvous with the friendly forces near Arcos de Canisi on the northeastern coast. As they came within sight of the coastal lights of Cuba about 3 A.M., the Cuban boat pilot, Eugenio Rolando Martinez (affectionately known as "El Musculito," owing to his diminutive but potent proportions), began taking readings and sightings to effect the landing.[73] Recarey felt his skin crawl. A jolt of fear struck the bottom of his stomach as he readied himself. He popped a tablet of Benzedrine to keep his energy up for the travail ahead, and waited. The boat maneuvered within several hundred yards of the surf, the engine idling down. Everyone searched the shore for some signal.

Nothing. After thirty minutes of fruitless searching, the decision was made to abandon the mission and return to Florida. Recarey's dangerous mission would have to wait for another day.

In that same third week of October 1960, Mafia leaders, in an effort to collect on Meyer Lansky's $1 million bounty on the life of Castro and restore their billion-dollar enterprise in Cuba, put their assassination plan into operation. An FBI bug (code-named "Little Al") in a tailor shop in downtown Chicago frequented by the leaders of the Chicago Outfit picked up a conversation in which Sam Giancana "assured those present that Castro's assassination plot would occur in November." Giancana was recorded as saying that he had already met the assassin-to-be.[74]

Although the intercepted conversation landed like a rocket back in FBI headquarters, Hoover chose to withhold the information from the CIA (which, given its own approach to the mob, would have been edified by the news) as well as from the Justice Department. His reasons? First, he trusted neither the CIA, for which he reserved a jealous animosity given its Cold War ascendance, nor Justice, most of whose chieftains were political appointees and therefore incapable of keeping secrets. Second, given that bugging was illegal under the Fourth Amendment and inadmissible in a prosecution, sharing it would have exposed Hoover and the Bureau. Third, as Anthony Summers and other writers have demonstrated, Hoover himself had been compromised by the Mafia.[75] His homosexual relationship with his assistant, Clyde Tolson, was a known fact within mob circles. During Hoover and Tolson's twice-yearly betting sojourns at the Santa Anita and Del Mar tracks, underworld figures like Costello and Rosselli fixed races and, for good measure, introduced Hoover and Tolson to lesser mob lights.

One such was Eugene Hale Brading, a West Coast shooter who would later become a Lansky courier. Brading, who subsequently claimed to have met Hoover at Del Mar in the early 1950s, was the same man who was flown to Dallas on November 21, 1963, in a private plane and who was arrested on November 22, 1963, minutes after the Kennedy shooting, near the Dal-Tex Building facing Dealey Plaza. Testifying in 1978, Brading admitted to being in the building, claiming that he had gone there in search of a pay phone on the third floor.[76]

In its intercept of Giancana's conversation in October 1960, the FBI paraphrased Giancana as stating that "the assassin had arranged with a girl . . . to drop a pill in some drink or food of Castro." It is now clear that the assassin being referred to was Richard Cain, a blond, fair-complexioned twenty-nine-year-old with, as FBI Special Agent William Roemer described him, "a confident air, a jaunty step, and a big smile . . . too handsome, too charming, too sure of himself." Cain also had an intelligence level that was off the charts.[77]

Cain was then serving as the Mafia's infiltration agent in the Chicago Police Department. He was in charge of paying off hundreds of Chicago cops and detectives as well as tipping off the mob to the movements and investigations of the Chicago police. But Cain was never one to sit still for long. In March 1960, he got himself in trouble for beating to death a "jack-roller" (a mugger of gay men) in a Chicago police station, and a few weeks later led a police raid on a bordello during which he pocketed some $30,000. This was not consistent with the rules of either the Chicago mob or the police department but, given his close relationship with Giancana — it was rumored that he was Giancana's illegitimate son — Cain was covered until he tried to bug the office of Mayor Daley's chief investigator (to assist Republican state attorney Ben Adamowski, a fierce Daley opponent). He was caught in the act and suspended from the Chicago Police Department in September 1960.[78]

For Cain, the Castro hit represented a fresh opportunity. Within two weeks of his suspension, he showed up in a top-secret CIA telex regarding his plans to fly to Cuba with Jack Mabely, a *Chicago News* columnist.[79] The head of the CIA's office in Chicago, Robert P. B. Lohmann, reported that he was unclear about Cain's purpose, only that he was fully fluent in Spanish and a pilot. In Miami, Cain worked out of Accurate Laboratories (a private investigation service that was a CIA front) and had meetings with Tony Varona (the Mafia's Cuban strongman-in-waiting who was supposed to replace the assassinated Castro) and Angel Solano, a Trafficante henchman. He also met with Rosselli, who had flown down to Miami for his third round of assassination meetings with the CIA's Jim O'Connell at the Aztec Hotel. The Castro hit was bringing together a hellish brew of murderous interests. The United States government was adding the ingredient Rosselli thought most critical to the advancement of Mafia interests — cover.

The Cain plot was to hit Castro at the Nacional Hotel in Havana (still nominally owned by Lansky associate Michael McLaney) when the Cuban leader dropped by, as he did on a regular basis, to visit one of his paramours. "The young woman," a CIA memorandum said, would "service Castro and attempt to poison him." Cain, a man who prided himself on never farming out any of his contracts, would be the team leader on the ground. He would then fly himself back to the United States. However, Cain was unable to get assurances of a secure place to land in Cuba. Castro, expecting to be invaded at any moment, had placed Cuban police and militia on high alert.

Reviewing the entire FBI and CIA file from the period, the staff of the House Select Committee on Assassinations summarized the situation in 1978: "The mob was then in a perfect position. If their private plot actually worked, and Castro died, then the syndicate had enormous blackmail potential against the CIA, which it could exercise at the opportune moment. However, if their intrigue backfired, then their position would be that they were only attempting to execute the wishes of their government."[80]

November 8–9, 1960

Hyannis Port, Massachusetts, and Forest Park, Illinois

Jack Kennedy walked alone across the wide, sand-patched lawn that divided his Hyannis Port cottage from his brother Bobby's within the oceanfront compound that Joseph Kennedy had purchased in 1928. It was 6:50 P.M., already dark. At a point between the two white clapboard cottages, the dunes fell away and the wind coming off the freezing water buffeted his face and snapped and pulled at his clothes.

As he climbed the wooden steps to the porch, he heard cheering coming from within the house. The thirty-five or so family members and key staff who had gathered to await the returns were delighted by the report of the first complete precinct from Cleveland: Kennedy 158; Nixon, 121.[81] The report was largely meaningless, but as with any election-night vigil, returns — even bad returns — at least slake the tension of long-deferred wonderment about the outcome.

Kennedy walked into the dining room of his brother's cottage, which had been transformed into a command control center. A tangle of cords and cables laid on the floor. There were tables with phones staffed by fourteen operators and a separate set of phones with dedicated lines for the chieftains — Kenny O'Donnell, Dick Donahue, Larry O'Brien, Ralph Dungan, and the campaign manager himself, Bobby Kennedy. Around the room were lounge chairs, typewriters, and four television sets, and trays full of finger sandwiches, compliments of the Mayfair Catering Service, on the tables.[82]

The candidate, his face puffy from his recent nap and bone-deep fatigue, was nattily dressed. He wore a Scottish tweed jacket over a white cotton shirt, tan twill trousers, green necktie, and brown loafers. He walked over to his father, who stood next to Bobby, arms folded, both staring expressionlessly at a TV screen. Neither looked up as Jack joined them.

The election-night drill for Democrats normally followed predictable patterns, but that evening even hard-bitten pros like O'Donnell and O'Brien lost their bearings in the seesaw that was about to take place. The quadrennial rule for Democrats was to ignore the early-evening trickle of Republican votes (and certainly any projections based on it), and wait and pray for a huge, urban industrial Mid-Atlantic, Midwest, and Eastern tide between about nine and midnight that would reach a crest with the southern returns, and then hang on as the long, slow Republican countertide of the Farm Belt, the Rocky Mountain states, and the far West rolled in from midnight till about 3 A.M.[83] The characteristically trenchant Bobby Kennedy had concluded that morning, "We better see a margin of 2.5 million or better by midnight."[84]

Associated Press's first summary total, which chattered out at 7:15 P.M. in an upstairs baby room, fell along predicted lines: Nixon 203,628; Kennedy 166,963. Jack look a little peeved when his brother-in-law Peter Lawford, just in from Hollywood, came sprinting down the stairs in his socks with the torn-off sheet, presenting it to the candidate as if it were some wounded bird. Some minutes later there was better news: Walter Cronkite announced that Kennedy was winning Connecticut by 100,000. Kennedy's three sisters, Jean, Eunice, and Pat, along with Ethel, cheered. Jacqueline Kennedy, eight months pregnant and recently arrived at the cottage, sat on a white loveseat behind them with a polite smile on her face.

Jack went upstairs to talk to his pollster Lou Harris, who was working off his calculations (essentially based on Truman's victory in 1948 and Stevenson's loss in 1952) to project the Kennedy vote. Just then, CBS News, touting its IBM mainframe and a small sea of number-crunchers in the background, made the startling projection (based on 500 precincts) that Nixon would win in an electoral landslide, placing the odds against Kennedy at 100 to 1. A low groan emanated from downstairs, but Jack was matter-of-fact: "That's bullshit."[85] Looking at the thirty-two-year-old Harris, surrounded by reams of paper and holding a slide rule, he gleefully encouraged him to prove it: "It's Lou against the machine," Kennedy said with a broad grin on his face. He bit off the end of a Havana Royal panatela and lit up.[86]

Moments later he returned downstairs, went over to Jackie, helped her up, and announced, "Well, we're off to dinner." As they walked out, their friend Bill Walton joined them for the walk back to their cottage. Over dinner, as Mrs. Kennedy was putting five-year-old Caroline to bed, Kennedy asked Walton, an internationally recognized painter, to appraise a seascape he had painted. "A primitive," was the reply from Walton.

About an hour and a half later at 10:45 P.M., the Kennedys returned with Walton to Bobby's cottage. The urban industrial tide from Pennsylvania, New York, Massachusetts, and New Jersey was now flowing strongly in Kennedy's direction. On the so-called "totalizers," or number tabulators, Kennedy was now ahead by over 1 million votes. Jackie, who had joined them, went over to her husband upon seeing the numbers and quietly said, "Oh, Bunny, you're president now." "No . . . no . . . it's too early yet," he replied.

In the Hyannis Port Armory, where two hundred or so press people were gathered, anxious to file their stories, a burly man with a sour face and the suspicious manner of a detective mounted the platform. As Theodore White later described it, "[H]e jounced heavily to see whether it would bear the weight of the full presidential party." All eyes watched him as he was joined by other plainclothesmen. In their effort to extract the most immediate common denominator of meaning, the press took this to mean that Kennedy had been elected. CBS then ran the tape of California's Governor Pat Brown, who predicted that Kennedy would take the state by 800,000.[87] Kennedy, either out of tension or disbelief, shook his head; he had never thought of California as a Kennedy state.

At about 11:30, Jack walked Jackie back to their cottage to wish her good night. By this time, a mobile TV unit, using the justification that it would take klieg lights forty minutes to warm up, had illuminated the cottage in a blinding glare. The country and its politics were on the threshold of a medium whose essential achievement was its intrusive immediacy, and whose justification was technique. History was about to become entertainment.

About a half hour later Kennedy crossed back to the command center to find a very different situation. In a low voice, Larry O'Brien gave Jack an update: the news was bad. They were losing Ohio, Wisconsin, Kentucky, Tennessee, the Farm Belt, and Illinois and Michigan. "We're running under our projections with about half in," O'Brien told him. Kennedy listened impassively. His father was on the phone. Jack walked over to his father and raised a fist in greeting. In their family style, the old man grabbed the top of his fist with his free hand, enclosing it completely. Bobby continued to stare transfixed at the TV monitor.

As they watched Ohio fall out of reach, Jack's composure finally broke. He shook his head and said disgustedly, "Ohio." He rolled up his sleeve to reveal a swollen hand and distended thumb. There were bruises and scratches all the way up his forearm. "Ohio did that to me," he said referring to his six trips to that state and final headlong run through southern Ohio toward the end of the campaign.

A few minutes later, someone called out, "Jack, we got Lyndon on the phone."

Kennedy signaled for the phone. After greeting Johnson, he listened for a moment, smiled, and said, "Well, that's good to hear." He continued to listen, laughed, and said, "I don't know." After the usual salutations, Kennedy hung up.

"What did Lyndon have to say?" Bobby asked.

"He says, 'I see we won Pennsylvania. What happened to *you* in Ohio?'"

There was laughter. Jack approached his brother and asked for an update. Bobby explained that four states were outstanding: Minnesota, California, Michigan, and Illinois.

There was silence as Jack looked at his father and Bobby. "Talked to Mayor Daley?"

Bobby shook his head and reached for a phone. Jack listened as Bobby spoke into the receiver. The tone was dry and sharp. "Mayor, we don't have your vote." He listened briefly. Jack, obviously displeased by the tone of his brother, took the phone. He greeted Daley, thanked him for all his help, and asked him how it looked. The room went silent except for the drone of the televisions and the intermittent ringing of phones. After Jack signed off, he looked at his brother and said, "He said we're going to make it with the help of a few close friends."[88]

Johnny Rosselli came out of the small office in the back of the Armory Lounge that served as Sam Giancana's inner sanctum. The bar, which was located at 7247 West Roosevelt Avenue, in Forest Park, Illinois, was a nondescript one-story brick structure that dated back to the 1920s, when it served as a Capone-run speakeasy. Rosselli walked into a large room, where eight women sat behind tables on the phone. He went quietly from one to the next, listening as each woman reported the vote total from the wards each was covering. Sam Giancana stood at the office door watching Rosselli make the rounds.[89] With him were two of his *capo regime,* Charles Inglese (known as Chuckie English), the boss of the 29th Ward, and Dave Yaras, whose central skill was execution but who also served as the leader of the 24th Ward. (Several months later the FBI would install a microphone behind the baseboard of Giancana's inner office and gain critical information about the Chicago Oufit's most secret workings, including its connection to the Kennedys.)[90]

Rosselli's presence in Chicago was unusual since he had left it some thirty years before to do the Outfit's business out west. But his diplomatic and organizational skills were critical in situations such as this and he had been called home. Doris Mulcahy, interviewed in October 1996, could no longer link particular hours with particular incidents that evening, only the apparition of Rosselli making the rounds and calculating the totals in his head.

The problem for the Kennedy campaign was that the Kennedy-Johnson ticket was doing even worse than expected downstate, ultimately losing 93 of Illinois's 105 counties. The critical question was: How much could Cook County deliver? Rosselli was probably working off Daley's estimate that the necessary Kennedy vote margin from Chicago was 300,000.[91] Whatever the case, there was the other unanswered question of *when* Chicago would report its vote. In their time-honored, statewide cat-and-mouse game, the Republicans and Democrats would hold back reporting votes, and then try to one-up the other by providing partial vote reports, nearly all vitiated by corruption.

At 3 A.M., in the very accurate memory of Kenny O'Donnell, Mayor Daley called him at Bobby Kennedy's house to explain the ongoing dialectic: "Every time we announce two hundred more votes for Kennedy in Chicago, they come up out of nowhere down-state with another three hundred votes for Nixon. One of their precincts outside of Peoria, where there are only fifty voters, just announced five hundred votes for Nixon."[92]

Daley's claim that there was plenty of vote fraud downstate was undoubtedly true, but it obscured the greater reality that in Chicago a substantial percentage of election day votes had either been created, purchased, destroyed, or simply stolen in the manner of a very efficient Third World dictatorship. Many Chicago voters were no longer living; many of those living no longer lived in Chicago. In addition to the ghosts on the rolls, the prevailing practices of election officials at the polls bordered on subornation. An investigation in 1962 revealed, for example, that of the more than 300 votes cast in the 41st Precinct, 27th Ward, "not more than ten votes were cast in private."[93] The curtains of voting booths were often left open and voters were "assisted" in the act of voting by judges and precinct captains whose operating motto in terms of their total control of their habitat was later memorialized in a book title: *We Don't Want Nobody Nobody Sent.*[94] In mob-controlled precincts, unwanted votes on paper ballots were often destroyed. For Giancana and his confederates, voting was an essential racket. To get the results they wanted that election day, they deployed some 900 *soldati*, as well as temporary operatives. On the mob-controlled West Side, Kennedy was averaging well over 80 percent; in the 29th Ward, legendary ward committeeman Bernard Neistein estimated the Kennedy-Nixon "take" at 27,000 to 500 (a 95 percent plurality).[95]

At a little before 4 A.M. back at Bobby Kennedy's cottage, Jack called it quits for the night, saying, with no trace of irony, "The votes are all in. I can't change any of them now."[96] He walked in silence with Cornelius Ryan (author of *The Longest Day*) across the illuminated expanse back to his cottage. Kennedy was still seven electoral votes short of the 269 needed to win. Shortly thereafter, the rest of the team wearily boarded the bus outside the compound on Scudder Avenue for the trip back to the Yachtsman Hotel.

Only Bobby Kennedy stayed, his voice gone hollow, the orbs of his eyes now slits, standing like a lone sentry. Waiting. Watching. Sometime later that morning, probably around 5:15, Daley called him with the news that Illinois would go to his brother. The margin was 8,858 votes — out of 4.75 million cast. Was the Chicago Mafia pivotal in the result? In the judgment of Notre Dame law professor and former chief counsel to the House Select Committee on Assassinations G. Robert Blakey, it was. Blakey told Seymour Hersh that based on his review of the transcriptions of FBI bugs in Chicago, "Beyond doubt, in my judgment, that enough votes were stolen — let me repeat that — stolen in Chicago to give Kennedy such a significant margin that he carried the state of Illinois."[97]

In the end, Kennedy's victories in Michigan and Minnesota put him over the top, but it was Texas and particularly Illinois that the Republicans jumped on. It quickly became a subject the Kennedy staff would not talk about. When Larry O'Brien asked Bobby later that morning about the possibility that Nixon would call for a federal investigation of vote fraud in Illinois, Bobby's answer was direct: "There's nothing he can do about it and therefore we don't need to talk about it." Throughout that day, however, as Ethel later remembered, "Bobby had that awful gnawing feeling that it could be reversed."[98]

But it was not only the fractional victory and the manner of its achievement that gnawed at Robert Kennedy. He suspected something else: for all his work (fifteen months of eighteen-hour days); for all the distance (some 220,000 miles) his brother had traveled, most of them in physical pain; for all the money his father had spent, that at the end of this picture-perfect campaign, the Kennedy dream may well have been delivered by people who murdered for a living.

At the moment of victory he must have sensed that there was trouble ahead.

December 15, 1960

Washington, D.C.

At 6:45 on this December morning, Bobby Kennedy walked out of his home in McLean, Virginia, accompanied by his best friend John Seigenthaler, a lanky thirty-three-year-old former reporter for the *Nashville Tennessean*. Seigenthaler had lived upstairs in Kennedy's home in October 1959 while editing Kennedy's book on the Mafia.[99] It was cold. A snowstorm the previous weekend had left a ghostly five-inch carpet that had drifted against the trees and hollows of Hickory Hill, his white brick antebellum home, which had once served as the Civil War headquarters of General John McClellan.

Kennedy and Seigenthaler got into the dead-cold Cadillac convertible. They were driving to President-elect John F. Kennedy's Georgetown home to inform him that Bobby would not be serving in his administration. Bobby had already told Jack in Hyannis Port the morning after the election that he didn't want to be his attorney general. There was one problem: Joe Kennedy was absolutely insistent that Jack appoint Bobby attorney general; he told Jack he would need someone he could trust utterly. On the night of December 14, Bobby called Jack to confirm that he wanted out. "This will kill my father," Bobby said as he dialed his brother's number. Jack, however, insisted they discuss it in person in the morning over breakfast.[100]

Bobby and Seigenthaler crossed the Potomac on Chain Bridge en route to Georgetown. Kennedy, deeply tanned from a post-election vacation in Mexico, had celebrated his thirty-fifth birthday three weeks before. Except perhaps for his deep-set blue eyes, which projected an opaque, hardened, and at times brooding gaze, he looked five years younger than his age. His weight since the elec-

84

tion was back up and gave him the appearance of a middleweight wrestler — compact, slump-shouldered, with thick, articulated forearms and heavily muscled legs. During the eight-mile trip to Jack's, Bobby had nothing to say. His mind was made up. He wanted out. He had told Jack he was "tired of chasing bad guys." But it probably went beyond that.[101] In the long, cruel grind of the campaign, he had angered and disturbed a great many people. Even within the tribe there were now reservations about him. Dave Powers, as loyal a lieutenant as the Kennedys ever had, likened him in print to the ferocious Ty Cobb, a man who would win at any cost, who would attack other players in the clubhouse, spike them with his cleats when he slid into a base.[102] When Texas billionaire H. L. Hunt sent a substantial cash contribution to the campaign, Bobby ordered Ralph Dungan to take a plane straight to Texas and hand the money back. "This man will have to be prosecuted if we're elected."[103]

Winning at any cost meant the pursuit of ends over means and, for a man like Robert Kennedy, who believed in sin, this was immoral. It also violated Oscar Wilde's maxim, "One should be very careful in the choosing of one's enemies." Bobby's tendency to play his politics for keeps, keeping score, holding ground, and hitting back with a vengeance, was now extending beyond the campaign. After the election, he put in a call to William Mahoney, a Phoenix lawyer who had run the Arizona campaign. He told Mahoney he needed a "shit list" of those who had promised to help and then had sold out to Nixon.[104] It was as if he couldn't help himself from pouring it on, and so he wanted out, wanted to travel around the world, or write a book, or become a college president, or run for governor of Massachusetts. He lunched with his old traveling companion and fellow radical, Associate Supreme Court Justice William O. Douglas, who agreed with him that he should try something new.

Over a breakfast of bacon and eggs in the small breakfast nook of the president-elect's narrow brick townhouse, Jack ticked off the emerging roster of cabinet appointments, commenting on them in terms of the politics or the merits of their selection. Finally Bobby said to him, "Now, Johnny. Can we talk about my situation?"

The president-elect replied at length, directing his observations more to Seigenthaler than to his brother. "There really is no person with whom I have been intimately connected over the years. I need to know that when problems arise I'm going to have somebody who's going to tell me the unvarnished truth, no matter what." Giving examples of Robert McNamara and Dean Rusk as people he respected but did not really know, he spoke of the critical nature of civil rights: "I don't want somebody who is going to be faint-hearted. I want somebody who is going to be strong, who will join with me in taking whatever risks . . . and who would deal with the problem honestly."[105]

Then Jack spoke directly to Bobby. "If I can ask Dean Rusk to give up a career; if I can ask Adlai Stevenson to make a sacrifice he does not want to make; if I can ask Bob McNamara to give up a job as head of that company — these men I don't even know . . . certainly I can expect my own brother to give me the same sort of contribution. And I need you in this government."

With that, Jack pushed back his chair, got up, and left the kitchen. Seigenthaler looked at Bobby and said, "Let's go, Bob." "No, wait," Bobby replied. "I've got some points to make." Seigenthaler said, "There's no point to make." Jack walked back in. "So that's it, General," he said. "Let's go." That ended it. For a man as hard-headed as he was, Bobby didn't put up much of a fight. His fealty to his father and his love and concern for his brother once again took precedence over his own wishes.

The announcement of the selection took place later that day on Jack's front steps. Bobby later remembered: "Jack told me to go upstairs and comb my hair, to which I said it was the first time the president had ever told the attorney general to comb his hair before they made an announcement." As they walked outside, Jack gave him further advice: "Don't smile too much, or they'll think we're happy about the appointment."[106]

Sam Giancana received the news "like a rabbit punch in the dark." He immediately called Sinatra and harangued him. Giancana's brother Chuck was to remember that Hoffa, Marcello, and Trafficante all had the same question for Giancana: "What the fuck is Jack Kennedy up to?"[107] In a more generic sense, Robert D. Novak, writing for the *Wall Street Journal,* saw the same problem: "Place a free-swinging, relentless political warrior named Robert

Francis Kennedy in the Attorney's General office, where even the most cautious of lawyers can collect enemies by the carload, and the result could be a mammoth record of accomplishment . . . or an unqualified disaster."[108]

Joseph Kennedy must have at least sensed the dangers inherent in persuading Jack to make Bobby attorney general. In one sense, Joe was right to insist on the appointment. Bobby's total loyalty and decisiveness were qualities the president-elect could not do without. Moreover, Bobby knew how to cover for Jack, whose health and marital truancy could damage or even ruin his presidency. But Joe also knew that on the matter of the Mafia, Bobby would do nothing but attack. As he reportedly told a chieftain in the Teamsters, "Everybody in my family can forgive — except Bobby."[109]

Johnny Rosselli and Sam Giancana had made their cash contribution for precisely that reason — a little slack, a little forgiveness. And they thought, as did nearly everyone else, that the old man still gave the orders. But Bobby had already shown he would resist his father's blandishments, and now he was the internal leader of the new administration. The irony, of course, was that Bobby was like his father — fearless in the fight and seemingly oblivious to the prospect of destruction. "Bobby is more like me than any of them," as Joe Kennedy had observed. "He hates the same way I do."[110] In *The Enemy Within,* there is this phrase: "If we do not attack organized criminals with weapons and techniques as effective as their own, they will destroy us."

For Christmas that year, Jack and Jackie gave Bobby a red leather, gold-embossed copy of *The Enemy Within.* Jack teasingly inscribed it, "To the Brother Within — who made the easy difficult, Jack, Christmas 1960." Jackie's inscription read, "To Bobby, who made the impossible possible and changed all our lives. With love, Jackie."[111]

Jacqueline Kennedy was right: Robert Kennedy, unlike his brother, believed in the impossible. This made him both very promising — and very dangerous.

Ordeal

1961

January 18, 1961

Léopoldville, the Congo

Two days before his inauguration, John F. Kennedy spent the morning in Georgetown, conferring with his advisers and working on the final draft of his inaugural speech. He canceled his appointments that afternoon because a howling snowstorm had descended on the city. When Jackie told him that he couldn't possibly remain in the house with his meetings and the coming and going of staff while she was trying to pack, he moved off to Bill Walton's house to spend the rest of the day and night.

A world away in the Congo, deposed premier Patrice Lumumba was loaded onto a plane bound for Elisabethville, located in the eastern part of the country. His transfer was ordered by Congolese on the CIA payroll. En route Lumumba was beaten nearly to death. Sometime the next morning, in a home outside the mining capital of Elisabethville, he was shot through the head.[1] His fate may well have been the result of intertribal ferocity, but it provided a treacherous prologue to Kennedy's thousand days in office, and posed immediately for the new president the question of whether murder should be used as an instrument of statecraft.

In November and December of 1960, ZR/RIFLE, a highly secret division within CIA headquarters under the command of William K. Harvey, had begun assembling a squad of assassins recruited from the ranks of organized criminals in Europe. Harvey, a squat, balding tank of a man with eyes that bulged because of a thyroid condition, had gotten the critical assignment after distinguishing himself as the commander of Operation Gold in 1955, which succeeded in tapping Soviet phone lines via a 500-yard tunnel into East Berlin. Until it was detected a year later, the tap gave the Americans key information about Soviet military plans and movements.[2]

Harvey's reputation among the tweedy Ivy League set then dominating the CIA was thereby made. He was a rough man for rough assignments, a "boom and bang" type. He drank martinis to excess, packed a .45 wherever he went, and freely resorted to obscenity in all kinds of company. With his aspect of an insolent fat plumber, he was not considered especially bright among the better born, but the appearance was misleading. Trained as an attorney, he had a penetrating command of intelligence work, with ten years experience in the field, and was a former FBI agent who understood the Hoover method of disguising tracks and disposing of enemies, bureaucratically or otherwise.

Harvey's inventory of potential killers included two Corsicans holding French passports, Santelli and Garioni, Italians from the Trieste area "of questionable morality" who were "willing to use gun . . . ready to go to the end," and a Belgian, Mozes Maschkivitzan, using the code name, QJ/WIN, who was asked to help with recruitment. After discussion through discreet intermediaries in Belgium, QJ/WIN boarded an Air France flight in Paris bound for Brazzaville on November 7. Two high-powered, scoped rifles as well as a poison potion derived from equine encephalitis (sleeping sickness) produced by the CIA's Technical Services Division had already been sent by diplomatic pouch by ZR/RIFLE to Leopoldville, the capital of the Congo, for use against Lumumba.

Lumumba's sin, in the view of the Americans, was his request for military assistance from the Soviet Union to repulse the Belgian intervention. In early September 1960 Congolese president Joseph Kasavubu removed Lumumba from office and placed him under house arrest. Recognizing Lumumba's "magical powers" of persuasion, however, the CIA regarded this as only the first step — Lumumba should be assassinated. Declassified CIA cable traffic reveals that clandestine efforts by the CIA mission to get the poison into the house where Lumumba was incarcerated and then into something he would ingest had failed; hence the Agency initiated the sniper operation. In mid-December, another CIA-hired shooter from Europe, code name WI/ROGUE, also arrived in Léopoldville and approached QJ/WIN, telling him he was to be part of the execution squad.

In mid-November, as part of a foreign policy briefing provided by senior government officials, the president-elect learned in detail about Lumumba's plight (though nothing at all about the CIA's role in it). Having chaired the Senate's African Subcommittee in 1959 and 1960 and having referred to Africa more than a thousand times in speeches during his campaign for the presidency, Kennedy brought a fairly probing understanding of the crisis to the discussion. A few days after his election, he had conferred with W. Averell Harriman, who had visited with Lumumba in August 1960 as part of a fact-finding trip for Kennedy. Harriman remembered the president-elect asking him, "Should we save Lumumba?" Harriman replied that he was not sure we could help him even if we wanted to.[3] With regard to the incoming administration's attitude toward Lumumba, the State Department advised caution, but Washington was alive with rumors that Kennedy would seek Lumumba's release.[4]

On December 28, 1960, Lumumba broke out of his detention and made a desperate run to his stronghold in Stanleyville (now Kisangani). He was captured three days later, imprisoned in Léopoldville, but nearly escaped again. At this point, the American hirelings in place, Internal Security Chief Victor Nendaka and Colonel Joseph Mobutu, prevailed on President Kasavubu to give the order to eliminate him. The American role in the final days may well have been oblique, but ZR/RIFLE chief Harvey, perhaps looking to broaden executive action in Cuba and possibly the Dominican Republic, informed his superiors at the CIA that QJ/WIN had performed his mission: "(I)t should be noted that QJ/WIN was sent on this trip for a specific, highly sensitive operational purpose which has been completed." Lumumba's death was not confirmed until a month later.

On February 13, 1961, in the Oval Office, Kennedy family photographer Jacques Lowe was taking some shots of the president when Evelyn Lincoln, the president's secretary, announced that United Nations ambassador Adlai Stevenson was calling and that it was urgent. Kennedy told Mrs. Lincoln to put Stevenson through. He picked up the phone and listened for a few seconds before bringing his right hand to his face in shocked dismay at the word of Lumumba's murder. Lowe's photograph captured a face seized in a furrowed and anguished grimace.

Beyond his reaction to Lumumba's murder, the specter of assassination, shadowed the new president. He spoke of it often with close friends like Dave Powers and even appraised his own prospects for it matter-of-factly. It also haunted Jackie. Arthur Schlesinger Jr. wrote of a post-election day in fall 1960 in Hyannis Port. Labor leaders Walter Reuther and Jack Conway were spending an afternoon on the beach with the Kennedys. Conway later remembered his talk with Jackie. "She was really obsessed with this whole idea of the change in her life, in Kennedy's life. How do you protect against assassinations?" Reuther, who like his brother Victor had himself narrowly escaped an assassination attempt, observed that you can't let precautions run your life; you can't stop living.

After the Lumumba murder came a torrent of accusations from Africa and Asia about the role Western powers, specifically Belgium, had played in the killing. Nonaligned leaders such as Egyptian president Gamal Abdel Nasser and Ghanaian president Kwame Nkrumah sent accusatory letters to Kennedy about America's role. In reply, Kennedy was emphatic about his position on assassination: "It . . . should be . . . vigorously investigated and condemned," he wrote Nasser. But the new president's view did not stop — or even slow — the murder train gaining speed in south Florida.

Two weeks after the president's letters to Nkrumah and Nasser, Jim O'Connell flew down to Miami for his third round of meetings about Castro with Giancana, Rosselli, Trafficante, and their go-between Robert Maheu. On March 12, 1961, in a suite at the luxurious Fontainebleau Hotel, the poison pills and $10,000 were passed to Rosselli. The choice of the site for this transfer foreshadowed what lay ahead.

The Fontainebleau was as close to an arch of triumph as the Mafia ever erected in the United States. Built in 1954, the hotel contained a vast open mezzanine of polished white marble with black bow-tie pattern trim.[5] The three garish chandeliers in the lobby were said to weigh a ton apiece. Joe Fischetti, the man who scheduled performers and events, and who also happened to be Al Capone's cousin, was the Fontainebleau's greeter. Downstairs was a shadowy bar-disco named the Boom Boom Room. When he arrived on that particular weekend, O'Connell found the Fontainebleau fairly swarming with mafiosi in town to attend their favorite sporting event, a heavyweight championship fight. In this case it was the third match between Floyd Patterson and Ingemar Johansson, the Swede who had beaten Patterson in their initial match but lost to him in the second. If that were not attraction enough, the mob's favorite entertainer, Frank Sinatra, was headlining.

When Washington, D.C., police inspector Joe Shimon arrived at the Fontainebleau to accompany Rosselli to the fight, he found the hotel filled with FBI agents in their mass-merchandised suits following their charges around as part of Hoover's Top Hoodlum Program (THP). Shimon did not recall in later years whether any of the special agents recognized him or Maheu (a former FBI agent) and the rather unusual company they were keeping, only that Rosselli and Giancana led two of the agents on a "wild goose chase" with Maheu, in turn, tailing the agents.[6]

All of this made Giancana nervous, particularly when Sinatra (who tended to turn from bully to bootlick in the presence of mafiosi) kept calling Giancana's suite. The Chicago don considered Sinatra an "untrustworthy bigmouth" who liked to brag about the heavy company he had been keeping. Late one evening, probably March 13, Rosselli passed the poison pills and the money to a small, reddish-haired Afro-Cuban by the name of Rafael "Macho" Gener in the Boom Boom Room, a location Giancana thought "stupid."[7]

Rosselli's purpose, however, was not just to assassinate Castro but to set up the Mafia's partner in crime, the United States government. Accordingly, he was laying a long, bright trail of evidence that unmistakably implicated the CIA in the Castro plot. This evidence, whose purpose was blackmail, would prove critical in the CIA's cover-up of the Kennedy assassination.

April 4, 1961

New Orleans, Louisiana

On April 4, accompanied by one of his lawyers, Carlos Marcello, the rotund little Louisiana crime boss whose organized reign of terror had proceeded untouched for nearly twenty years, walked into the offices of the Immigration and Naturalization Service in the Masonic Temple on St. Charles Avenue in New Orleans. As a resident alien, Marcello made such visits every three months or so, but this one proved different. An INS official read Marcello a letter on Justice Department stationery, informing him that he had entered the United States illegally from Guatemala and therefore would be deported forthwith. Two INS officers handcuffed him. Marcello demanded to call one of his attorneys but was refused. He asked if he could call his wife to get a toothbrush and some money. This too was refused.[8]

Marcello was immediately driven to New Orleans Moisant International Airport, bundled aboard a waiting INS plane by a small army of police and immigration officials, and flown 1,200 miles to Guatemala City. Along with his Shreveport attorney Mike Maroun, Marcello was later expelled from Guatemala to neighboring Honduras. After the bus carrying the two men crossed the border between the two countries, they were dropped off on the side of the road. They walked in the direction of a village in the high altitude, but the portly Marcello soon collapsed with exhaustion. Lying on the side of the road, his enjoinder to Maroun was to become a staple in the saga of the Marcello vendetta: "If I don't make it, Mike, tell my brothers when you get back about what that kid Bobby done to us. Tell 'em to do what they have to do."[9]

During the first weeks of the Kennedy administration, the new attorney general moved with emergency dispatch against organized crime. Asked how he hoped to be remembered, Bobby's response was blunt: "As the guy who broke the Mafia." He set about to recruit the best and the brightest for the assault. When, at a meet-the-new-boss discussion, twenty-six-year-old attorney William French expressed his desire to leave Justice because it was doing so little against organized crime, Kennedy took him aside and invited him to his office for a chat. He persuaded French to stay on and join a new task force investigating the Detroit mob. He then led French to a conference room in which there was a table covered with the green-bound transcripts of the McClellan Committee hearings and referred him to their contents.

Marcello was not the only candidate for deportation. Another was Johnny Rosselli, who had probably learned that FBI agents in Chicago had already pulled his phony affidavit of birth and were searching for some record of his real parents.[10] It was now clear that Robert Kennedy would act against, even manhandle, mafiosi without warning or due process and deport them at will. (Kennedy initially had planned to deport Marcello to Formosa.) In a foreign country, with no money in their pockets, the mafioso could be imprisoned by the locals, or worse.[11]

But Rosselli was already on the move to "throw some fear"— as the Chicago Outfit liked to say when it applied low levels of terror — into the federal hunting party. If the mob contribution to the Kennedy campaign wasn't having the desired effect, perhaps a little blackmail regarding Jack Kennedy's amorous pursuits would. On March 21, 1961, Rosselli invited private investigator Fred Otash to lunch at the Brown Derby in Beverly Hills. Otash, who did spot jobs for the Los Angeles mob, had been retained by Peter Fairchild in a divorce action against his wife, actress Judy Meredith. To reduce the alimony settlement to his wife, Fairchild, through Otash's snooping, was prepared to document that she had sexually consorted with Frank Sinatra, Jerry Lewis, Dean Martin, and Jack Kennedy. Rosselli told the stupefied Otash that "at the request of the attorney general" he was offering Fairchild $15,000 cash to get rid of the documentation. The fact that Otash brought Rosselli's overture to the attention of the L.A. office of the FBI within days of the lunch strongly suggests the blackmail at hand. The FBI special agent in charge noted in his telex to J. Edgar Hoover that Rosselli had done this to "avoid derogatory publicity."[12] By this time, the mob knew that Hoover, a known purveyor of blackmail, feared the new attorney general, whom he described to former vice president Richard Nixon around this time as a "sneaky little son of a bitch."[13]

News of the Rosselli move must have pleased Hoover, who railed against Bobby Kennedy's intrusion into his fusty little kingdom of G-men, and in particular against the attorney general's peremptory way of summoning him by means of a buzzer he'd installed between the two offices. Kennedy was openly derisory about Hoover, poking fun at the sixty-six–year-old's collapsing jowls and wondering whether he had to "squat to pee." He told Kenny O'Donnell on one occasion that "J. Edna" was "the kind of guy we can deal with."[14]

In retrospect, however, Bobby Kennedy misjudged Hoover, who, like a crouched and glistening toad, could deliver a poisonous charge when a larger creature entered his lair. In early April, Hoover sent a letter — with damning enclosures — to Kennedy's brother-in-law Peter Lawford, accusing him of financially consorting with a Mafia financier. A frightened Lawford immediately relayed this to the attorney general, observing "his [Hoover's] intimation is nothing less than extraordinary."[15] Kennedy's reaction to these venomous emissions was notably nonplussed. He reported in his 1964 oral history for the Kennedy library that Hoover had given him a memorandum detailing FBI findings that the president and the attorney general had sexual "assignations" with a "group of girls" on the twelfth floor of the LaSalle Hotel in Washington. "He would do this," Kennedy later said, "to find out what my reaction would be."[16]

Why Bobby did not see Hoover as dangerous is unclear. Could he actually have been ignorant of the president's philanderings? The LaSalle, along with the Carlyle in New York, was indeed a sexual watering hole for Jack Kennedy. Perhaps, Hoover's relationship with Joe Kennedy — "Father was a good friend," Bobby reports in his oral history — may have reassured Bobby that Hoover would ultimately not go for the family's throat. Finally, Hoover was clever. He would do his destructive business and then assume a benign pose. "Dear Bob," he wrote in a note dated June 9, 1961, "[Y]our confidence and support mean a great deal to me and I sincerely trust I shall always merit them."[17]

All of this pointed to Bobby Kennedy's chief failing: underestimating his enemies. His idea of political battle was frontal, but the attacks of men such as Hoover were often oblique and disguised. General Maxwell Taylor wasn't exaggerating when he said that Bobby Kennedy would have made it in his 101st Airborne Division — "the kind of guy we wanted around to take a hill or a trench."[18] Such bravery conduced to forward movement but it could also result in sudden casualty. He was brave in taking risks, but he was not always capable of calibrating them.

Hoover already had a scandal file on John F. Kennedy dating back to the early 1940s.[19] By 1961 the file was said to be six inches thick. "Joe always told me he should have gelded Jack when he was a boy," Hoover observed around this period.[20] The president was stunned to read the contents of Hoover's dossiers about his potential appointees. "I don't want any part of that stuff," he told Kenny O'Donnell. "I don't want to hear about it. I'd like to see the report they've got on *me*."[21] For all of his rhetorical counterpoint about sacrifice in the cause of national greatness and his earlier literary exercise in "profiles in courage," Jack accepted moral compromise. But such was not the case with his brother, whose zeal about destroying the Mafia, ironically enough, handed Hoover license to continue using his favorite instrumentality of blackmail — bugs — and further expose the president to harm.

Electronic eavesdropping fit neatly into Hoover's métier as voyeur-in-chief. Bugs revealed highly charged information about mob hits, schemes, crimes, disputes, etc., while granting the bugged mafiosi immunity from prosecution since the information was illegally gathered.[22] Moreover, the director made it clear to his agents that if ever they were caught installing such devices, the Bureau would fire them outright and cooperate in their prosecution.[23] The real targets of the bugs were not the hoodlums but the politicians they compromised with payoffs and the provision of women. Outside of the anticommunist headhunters on Capitol Hill, Hoover's singular following was drawn from among this worried throng of potential blackmail victims. In July 1961, Attorney General Kennedy formally countenanced the expansion of this tricky practice when he told FBI assistant director Courtney Evans to use more "technical equipment" against the mob.[24]

In his war against the mob in 1961 Bobby moved on several fronts of investigation. He ordered up hundreds of FBI files on Mafia figures and rackets and personally read through them, producing a "hit list" of mob personalities. He asked his old law professor at the University of Virginia, Mortimer Caplin, to become an IRS commissioner and targeted leading Mafia figures for audits and indictments. It was the gambit that had finally ruined Capone. In 1957, the IRS had netted Chicago underboss and Paul "The Waiter" Ricca and put him in prison for two and a half years. In 1960, Tony Accardo was indicted for deducting a sports car as a "beer salesman."[25] The IRS charges were usually petty — and the manner in which mob leaders were targeted probably illegal — but they tied them up in audits of their huge incomes and dubious deductions and sometimes put them in prison.

To head the Organized Crime Division Kennedy appointed Edwyn Silberling, a New Jersey attorney he had come to know through the McClellan Committee. He increased the number of attorneys on staff in Washington from 15 to 60. As Victor Navasky described it, "Operating with a direct line to the top, the Organized Crime 'whiz kids' fanned out across the country and began raiding gambling establishments, closing down bookies' services, indicting corrupt mayors and judges and generally picking off, one by one, the names on the 'hit list.' "[26] The new attorney general also established field units that drew together all federal agents in strike forces in the major cities of the United States. These strike forces were put under the command of assistant attorneys general, such as Bill French in Detroit. They shared intelligence on taxes, gun transfers, immigration status, cross-state trafficking, and the full range of Mafia rackets. Kennedy's idea was to create a martial level of synergy within the twenty-two different agencies of federal law enforcement. At the national level, he proposed the creation of a national crime commission to consolidate federal leadership. Although Hoover successfully had excised the crime commission idea from all proposed legislation, Kennedy was able to push five anti-crime bills through the Congress so quickly, William Geoghegan remembered, that nobody on the Judiciary Committee even had a chance to read them.

Mafia chieftains soon felt the squeeze. They began calling in their political markers. California governor Pat Brown, a strong supporter of John Kennedy in 1960, fairly demanded — and got — an appointment with the attorney general for John Alessio, a California hoodlum, whom the governor described as "one of the finest men I have ever met [who] has done as much for the Democratic Party as anyone I know."[27] Kennedy gave the man five minutes — and no relief from the money-laundering probe that had caused Alessio to seek the meeting.

Kennedy's McClellan Committee experience led him to conclude that narcotics would eventually become one of the underworld's premier industries, and as attorney general he moved aggressively against its chieftains. Harry Anslinger, the federal commissioner of narcotics, remembered Kennedy "traveling the country, calling special meetings with our agents, exhorting them to nail the big traffickers. . . . He would go down the line, name by name, and ask what progress had been made. . . . He demanded action and got it."[28]

No project in his war against organized crime was so personally prized by Bobby as the making of *The Enemy Within* into a movie. Producer Jerry Wald, among Hollywood's finest at the time, had agreed to develop the book. Scriptwriter Budd Schulberg of *On the Waterfront* fame was retained to do the script. He and Kennedy soon became good friends. One evening at Hickory Hill, Schulberg told Kennedy that he liked the deeper theme of the book that "something at the core of our society was beginning to rot." "Good," Kennedy responded. "I wrote those last pages very carefully."[29] But no sooner had the formidable Wald (whom Schulberg later described as the man who "alone had the courage to produce it") started putting the project together than he encountered strong resistance from key industry people like Jack Warner, an old and singularly powerful friend of Johnny Rosselli. There were rumors that the entertainment unions would strike the film. On May 3, 1961, *Variety* headlined a stinging article about the project: "Will Bob Kennedy-Written Film Bum-Rap All of U.S. Unions?"[30] It is not known whether Rosselli, with his entrée into the studios and proven clout with the entertainment unions, had a role in all this. But he certainly must have recognized the danger for the Mafia if such a searing indictment of his trade ever made it to the screen. Kennedy and his press aide Ed Guthman continued to work with Wald and Schulberg on the script throughout 1961. Actor Paul Newman was approached to play the part of Robert Kennedy. On July 2, 1962, Wald reported to Kennedy that the final draft of the script was finished.[31] Four days later, however, Wald was found dead, reportedly of a heart attack, in his Beverly Hills home. He was forty-nine years old. The project was put on hold.

Kennedy's biggest challenge in his assault on the mob was the FBI. Hoover had instructed his agents to avoid all collaboration with other federal law enforcement agencies.[32] The attorney general's initial soundings about FBI preparedness were not promising. When he asked J. F. Malone, the special agent in charge of the New York office, to bring him up to date on organized crime, Malone replied, "To tell you the truth, Mr. Attorney General, I'm sorry but I can't, because we've been having a newspaper strike here."[33] In New York, where Hoover periodically communed with mobster Frank Costello, special agents tagged along with the mobsters the way reporters do celebrities. In Los Angeles, Rosselli kidded around with his retinue and held doors open for them on occasion, saying with a smile, "I know. I know. You're just doing your job."[34] As far as Hoover was concerned, it was a case of the blackmailer being blackmailed. Both Costello and Rosselli were fully apprised of Hoover's homosexuality as well as the fact that Meyer Lansky had a photograph of the director with another man in *flagrante fellatio*.[35]

But in cities such as Chicago, the FBI was on the attack. A highly aggressive FBI mob detail led by William Roemer, Marshall Rutland, and Ralph Hill had already succeeded in planting a microphone in the Outfit's downtown headquarters on Michigan Avenue. With Kennedy's urging the skirmish moved to siege. He increased the FBI's Mafia detail in that city from five to seventy and flew there every few months to urge the agents on.

One such trip occurred in May 1961. Kennedy and press aide Guthman met with special agent in charge Marlin Johnson, Roemer, Hill, and the others assigned to follow the Outfit. When Johnson began reading a prepared statement to the attorney general, Kennedy interrupted him. "Mr. Johnson," he said, "I didn't come here to hear a canned speech about how magnificent you are. I didn't come here to hear from *you* at all. . . . You can sit over there in the corner and we'll listen to the agents who are out on the street, the men who are doing the work you think is so great." With that, he turned the briefing over to the foot soldiers. "He impressed all of us," Roemer remembered. "His questions showed that he had been reading our daily summary airtels. He was most knowledge-able about the Chicago mob. . . . I was surprised he knew so much about one guy in particular: Sam Giancana."[36]

Kennedy continued the exchange over lunch between mouth-fuls of turkey salad sandwiches and potato salad, pulling more and more information out of the agents as he peppered them with ques-tions. Emboldened by Kennedy's encouragement, Roemer told him about a tape he got from a secret microphone placed in the headquarters of the Regular Democratic Organization of the First Ward in Chicago. The tape contained a series of conversations in-volving Pat Marcy, a Democratic organizer Kennedy had met dur-ing a campaign trip there in 1960, and various others. Roemer explained to Kennedy that Marcy (whose real name was Pasqualino Marchone) was a mob capo, then turned the tape recorder on, let-ting it run as Marcy spoke to two Chicago police officers about a third police officer on the vice squad they couldn't control because he wouldn't go on the take. After expressing frustration with this third officer, Marcy and his police confederates decide to kill him. "When the tape ran down," according to Roemer, "Bobby looked at Guthman and then looked at the floor for ten seconds or so. He then asked that the latter part of the tape be replayed — the crucial part where the decision to kill was made." As it played, Kennedy, saying nothing, looked from face to face in the room. "We got the message," Roemer later recalled.[37] Roemer, Hill, and the other FBI agents took Kennedy's silent reaction to the tape as a wordless call to arms. In all probability, it was that. But it may have also been Kennedy's mute recognition of the blood price of political power.

Toward the end of May, the attorney general was shocked to learn that Carlos Marcello had secretly reentered the country. He was flown in either via jet, compliments of Dominican dictator Rafael Trujillo, or by a private plane piloted by David Ferrie, who would later figure centrally in President Kennedy's assassination.[38]

The attorney general immediately dispatched twenty United States marshals to south Louisiana to hunt for Marcello, who surrendered voluntarily to INS officials a few days later. Kennedy moved to have him deported again, using a federal grand jury indictment. Marcello, through his attorney Jack Wasserman, had already sued the attorney general for his kidnap-style deportation the previous April, and was seeking to set aside the $835,396 tax lien the IRS had placed on Marcello and his wife.

The war was on. Marcello had two new collaborators in his counter-attack against the government: Guy Banister, a former FBI SAC in Chicago who was then stockpiling weapons in his New Orleans office for the anti-Castro Democratic Revolutionary Front, and Ferrie, who, according to an FBI report in April 1961, was distributing Marcello money to anti-Castro exiles.

April 17, 1961

Bay of Pigs, Cuba, and Washington, D.C.

John F. Kennedy came into office publicly committed to ridding Cuba of Castro, having blistered the Eisenhower administration for allowing him to survive. In the interregnum, the president-elect was briefed on a plan to infiltrate bands of thirty to fifty exile commandos on the island to foment rebellion. By the time Kennedy took office, the plan had mushroomed. The new proposal was to land an amphibious force of several hundred exiles. The CIA's Richard Bissell told Kennedy that unless Castro was quickly forced from power, the Soviet Union would arm and garrison a client state in the Americas. The question was, would the new president approve of the invasion plan?[39]

At the first National Security Council meeting on Cuba, the president was "wary and reserved" about the plan. The Joint Chiefs expressed concern about the prospect of military intervention, but were assured there would be none. Some, like Senator J. William Fulbright and Special Assistant Arthur M. Schlesinger Jr., argued that intervention was foolhardy and would "fix a malevolent image on the new administration." These objections hardly registered in the barrage of "intelligence analysis" about logistics, weaponry, and the claim that Castro would have Russian MIGs in a matter of weeks. CIA director Dulles pointed out that if the exiled Cubans did not attempt the invasion, there would be a "disposal problem." Kennedy agreed that the "simplest thing might be to let the Cubans go where they yearned to go, Cuba, with a minimum of risk to the U.S."[40]

Such was the case with Jorge Recarey, who on February 13 made his seventh nighttime trip across the Windward Straits. At Arcos de Canisi on Cuba's north coast in the early morning hours, his craft was met by farmers in rowboats. They brought him aboard and took him through the rough surf. He was then taken to the house of a local landowner, Jorge Fundora, and smuggled into Havana for his meeting with the head of the anti-Castro underground in Cuba, Rogelio Gonzalez Corso, code-named Francisco. On his person, Recarey carried a sealed envelope containing his instructions to be given to Francisco. Shortly after Recarey left Fundora's home, Cuban security police arrived. Fundora was arrested and shot.[41]

In Havana, at a house deemed secure, Recarey, now operating under his code name Julio Cesar Blanco, met with Francisco. The instructions were to organize and lead the underground in Matanzas, a city of some 25,000 situated in flat, scrubby terrain east of Havana. In Matanzas, Recarey encountered widespread opposition to Castro. Some two hundred active opponents operated scores of safe houses through which they were smuggling weapons, explosives, agents, propaganda, and counterfeit money. Recarey moved from safe house to safe house, changing location every night, organizing the underground in hard-to-penetrate five-man cells. (A single individual in each group knew a single person in another group; if one cell was captured or penetrated, the single individual in the other cell would be exfiltrated.)

In the weeks that followed, Recarey became increasingly aware of the CIA's incompetence. Shipments dropped at Punto Fundora (named after the executed landowner) contained weapons that didn't work, counterfeit bills that bled when wet, and motor oil that had been blended (unbeknownst to Recarey) with an explosive substance. When Recarey's driver added oil to their 1959 Olds 88, the front of the car blew up as they were riding down a highway. They walked away unscathed, but others, following the Agency enjoinder to prepare the resistance for the coming invasion, were not so lucky. Underground leader Francisco attended a large anti-Castro meeting in Havana that contained informants, and soon after was arrested and executed. Recarey's radioman, Jorge Rojas, met the same fate. Disposal indeed.

With no CIA guidance and little coordination with other units, much less with the invasion force itself, Recarey and other anti-Castro sappers did what they could. They attacked targets with

C-4 *plastique* and incendiary compounds, blowing up communications linkages and the country's largest department store, El Encanto, which burned to the ground on the night of March 16.

Back in Washington, indecision reigned. On March 15, President Kennedy rejected the concept of direct American military intervention — air strikes — as well as the recommended landing locus at Trinidad. He informed his advisors that they should continue to plan the invasion with the contingency that it could be called off within twenty-four hours before it was due to begin. To "maintain options," in the favored phrase of the day, made sense in the shifting sluice of events, but in war-making it is often a recipe for disaster. Armed with the president's ambivalence, the CIA "ops" leadership (which had excluded the CIA's intelligence wing from any role in, much less knowledge of, the operation) prevaricated. They led the White House and the Joint Chiefs to think of the landing as a large-scale infiltration that would coincide with a mass uprising against Castro on the island. Down on the ground, CIA trainers told the brigade leaders that the United States would provide air cover and follow up with its own forces once the beachhead was established at the new location — the Bahia de Cochinos, the Bay of Pigs.

Marine colonel Jack Hawkins, who was exercising overall command of the paramilitary aspects of the landing, informed Bissell that the Bay of Pigs was a bad location. It was hemmed in by a huge swamp.[42] But Bissell, banking on Rosselli's assurance that the Mafia was within striking distance of killing Castro, was unmoved. "Assassination was intended to reinforce the plan," Bissell later observed. "There was the thought that Castro would be dead before the landing. Very few, however, knew of this aspect of the plan."[43]

Did President Kennedy know about the murder plot? Seymour Hersh in *The Dark Side of Camelot* asserts that Kennedy did: "Jack Kennedy had every reason to believe in April 1961 that Sam Giancana and his men in Miami and Havana would do the deed. Giancana had delivered, as promised, on the 1960 election. And, as Kennedy surely knew, no one was more adept at murder."[44] Hersh cites Judith Campbell (later Exner), a woman who was consorting sexually with both Jack Kennedy and Sam Giancana, as the confessed conduit of manila envelopes containing documents that dealt with the elimination of Castro. After her sexual encounters with Kennedy, she later claimed, he instructed her to pass these documents to Giancana. Campbell's story has changed over the years, but in the version given Hersh she alleges she knew about the contents of those secret missives. The reflection of Exner's former husband William Campbell suggests the unlikelihood of such a role: "I couldn't imagine her being privy to any sort of secret information. She wouldn't understand it anyway. I mean they weren't dealing with some sort of Phi Beta Kappa."[45] The notion that Kennedy was communicating directly with Giancana regarding the assassination of Castro strains credulity in any case. Later, in an article written by Liz Smith for *Vanity Fair,* Exner repudiated *My Story,* her earlier book about the affair, and claimed that she became pregnant by President Kennedy in 1963.[46]

To support his conclusion that the president gave the order to kill Castro, Hersh offers Bissell's disclosure in January to National Security Advisor McGeorge Bundy that the CIA was developing an executive action capability. But both Bissell and Bundy denied that Castro's name was ever specifically named, or that President Kennedy was ever informed about either ZR/RIFLE or the plot against Castro. Bissell, of course, may well have told Bill Harvey and other CIA operatives, such as Jacob B. Esterline and Samuel Halpern, that he had such authorization, but the established etiquette was neither to ask presidents for such an order nor to tell them about executive operations. Richard Helms, who was then Deputy Director of Plans, later observed: "Nobody wants to embarrass a president . . . by discussing the assassination of foreign leaders in his presence."[47] Hersh's conclusion rests on the testimony of officials down the chain of command. It is essentially a circumstantial projection of what he believes must have happened.

Senator Fulbright, who was privy to the planning of the operation, wrote the president on March 30 that no matter the denials and the disguise, the world would see it as an American invasion, and that if things went wrong the United States would be sorely pressed to intervene directly. He registered his complete opposition, likening Castro to a "thorn in the flesh, not a dagger in the heart." But the opposition of Fulbright, UN ambassador Adlai Stevenson, and special assistant Schlesinger was no match for the authority of Cold

War titans like CIA director Dulles and Bissell. At the decisive meeting of April 4, Dulles played his trump card: Castro was about to receive MIGs from the Russians. It was now or never. Even if the beachhead failed, the exiles could repair to the "nearby Escambray mountains." In fact, these mountains were more than 100 miles from the coast and separated by a huge, impassable swamp. Kennedy, still troubled, gave the go-ahead: April 17, 1961.

By early April, Castro had his forces on full alert and daily taunted the exiles in radio broadcasts, saying that everywhere he went people were asking: "When are they coming?" With literally scores of agents in Miami and at the training camp of Brigade 2506 in the Guatemalan mountains, Castro had a complete view of the coming invasion. He sensed that the American-led invaders would first try to destroy his tiny air force, so he scattered and concealed the operative fighters and bombers and grouped the disabled planes in obvious locations.[48] To make the infiltration "less noisy," President Kennedy meanwhile cut the number of B-26s provided the exile air squadron from 16 to 8.

On April 14, Brigade 2506, with 1,500 men in the bowels of seven ships, put to sea from Puerto Cabezas on the Nicaraguan coast for the two-day trip to Cuba. Only 135 were soldiers; the rest were lawyers, doctors, businessmen, and students. Among the latter was Blas Casares Rovirosa, native of Camaguey province and the son of a doctor. In 1960 Casares had dropped out of the University of Oklahoma, where he had been studying geological engineering, to join the anti-Castro front. Trained as a frogman, Casares was assigned to put markers that would guide the landing craft through the reefs leading in to the beaches.[49] Analyzing aerial photographs of the Bay of Pigs, CIA photo experts had concluded that a series of dark ridges in the bay were seaweed formations. They were not; they were reefs.

At the Puerto Cabezas dock, Nicaraguan dictator Luis Somoza, surrounded by his bodyguards, his face heavily powdered, shouted to the departing volunteers: "Bring me a couple of hairs from Castro's beard."[50] Although there had been a near mutiny in the exile training camp three weeks before, the flat assurance by CIA trainers that American forces would follow after the Cubans established a beachhead had a cheering effect on the rebels.[51] A dispatch sent directly to President Kennedy of an eleventh-hour evaluation, done at his insistence by a Marine Corps colonel (and decorated combatant at Tarawa), corroborated this mood: "My observations have increased my confidence in the ability of this force to accomplish not only initial combat missions but also the ultimate objective, the overthrow of Castro. . . . These officers are motivated by the fanatical urge to do battle."[52]

When the brigade was at sea, rebel pilots, guided by CIA command and control, struck at Castro's air force. At about 6 A.M. on April 15, eight B-26s began bombing airfields and military bases in Cuba. They destroyed Castro's junked-together decoys, but missed several of his operative bombers and jet trainers. Several of the 500-pound bombs hit downtown Havana, causing civilian death and injury. Castro now moved on all suspected and identified members of the opposition, rounding up tens of thousands in the days that followed the attack and detaining them in the Principe castle, the La Cabana moat, the baseball park in Matanzas, and a host of other locations.[53] Recarey managed to elude this roundup.

Castro then led a huge cortege through the streets of Havana to the cemetery at Colon, railing for two hours against the United States, likening the bombing to Pearl Harbor, remembering the sinking of *La Coubre,* and telling of one loyal *miliciano,* who, lying mortally wounded from a bomb fragment, wrote the name Castro with his blood on a wall.[54] No one had advised Kennedy of the worst-case contingency for the United States in the invasion plan — that Castro, no longer having to live with protest within Cuba, would gun down the internal opposition once and for all. The Cuban leader ordered his pilots to sleep under the wings of what was left of his air force and to take turns around the clock in the cockpits. Faced with embarrassing revelations that the bombing raids were orchestrated by the United States, President Kennedy countermanded the order to permit Cuban exile pilots, then waiting in their cockpits, to make another series of runs over Cuba.

Back in Miami, the nominal political leadership of the exiles, the Democratic Revolutionary Council — which Castro referred to as the Consejo de Gusanos (the Council of Worms) — were put under house arrest by their CIA advisors as a matter of "security." Incredibly, these men knew nothing of the launching, in which four of their sons and two of their brothers had participated. The CIA turned over all public communications for the waiting world to the Lew Jones Agency, an advertising group in New York. President Kennedy spent an anxious weekend in Glen Ora, Virginia, at one point pounding golf balls into an empty cornfield with his old friend Charles Spalding, and then heliocoptering back to the White House for the first reports from the beach.[55]

An hour or so after midnight on April 17, the troop ships of Brigade 2506 rendezvoused 2,000 yards off the principal landing site at Playa Giron. In Havana, the now-sleepless Recarey heard the CIA's Howard Hunt (later of Watergate fame) issue supposedly coded messages in an early morning broadcast from "Radio Swan" island: "Look well to the Rainbow . . . The fish will rise very soon . . . The fish is red." This nonsense was supposed to panic Castro and his lieutenants the way the CIA had panicked the hapless Guatemalan populist Jacobo Arbenz in 1954. It did nothing of the sort. In fact, the CIA attempted no radio contact of any operational nature with the anti-Castro underground in Cuba on the eve of the invasion. The Agency simply did not trust the Cubans. Through the entire charade, there was that cruel word — *disposable*.

As the force of Brigade 2506 waited in their ships in the morning darkness, a squad of frogmen led by two Americans, Grayston Lynch and Rip Robertson, reconned the beach area. Suddenly, they ran into a Cuban patrol and had no choice but to open fire. From the ships, the soldiers, now starting to scale down the ship nets to the landing craft below, could see the flashes of light on the beach and hear the choppy report of automatic arms fire. The advantage of surprise was lost. Using the inaccurate reef maps provided by the CIA, frogman Casares and his team dropped markers to guide the landing craft between the reefs. The widest point between the reefs was no more than 25 yards. An hour later, half of the landing craft were hung up on the reefs. When members of the Brigade's Fifth Battalion exhibited doubts about getting into the LCVs, the CIA's Robertson pulled out his sidearm and shouted: "Get into the boats. This is your fucking war."

Fidel Castro was awakened at about 2:30 A.M. at Celia Sanchez's apartment on Eleventh Street in Havana. He immediately phoned his old friend Captain José Ramon Fernandez, "El

Gallego," in Managua, south of Havana, and ordered him to move the elite Militia Officers School Battalion, numbering 870 men, to Playa Giron, along with as many Soviet T-34 tanks as he could get onto flatbed trucks.[56] Sometime early that morning, sensing that something was happening, Recarey woke his driver and sped to the outskirts of Havana. There, in the early morning dark, they saw a long line of Cuban troop and tank trucks, bumper to bumper, crossing the lone bridge that led toward the Bay of Pigs, the bridge that Recarey had scheduled for demolition. He began to cry.[57]

By 3 A.M. Castro was at his Punto Uno command post. He phoned the air force base at San Antonio de los Banos and spoke with its senior pilot, Captain Enrique Carreras: "Chico, you must sink those ships for me." At first light, two of the Sea Furies, armed with rockets and four 20mm cannons, and a B-26 bomber, started strafing the troop and supply ships, grounding the *Houston*, damaging the *Barbara J*, which was serving as the CIA command vessel, and sinking the freighter *Rio Escondido*, which was carrying most of the Brigade's ammunition and supplies. Castro's T-33 jet trainers then intercepted six of the exiles' lumbering B-26s, shooting down four of them.

The main exile force of about 1,350 men had established a deep beachhead, and now exchanged mortar and artillery fire with Castro's force of some 2,000. By the afternoon of April 17, there was heavy fighting. Led by Commander Erneido Oliva, the exile forces attacked with tanks, armored personnel carriers, and bazooka teams that took out several of the T-34s. After several hundred yards of progress, they were met by a blanket of 122mm howitzer fire, and dug in.[58] Castro, now at the front in battle dress with his M-1 in hand, supervised the emplacement of Cuban reinforcements of some 20,000. It was now obvious that without American intervention the brigade would eventually be overwhelmed.

As Castro's T-33s strafed brigade positions, Commander José "Pepe" San Roman radioed for help: "Blue Beach attacked by three jets . . . . Where is our cover?" From the *Barbara J*, the CIA's Grayston Lynch radioed back that the "jets are coming." This cheered the beleaguered invaders but was untrue. American Sabre jets made passes over the field of battle and viewed the havoc below, but did nothing more. When navy aviator Commander Mike Griffin, who had piloted one of those jets, returned to his carrier, he was crying uncontrollably in shame and frustration. But President Kennedy was moved more by Khrushchev's stinging message that came the next day, April 18. The Soviet premier intimated that the Soviet Union might come directly to Castro's aid, or even move on West Berlin, if the Americans invaded the island. At midnight, Bissell and Navy chief of naval operations, Admiral Arleigh Burke, asked that the president authorize an air strike to relieve the brigade. Kennedy refused. Later, disconsolate at the predicament in which he had put himself and the hapless men in the Bay of Pigs, he called Bobby. "How could I have been so stupid?"

Castro's forces now massed for the final assault on the brigade positions. Kennedy read the desperate series of radioed messages from Commander San Roman, which were forwarded to him from the carrier, USS *Essex:*

> Do you people realize how desperate the situation is? Do you back us up or quit? All we want is low jet cover and jet close support. Enemy has this support. I need it badly or cannot survive. Please don't desert us. Am out of tank and bazooka ammo. Tanks will hit me at dawn. Pepe.

Back at CIA command in Quarters Eye in Washington, one CIA officer vomited into a wastebasket after he read this.[59]

Later, on the 19th, this message was received from the beach: "We are out of ammo and fighting on the beach. Please send help. We cannot hold. Pepe."[60]

Later still on the 19th: "In water. Out of ammunition. Enemy closing in. Help must arrive in this hour. Pepe."

By afternoon, the brigade forces started to surrender. Back on the sinking *Blagar*, hit again by a Sea Fury cannon, the commander yelled, "Everybody for himself." As the crew abandoned ship, Casares grabbed the radio message log and stuck it in his pocket before jumping into a 20-foot catamaran. They were eventually picked up by the American destroyer USS *Eaton*. In the days that followed, Casares and four other volunteers went back into the swamp near Giron in a small boat to look for brigade survivors. They rescued thirty-six of them.[61]

In Washington, the recriminations had begun. At a National Security Council meeting on April 19, the participants argued bitterly about how to destroy Castro — by an invasion of American forces, naval blockade, or other means. McNamara later characterized the mood regarding Castro as "hysterical." Attorney General Kennedy, reverting to his role as his brother's enforcer, ripped into Undersecretary Chester Bowles outside the cabinet room for disloyalty to the president. Bobby accused Bowles of leaking his opposition to the invasion after the fact to his liberal friends on the editorial board of the *New York Times*.[62] Bowles was outraged. The president, although insistent in shouldering the blame publicly, was privately appalled at "those fucking brass hats," namely the Joint Chiefs, for their indifferent review of the military aspects of the plan. He told Schlesinger that he was considering asking Bobby to take over the CIA. The president asked that the Cuban exile leaders be flown from Miami, where they were still languishing under house arrest, to Washington. Upon arrival they were whisked from National Airport directly to the White House, and then through the East Wing to avoid the swarming press.[63]

Kennedy, looking exhausted, greeted them somberly as they walked into the Oval Office. Sitting in his rocking chair, the president tried to explain why he had backed away from full intervention and why he had supposed that the operation might succeed on its own. He took out the dispatch from the Marine colonel who had done a final evaluation of the brigade on the eve of setting off for Cuba and read its rousing prognosis out loud.

Kennedy told the exile leaders that the struggle against communism had many fronts and that leadership in that struggle imposed many responsibilities. The United States had to consider the balance of affairs all around the world. However tragic this episode, no one could doubt our commitment to the eventual freedom of Cuba, Kennedy said. He added that he himself "had fought in a war, that he had seen brave men die, that he had lost a brother, and that he shared their grief and their despair."[64]

Later the president called his father in Palm Beach. The senior Kennedy was so surprised by his son's piteous tone that he told Jack that if he couldn't take it then "give it to Lyndon." Kennedy later told family friend and former Truman cabinet officer Clark Clifford,

"For two days I haven't slept. This has been the most excruciating period of my life."[65]

The next evening, Jack watched CBS News with Bobby and Kenny O'Donnell in the family quarters. The president stood several feet from the set, flanked by the other two. The sense of humiliation was almost palpable, O'Donnell remembered. Kennedy's arms were crossed, one of his hands gripping deeply into the sides of his face, as he watched the report. CBS showed videotape of Castro (apparently from 1959), jut-chinned, screaming in high-pitched Spanish, as he stood over some wrecked and smoking armament, waving his arms to dramatize his invective. Walter Cronkite then quoted Castro as calling Kennedy "a coward."

Bobby shouted "Fuck!"— and stormed out of the room.[66]

May 14, 1961

Anniston, Alabama, and Washington, D.C.

After the Bay of Pigs, Robert Kennedy emerged as the most forceful man in the Kennedy administration's foreign policy. Although he did not, as the president had proposed, take over the CIA, Bobby administered the replacement of its leadership (Dulles stepped down in favor of John McCone as CIA director in December 1961) and rammed Cuban policy into paramilitary motion. During the month of May, Bobby added five or six hours a day of deliberations on Cuba to his duties as attorney general. He worked on an emergency basis, walking in and out of meetings at will, excoriating top policymakers in the hall, and lashing out at the laggard work of the State Department. He told the president's advisors, "You people are so anxious to protect your own asses that you're afraid to do anything. All you want to do is dump the whole thing on the president. We'd be better off if you just quit." The president sat there listening to this, tapping his front teeth with a pencil. It was then that Richard Goodwin realized, as he later wrote, that "Bobby's harsh polemic reflected the president's own concealed emotions."[67]

In mid-May, a racial crisis erupted that put Bobby's emotional endurance to the test and challenged the administration's commitment to civil rights. On May 4, a group of six whites and seven blacks boarded a Greyhound bus in Washington with the purpose to "challenge every form of segregation by the bus passenger" in the segregated South. They called themselves the Freedom Riders. They passed peacefully through the first three states — Virginia, North Carolina, and Georgia — entering washrooms, eating facilities, and waiting rooms in violation of Jim Crow laws. On May 14 in Anniston, Alabama, the situation changed. A mob of angry whites forced the Freedom Riders off the bus, beat them bloody with clubs and chains, and then burned the vehicle.

The administration, tense and gloomy in the aftermath of the Bay of Pigs, saw the incident as needless provocation that further undermined the president on the eve of his reckoning with Premier Khrushchev in Vienna. Kennedy called his special assistant for civil rights, Harris Wofford, and angrily told him: "Stop them. Get your friends off those buses." But there was nothing much Wofford could do, and he told the president so.[68] "The dream deferred," as the poet Langston Hughes had once termed it, was about to explode.

Until May 1961, "defer" was precisely the Kennedy technique when it came to civil rights. As senator, Kennedy had zigzagged through the long obstacle course of civil rights legislation, siding in most cases, as a Ted Sorensen memo to Bobby proudly explained in December 1959, "with our friends in the South." He meant white friends.[69] Notwithstanding the strong plank in the 1960 Democratic platform and the September 1960 pledge to eliminate segregation in federal housing with the "stroke of the pen," the Kennedys were engaging in electoral gamesmanship. "I didn't lie awake at night," Bobby later remembered in a particularly unvarnished phrase, "worrying about the plight of the Negro."[70]

Powerful political realities militated against active support for racial equality. Kennedy's razor-thin victory as well as the Democrats' unsteady majority on Capitol Hill both depended on the "solid South." The most entrenched and skilled leaders of that majority in the Senate — McClellan of Arkansas, Eastland of Mississippi, Ervin of North Carolina, and Fulbright of Arkansas — were all vehement opponents of civil rights as well as close friends of Bobby Kennedy. Eastland and McClellan had proudly shepherded his nomination as attorney general through the Senate.

Beyond this, Jack Kennedy simply did not like the "tar baby" issue, as he called it. He thought it messy and ultimately insoluble. He saw himself as a foreign policy president; everything in his formation led him to that self-concept. By the time he ran for Congress in 1948, Jack had probably crossed the Atlantic more times than he had the Mississippi. His growth as a public thinker had come in the course of extended trips through Europe in 1936 and

117

Asia in 1951, trips that resulted in prescient statements on democratic preparedness in the face of aggression and the power of anti-colonial nationalism, respectively.

In his inaugural address, with all its inspired rhetoric about sacrifice in the anticommunist struggle, there was scarcely a word about America's challenge in undoing the systematized hatred within its borders. A few weeks later in his State of the Union speech, Kennedy invited his listeners in stark, almost metallic language to join with him in the country's "hour of maximum danger." In the pure, frozen twilight of the Cold War, there was the need and the space for a great president. In civil rights, there was only bitter trouble and the prospect of a ruined reelection. So when word came in of the racial violence in Alabama, the president did what he thought he had to do — duck.

Bobby was already charting his own course. In March 1961, he agreed to address Law Day exercises at the University of Georgia in Athens on May 6. As he worked on the speech in his lonely, dogged way, slogging through no fewer than four drafts with the assistance of his aides Burke Marshall and John Seigenthaler, something unusual happened: the speech changed from a statement about the challenge of organized crime to one about civil rights.[71] Part of the reason may have been that ten days before the speech, Kennedy had used a court order to open the public schools of Prince Edward County, Virginia, to 1,700 black schoolchildren who had not been allowed in school for two years. But there was something in the method of his preparation that harkened back to the McClellan Committee days, when he would bear down over long hours and forge his way to a new level of understanding.

On May 6, before a crowd of 1,600, his hair combed and wearing a new blue suit (it was said that Ethel had forced him to be fit for it), the attorney general compared racial segregation to organized crime and explained why he had intervened to open Virginia's schools to black children. "In this case — in all cases — I say to you that if the orders of the court are circumvented, the Department of Justice will act." He then offered a broader vision:

> I happen to believe that the 1954 [*Brown* v. *Board of Education*] decision was right. But my belief does not matter — it is the law.

> Some of you may believe the decision was wrong. That does not matter. It is the law. . . . On this generation of Americans falls the full burden of proving to the world that we really mean it when we say all men are created free and are equal before the law.[72]

The speech startled his listeners and drew a chorus of protest from across the South. The reaction had scarcely subsided when the Freedom Riders encountered the brutal gauntlet of racist attack in Alabama. Kennedy's words were put to the test. His first move, after consulting the president, was to try to get the riders out of harm's way by moving them from Birmingham, fifty miles west of Anniston, to Montgomery, the capital. Although Hoover had received word from one of his agents in Birmingham that the Ku Klux Klan was planning an ambush, he chose not to report it to his boss.

With a menacing crowd gathering around the Birmingham bus terminal, Kennedy telephoned the Greyhound terminal superintendent, George E. Cruit, and demanded in heated language that he find a bus driver to drive the Freedom Riders out. "We have gone to a lot of trouble to see they get this trip," Kennedy told him, "and I am most concerned to see that it is accomplished." Listening on another phone, Cruit's secretary took this down and the next day Kennedy's rather infelicitous choice of words was all over the country. In the view of many in the South, it indicated that the Kennedys had sent provocateurs to the South to crack Jim Crow.[73]

The besieged Riders were eventually flown out, but more kept coming in from the northern states, and tension mounted swiftly across Alabama. At a meeting at the White House on Friday, May 19, the president insisted that the federal government not step in until a "maximum effort" had been made to let local authorities handle the problem. Alabama Governor John Patterson would have none of this; he told the press that state law did not guarantee "the safety of fools" and resolutely refused to take the president's calls.[74] When a bus bringing Freedom Riders from Birmingham reached Montgomery on May 20, a crowd of white segregationists set upon the group and brutally beat them. When John Seigenthaler, the president's representative in the crisis and Bobby's good friend, tried to rescue a girl who was being beaten, he too was knocked unconscious.

Bobby called Jack and insisted on interposing federal officers. Several hours later, 303 federal law enforcement personnel moved into Montgomery. A tense state of calm ensued. After a couple of hours of sleep at Hickory Hill, the attorney general attended early morning mass before returning to his office. It was then that the second phase of the crisis erupted: thirty-two-year-old Reverend Martin Luther King Jr., despite Kennedy's appeal to desist, drove to Montgomery to congregate with the Riders at the First Baptist Church. A white mob, this one with armed Klansmen, soon descended on the church, apparently intent on burning it down. The deputy attorney general on the scene, Byron White, could get only 150 marshals in position before the crowd closed in. With the Reverend King inside preaching and leading the congregation in prayer, and the white mob outside howling its discontent, Kennedy finally got through to Governor Patterson, who had himself gone apoplectic.

After several heated exchanges through the long night (the two knew each other from the 1960 campaign when Patterson had been an early and ardent supporter of Senator Kennedy), the governor finally pledged that the National Guard would be immediately called in to protect the church. At around 4 A.M., the Reverend King placed a call to the attorney general. "Well, Reverend," Kennedy asked King impishly, "are you praying for us?" King reacted negatively to this. He told Kennedy he could summon 100,000 students into Alabama. "They will use their lives and their bodies to right a wrong. They will give witness by their lives if necessary."

Bobby was angered by the melodramatic tone and tragic implications of such a claim. "Don't make statements that sound like threats," he told King. "That is not the way to deal with us. You'd be dead as doornails without those marshals," he added.[75] He called for a "cooling-off period" the next day, but this too was rejected by Ralph Abernathy of the Southern Christian Leadership Conference: "We've been cooling off for a hundred years."

By the end of May, tempers did cool, enough for Kennedy to craft a disengagement strategy based on using the Interstate Commerce Commission to press for the desegregation of all bus facilities in the nation. It was a tactical victory made possible by Bobby's detached judgment, which in turn derived from his prodding style of negotiation. As he once quoted Francis Bacon to one of his lieutenants, "A wise interrogation is half the knowledge." When the president was asked in a press conference to state his opinion of the Freedom Riders, his response reflected not only a change in his own outlook toward civil rights but a recognition of the emerging locus of power within his administration: "I think the attorney general has made it clear that we believe that everyone who travels . . . should enjoy the full Constitutional protection given them by law."[76]

July 13, 1961

Chicago, Illinois

During most of 1961, Johnny Rosselli probed the perimeter of the Kennedy high command, looking for an opening, a way to neutralize Robert Kennedy's war on the Mafia. In March, he fired a warning shot involving the president's alleged adultery with actress Judy Meredith. In April, Sam Giancana, having joined Jack Kennedy as one of Judy Campbell's lovers the previous year, told her to tell the president that they were a threesome. In May, Frank Sinatra visited Ambassador Kennedy in Hyannis Port and, according to the attorney general's phone logs, called Bobby on two occasions. Later, there were offers to give Joe Kennedy a piece of the Cal-Neva Lodge and casino that Sinatra and Giancana were then building near Reno, Nevada.[77] According to the FBI, the elder Kennedy, after having been "visited by many gangsters with gambling interests," did indeed take a piece of the Cal-Neva through his son-in-law Peter Lawford.[78]

None of these overtures had any apparent effect on the attorney general's war against the mob, although it is important to note that Hoover kept him in the dark about the damning disclosures the FBI had in its possession. Had Kennedy known of them he might have pulled back a bit. But he knew nothing, and after his May trip to Chicago, in which he heard Mafia capo Pat Marcy conspire with two Chicago cops to murder a third, Bobby opened up on the Chicago Mafia. In early July, he approved a Chicago federal grand jury subpoena to be served on Giancana's girlfriend — in his presence.

On July 11, Sam Giancana and his girlfriend, singer Phyllis McGuire, flew to Phoenix, where their hotel was bugged by the FBI. The couple then took an American Airlines flight to New York with a stopover in Chicago O'Hare. The date was July 13. At O'Hare, FBI agents Ralph Hill and William Roemer accosted McGuire and gave her a choice: either she could answer their questions on the spot (in which case she would not be served) or refuse and later face questioning before the federal grand jury. McGuire coolly agreed to be questioned on the spot and was led off by Agent Hill.

Roemer stayed with the incredulous Giancana, who became abusive after his girlfriend was led away. "Have you guys figured out how many men I've killed?" he asked the towering Roemer, a former Marine and heavyweight boxing champion at Notre Dame. "Why don't you tell us, Mo?" Roemer sarcastically replied, using Giancana's nickname.[79] When Giancana realized Roemer would not be shaken by threats, he stormed back on the plane to retrieve McGuire's coat and purse, figuring that he and McGuire were going to miss the flight to New York.

As Giancana walked back up the gangway, Roemer resumed his taunting: "I heard about you being a fairy but now we know, don't we?"

Giancana went crazy. "You fucking cocksucker. Do you know who you're talking to? I could have Butch come here right now with his machine gun and take good care of you." When Roemer asked if Giancana was threatening a federal officer, the mob chieftain took another tack.

"Fuck Bobby Kennedy and your super, super boss."

"Who is that?"

"John Kennedy," Giancana snarled.

"I doubt if the president of the United States is interested in Sam Giancana," Roemer responded.

"Fuck John Kennedy! Listen, Roemer. I know all about the Kennedys, and Phyllis knows more about the Kennedys and one of these days we're going to tell all."

The acrimonious exchange continued until Roemer, nothing if not fearless, announced to the crowd of onlookers that they were all in the presence of "this piece of slime, Sam Giancana. Boss of the underworld here in Chicago."

Giancana concluded the exchange by noting darkly: "Roemer, you lit a fire tonight that will never go out."

What exactly Giancana had on the Kennedys was unclear to

Hoover, until he authorized the FBI in Chicago to install yet another bug, this one in the Armory Lounge, Giancana's inner sanctum. In August, Roemer and company, after having detained the janitor and surreptitiously made a copy of his key, broke into Giancana's hideaway office and placed a pineapple-sized microphone behind a baseboard. The agents strung the wire down through the basement and out through the parking lot, which they trenched to bury the wire. Giancana immediately gave the Bureau a full view of the complex and wide-ranging interests of the Chicago Mafia.[80] The bug also revealed the deal Rosselli and Giancana thought they had with the Kennedys. As was his practice, Hoover shared the tapes with no one outside the Bureau, but one immediate result was that the FBI stepped up its surveillance of Rosselli.

Rosselli continued to work the murder-Castro operation in south Florida. Although the CIA had provisionally discontinued its joint venture with the mob, pending the reconsideration of Cuba policy in Washington, Rosselli "stayed in position."[81] He set up shop at an upscale motel in Key Biscayne and hosted barbecue cookouts for his Cuban friends. Always the sybarite, "there were speedboats on crystal waters and women in abundance," as well as "optimistic projections of casino shares and cabinet positions once Fidel Castro was run out of Havana." Rosselli also hooked up with John V. Martino, a former mob electronics technician in the Havana casinos who had just been released from prison in Cuba by the Castro regime. Based on his association with Rosselli, Martino would eventually end up on the periphery of the plot to kill President Kennedy and provide critical testimony of what really happened.

When Rosselli left Florida, the FBI had difficulty tracking his movements, as FBI telexes of the time attest. The tap they had put on Rosselli's apartment phone in L.A. revealed little of value. (Rosselli likely knew of its existence and played along; a telephone, he once told an associate, "is a stool pigeon.") Rosselli was also hard to track because he either rented cars or used those of friends, which impeded FBI physical surveillance.[82] He had no retinue of bodyguards or backup cars, except on the rare occasion when West Coast shooter Jimmy Fratianno drove him. When he traveled by air, which was often, Rosselli never made reservations. He would show up at the airport ten minutes before a flight and pay for his ticket in cash.

Accordingly, Rosselli rarely showed up on the flight manifest. Like a wolf trotting along a distant timberline, he was visible only when he chose to be, otherwise disappearing, as if by instinct, into the underbrush he knew so well.

On December 13, 1961, he did appear on the FBI radar screen — in the course of a visit to Giancana's bugged office at the Armory Lounge in Forest Park. The Chicago office of the FBI listened as Rosselli explained to Giancana about Sinatra's efforts to slow down Bobby Kennedy.

ROSSELLI: I said, Frankie, can I ask you one question? He says [answer deleted] I took Sam's name and wrote it down and told Bobby Kennedy, this is my buddy. This is what I want you to know, Bob . . . Between you and me, Frank saw Joe Kennedy three different times. Joe Kennedy, the father — he called him three different times.

GIANCANA: Called who?

ROSSELLI: Called Frank. So maybe he's starting to see the light . . . you're friends. He's [Frank's] got it in his head that they're not faithful to him.

GIANCANA: In other words, the [campaign] donation that was made . . .

ROSSELLI: That's what I was talking about . . .

GIANCANA: Well, one minute he tells me this and then he tells me that and then the last time I talked to him at the hotel down in Florida a month before he left, and he said, Don't worry about it, if I can't talk to the old man [Joseph Kennedy], I'm gonna talk to the man [President Kennedy]. One minute he says he's talked to Robert, and the next minute he says hasn't talked to him. So he never did talk to him. It's a lot of shit. Why lie to me? I haven't got that coming.

Giancana then told Rosselli that one of his shooters, Johnny Formosa, had offered to hit Sinatra and "take the nigger's [Sammy Davis Jr.'s] eye out."

ROSSELLI: He's got big ideas, Frank does, about being an ambassador or something. You know Pierre Salinger and them guys, they don't want him. They treat him like a whore. You fuck them, you pay them, and then they're through. You got the right idea, Mo, go the other way. Fuck everybody. We'll use them every fucking way we can. They only know one way. Now let them see the other side of you.

This was an ominous proposal for a measured man like Rosselli, but one Bobby Kennedy was never to know. Hoover now had a clearer view of the bargain Joe Kennedy had made with the Chicago Outfit. Hoover ordered the tapes to be flown to Washington for safekeeping and stepped up FBI surveillance of Sinatra, Giancana, and Rosselli, only to find out something even more shocking about America's first family — that Joe Kennedy was *still* doing business with the Mafia. As he was gathering this package of poison, Hoover was also penning a note to Bobby and Ethel in response to their invitation to the Justice Department Christmas party: "It was indeed thoughtful of you to remember me. With my very best wishes to you both for a very Merry Christmas and Happy New Year. Sincerely, Edgar."[83]

The world had changed for the Mafia. Over 250 racketeers were indicted in 1961; 96 were convicted, compared with 19 in 1960. IRS audits now numbered in the hundreds. The FBI, emboldened by their surreptitiously derived knowledge of the Mafia's inner workings, were shadowing and even publicly mocking Mafia leaders. Giancana told a friend: "I never thought it would get this rough. You told me when they put his brother in there we were gonna see some fireworks, but I never knew it would be like this. This is murder."[84]

November 9, 1961

Washington, D.C.

On November 9, journalist Tad Szulc, then covering Cuba for the *New York Times*, had a conversation in the Oval Office with the president. Kennedy suddenly leaned forward in his rocking chair. "What would you think if I ordered Castro to be assassinated?" he asked. Szulc was stunned and later recalled "blurting out a long sentence to the effect that I was against political assassination as a matter of principle and that, anyway, I doubted that this would solve the Cuban problem for the U.S." The president smiled and leaned back in his rocking chair, saying that he was testing him. Szulc wrote that Kennedy had told him that "he was under terrific pressure from advisors in the Intelligence community to have Castro killed, but that he himself violently opposed it on the grounds that for moral reasons the United States should never be party to political assassinations."[85]

It was the same position Kennedy had expressed ten months earlier when Lumumba was assassinated. Despite the president's opposition, there is persuasive evidence that Bobby Kennedy was the moving force behind a renewal of the effort to kill Castro.

In the weeks following the Bay of Pigs at top-secret hearings, a board of inquiry consisting of the attorney general, General Maxwell Taylor, Admiral Arleigh Burke, and Allen Dulles heard the testimony of everyone from brigade frogman Blas Casares to Marine commandant David Shoup about the genesis and gestation of the debacle — Castro's T-33s, the uncharted reefs, the nonexistent "mass uprisings," etc. What remained unadmitted was the president's own feeble display of management. "Johnny, you didn't say yes but you didn't say no," was Bobby's rather paternal admonition.[86]

The brothers communicated constantly on Cuba during those weeks and their joint position appeared to be seamless, but there were differences. The Bay of Pigs confirmed the president's gut-level distrust of the generals and admirals, with their tidy and categorical prescriptions on the efficacy of force. Kenny O'Donnell would remember Kennedy mocking air force general Curtis LeMay after a meeting, making fun of the "fruit salad" on his chest and his simple-minded pronouncements.[87] Kennedy did not follow up on his angry threat to "split the CIA into a thousand pieces," but it did reveal his antipathy to the paramilitary busybodies who had gotten him into the mess in the first place. It was also revealing that Jack forwarded a communication to Bobby from Senator Mike Mansfield, who had written him on May 1: "If we yield to the temptation to give vent to our anger at our own failure, we will, ironically, strengthen Castro's position." Mansfield recommended that the United States disengage from the anti-Castro groups and stop the verbal attacks.[88] Disengagement was probably not an option the president considered, but it is clear he opposed the idea of an invasion of Cuba. Reacting to the calls for military action against Castro, from Richard Nixon among others, he told his old friend Paul Fay, "We're not going to plunge into an irresponsible action just because a fanatical fringe . . . puts so-called national pride above national reason. Do you think I'm going to carry on my conscience the responsibility for the wanton maiming and killing of children?"

Jack Kennedy was at heart an ironist who recognized the limits of will and power. His close friend David Ormsby-Gore, the British ambassador to the United States, described his sense of "the fatality of activism."[89] His reading reflected this. The president liked Ian Fleming's new novel, *On Her Majesty's Secret Service* ("I think James Bond fucks about three women in four countries — or vice versa" was his amused précis) but it was Barbara Tuchman's *The Guns of August* that he encouraged friends and advisors to read. Tuchman depicts the vainglorious lock-step of the oligarchs of pre–World War I Europe as they steered their countries off the cliff and into the abyss of total war. Revisionists of the Kennedy record, perhaps rightly, might point to the martial rhetoric about "the hour of maximum danger," but Kennedy had little faith in military intervention. Gore Vidal thought that Kennedy's most unusual gift was "an objectivity which extends to himself. He can discuss his own motives with a precision not usual in public men, who tend to regard themselves tenderly and according to the rhetoric of the day."[90]

He was downright contrite about the Bay of Pigs and repeatedly expressed his personal sense of guilt. After Blas Casares appeared in early May before the board of inquiry, he was brought over to the White House for a visit with the president. "You fought bravely," Kennedy told Casares. "You're not responsible for the fiasco." Casares then reached into his pocket to pull out the radio messages he had saved from the *Blagar,* messages that detailed the brigade's abandonment. One of the president's military aides, thinking the twenty-one-year-old was about to draw out a weapon, grabbed his wrist to restrain him. Kennedy waved off the aide and Casares handed the messages to the president, asking if he had read them. Kennedy thumbed through them for a few seconds, then responded that he had. Casares asked why the United States had provided no air cover for the exiles. Kennedy replied, "I can't answer that question, Mr. Casares. Someday I hope to."[91]

There was no particular sense of contrition, much less perspective, evident in Bobby Kennedy's attitude toward Cuba — only action. His crusade against Castro, which took form during the Bay of Pigs postmortem, was a dark admixture of emotion and crude miscalculation. It had the character of a vendetta. Bobby saw Castro the way he saw Hoffa: as a betrayer of his people and a poseur, who, with the right formula of assault, could be taken down. Secretary of Defense Robert McNamara described his attitude at the time as "hysterical."[92] As in the 1960 campaign, shrouded in self-righteousness and determined to win at any cost, Bobby was willing to justify the means for the end.

On May 22, in a memorandum sent to him by Hoover, the attorney general was told point-blank that the Mafia had been recruited to eliminate Castro. The FBI had stumbled upon evidence of the joint venture by accident. Giancana had induced the CIA, through Robert Maheu, to bug the Las Vegas hotel room of comedian Dan Rowan, who Giancana feared was having an affair with Phyllis McGuire. The man sent to wire Rowan's room, Arthur J. Balletti, got caught, and the FBI was called in.[93] Hoover demanded to know from Colonel Sheffield Edwards, CIA director of security, just why the CIA was providing such favors for Giancana. After Hoover was fully briefed, he prepared a memo for the attorney general:

> Colonel Edwards said that since this is "dirty business" he could not afford to have knowledge of that action of Maheu and Giancana in pursuit of any mission for the CIA. . . . Mr. Bissell, in his recent briefings of General Taylor and the attorney general and in connection with their inquiries into CIA activities relating to the Cuban situation told the attorney general that some of the associated planning included the use of Giancana and the underworld against Castro.[94]

If any doubt remained in Kennedy's mind as to precisely what "dirty business" or "associated planning" meant, a simple call to Bissell would have confirmed that the connection involved plotting to murder Castro. In view of the administration's all-out attack on the mob, it might have seemed imperative for the attorney general to sever the CIA-Mafia joint venture, particularly since knowledge of it added ammunition to Hoover's arsenal of blackmail. Instead, Kennedy simply penned into the margin a rather pro forma instruction to his FBI liaison, Courtney Evans: "Courtney, I hope this will be followed up vigorously."[95] A year later, in May 1962, Bobby would have another chance to terminate the Mafia's role in plotting to kill Castro, but would only request that he henceforth be informed beforehand. Although he might countenance using the Mafia against Castro, Kennedy would again give them no quarter in his prosecutorial assault.

Why play such a dangerous double game? Bobby was clearly frustrated that all the deliberations at the State Department, White House, and CIA had produced nothing but endless harrumphing about the blight of Castro and no sense of what to do. On June 1, the attorney general wrote, "The Cuban matter is being allowed to slide because no one really has the answer to Castro. Not many are really prepared to send American troops in there at the present time but maybe that is the answer."[96] But with Khrushchev spoiling, at least rhetorically, for a showdown over West Berlin, for which the

Soviets had mustered an overwhelming array of armor and men, it seemed senseless to be contemplating an invasion of Cuba. George Ball said as much during a Cuba Task Force meeting when he asked pointedly what it would take to invade the island: "A half-million men? One million men?" What if the Soviets seized West Berlin when the United States invaded Cuba? he asked. The attorney general bristled at this, but Ball pressed his point.[97] And what of the costs in civilian deaths, or the bitter prospect of garrisoning the island and brutalizing its population, as the United States had done during its occupation of Haiti during the 1920s? Bobby Kennedy knew little if anything about Latin American history, much less about what was involved in an airborne or amphibious assault. In matters of foreign policy, he was willful but unschooled, the moralist at large. Even Averell Harriman, one of his best friends, later conceded in an interview: "He was totally wrong [on Cuba]."[98]

What chance there was for restraint in Cuban policy was lost after President Kennedy's disastrous summit with Khrushchev in June 1961. Kennedy had come to the talks hoping to achieve some degree of peaceful entente with the Soviet premier, and maybe even to extract a nuclear test ban commitment. But Khrushchev simply mugged Kennedy. He engaged in open talk of war if the United States did not accept Russia's position on access to Berlin. Kennedy left the last five-hour session "dazed," in the observation of British correspondent Henry Brandon. James Reston gave an even starker account of Kennedy's emotional condition in Vienna, describing him with his hat "pushed over his eyes like a beaten man."

> "Pretty rough, was it?" I asked.
> "The roughest thing in my life," Kennedy replied. " I have two problems. First to figure out why he did it, and in such a hostile way. And the second is to figure out what we can do about it. I think he did it because of the Bay of Pigs. I think he thought that anyone so inexperienced as to get into that mess could be taken, and anyone who got into it and didn't see it through had no guts. So he beat the hell out of me."[99]

Part of the problem was Kennedy's own unrealistic expectations. As President de Gaulle had warned him only days before the meeting,

Khrushchev was a demagogue, full of bluster but not meaning half of it. Back in Washington, however, Khrushchev's rhetoric was read differently, and the hawks were soon circling over a Soviet-American showdown on Berlin.

On July 13, the president listened expressionlessly as former secretary of state Dean Acheson recommended that the United States be prepared to go to nuclear war over Berlin, and that it should avoid all negotiations "until the crisis is well-developed." Kennedy's own secretary of state, Dean Rusk, essentially agreed with this position.

But the president was troubled. "All wars start with stupidity," he remarked to Kenny O'Donnell. "God knows, I'm not an isolationist, but it seems particularly stupid to risk killing a million Americans about access on an Autobahn."[100] Later, at a top-secret briefing, an air force general analyzed the chances of nuclear war for the president and the national security council. Kennedy was so disgusted by the "kindergarten" quality of it that he got up and walked out. "And we call ourselves the human race," he said in exasperation to Rusk.[101] In a speech to the nation on July 25, Kennedy adopted a tough posture, announcing that he would call up 150,000 reservists and authorize a national civil defense program, but he alluded openly to his resistance to the hard-line position. "Miscommunication," he said, "could rain down more devastation in several hours than had been wrought in all of human history." As would be critically important in the missile crisis of the following year, Kennedy's sense of historical irony and his visceral distaste for the military establishment ultimately confirmed him as a diplomatist.

Bobby, with his more red-blooded view, was meanwhile attending the marathon meetings on Cuba, which at one point in May–June 1961 were running four hours a day, five days a week.[102] He increasingly sought the company of military men who might supply the forceful answers. General Maxwell Taylor, whom the president had summoned out of retirement to do the postmortem on the Bay of Pigs, was by any measure an exceptional man. The jumping general of the 101st Airborne was one of the most decorated officers of World War Two. He was also a linguist, and had the polish and demeanor of a European prince. Bobby and Taylor became close. Kennedy was to name a newborn son after the general.[103]

The other general mustered to do battle over Cuba, Edward G. Lansdale, was the opposite of Taylor — a noisy martinet who had more answers than there were questions. But Lansdale had something everybody was looking for in that angry summer and fall of 1961: a means short of invasion to stop communist revolution. It was called counterinsurgency. Nothing if not a legend in his own mind, Lansdale claimed to have the experience necessary from his anticommunist adventures in the Philippines and Indochina.

In *The Quiet American,* Graham Greene had likened his Lansdale-like character Pyle to "a dumb leper who has lost his bell, wandering the world meaning no harm."[104] In 1961, operating out of his office in the Pentagon, Lansdale was back looking for his bell and spreading his infectious creed. This time, however, weaponry was being distributed on American soil in southern Florida. The problem that was arising was in many ways the same that had bedeviled Athens during the fourth century B.C., when the city-state democratically poisoned itself by unrestrained warmongering.

Lansdale was to develop thirty-three different ways to eliminate Castro: chemical attacks on the Cuban sugar crop, dumping counterfeit Cuban currency into Cuba, dropping "para-dummies" to panic the population, introducing "cheap marijuana" (or, alternatively, accusing Cuba of narcotics trafficking), announcing a "misfire" of an American nuclear missile that was heading toward Cuba, and so on.[105] Lansdale's own favorite, one he told the so-called Special Group (Augmented) he had used against the communists in the Philippines, was to spread a rumor within Cuba's large Catholic population that the Second Coming was en route, and that Christ would "return to Cuba." (The Book of Revelations does not report Christ in Cuba in the first place, but no matter.) The condition for Christ's reentry was the removal of Castro, whose anti-Catholic activities had inspired divine rage. Once this rumor was circulated, an American submarine positioned off the Cuban coast would fill the night sky with exploding star shells, the sign of Christ extant. The frenzied Cubans would then overthrow Castro. Walt Elder, CIA director John McCone's executive assistant, termed this "elimination by illumination."[106]

Bobby Kennedy was a rapt apostle. He sent his new administrative assistant James Symington over to the Pentagon to commune with Lansdale. Symington thought Lansdale an idiot. He wrote the attorney general that Lansdale was "the 800-pound all-American gorilla," a description that offended Kennedy. Bobby was smitten by the notion of counterinsurgency.[107] He would import Green Berets for weekends at Hyannis Port, where they would demonstrate their prowess by swinging from trees and climbing over barricades.[108] A green beret sat on the attorney general's desk. The hard-bitten CIA and former U.S. Navy frogman Rip Robertson paid a visit to Hickory Hill and on his return to south Florida was able to report to his colleagues that Bobby Kennedy was "OK." Harris Wofford later wrote that "the attorney general was the driving force behind the clandestine effort to overthrow Castro. . . . He seemed like a wild man who was out-CIAing the CIA."

Ethel Skakel Kennedy too played her part. Her family's business, Great Lakes Carbon, had maintained an office in Havana and sold filters to sugar refineries during the Batista regime. The Skakels had also wintered in seaside Varadero, outside Havana, and Ethel was acquainted with the children of several upper-class Cuban families. Shortly after Castro's takeover in 1959, certain *fidelista* irregulars had tried to commandeer the Skakel's 55-foot luxury craft. This incident sealed the family's dire opinion of Castro. In the summer of 1961, Ethel took several young brigade veterans who had escaped from Giron under her wing. She even set up Blas Casares on a date with a good Catholic girl. As always, the Kennedys threw themselves into everything they did.

By October–November 1961, the CIA, in Richard Helms's words, "was instructed to get going on plans to get rid of Castro by some device which obviously would have to be covert because nobody had any stomach anymore for any invasions or any military fiascoes of that kind." Helms, then serving as the deputy director of plans at the CIA, described the atmosphere as "very intense. . . . Nutty schemes were born of the intensity of the pressure. And we were quite frustrated. . . . No doubt about it, it was white heat."[109] The interagency Special Group, which met every Thursday at 2 P.M., would metamorphose into the Special Group (Augmented), informally known as Mongoose, when the attorney general arrived, usually as the Special Group's business was concluding. ZR/RIFLE chief Bill Harvey and General Lansdale routinely showed up for the Mongoose meeting and it was in this forum that a clear — if bureaucratically deniable — signal was sent to kill Castro. Certainly this is the conclusion of John Ranelagh, author of *The Agency: The Rise and Decline of the CIA*, generally acknowledged as the most comprehensive history of its kind.[110]

When word of the decision (possibly via the attorney general) reached the president, he was deeply concerned. It was in this circumstance that he spoke to *New York Times* correspondent Tad Szulc of the "terrific pressure" on him to order the murder of Castro. Wofford's judgment as to who in fact was behind this terrific pressure is persuasive:

> If Robert Kennedy understood and supported this secret plan within the larger covert operation, he himself may have been the source of "terrific pressure" for the assassination. Nothing in the testimony before the Senate [Chuch] committee suggests that the circumlocutious and evasive leaders of the CIA would have put such direct pressure on the president. Then who did? "Terrific pressure" is what anyone, including his brother the president, would have felt if he tried resist a course strongly advocated by the Attorney General.[111]

A few days after the president's exchange with Szulc, White House aide Richard Goodwin discussed the matter of assassinating Castro with the president. It was to Goodwin that Kennedy observed, "If we get into that kind of thing, we'll all be targets."[112]

The president's view did not prevail. On November 13, in evident anticipation of "Phase II" of the assassination effort, Bill Harvey cabled the Mexico City CIA station to dispatch David S. Morales to JM-WAVE (the CIA's base in south Florida) for permanent posting.[113] Morales, a Mexican-American CIA agent from Phoenix, was well known as the Agency's top assassin in Latin America. He had served in Cuba from 1958 to 1960 in the American consulate in Havana. He had played a supporting role in Mexico City during the Bay of Pigs planning. Afterward he had openly described what Kennedy had done as *traición* (betrayal).

Nicknamed El Indio because of his dark skin and Indian features, Morales was a man of explosive temperament and exceptional cunning, a master at his deadly game. In south Florida he was to team up with Johnny Rosselli. This would be a murderous coupling.

In New Orleans, another alliance had formed by the end of 1961. David Ferrie, having lost his job as an Eastern Airlines pilot for seducing young men, was spreading Marcello money among violently anti-Castro exiles, one of whom, Sergio Aracha-Smith, was a CIA informant. In June Ferrie had made a fiery speech to the Military Order of World Wars in New Orleans about the Bay of Pigs, saying "anyone could lie in the bushes and shoot the president." The FBI field office noted that Ferrie was known in the New Orleans area for his work with the local Civil Air Patrol. One of Ferrie's trainees, as a photograph would later show, was a teenager by the name of Lee Harvey Oswald.

December 19, 1961

West Palm Beach, Florida

Bobby liked to describe Jack as having "the guts of a cat burglar," adding that it was their father who had bequeathed him this trait. Joe Kennedy may have given his sons the singular advantage of money, but he also passed on his intense fearlessness in taking risks. For both Jack and Bobby, he remained both a figure of awe, a titanic presence in their public and personal lives — shouting instructions to one or the other on the phone from Hyannis Port, telling Jack with a heavy arm across his shoulders that he would one day be regarded as a great American president, or warning Bobby to stay straight with Hoover. For all his flaws, he was there for them every day, as he had been for all his children, unstinting and devoted. In December 1961 this changed.

On his way back from a six-day trip to Latin America on December 19, the president stopped off for a quick visit with his father at his home in West Palm Beach. A few hours later, Jack reboarded Air Force One and continued on to Washington. His father went for a round of golf with his niece Ann Gargan. Suddenly feeling faint on the fairway of the 16th hole, the Ambassador — as his children continued to call him — returned home and went to bed. Hearing that he was not feeling well, Rose looked in on him. "There's nothing I can do but pray," his wife told the staff and went off for her own scheduled golf game.[114] Hours later, when his condition seemed to have become more serious, an ambulance was called. Within minutes of returning to the Oval Office late that afternoon, Jack got a call from St. Mary's Hospital in Palm Beach advising him that his father had suffered a stroke. He immediately called Bobby, who was conferring with his Detroit organized crime strike force, and told him the news in a strangled voice, "Dad's gotten sick."[115]

Together the brothers flew down on Air Force One to West Palm Beach and went straight to the hospital. Their father hovered near death; he was given the last rites. In the days that followed, Joe Kennedy inched back toward normality, but remained paralyzed from head to toe on his right side. He seemed to understand people when they talked to him, but in reply could only blurt out in a ruined, angry way: "No . . . No . . . No." His doctors informed family members that the prognosis for recovery was not good. The family's strong mast was broken.

Over the weeks that followed, no one seemed to take Joe's stroke harder than Bobby, who surveyed doctors and experimental procedures all over the country in a search for a cure. There was none.[116] Bobby flew to West Palm Beach twice before Christmas. James Symington, who accompanied him on one of those trips, remembered that each time Bobby saw his father he himself would go into a state of disconsolate shock.[117]

One year before, Joe had pressured Bobby to become attorney general and, as his father had predicted, Bobby had progressively taken command of the administration in the same way he had Jack's 1952 and 1960 campaigns. But Bobby's indispensable resource in every sense during "the very mean year of 1961," as he later put it, had been his father.[118] Now he was alone.

Well before Joe's stroke, General Maxwell Taylor had concluded that the fraternal order was not what rank or age suggested: Bobby was the senior brother.[119] Taylor had his reasons for thinking this. The president's chronic state of pain transformed each day into something of a question mark. There were days Jack could tie his shoes by himself, and days he couldn't. Despite his stoic drive, he was forced to take frequent baths, shots in his back, and to curtail his schedule. At times, such as when Ghanaian president Kwame Nkrumah visited him in the first week of March 1961, his face was unusually bloated. Under the care of Dr. Janet Travell, whose regimen included novocaine injections, barbiturate painkillers, orally ingested cortisone, baths, exercise, a shoelift that relieved the seesaw caused by his curved spine, and a braced corset, Jack's health improved. But there were always episodes. A tree-planting ceremony during a state trip to Canada in the second week of May had re-injured his fragile lower back and transformed his trip to Vienna for the summit meeting with Khrushchev into an ordeal.[120]

As always, Jack rarely complained, but during the dark days of the Bay of Pigs, Bobby saw disturbing physical manifestations that were induced by either sleeplessness, stress, pain, or some combination. The president would rub his eyes, roll his head, and sit down suddenly as if he were dizzy. Bobby's calls to Jack's aide Kenny O'Donnell always began with a pointed inquiry: "How's the president?"[121]

The womanizing, which resumed after a postinaugural hiatus of a month or so, probably didn't help, although Kennedy claimed it was the one thing that relaxed him. The "talent," as the president called them, varied. There was a continuing stream of actresses and starlets, usually procured by Peter Lawford. Angie Dickinson, Lee Remick, and Marilyn Monroe were among the more notable and long-standing.[122] Through former Lyndon Johnson aide and bagman Bobby Baker and other wheeler-dealers, Jack was able to troll Capitol Hill waters for party girls like Ellie Rometsch. Closer to home were Jackie's secretary, Pamela Turnure, and two secretaries in the White House pool Jack referred to as "Fiddle" and "Faddle." (The observant Jackie referred to these latter two as "the White House dogs.")[123] Beyond this, there were prostitutes and call girls that materialized at their appointed hour (it rarely took longer than that). Some of these, perhaps accepting their status, required little maintenance. Others, like Judy Campbell, came to believe that the president might leave his wife for them. Only one might have posed that contingency — Mary Pinchot Meyer, a sophisticated divorcee and successful painter of the colorist school whose affair with the president began in March 1961 and continued off and on until his death.[124]

Through all of this manic coupling, the Secret Service was obliged to perform extra duty — staking out trysting locations or hustling women in and out of the White House sub rosa. This caused discomfort among certain agents, particularly the more monogamous ones. Jackie, if not fully aware of all the names and faces, knew of her husband's relentless philandering, but dealt with it as she always had — with a combination of occasional hurt and consistent hauteur. It did not prevent her from sharing her sexual favors with her spouse, nor at the same time from taking the children away for the weekend, knowing the predictable consequence back in the White House. Trained by both Jack and her father Black Jack to accept adultery as an ugly fact of family life, Jackie was capable of carrying on. Her sense of self-direction as well as her deep attachment to her children were somehow untouched, perhaps even strengthened. Jacqueline Kennedy emerged as a strong, driven, lonely woman who loved her husband in her own way and occupied a central space in his life with pride and supremely sure taste.

Joe Kennedy had always been Jackie's closest ally in the family. His incapacitation not only jeopardized her access to money (since Jack never concerned himself with the family's finances) but deprived her of the one person who sought to contain Jack's extramarital sorties. Bobby had also been loyal and episodically attentive to her, as the stillbirth in August 1956 revealed, but he either didn't realize or simply ignored Jack's pursuit of other women.

This began to change in 1961 when Bobby began rallying to Jack's side on national and international crises. As soon as the president heard the East Germans were constructing a wall in the middle of the night to stanch the flow of refugees into West Berlin, he said, "Go get my brother." On the issue of American funding of Ghana's Volta Dam, on the other hand, Jack found Bobby's presence less welcome. The attorney general opposed American aid because he thought President Nkrumah to be a "Black Castro," a characterization bordering on the absurd. Bobby arrived late at the National Security Council meeting on September 5 in which the matter was to be decided and sat directly behind the president, who commented that he knew the attorney general had arrived because he could "feel the hot breath of his opposition down the back of my neck." The president gave his brother the floor, listened to his strong disapproval of the funding, then gave the green light to the Volta River Project.[125] At least on foreign policy, Bobby was more of an enforcer and intimate interlocutor than a decision maker. But this too was changing.

The Washington press began to refer to Bobby as "the second most powerful man in Washington." In the presence of several

White House reporters in the Oval Office, the president took a call from his brother, and with his hand over the phone whispered to them that it was indeed "the second most powerful man in Washington" on the line.

Bobby's stick on policy matters was soon being brandished in personal areas. During the first months of 1961, the president had come under the treatment, if it could be termed that, of a New York doctor by the name of Max Jacobson, a veritable Dr. Feelgood. Jacobson's specialty was to give his patients (among them Eddie Fisher and Jackie's brother-in-law, Stanislaus Radziwill) cocktail injections of vitamins, enzymes, and amphetamines. The president grew so fond of Dr. Jacobson's treatments that he brought him along on his trip to the Vienna summit with Khrushchev. In September 1961, Jacobson gave the president a shot directly into his throat before the hoarse-voiced Jack was to address the UN General Assembly. When Bobby got wind of this, he immediately procured the substance, sent it to the FDA for testing, and then confronted his brother with the fact that he was being injected with narcotics. "I don't care if it's horse piss," Jack replied. "It works."

Joe Kennedy's stroke only elevated Bobby's preeminence within his talented family, but the cost was high. Having bought, bullied, and bulldozed his family's way to power, Joe Kennedy understood the price and terms of its thirty-year trajectory. Bobby did not. Moreover, Joe Kennedy was feared by everyone, even by those who hated him and his sons. Gone now was the broker of the family's dangerous alliance with the Mafia. Gone too was Hoover's single ally in the Kennedy family. Bobby's contempt for his enemies was now unleavened by any sense of limits or by the remotest calculation of their destructive power. He would cleanse them from his family and his country once and for all.

The Kennedy children rallied round their fallen patriarch. Jack flew up every weekend he could to Boston and would helicopter over to Hyannis Port; the old man watched from the porch as the helicopter landed. Jack would tease his father by telling him how closely he was consulting with all the people his father detested.[126] Bobby and Ted were there as well every weekend. On one occasion, when the senior Kennedy staggered as he tried to get out of his wheelchair, Bobby rushed over the help him. The old man started screaming and tried to hit his son with his cane. Bobby fended off the blows and grabbed his father and kissed him: "That's what I'm here for, Dad. Just to give you a hand when you need it. You've done that for me all my life, so why can't I do the same for you now?"[127]

But it was Jackie who seemed to reach the Ambassador the most. One weekend at Hyannis Port, Dave Powers found them sitting together on the loveseat in the front room. She was holding his deformed right hand in hers, occasionally wiping away drool from the corner of his mouth and kissing him on the paralyzed side of his face. "Grandpa, I'm praying for you every day," she told him. At this point the president walked in behind the two of them from the dining room. He stood there listening as Jackie continued talking to his father. "You know that Jack never would have married me without you," she said, and put her arms around the crumbling old man.[128]

Powers remembered that Jack paused and lowered his head as he heard this.

Triumph

1962

February 2–28, 1962

World Trip

At the beginning of 1962, when the Washington press corps collectively alighted upon the obvious with a sense of discovery, namely that Bobby Kennedy was "the second most powerful man in Washington," certain reporters like *Life*'s Paul O'Neil and the *New York Times*'s Anthony Lewis dug beneath the opaque surface of the attorney general. There they found a matrix that was far more complex and contradictory. O'Neil wrote:

> He is motivated — in his concern for his friends and allies, in his almost emotional refusal to be swayed by wealth and social position, and in his pugnacity as well — by a stern and literal belief in concepts of good and evil which most humans abandon after childhood, and by a sense of duty to family and country which overrides his own considerable ambition. . . . Though he clings to attitudes the world considers impractical in the extreme, he practices them with a calculating pragmatism.[1]

Even the magazine cover portraits of Bobby seemed to convey the contradictions. On *Life*'s January 1962 cover, Bobby, with his unlined face and Vitalis-coiffed hair, looks like an altar boy. *Time*'s February cover, an impressionist portrait of multicolored brushstrokes, catches the sharp angles in his face, the raptor nose, and the brooding eyes that suggested anger or aggression.[2]

The press's primary point of reference to Bobby was of course Jack, but in essential ways they could not have been more different. The president had migrated from his family's Irishness. In many ways he was more like his friend British ambassador David Ormsby-Gore, a detached gamesman whose tastes in books, women, and public affairs were those of an aristocrat. Jack Kennedy went to church the way one might go to a club, drank sparingly, and avoided all forms of ethnic chauvinism.[3] He moved through his days, as John Kenneth Galbraith later wrote, "alert, alive, amused, amusing."[4] However taut, he was an upbeat, charming character who made it a point to carry the burden lightly.

Bobby was a throwback to his immigrant great-grand-parents — moody, unappeasable in his distaste for the powerful, fatalistic with flashes of joy and humor, and profoundly and actively Catholic. Watching Bobby at work one day in his cavernous office, a journalist described him "patting the arms of his chair in a slow and feverish rhythm, looking off into the beyond with that expression of muted despair."[5] This was not a happy man. His best friend in prep school, David Hackett, said that at school Bobby was a "misfit" and an awkward young man. From this uncenteredness sprang his compensatory ferocity, with its complement of brilliance and blindness. Bobby did not regard politics as the art of the possible. He instead saw politics as a moral crusade in which causes were both lance and shield. Anthony Lewis, who was no uncritical admirer of Bobby's at the time, thought that "in a tormented way, he was trying to do everything on the merits."[6] Everything, Lewis might have added, except when it came to the ultimate cause — Jack. There the merits gave way to an unsparing ruthlessness.

Commanding the Kennedy sanctum, Bobby was fiercely loyal and fiercely demanding of loyalty, and unusually protective, even solicitous, of clan members. When the mother of Bill French became seriously ill, Kennedy arranged for French to be flown to Ohio and later called him to ask how she was.[7]

Outside that sanctum, the idealist emerges, armed with a vaulting ambition to change the world, particularly that of the poor, the young, and the sick. But whichever dimension of Robert Kennedy's personality prevailed, they all, as Gore Vidal once said, had a moral essence, making his temperament basically that of an authoritarian.[8]

No one in the press understood him as well as the newspaper columnist Mary McGrory, and she ascribed his nature to his ethnic origin; he was a Celt, and a Celt at heart is a pessimist — a victim of fate or history who goes down lyricizing his defiance, as Robert Emmet did.[9] At times McGrory communicated with him in a sort of ethno-historic shorthand. One message she left for him read: "Maud Gonne called to inquire if Kevin Barry still intends to bomb the Post Office."[10] The integument of Irish Catholicism sealed Bobby's view of man as fallen, but added, paradoxically, the notion that the world, though temporally doomed, could be redeemed through corporal acts of mercy. Thus his ministrations in the realm of the mentally ill, the poor, and the distressed youth. Late one morning, Kennedy disappeared from his office and turned up in East Harlem a few hours later. He had decided to track down members of a gang called the Viceroys, and, once he did, sat on a curb, tie loosened, hair askew, listening to what the gang members had to tell him. He returned to his office late that afternoon. "He looked like a bop himself," one Viceroy later told a journalist admiringly.[11]

The final twist in the multiveined matrix of his personality — his gentility — was evident in his fascination with children and his own childlike devotion to those who served him. When his secretary Angie Novello sent him a memo appealing to him to "notify his immediate staff of his whereabouts at all times," he jotted a laconic reply: "What if I'm lost. Love."[12]

Ben Bradlee of *Newsweek* asked the president for an estimate of Bobby — "and never mind the brother bit." Jack replied, "First, his high moral standards, strict personal ethics. He's a puritan, absolutely incorruptible. Then he has terrific executive energy. We've got more guys around here with ideas. The problem is to get things done. Bobby's the best organizer I've ever seen."[13] Despite his deep admiration for Bobby, Jack tried to steer clear of the "puritan" during off-hours on weekends and evenings. Sometimes this was difficult. At a White House dinner in November 1961 for Fiat chairman Gianni Agnelli, Gore Vidal was amazed to feel a hand — Bobby's — peeling his hand off of his step-sister Jackie's shoulder. Bobby apparently could not brook the fact that Vidal, a known homosexual, was touching Jackie. A violent argument erupted between the two men.[14] Hearing of the confrontation, Jack, who liked Vidal, blithely remarked, "Just don't get me involved, would you?"[15]

Bobby's faith was deep, constant, and literal.[16] His Jansenist Catholicism carried over into reflections about the afterlife. When the wife of Protocol Chief Angier Biddle Duke suddenly died,

Bobby dictated a telegram: "Still it must be a consolation to you to know that she is now raised above all earthly problems, the everlasting joy and light of heaven are hers and that she smiles down on you from what must be a very high place in Paradise."[17] One Sunday morning at St. Francis Xavier Church in Hyannis Port, when an altar boy failed to show, Bobby came forward and substituted flawlessly — Latin, presentation of the cruets, and all. One of his briefs against Castro was the destruction of the Catholic Church in Cuba.[18]

Insiders in Washington were starting to conclude, as *Time* put it, "that while Jack may now be president of the United States, Bobby is fast becoming the chief of the clan — perhaps by Kennedy standards a more enduring and more important position — and toils to protect the prestige now reflected from the White House as Father Joe toiled to protect and enlarge the family's investments in Wall Street."[19]

Jack had always felt that one area where Bobby needed development was in foreign affairs. Sometime in December 1961, he suggested that Bobby go on a trip around the world. Bobby's initial reply was that he couldn't spare the time, but the president insisted. There were other factors that encouraged such a trip. An elderly Japanese acquaintance of the brothers, Hosono Gunji, who had squired Congressman Kennedy and his younger brother around Japan in 1951 (and had corresponded with Bobby for ten years thereafter) relentlessly proposed a visit. Additionally, there was pressing diplomatic business Bobby could do. Heightened tension between the United States and Indonesia's flamboyant nonaligned leader, Achmed Sukarno, over the status of Dutch West New Guinea (as well as Sukarno's refusal to release a captured CIA pilot named Allen Pope) had strained relations to the breaking point. A visit by the attorney general, given his political standing, offered the prospect of negotiated resolution. Ethel Kennedy too was all for the trip, seeing it as an opportunity to showcase the fashions of Madame Paul, her Swiss-born couturière. By early January 1962 it was settled; the four-week trip was on.

Before leaving for their first destination, Japan, Bobby and Ethel flew to Los Angeles for a send-off party hosted by Peter and Pat Lawford at their beachfront home in Santa Monica. At Peter

Lawford's direction, the attorney general was seated between actresses Kim Novak and Marilyn Monroe; Ethel was seated a couple of tables away.[20] In an interview years later, Lawford rejected any suggestion that he was deliberately dangling forbidden fruit before the Kennedy family's puritan; it was simply that Monroe "had wanted to meet him."[21]

The Hollywood press turned the party into something of a political premiere, flashing pictures and shouting questions at the guests as they alighted from their Cadillacs, Aston-Martins, and so forth. About two hours into the party, Monroe arrived in a VW bug driven by a young man she described to the press as "a sailor," who had picked her up earlier that afternoon. After taking her seat next to Bobby, she scrawled a note in red lipstick on a napkin and handed it to him: "What does an attorney general do?" Sometime later, Bobby asked her to dance the twist, which he had slightly mastered after a lesson from Harry Belafonte at Hickory Hill. According to Lawford, Ethel watched this with a steady gaze.[22] It was the beginning of a perilous tangent. A few days later in Tokyo, while touring the famous Ginza district with his Japanese hosts, Bobby was asked what he thought of the beauty of Japanese women. He quickly reminded his hosts (and possibly himself), "I am a married man."[23] Married or not, he was now entering into the heady precinct of celebrity.

Time likened the impact of the Kennedys' visit to Japan to the minor earthquake that hit Tokyo during their stay. The Kennedys encountered a political situation that was highly uncertain. There had been periodic strikes and violent anti-American protests. The attorney general's first address at Nihon University in Tokyo was a success, in part because Bobby made fun of his murderous attempt at Japanese. The Japanese press the next day depicted this as *honne*, their word for true feeling. But at his next stop, Waseda University, he was hissed and booed by several hundred Marxist students. As he was being drowned out, Bobby reached down and pulled one of the hecklers up on stage and offered him the microphone. The young man launched into a high-pitched diatribe while the attorney general, smiling, stood alongside him, seeming to listen to the nonstop, anti-American imprecation.[24]

When the young man finally finished, Bobby took back the

microphone. Suddenly there was a blackout. Someone located a battery-operated bullhorn and Kennedy resumed telling the students that the reason his brother had sent him to Japan was to hear from young people who wished to speak out. United States ambassador Edwin O. Reischauer, a former Harvard professor, translated these sentiments into flawless Japanese, and soon the crowd began to turn. Finally, the school cheerleader led the audience in the school song, "Miyako no seihoku," which Bobby and Ethel insisted on learning. (It later became the favorite party song at Hickory Hill.)

After this unusual encounter, the press coverage became enormous. Bobby did a succession of interviews through the skilled interlocution of Reischauer, who would later comment on how fascinated the Japanese were by Kennedy's blunt responses. The newspaper *Yomuri* praised his "frankness, simplicity, and courage." Kennedy, it noted, would go anywhere, see anyone, and try anything in his quest to understand Japan. Only his Catholicism seemed to get in the way. Outside Osaka at an ancient Buddhist temple, Bobby was asked to light an incense stick. "What are the implications if I do this?" he asked Ambassador Reischauer. When the ambassador told him it simply showed respect, Bobby reminded him that he was a devout Catholic. "You're sure it won't look like I'm worshiping Buddha?" he asked. When reassured, he lit the stick.[25] (This became another of Jack's sarcastic anecdotes about his brother, who, he would inform people with straight-faced mockery in Bobby's presence, was a sophisticated and ecumenical Catholic.) Whatever the case, the trip did reveal something unexpected — that Bobby, although lacking Jack's witty self-possession, had a powerful effect on people because of his unaffected openness.

Ethel, in her own Panglossian way, complemented him perfectly with her tanned, lithe presence and consistent demonstration of enthusiasm over erudition. The first night in Tokyo, she left the water running in the bathtub and it flooded down to the next floor. The next day, she started a speech she had clearly never seen before, stopping and commenting, "Gosh. This sounds like a terrible graduation speech," then inviting the audience to "just call me Ethel." At a formal luncheon, Ethel asked Japanese politician (and later prime minister) Yasuhiro Nakasone, "Did I read that your cats have

no tails?" There was silence. The Japanese couldn't quite comprehend this one, either.[26] Nor did Madame Paul's hairbows, which
appeared regularly on Ethel's beehive (matching the color of her
dresses), conform in the slightest with Tokyo's understated couture.
But Ethel's sheer vivacity did conform to the Japanese idea of Americans as enthusiasts. The Kennedy visit, in good part because of its
shock value, was a total success.

And so it went. In Jakarta, while staying at Sukarno's presidential palace, Ethel stuck the plug of her hairdryer into the wrong
outlet and plunged the entire building into darkness. At the University of Indonesia, after having been hit in the face by a piece of
fruit during his speech, Bobby talked down yet another large as-
semblage of anti-American communists.[27] Three days before his arrival, the American embassy had been stoned in anticipation of his
visit. Within days of his appearance, Bobby was walking Jakarta's
streets followed by tens of thousands of cheering Indonesians who
seemed inspired by his youthful sincerity. As would happen in the
1968 campaign, the press, wary at first because of Bobby's reputation as a ruthless enforcer, came to see him at close quarters as open
and without affectation, seemingly tireless in his quest to understand. They became his uncritical admirers.

In his negotiations with the wily Sukarno, Bobby was at his
bulldog best, alternatingly complimenting and excoriating the old
man. At one point in their exchanges over Dutch West New Guinea
and the release of the CIA pilot from an Indonesian jail, Kennedy
angrily walked out of the room in which they were sitting only to
return with the inquiry: "Am I to go back to the president and say
that you will not tell us that you'll stand by your word? Everybody
tells me you're a man of your word and the president believes
that."[28] The negotiation produced no immediate results, but eventually Pope was released and war between Holland and Indonesia
was averted.

After visiting India and Thailand, the Kennedys flew to Europe.
In Rome, the press brought a motor scooter into Alfredo's restaurant for Ethel, who promptly tried to drive it among the tables. (She
later crashed a Vespa into a bus.) Bobby met with de Gaulle in Paris
and Adenauer in Berlin, through which he made a triumphal tour
on a snowy, bitter cold day. On February 28, they flew home —

having covered 30,000 miles and fourteen countries in twenty-eight days. It was an exhilarating and edifying trip for them both. Bobby's subsequent correspondence and schedule reveal that he nurtured relationships with scores of people he had met along the way — from prime ministers to chauffeurs, Marxist students to members of the United States armed forces.[29] Over the months that followed, there was a steady stream of Japanese, Italian, Indonesian, Indian, German, and Ivoirien (from an earlier trip Kennedy had made to the Ivory Coast) visitors who came to receptions and dinners at Hickory Hill, where Ethel presided in her exuberant style.

Much was made in later years about the high culture Jackie Kennedy brought to the White House — from her elegant refurbishing of it, to the concerts given by cellist Pablo Casals. But as Peter Collier and David Horowitz have written, Hickory Hill, with its boisterous élan, was the real home of the New Frontier. There intellectual and physical engagement were equally prized and tested.[30] Aside from the touch-football matches, the Hickory Hill seminars brought some of the best minds, from the pioneer environmentalist Rachel Carson to the political philosopher Isaiah Berlin, into direct exchange with senior policymakers in the administration. The president usually didn't attend, but on one occasion when he did he pressed Princeton historian David Donald about whether Lincoln was regarded as great because he was assassinated. Was that what it took?[31]

At times, the Hickory Hill seminars said as much about the sophistication of their hosts as they revealed about the state of American arts and science. When philosopher and Oxford don A. J. Ayer presented his theory of logical positivism, Ethel interrupted him. Where was God in all of this? she asked. Ayer pointed out that his field was philosophy, not theology, but Ethel asked again about the relevance of God. Bobby then muttered, "Can it, Ethel." It remained canned until Ayer's talk was concluded. Bobby then asked, "But don't you believe in right and wrong?"[32]

There was something peculiarly American in the roving assembly of children and animals at Hickory Hill. There were seven children and fifteen animals (which included a horse, four ponies, a burro, three geese, three dogs) both inside and outside the house. When asked by a Japanese reporter how the attorney general relaxed, Ethel replied: "When he comes home, the children jump on his back." Jackie made a comic drawing of the Hickory Hill scene, showing children hanging out of windows, on the roof, an old cook leaving by the back and the new one on the front porch, with Ethel looking frazzled by it all. Ethel was delighted by the drawing and hung it in the kitchen. Hickory Hill had a tennis court, a touch-football field, and two swimming pools. Ethel liked to initiate stuffy potentates like Defense Secretary Robert McNamara and General Maxwell Taylor at dinner parties by pushing them into a pool fully clothed. At a Saint Patrick's Day party, she put live bullfrogs on the tables as centerpieces. The pets ran wild over the large property; Brumus, a large, ill-tempered Newfoundland dog, ventured onto an adjoining property, mauled a neighbor's dog, and tore the clothes of two of the neighbor's children. Furious, the neighbor, James Brent Clarke Jr., wrote the attorney general, who after making amends to Mr. Clarke thereafter brought Brumus to his office, where the dog lay in a corner growling at unsuspecting visitors.[33]

For a host of unlikely people — from exiled Cubans to Washington orphans (the *Washington Star* of August 13, 1962, shows Bobby hosting one of his periodic weekend swimming parties for the children of Saint Ann's Infant Home) — Hickory Hill was a sort of home away from home, open, unguarded, completely informal, and somehow, in retrospect, the symbol of a more innocent age.

Bobby Kennedy may have had a way with errant animals, children, and even the hard-bitten doubters in the press, but among the political insiders in Washington he was pure anathema. "You won't have any trouble finding my enemies," he once told a reporter. "They're all over town."[34] The reason Washington players took exception to Bobby Kennedy was that in their world of posture and compromise, he would not play along. All of their seamy little deals and self-serving arrangements stood to be exposed, publicly audited, or even prosecuted, they feared, because he ranged so freely. A reporter once told him that a Republican would probably win state office in Illinois. "I hope so," he replied. "The Democrat is a crook."[35]

The steel crisis of April 1962 only exacerbated this impression of arrogant interposition. The ostensible issue was control of inflation through negotiated wage and price restraints. After getting commitments from the leading steel companies not to raise their prices and from the United Steelworkers not to move for wage increases, U.S. Steel CEO Roger Blough informed the administration that his company was raising its steel price. The president was furious. When the other steel companies followed suit, Kennedy suspected collusion and asked his brother to investigate. Bobby immediately ordered FBI agents to conduct interviews with those involved. Since the press had been covering the contest, this included reporters. In several instances, FBI agents made predawn visits without warning to those under suspicion. The attorney general then convened a grand jury to examine the prospect of criminal violations and to subpoena the records, both corporate and personal, of the steel executives.[36]

After seventy-two hours of nonstop government harassment and recriminations, including the president's famous line, "My father always told me that steel men were sons of bitches," Blough and the other steel executives threw in the towel and rolled back their prices. But the press and the business community raised a chorus of complaint about Robert Kennedy's use of "naked power," as the *Christian Science Monitor* put it, and his "agents of the state security police," in the view of the *Wall Street Journal*. Professor Charles Reich of the Yale Law School wrote, "It was dangerously wrong for an angry president to loose his terrible arsenal of power for the purposes of intimidation and coercing private companies."[37] The fact that national security was not even remotely involved made the tactics particularly reprehensible. Bobby himself conceded in 1964 that the whole episode was "rather scary. There's no question about that."[38]

But a few months later, the episode was nothing more than grist for the Kennedys' insouciant humor. At a party given by Steve and Jean Kennedy Smith, the president toasted the attorney general by relating a telephone conversation he had recently had with the president of Republic Steel, Jim Patton.

And I was telling Patton what a son of a bitch he was. . . . And he was proving it. Patton asked me, "Why is it that all the telephone calls of all the steel executives in all the country are being tapped?" And I told him that I thought he was being totally unfair to the attorney general, and that I was sure that it wasn't true.

And he asked me, "Why is it that all the income tax returns of all the steel executives in all the country are being scrutinized?" And I told him that, too, was totally unfair, that the attorney general wouldn't do such a thing.

And then I called the attorney general and asked him why he was tapping the telephones of all the steel executives . . . and the attorney general told me that was wholly untrue and unfair.

With his usual perfect sense of timing, Jack paused before continuing. "And, of course, Patton was right."

Bobby then got to his feet to explain in mock seriousness the use of such extreme tactics. "They were mean to my brother. They can't do that to my brother."[39]

The spoof did reflect an evident truth about the fraternal order of power: Jack Kennedy could dance above it all, could even joke about the use of police-state tactics with a member of the press in the room, because the motive of family loyalty tended to make things excusable. Moreover, Jack remained popular among the insiders because he didn't need to play the game for keeps — precisely because Bobby did.

March 22, 1962

Washington, D.C.

The business of Hoover's lunch with the president on March 22 was blackmail; the concession the director sought was confirmation in his post as head of the FBI. Tensions between Bobby and Hoover had erupted in the press on January 6, when columnist Drew Pearson predicted that the attorney general would get rid of the FBI director.[40] The Kennedy brothers in fact had already lined up a replacement for Hoover in the person of State Department security director William Boswell. The timing was poor. During Bobby's month abroad, Hoover had had the time to prepare his trap. He sprang it on February 27, the day before Bobby's triumphant return home, in the form of a top-secret memorandum to the attorney general that summarized Judy Campbell's telephone contact with the president as well as her association with Sam Giancana. Another copy of the memo was sent to O'Donnell: "I thought you would be interested in learning of the following information which was developed in connection with the investigation of John Rosselli, a West Coast hoodlum."[41] As always, Hoover justified his blackmail of public officials in terms of information learned in the course of an ongoing FBI investigation.

Hoover arrived in his limo that day at the northwest entrance of the White House at one o'clock, greeted the president in the Oval Office, and then proceeded with him and O'Donnell to the dining room in the executive mansion. There is no record of the conversation, either in FBI files or the president's office files. O'Donnell later described it as "bitter" and we know it went on for no less than four hours.[42] The attorney general, as Hoover's superior as well as the singular power in the administration, should have attended but did not. Perhaps in their desperation the brothers decided to two-track Hoover, or perhaps Bobby's exclusion was a condition Hoover had exacted before agreeing to the meeting.

Whatever the case, President Kennedy was confronted with the fact that Hoover not only knew the full extent of his extramarital liaison with Campbell and her relationship with Rosselli and Giancana but had documented it. Did he also tell the president about the murder plot against Castro and Rosselli's role in it, and the fact that the attorney general had, in fact, silently countenanced such a plot in May 1961? We do not know. He certainly informed Bobby of all of this. Harris Wofford later wrote, "Aside for the moral issues, the morass of potential blackmail in which the attorney general found himself must have appalled him and added to the revulsion he felt."[43]

We have no account of Bobby's reaction to this meeting, only that his own telephone log bulged with exchanges with the president during the third week of March 1962.[44] The unfolding disaster was one of their own making: Jack for his own rank womanizing; and Bobby for a sin Machiavelli would have thought greater: wounding a prince rather than killing him outright.

Hoover may have been manipulated in the blackmail scheme by a more distant puppet master — Rosselli. First, Rosselli arranged the introduction of his former paramour and friend Judy Campbell to President Kennedy.[45] Second, Rosselli knew about the FBI wiretap of his phone in his L.A. apartment, and therefore that the surveilled contents of his conversations would be transcribed and analyzed by federal authorities. He also knew of the war going on between the attorney general and the FBI director. Finally, Rosselli allowed Campbell to stay at his apartment when he was away from Los Angeles, which was often.[46] In all probability, Hoover not only had evidence that around seventy calls were exchanged between the Oval Office and Campbell but actually had transcribed copies of some of the exchanges that came from the tap on Rosselli's phone.

Shortly after his meeting with the president, the director called Richard Berlin, a top executive in the Hearst newspaper chain, and fed him a blind item for Walter Winchell's nationally syndicated column. Gossip columnist Liz Smith later surmised that the item probably touched off "backstage maneuvering and rewriting at Winchell's paper" when it finally surfaced on May 9, 1962: "Judy

Campbell of Palm Springs and Bevhills is Topic No. 1 in Romantic Political Circles."[47]

The blind item meant nothing in particular to the millions of Americans who read Winchell's gossip column, but it had the impact of a torpedo on the White House. A short time later, Hoover detonated another charge in the press — a leading report that Jack had been previously married to a Florida socialite, Durie Malcolm, a petite blonde who was the recipient of his sexual attentions sometime in the late 1940s. When *Newsweek* decided to run a story relaying the rumor, Bobby ordered the FBI to provide *Newsweek*'s Washington bureau chief Ben Bradlee with the full file on the case. To get to the documents, Bradlee had to agree to show the president the finished story, which he did.[48] The Kennedys were taking no chances. *Newsweek* ultimately debunked the marriage story, but Hoover had succeeded in terrorizing the president and the attorney general. The FBI director was confirmed in his position. Seymour Hersh later made a plausible case that Jack had indeed married Durie Malcolm sometime in 1947 as a kind of lark after a long night of drinking. There remains no documentation of this and Ms. Malcolm has always denied it.[49]

Bobby now tried to shore up the flank exposed by Hoover. The day the director lunched with the president (and a day before Jack left on a trip to the West Coast), Bobby called Jack and told him that he had to cease all contact with Frank Sinatra — that under no circumstances could he stay, as planned, at Sinatra's home in Palm Springs. By this time, Sinatra, in a state of high excitement and expenditure in anticipation of the president's visit, had installed twenty-five phone lines, built cottages for the Secret Service near his home, and even put a gold plaque in the bedroom where the president was to stay to commemorate the visit. Bobby called his hapless brother-in-law Peter Lawford and told him to tell Sinatra that the visit was off. Lawford, whose medium-sized star was very much hitched to Sinatra's larger one, protested, but to no avail. When Lawford informed Sinatra of the decision, the singer went berserk. A short time later, according to his valet George Jacobs, he picked up a sledgehammer and began smashing the concrete pad that had been specially built for the president's helicopter.[50]

The president's entourage arrived in Los Angeles on the

evening of March 23 and proceeded directly to Palm Springs, where the president stayed with singer Bing Crosby. The next day, who should show up at the Crosby compound wearing a dark wig but Marilyn Monroe, who spent the night with the president.[51] Given his brother's furious admonition to control himself, Jack's behavior seems pathologically reckless. A comment to his old partying buddy Senator George Smathers may provide a glimpse into the symptom formation: "While I'm alive, they'll never bring it out. After I'm dead, who cares?"[52]

Hoover, meanwhile, was busy trying to dig deeper into the Kennedys' role in the earlier CIA-Mafia plot to murder Castro. His purpose, again, was blackmail. In a memo to the attorney general the day after his meeting with the president, Hoover asked Kennedy to make a decision on whether or not to prosecute Arthur Balletti, the wireman who had been arrested a year earlier during the break-in that first revealed the CIA-Mafia alliance. If prosecuted in open court, Balletti might expose the whole plot. The CIA, Hoover informed Kennedy, was demanding that there be no prosecution as a matter of national security. Realizing that Hoover was setting him up, Kennedy immediately distanced himself from the whole matter. The head of Justice's Criminal Division, Herbert J. Miller, conferred with his counterpart at the CIA, General Counsel Lawrence Houston, and reported back to the attorney general that he agreed with the CIA: Balletti should not be prosecuted. "This would not necessarily affect prosecution of Giancana for any other offenses," Miller added. Translation: The attorney general's war on the Mafia was still on, despite the non-prosecution of Balletti.[53]

On May 7, Houston and the CIA's director of security, Colonel Sheffield Edwards, briefed the attorney general about the details of the CIA-Mafia plot to kill Castro, including Rosselli's recent operational prominence. Kennedy said very little. When the briefing was concluded, he observed, "I trust that if you ever try to do business with organized crime, with gangsters, you will let the attorney general know before you do it."[54] Of course, the whole briefing was phony, as the Church Committee — formed in 1974 to investigate intelligence activities — later suggested. Kennedy had known of such plots for over a year and done nothing to stop them. To the contrary, throughout the summer and fall of 1961, he had demanded action to eliminate Castro. Meetings to do just that had taken place within the Justice Department and CIA. In June 1961, Lansky protégé Norman "Roughhouse" Rothman, an acquaintance of Rosselli and Jack Ruby who had supervised slot machines at mob casinos in pre-Castro Cuba, met CIA officials in the deputy attorney general's office in the Justice Department. Rothman claimed that he had "the personnel and capabilities to attack or sabotage any target in Cuba," including the elimination of Fidel.[55] It seems impossible to believe that Kennedy did not hear of this. Nor is it possible to believe that he also did not read Hoover's memo of April 1961, setting forth the use of the Mafia against Castro. The fact that there is a notation in his handwriting on the May 22, 1961, memo from Colonel Edwards is but one confirmation of the obvious.[56]

Ardent Kennedy biographers would later alight upon a description of Bobby's unhappy visage at the May 7 meeting ("steely eyes . . . jaw set . . . voice low and precise") provided by the CIA's Lawrence Houston during testimony before the Church Committee to suggest his surprise and disaffection. The evidence suggests the opposite: Bobby had long known about the Mafia's role.[57] Were he so surprised and angered when he supposedly first learned of the plotting at the May 7 meeting, why did he not simply give the order to stop it? In the memorandum of record prepared after their meeting with Kennedy, Houston and Edwards stated that they had told him the plot to kill Castro had been suspended. The fact that it had not been suspended is yet another indication of the cover-up involved. On May 9, to lengthen the paper trail, Bobby met with Hoover, who noted in his memo after their meeting of his "great astonishment" at the use of *mafiosi* — though he too had known about such use for over a year.[58] Despite this charade, the CIA continued to consort with Rosselli for the purpose of murder.[59]

The entire spectacle showed both arrogance and remarkable deficiency of judgment on the part of the attorney general. To abandon the whole enterprise and bury the record of his knowledge seemed the expedient course. But Bobby wanted it every way: he wanted the Kennedy name protected, the Mafia destroyed, and Castro eliminated. This was hubris of destructive proportions, calling to mind Jack's prophetic comment about the idea of killing Castro: "If we get into that kind of thing, we'll all be targets."

As Jack's sexual policeman and political protector, Bobby undertook another tricky rescue mission in late May — to contain the increasingly outspoken disaffection of one of the president's jilted lovers, Marilyn Monroe. The affair might have tailed off into sullen oblivion were it not for Peter Lawford, who had the idea of helping Marilyn revive her lagging career by singing "Happy Birthday" to the president at a gala event at Madison Square Garden on May 19, 1962. It turned into something more than that. Sans bra and panties, Monroe appeared in a $12,000 dress made of nothing but beads and designed by Jean-Louis of Marlene Dietrich fame. As the panicky Monroe — who was in a holding room, fortifying herself with drink as she tried to remember the special lyrics to the song — dallied, master of ceremonies Lawford milked the emotions of the largely male crowd by twice announcing the entrance of Monroe to a drum-roll, then shrugging his shoulders when she failed to show.[60]

Finally the moment came. Lawford did his tongue-in-cheek best: "Because, Mr. President, in the history of show business, perhaps there has been no one female who has meant so much . . . who has done more . . . Mr. President, the *late* Marilyn Monroe!" The Garden fairly exploded in applause as Milt Ebbins pushed a tipsy Monroe out onto the stage, across which she fairly shimmied to the podium (the dress was so tight she had to be stitched into it). Lawford removed Monroe's white ermine stole and she stood there like a celestial vision, throwing off a thousand shafts of reflected light. "It was like a mass seduction," said Richard Adler. *Time* columnist Hugh Sidey later told historian Ralph Martin, "You could just smell lust." She breathed heavily into the microphone, tapped it a couple of times with her nails (this occasioned another roar from the crowd), and slowly and languorously sang "Happy Birthday, Mr. President."

As if this was not enough, the president then walked onstage and, with Monroe standing beside him, took over the microphone. He thanked her with a grin on his face: "I can now retire from politics after having had 'Happy Birthday' sung to me in such a sweet, wholesome way." The gamesman was just where he wanted to be — right on the edge.

Afterward there was a party hosted by entertainment chieftain

Arthur Krim. Attendee Adlai Stevenson later wrote about Monroe: "I do not think I have seen anyone so beautiful . . . my encounters, however, were only after breaking through the strong defenses established by Robert Kennedy, who was dodging around her like a moth around the flame."[61] Stevenson's metaphor could hardly have been more precise. There was a wild and consumptive quality to Bobby's interest in the actress. He was clearly smitten. Monroe only stoked the flame by backing Bobby up against a wall, to his total consternation, while Jack and Bill Walton looked down on them from a staircase above, "rocking with laughter" at the scene below. Jack spent that night with Monroe but thereafter ignored her calls. She was alternatingly depressed and incensed by this. Anthony Summers, author of the biography *Goddess,* reports that Monroe went into another "narcotic nosedive."[62] Out of personal concern for her and political concern for the president, Lawford telephoned the family protector. Bobby flew out to Los Angeles in late May. In the course of the afternoon with Monroe at the Lawfords' Santa Monica home, he fell into her sexual embrace in a bedroom that was bugged.[63]

Summers has amply detailed the extraordinary cross-fertilization of FBI and Mafia surveillance of Bobby's affair with Monroe. There were FBI memos detailing his comings and goings to the Lawford house, as well as Monroe's Brentwood home and the apartment she continued to keep nearby in Beverly Hills.

Bobby seemed as much drawn to her vulnerability as to her ripe allure. In his biography of RFK, Arthur Schlesinger may have caught the quality of their longing: "There was something at once magical and desperate about her. Robert Kennedy, with his curiosity, his sympathy, his absolute directness of response to distress, in some way got through the glittering mist as few did."[64] Her attraction to him, it seemed, was the hunger of the marooned, and his was like the frozen current that once thawed sweeps all before it. At points, Monroe sent Bobby droll telegrams, such as the one responding to his invitation to a party at Hickory Hill: "Unfortunately I am involved in a freedom ride protesting the loss of the minority rights belonging to the few remaining earthbound stars. After all, all we demanded was our right to twinkle."[65]

Monroe's diary, according to her friend and neighbor, Jeanne

Carmen, reflected her hopes about Bobby: "She thought Bobby would be her passport to becoming a great lady. I saw the stuff in Marilyn's diary — things about Jimmy Hoffa and Fidel Castro. It didn't mean anything to me because I was just a stupid young girl and couldn't have cared less if they all killed each other."[66] Monroe believed that Robert Kennedy was going to marry her, and she said so to more than one person. It was probably this as much as any intimation of the mass surveillance going on that fractured their affair. Around the third week in June 1962, Bobby stopped taking her telephone calls. The affair, from his standpoint, was over.

But for Monroe it was not. Furious and disconsolate, she told Lawford that she was going to tell the world what the Kennedy brothers had done to her. Had this happened, it is difficult to see how Jack and Bobby could have survived politically. But between her psychiatrist, Ralph Greenson, who administered sedatives of all kinds, and the intermittent application of human palliatives like Lawford and Jeanne Carmen, she held her tongue. The Lawfords took her up to the Cal-Neva Lodge at Lake Tahoe for a weekend in late July. That night Monroe imbibed a nonstop diet of barbiturates and alcohol and, if Rosselli is to be believed, had sex with both Sam Giancana and Frank Sinatra. In Chicago for a meeting, Rosselli observed sardonically to Giancana, "You sure get your rocks off fucking the same broad as the brothers, don't you."[67]

Lawford was worried enough about Monroe's threat to hold a press conference that he called Bobby Kennedy to tell him that unless he told Marilyn face to face why the affair was over, she could well go public. Lawford later denied that Bobby actually flew to L.A. from San Francisco (where he was scheduled to address the American Bar Association) on the weekend of August 4.[68] But Lawford's recollection, which he later changed, differs from the persuasive evidence of Peter Spada and Anthony Summers that Kennedy did indeed travel to Los Angeles and saw Monroe during the final hours of her life. Whether or not Bobby was in fact there on August 4–5, one thing is certain: the FBI and various members of the Los Angeles Police Department scrubbed the entire scene clean.

For both Jack and Bobby, the whole episode and its tragic conclusion now threatened their marriages. According to Lawford, Bobby was deeply shaken. Jackie didn't need to know all the details to get wind of a full-court cover-up and, furiously, took Caroline and a dozen Secret Service agents with her to Ravello, Italy, to stay with her sister. According to George Smathers, "It was her way of telling him that he'd gone too far this time. The possibility that she might be humiliated or embarrassed really got to her. She didn't like it, not one damn bit."[69] As *Time* reported, "Jacqueline Kennedy originally planned to stay at Ravello for two weeks. But the two became three, and now they have stretched into four. . . . [S]he might yet declare herself a permanent resident." When Jackie showed up in AP photographs with handsome billionaire Gianni Agnelli, Jack angrily sent her a cable: "A LITTLE MORE CAROLINE AND LESS AGNELLI." Bobby also went on an extended vacation, but no record exists of the nature of his reconciliation with Ethel.

The Kennedys may have dodged a deadly projectile of their own reckless launching, but they were now wholly compromised by J. Edgar Hoover. When W. H. Ferry of the Fund for the Republic publicly criticized Hoover for his shameless and absurd campaign against communism in the United States, who should rise to Hoover's defense but Bobby Kennedy. "Attorney General Kennedy defended FBI Chief Hoover against the charge that he magnifies Communist strength at home and abroad," the AP reported. "To the contrary, Kennedy said, Hoover's dedication and effort is the major reason for the numerical weakness of Communists in the United States."

The *Baltimore Sun*'s Phil Potter, then in New Delhi, couldn't believe Kennedy's statement. "Is this the price you pay for the privilege of passing in and out through the doors of the Justice building?" he wrote Kennedy on August 7. "How do we preserve the union when he's dead?"[70] Kennedy sent him a jocular reply: "In answer to your question of what we'll do when Edgar is dead — we'll always have you, my friend."[71] But Hoover was not satisfied. On August 16, he sent the attorney general a "personal memo" smearing his stricken father, the very man who had secured Hoover's reappointment in December 1960:

Before the last presidential election, Joseph P. Kennedy (the father of President John Kennedy) had been visited by many

164

gangsters with gambling interests and a deal was made which resulted in Peter Lawford, Frank Sinatra, Dean Martin and others obtaining a lucrative gambling establishment, the Cal-Neva Hotel, at Lake Tahoe. These gangsters reportedly met with Joseph Kennedy at the Cal-Neva, where Kennedy was staying at the time.[72]

Bobby's reaction is not known.

July–August, 1962

Washington, D.C., Havana, Point Mary, Key Largo

The irony about Bobby Kennedy's bureaucratic backfilling during the first two weeks of May 1962 was that it gave Johnny Rosselli new standing in the CIA. After his meeting with Kennedy, Sheffield Edwards informed Bill Harvey, chief of ZR/RIFLE, that "tacit approval" of Richard Helms would be necessary were Rosselli to be further involved in the murder-Castro plot. (Doing his own backfilling, Edwards claimed in an internal memorandum that Harvey had promised he was "dropping any plans for the use of Subject [Rosselli] for the future." In testimony before the Senate Intelligence Committee in 1975, Harvey called this a lie.)[73] After Rosselli received Helms's "tacit approval," he was given the nominal rank of colonel, and David Morales, JM/WAVE's hotheaded chief of operations, was formally seconded to the assassination mission. Toward the end of May, the CIA built a small base for Rosselli's unit on Point Mary, Key Largo, clearing out an acre or so of the thick mangrove forest for rough-hewn sheds and two crude structures. Offshore, a floating dock was anchored into the coral reef. The purpose of the base was to train snipers.

Rosselli had soon charmed everyone in sight. He was the only person who could make the incendiary Morales laugh. They would drink until the sun came up, usually joined by Rip Robertson, the hard-bitten Texan and decorated veteran of World War II who was the favorite "boom and bang" guy among the exiled Cubans. A favorite bar was Les Deux Violins, where, according to one of his Cuban operatives, "Johnny knew all the help by their first name, tipped hugely, and would tell farcical stories about his days with Al Capone."[74] Throughout his criminal life, Rosselli had befriended men more dangerous and sociopathic than these. As before, defenses were dismantled and egos enhanced in the course of hard drinking. The Rosselli touch — his seeming ability to seduce anyone — was made evident in Colonel Bradley J. Ayers's memoir. Ayers and his wife had invited over a man named Wes, a major then working for the CIA. "Wes had been drinking before he got to the house that night. He and John Roselli [*sic*], the dapper American agent in charge of the continuing attempts to assassinate Fidel Castro, had been on a weekend binge together. They'd become close friends as they worked together, and with Roselli a bachelor and Wes without his family in Miami, their drinking relationship was a natural extension of their duty relationship."[75]

Colonel Ayers, who was training commandos in small-team tactics at his own base on a nearby key, visited Rosselli's encampment on Point Mary. There he met Rosselli's commander, a tall young Cuban called Julio who spoke excellent English. Julio told Ayers that his teams operated independently, without direct supervision of a CIA case officer. According to Julio, Colonel Rosselli used the team from time to time for raids and other operations. Rosselli was one of only two Americans authorized to go into Cuba on clandestine missions.

After spending the night on Point Mary with Rosselli's commandos, Ayers was jolted out of his sleep early the next morning by the crack of a rifle. "It's just our sharpshooter doing his daily marksmanship practice," Julio explained. To Ayers's amazement, the sniper then nailed a cormorant perched on a mangrove stump some 500 yards offshore. Julio further explained that the man was rehearsing "for the day when he could center the crosshairs of his telescopic sight on Fidel Castro." Upon hearing of President Kennedy's assassination the following year, Ayers wrote, his mind flashed back to that morning on Point Mary and the explosion of purple cormorant feathers on the distant mangrove stump.[76]

The scene on Point Mary was the direct result of an Operation Mongoose meeting in the attorney general's office on January 19. "No time, money, effort or manpower is to be spared," the memo summarizing the meeting stated. "Yesterday . . . the president indicated that the final chapter had not been written — it's got to be done and will be done."[77] On the basis of this meeting, General Lansdale produced a nine-page memorandum outlining everything from political intrigue, economic warfare, psychological operations, and paramilitary action. Within the interstices of this policy lay the mandate of assassination, Phase II.[78]

Even if a more reasoned American policy were possible, Castro did nothing to encourage it. On January 23, he publicly observed: "How can the rope and the hanged man understand each other, or the chain and the slave? Imperialism is the chain. Understanding is impossible."[79] The modus vivendi Che Guevara had spoken about to Richard Goodwin at the Punta del Este Conference the previous August was probably a delaying tactic to buy time for the Castro regime.[80] Neither Fidel nor Che felt an entente with Washington was possible; imperialism, they believed, was conceived in violence and dedicated to conquest.

Under the expanded mandate of Operation Mongoose, south Florida became a huge staging area for the not-so-secret war against Cuba. Located south of Miami in a heavily wooded 1,571-acre tract, JM/WAVE was now the largest CIA station in the world. Its code name was Zenith Technological Enterprises, and phony charts and business licenses adorned the offices of the wooden clapboard buildings to provide the thinnest possible semblance of cover. Behind these buildings was a huge rhombic antenna scanner pointing south. By the spring of 1962, JM/WAVE employed more than two hundred American operatives who, in turn, deployed about 2,200 Cuban agents, each one ensconced in front operations that ranged from insurance agencies to boat-repair yards. JM/WAVE had a navy of over 100 craft, including the 174-foot former sub chaser *Rex*, stuffed with electronic gear and studded with 40-millimeter and 20-millimeter cannons, and capable of lowering 20-foot fiberglass speedboats via crane into the water, to dozens of V-20 Swift craft with exhaust deflectors or black rubber rafts powered by Mercury outboards. According to one former agent, the Miami River experienced late-afternoon traffic jams of CIA boats on their way back to their moorings. The air force included 50 amphibians, dozens of single-engine patrol craft, and, on select occasions, F-105 Phantoms from nearby Homestead Air Force Base. The sound of detonations of *plastique* on the outskirts of Miami — part of the CIA's training of anti-Castro sappers — alarmed citizens, who were routinely told they were demolitions for freeway excavations.[81]

By the first week in April 1962, the plot to kill Castro was again under way. On April 8, Rosselli flew to New York to meet with Bill Harvey.[82] A week later, the two met again in Miami to discuss the plot in greater detail. In good part, Harvey was taking the measure of his Mafia counterpart. At the Miami meeting he pulled a pistol out and slapped it on the table.[83] Rosselli proved suitably deferential. Rosselli's plan was again to pass poison pills through Tony Varona to a Havana restaurant where Castro liked to eat. In exchange, Varona wanted the CIA to provide him with high-powered rifles, handguns, detonators, and boat radar. Harvey agreed. On April 21 he flew from Washington to deliver four poison pills directly to Rosselli, who got them to Varona and thence to Havana. That same evening, Harvey and Ted Shackley, the chief of the CIA's south Florida base, drove a U-Haul truck filled with the requested arms through the rain to a deserted parking lot in Miami. They got out and handed the keys to Rosselli. Not fully trusting the mafioso, Harvey had the parking lot surveilled. Sure enough, two Cubans drove up and Rosselli gave them the keys. They took the truck somewhere and unloaded it.[84]

The manner of the exchange proved important. Rosselli was now handling conventional weapons for the CIA, beginning what would become his full incorporation into the Agency's south Florida war machine. He was also developing a personal relationship with Harvey, Operation Mongoose's point man, who briefed Attorney General Kennedy and other leading members of the administration on the get-Castro effort. Throughout April, there was, as the House Select Committee on Assassinations staff later termed it, "intense contact between HARVEY and ROSSELLI."[85] This gave Rosselli insight into a growing rift between Harvey and the attorney general. It was Harvey who introduced Rosselli to David Morales, who had been brought in the previous November in preparation for Phase II.[86]

Late that summer, Rosselli led his first nighttime mission across the Windward Passage in a pair of swift V-20s. The V-20 was the workhorse of the CIA fleet, admirably suited to its unique tasks. With its gun mounts and twin 100-horsepower Graymarine engines concealed by fishing nets, the boat looked like any other medium-sized craft plying the route. It also had a double hull made of fiberglass, capable of withstanding the pounding of the open sea as well as collisions with coral reefs. The V-20's top speed was 40 knots. By the summer of 1962, the Cubans were deploying the best Soviet patrol craft. One such Cuban patrol boat spotted Rosselli's raiders and gave chase, ripping the bottom out of Rosselli's boat with machine-gun fire. Rosselli jumped into the water and swam to the second craft, which managed to make it back to camp.[87]

On his second run toward the coast of Cuba, Rosselli's V-20s were again intercepted and the lead boat was sunk. Rosselli managed to get aboard a small dinghy before the speedboat went under. He drifted alone for several days in the boat and was given up for dead back in Florida until an American patrol cutter rescued him and brought him back to camp.[88] Giancana, for one, thought he was crazy to risk his life, but Rosselli had always been an over-the-top type who fed on the intensity of camaraderie in combat. On Point Mary today, aside from a couple of ruined docks, you can find a great profusion of beer and liquor bottles among the mangrove roots — the detritus of good times and cruel dreams.[89]

At the same time Rosselli was putting his life on the line off the coast of Cuba, FBI agents back in Chicago were trying to track down his fictive birth records in an effort to deport him as an illegal alien.[90] Rosselli was closing in on Castro in the name of national security; Bobby Kennedy was closing in on Rosselli as a matter of national interest. But Rosselli fought on. In addition to the words commonly used to describe him during this period — charming, dapper — the word "patriotic" comes up again and again.[91] Johnny Rosselli, who had once signed up with the U.S. Army to fight in World War Two only to be mustered out of the military in 1943 and then tried and imprisoned for extortion, was once again trying to prove that he was a true American.[92]

It is certain that Bobby was aware of Rosselli's unusual qualities and far-flung pursuits. The overlap of their activities is extraordinary. Harvey, who was in "intense contact" with Rosselli during this period, reported to the attorney general among others. Brigade exile leaders Pepe San Roman and Enrique Ruiz-Williams, both of whom spoke to Bobby at least once a week, were Rosselli acquaintances.[93] Former Eisenhower ambassador (and Flying Tiger co-founder) William D. Pawley, who had become a sort of godfather of Cuban exiles in south Florida, approached Kennedy through aide Richard Goodwin. Pawley wanted to raise money to pay the ransom of the imprisoned Bay of Pigs fighters through the sale of Cuban government bonds.[94] It was a venture long on creative quality and short on financial sense, but Kennedy looked at it. One of the major subscribers was Johnny Rosselli.[95]

Even their mutual dedication to the Catholic Church as well as to civil rights brought Kennedy and Rosselli into indirect contact. Unlike most of his Mafia confreres, Rosselli was a progressive on civil rights and had befriended a Jesuit priest, Father Albert Foley, then chairing the sociology department at Springhill College in Mobile, Alabama. At Rosselli's urging, Monte Prosser Productions had retained Father Foley to prepare a screen treatment on the true-life story of a priest who traveled from New England to the South during the Civil War. The film was to rally for desegregation.[96] Father Foley's civil rights activism (he served as chairman of the Alabama Advisory Board to the U.S. Civil Rights Commission) came to the attention of journalist Fletcher Knebel, who set up a meeting between the attorney general and the priest.[97] There is no record of their conversation, but it would have been news to the attorney general that the man charged with the task of killing Fidel Castro was also active in the cause of desegregation — through a Catholic priest, no less. As different as their backgrounds were, these two men shared a ferocity fortified by religious belief. The difference was, Rosselli was a murderer.

On one occasion Rosselli's henchmen came close to killing Castro. In September 1961, minutes before Castro was to pass through the intersection of Rancho Boyeros and Santa Catalina Avenues in Havana on his way out of Ciudad Deportiva, four assassins (led by Juan Basigulpe-Hornedo) in two Jeeps armed with bazookas, grenade launchers, and machine guns were arrested. They were parked in a garage on that corner.[98] On September 24, the Cuban government announced that it had smashed the so-called Amblood ring. Two of those arrested, Guillermo Caula Ferrer and Higinio Menendez, gave Cuban DGI interrogators the full details about the plot: they had been trained on Guantanamo, the American naval base in Cuba, and communicated with their CIA handlers in Miami via secret writing drops in Quito, Ecuador. They even alleged that the Swiss embassy in Havana had served as a contact point. They were all executed.[99]

To some CIA professionals, this attempt revealed some inescapable truths about trying to eliminate Castro. First, there were more than one thousand pro-Castro agents in south Florida, including some who were in evident contact with CIA case officers. Nothing JM/WAVE tried to do — whether launching a sustained counterintelligence effort, requiring tens of thousands of hours of interrogation and analysis, or separating covert operations into self-contained units insulated from pro-Castro penetration — seemed to work. Additionally, the Cuban exiles were preternaturally talkative and had formed some 300-odd movements, factions, parties, and so on, which only intensified the level of gossip and leaks. "A Cuban is someone who can't keep his mouth shut," one American official groused. Justin Gleichauf, chief of the CIA's Miami field office, held the same opinion. "To a Cuban," he said, "a secret is something you tell only one hundred people. The Agency and administration were naive in dealing with Cubans. They thought they were dealing with some breed of Europeans where self-discipline is part of the character. The Cubans had no self-discipline."[100]

It was the same old problem: the CIA had no real use and no respect for the Cuban exiles. They were only regarded as instruments for Castro's destruction. Whatever their effectiveness as covert actors, CIA principals like Bill Harvey, Jim O'Connell, Ted Shackley, Howard Hunt, David Phillips, Rocky Farnsworth, and David Morales all shared the same supercilious attitude toward the Cubans. For this reason, they aligned themselves with the most conservative (and usually corrupt) Cuban leaders — those who had demonstrated their fervent devotion to the American presence during the Batista regime. Thus it was perfectly natural that the poison should pass from O'Connell to Rosselli to Antonio de Varona under the watchful eye of Santos Trafficante.[101] The mind-set of the CIA and its criminal confederates was like that of the Bourbons: *Ils n'avaient rien appris mais rien oublié* (They had learned nothing but forgotten nothing). Varona was their type — hot-tempered, corrupt, and, if his nickname *El Tronco de Yucca* (Yucca Trunk) was accurate, dumb. When he failed to get the job done, Rosselli and Morales repaired to ex-president Carlos Prio Socarras (Prio was overthrown by Sergeant Fulgencio Batista in 1952). Prio's mass larceny of the Cuban treasury was only matched by his largesse with gangsters.[102] With neither faith in nor concept of Cuba's future beyond Fidel, the Americans could only plot to bring back the past.

Peter Wyden, in his account of the Bay of Pigs invasion, called this the "gook syndrome" and asserted that at its base was racism:

> The final arrogance, the failure to inform themselves about Castro's strength and his people's spirit or even to inform their own infiltration teams, I attribute to the gook syndrome. American policymakers suffer from it constantly. They tend to underestimate grossly the capabilities and determination of people who committed the sin of not having been born American, especially "gooks" whose skins are less than white.[103]

In the absence of the most elementary understanding of recent Cuban history and politics, Bobby Kennedy filled the void in his own knowledge of Cuba with Lansdale's counterinsurgency option. "Counterinsurgency," wrote Kennedy in 1962, "might best be described as social reform under pressure. Any effort that disregards the base of social reform, and becomes preoccupied with gadgets and techniques and force, is doomed to failure."[104] But that is exactly what happened. "Pressure" of the most violent kind took the place of "social reform." As in Vietnam the capture of hearts and minds ("the allegiance of man," as Bobby put it) was difficult in war zones where torture, terror, and execution had become the currency of power. The Mafia and the CIA's cloak-and-dagger types understood this. They also knew that America's association with the corrupt ancien régime was deep and would be difficult to change.

Bill Harvey was the one who brought this to Kennedy's attention. At issue was the infiltration into Cuba of trained teams of anti-Castro commandos. In "Lansdaleland," JM/WAVE would infiltrate 255 Cuban spies by mid-1962 — "an astonishingly unrealistic number," according to historian David Corn. At one meeting the impatient attorney general demanded to know why JM/WAVE had not infiltrated even a single team. Harvey answered that the Cubans had first to be trained. Kennedy supposedly replied that he would "take them out to my estate and train them." "What will you teach them, sir?" Harvey asked. "Baby-sitting?" No one in all Washington dared to speak to the president's brother like this. It must have done Rosselli's heart good, given the transgressions he thought Bobby Kennedy guilty of, to hear Harvey routinely refer to the attorney general as "that fucker."[105]

As was his nature, Bobby formed policy through people. In civil rights, this brought him close to potent and constructive figures like Martin Luther King Jr. and A. Philip Randolph. On Cuba it led him to Generals Lansdale and Taylor, the apostles of counterinsurgency, and to the anti-Castro Cubans, several of whom became devoted to Kennedy. Perhaps it was because his youth, Catholicism, and his vengeful anticommunism matched theirs; or perhaps they saw in him what they desired most from the Americans — a sincerity of allegiance.[106] Any number of rank-and-file Cuban operatives on CIA retainers of $150 a month called him at the office or at home with their concerns or demands, and usually they got what they wanted the next day. Other Cuban exile fighters attended receptions, or even spent the night, at Hickory Hill. George Ball thought the practice "completely disruptive to any settled development of policy. But nobody," he said, "dared question Bobby. He would have your head."[107] Interviewed in 1977, former National Security Advisor McGeorge Bundy thought that Kennedy's personal attachment to the Cubans "while it may have energized the covert war also had the effect of continuing it as a matter of human loyalty as opposed to considered policy. My distinct memory is that we [Special Group Augmented] never really believed that the covert actions against Castro had any chance of succeeding."[108]

The Cuban leaders Kennedy grew closest to were Roberto San Roman, Enrique Ruiz-Williams, and, in 1963, Manuel Artime. On at least one occasion, as Bundy suggested, Bobby's personal relationship with the exile fighters nearly backfired in a major way. After a Cuban exile agent the attorney general had met with in Washington was infiltrated into Cuba, he was captured by Cuban security and reportedly tortured. According to David Corn, Ted Shackley and the principals of JM/WAVE feared that he would confess he had conferred with the president's brother. The agent was tried by Cuban authorities, confessed to nothing, and was executed. The CIA leadership "let out a collective sigh."[109] There were other instances of Kennedy's indiscretion. On May 17, 1962, he met with Miguel Aleman, whose father José Aleman Jr. had close ties to Santos Trafficante.[110]

Beyond Kennedy's sophomoric dedication to counterinsurgency, the simple fact was that Miami was no longer controlled by Washington. Besides Rosselli's kill team, Operation 40, a ZR/RIFLE unit created prior to the Bay of Pigs, brought together Cuban mob henchmen like Eladio del Valle and Rolando Masferrer — both Trafficante couriers — soldiers of fortune like Frank Sturgis (Fiorini), and CIA case officers like Colonel William Bishop and David Morales, who managed assassins.[111] Sturgis later described them as a "group that would upon orders, naturally, assassinate either members of the military [or] the political parties of the foreign country that you were going to infiltrate, and, if necessary, some of your own members who were suspected of being foreign agents. . . ."[112] Operation 40's closest ties were with the violently anti-Castro group Alpha 66, the special charge of the chief of Cuba operations in the Mexico City CIA station, David A. Phillips. This assembly of malignant spirits had by 1962 quickened into a beast beyond the control or even bureaucratic comprehension of its putative handlers in Washington.

The incoherence of the Kennedy administration's Cuban policy was never more evident than in August of 1962. Despite Bobby's hectoring, neither the State Department nor the intelligence wing of the CIA believed that Operation Mongoose would bring down Castro. CIA director John McCone, Under Secretary of State Ball, and even the delphic secretary of state Rusk resisted efforts to expand the covert war. At a Cuban task force meeting in Rusk's office on August 10 (from which Bobby was absent), a new Lansdale proposal for large-scale sabotage raids called "stepped-up Course B" was rejected by the majority of the group. Secretary of Defense Robert McNamara, a close Bobby ally, got up to leave and voiced an opinion that "the only way to take care of Castro is to kill him. I really mean it."[113] Later, Lansdale referred to "the liquidation of leaders" in a memorandum to the group. Harvey described this as "stupidity."[114] Helms agreed with Harvey. Murder should not be advertised in print.

At the next meeting of the Special Group (Augmented) on

August 21, Bobby Kennedy was back in action, arguing for more sabotage raids. This time Kennedy and McNamara won the day. New attacks, including one on Cuba's largest copper mine in Matahambre, were ordered up.[115] (Incredibly, either because of appallingly sketchy intelligence from Cuba or complete operational impotence, JM/WAVE was never able to assist the large anti-Castro insurgency in the Escambray Mountains, which by mid-1962 numbered about three thousand men and ultimately caused about $1 billion damage.) Lansdale was soon waxing lyric about a hybrid weed that could be sown throughout Cuba via aerial bombardment. When combined with fire and chemical drops, the invasive weed would starve the Cubans into submission.

All this spiteful and ineffectual activity had an unintended effect: it persuaded Castro and Khrushchev that America was preparing to invade Cuba again. Given America's military superiority in the Caribbean, there was no way the Soviet Union could defend Cuba through conventional means. The only way to stop the Americans, Khrushchev reasoned in a conversation with First Deputy Premier Anastas Mikoyan in the Lenin Hills in April 1962, was with nuclear weapons.[116] Once Castro gave the go-ahead, these would be secretly emplaced. The Kennedy administration would be confronted with a fait accompli.

Sensing that missile deployment might be afoot, President Kennedy issued a warning on September 4 that if the United States had firm evidence of "offensive ground-to-ground missiles, the gravest issues would arise." On September 13, following rumors of missile shipments to Cuba being spread by New York Republican senator Kenneth Keating, Kennedy reiterated the warning. If the Soviets established "an offensive military base of significant capacity . . . then this country will do whatever must be done to protect its own security and that of its allies."[117]

But Khrushchev, perhaps as much for emotional as pragmatic reasons, "plunged" ahead.[118] And Castro, whose revolution was based on violent defiance of the United States, took the warrior's gamble. "We preferred the risks, whatever they were, of great tension, a great crisis," he told Tad Szulc years later, "to the risks of the impotence of having to wait . . . for a U.S. invasion of Cuba."

Khrushchev may have initiated the crisis by secretly planning to station offensive nuclear missiles in the Western Hemisphere, and Castro certainly facilitated it by agreeing to make Cuba a potential battleground, but ultimately the crisis was caused by the Kennedy administration's assault on Castro. The conclusion that emerged from the historic symposium of former Cuban, Russian, and American policymakers that took place in Havana in January 1992 was that "Kennedy's policy of isolation, harassment, and intimidation . . . forced Castro to turn to the Soviet Union for protection, ultimately in the form of nuclear weapons."[119] And no single person was more responsible for that than Bobby Kennedy.

September 30, 1962

Oxford, Mississippi, and Washington, D.C.

On Sunday evening, September 30, President Kennedy went on national television to explain why he had sent federal marshals to Oxford, Mississippi, to enable James Meredith, a black air force veteran, to enroll at the University of Mississippi. Unbeknownst to Kennedy, a few moments before he went on the air, the campus had erupted in violence. A screaming crowd of over two thousand, some crying in unison "Kill the nigger! Kill the nigger!" converged on the line of white-helmeted, orange-vested marshals standing in front of the Lyceum, the Ole Miss administration building.[120] As night fell, the cordon of Mississippi state troopers who, under an agreement hammered out between the attorney general and Mississippi governor Ross Barnett, would maintain order, vanished. The mob threw bricks and bottles, injuring several of the marshals. The federal officers were ordered by deputy attorney general Nicholas Katzenbach to fire teargas canisters. Suddenly, amid the rebel yells, came the sound of rifle shots. Several marshals fell to the ground wounded; two men, one a French reporter, were killed.

The president meanwhile was concluding his remarks to the nation by appealing to Mississippi's sense of honor "on the field of battle and on the gridiron." After Jack finished his speech, Bobby informed him of the bloody spectacle at Ole Miss, including the report that Klansmen had seized Meredith in his dormitory and were intending to lynch him. By this time, Katzenbach had gotten to a phone to call the attorney general to ask for permission to fire on the assailants with live ammunition if their position was about to be overrun. The president, who was listening to Bobby's conversation with Katzenbach, said no — only if Meredith's own life was at risk.[121] At this point, Jack decided to do what his brother had done everything he could in the previous week to avoid — send in army troops.

Like the tenuous zone between the marshals and their would-be killers, the Kennedy administration had searched for every expedient in its twenty months in office to hold neutral ground between the rising tide of black protest and the white riptide of murderous opposition. But the administration — and the country — were now engulfed, and the Kennedys' containment strategy on civil rights was itself about to be overrun.

When Jack took office, the administration's strategy could be summarized by something the president-elect had told Harris Wofford in an early meeting on civil rights: "Minimum civil rights legislation, maximum executive action."[122] The plan was to avoid Congress, where powerful Southern Democrats like Senate Judiciary Chairman James O. Eastland of Mississippi had used filibuster and committee trench warfare to mangle the civil rights initiatives of liberal members. Instead, the Kennedy administration planned to hire more blacks, make several key appointments, litigate voting-rights violations in the South, and, through private suasion, open closed doors.

President Kennedy's personal efforts to desegregate public and private facilities began as soon as he took office and, at least as compared to Eisenhower's, they were impressive. The president resigned from the segregated Metropolitan Club in Washington (as did every other member of the administration) and ordered Pedro San Juan of the White House Protocol staff to push for the opening of segregated restaurants, terminals, clubs, apartment complexes, and residential neighborhoods in the D.C. area. Although these efforts were targeted to help Washington's African diplomats, they had an impact on the lives of black Americans as well. In late 1961 the president went around the table at a cabinet meeting and asked each member to tell him how many black candidates had been appointed in each department. He was pleased with what he heard: in Labor, black appointments above grade 12 had risen from 24 to 41; in Agriculture, from 15 to 46; in Justice, the number of black attorneys had risen from 10 to 50 by the end of 1961. Kennedy had appointed a black foreign service officer, Clifton R. Wharton, as ambassador to Norway and had proposed Robert Weaver as the new housing secretary.

But, as the memoir of his civil rights assistant Harris Wofford reflects, Kennedy's determined preference was to control the pace of civil rights progress, so that it did not spoil the administration's working relationship with key segregationists on Capitol Hill.[123] The first casualty of this go-slow strategy involved an executive order to desegregate federal housing. Kennedy and twenty-two other elected Democrats had boldly declared in 1960 that the next Democratic president would enact it "with the stroke of a pen." Kennedy chose to put off signing it until November 1962, and the criticism from white liberals and black leaders was sharp. Civil rights activists began mailing in pens to the White House, first numbering in the hundreds and by late 1961 in the thousands. The president was both embarrassed and frustrated that he could not have it both ways. He reasoned that the do-or-die emotions of the civil rights activists and the fury of southern white reaction could only end in needless bloodshed, divide the country at a time of international reckoning, and endanger his own reelection chances. Kennedy's challenge to Americans to put a man on the moon by the end of the decade inspired Eisenhower Civil Rights Commission appointee Reverend Theodore Hesburgh, the president of Notre Dame, to offer a stinging rebuke of the administration's priorities: "Personally," he wrote, "I don't care if the United States gets the first man on the moon, if while this is happening on a crash basis, we dawdle along here in our corner of the earth, nursing our prejudices, flouting our magnificent Constitution, ignoring the central problem of our times, and appearing hypocrites to all the world."[124]

In an article in *The Nation*, the Reverend Martin Luther King Jr. offered a more measured view of Kennedy's ambivalence:

> The Administration sought to demonstrate to Negroes that it has concern for them, while at the same time it had striven to avoid inflaming the opposition. The most cynical view holds that it wants the votes of both and is paralyzed by the conflicting needs of each. I am not ready to make a judgment condemning the motives of the Administration as hypocritical. I

believe that it sincerely wants to change, but that it has misunderstood the forces at play.[125]

The basic problem with the Kennedy strategy of containment was that it forced black leaders to provoke peaceful showdowns against Jim Crow in the South — on buses, at lunch counters, and in polling places. And white public officials — from Arkansas senator J. William Fulbright to Birmingham police chief Eugene "Bull" Connor — were waving the bloody flag of resistance not just to civil rights leaders but to all forms of federal judicial and military force. Reconstruction, though nearly a century old, was nearly as incendiary an issue as desegregation. Bobby Kennedy's blunt communication in Athens, Georgia, in April 1961 that "if the orders of the court are circumvented, the Department of Justice will act" was about to be tested again.

The issue was voting rights. By April 1962, the Justice Department had brought no fewer than one hundred cases against election officials throughout the South for preventing blacks from voting. Bobby had tried to keep civil rights action in-house. "You're second-guessers," he told members of the Civil Rights Commission. "I'm the one who has to get the job done."[126] Getting the job done involved a delicate political trade with the administration's southern supporters like John Stennis, J. William Fulbright, and James O. Eastland: the administration would neither introduce nor put its weight behind civil rights legislation if these senators would countenance black judicial appointments and support other Kennedy legislation, principally trade expansion and an increase in the minimum wage. As Bobby later pointed out to journalist Anthony Lewis, Eastland would habitually delay appointments (such as that of Thurgood Marshall to the Circuit Court of Appeals) before letting them go through.[127] The attorney general's attitude toward the liberals was reflected in a comment he made to an attorney in Justice's Civil Rights Division: "It's easy to play Jesus and it's fun to get in bed with the civil rights movement, but all the noise they make doesn't do as much good as one case."

Kennedy had a point. The legal fate of James Meredith was at that moment winding its way through the federal courts. On the same day that John F. Kennedy took the oath of office, Meredith had written for an admission application to the University of Mississippi. When he was eventually denied admission, he brought suit in federal district court in Mississippi. Meredith's suit was dismissed, but he successfully appealed to the Fifth Circuit Court, which reversed the lower court in June 1962. In September, the Supreme Court considered Mississippi's appeal. The United States Justice Department had submitted an amicus brief supporting Meredith's case. On September 10, the Supreme Court upheld the circuit court's decision and ordered Meredith to be admitted to Ole Miss.[128]

Mississippi governor Ross Barnett publicly denounced the decision and promised to bar Meredith's admission "by force, if necessary." The attorney general made the first of twenty-eight phone calls to Barnett searching for a political solution. Their phone exchanges, which were recorded, reveal the essence of Bobby Kennedy's negotiating style — simple and unmoving adherence to the principle that the court order must be obeyed, accompanied by an open-ended consideration of options.[129] Although Barnett resorted to threats and flights of hyperbole, Kennedy drained much of the accusatory venom out of Barnett by asking practical questions about how together they might work this out, always leaving the door open to further exchanges. It was what the Harvard Negotiation Project would later characterize as "process" — as opposed to "power" — negotiation.[130]

> BARNETT: A lot of states haven't had the guts to take a stand. We are going to fight this thing. . . . This is like a dictatorship. Forcing him physically into Ole Miss. General, that might bring a lot of trouble. You don't want to do that. You don't want to physically force him in.
>
> KENNEDY: You don't want to physically keep him out. . . . Governor, you are part of the United States.
>
> BARNETT: We have been part of the United States but I don't know whether we are or not.
>
> KENNEDY: Are you getting out of the Union?
>
> BARNETT: It looks like we're being kicked around — like we don't belong to it. General, this thing is serious.
>
> KENNEDY: It's serious here.

BARNETT: Must it be over one little boy — backed by communist front — backed by the NAACP which is a communist front? I'm going to treat you with every courtesy but I won't agree to let that boy get to Ole Miss. I will never agree to that. I would rather spend the rest of my life in a penitentiary than do that.

KENNEDY: I have a responsibility to enforce the laws of the United States. . . . The orders of the court are going to be upheld. As I told you, you are a citizen not only of the State of Mississippi but also the United States. Could I give you a ring?

BARNETT: You do that. . . . Good to hear from you.[131]

Initially, the effort to find a political solution miscarried in the extreme. When Meredith showed up to register accompanied by federal marshals on September 20, he was accosted by the governor and a surly crowd of students and Oxford townspeople. Barnett read a lengthy proclamation in purple prose that set forth the reasons for denying Meredith admission. He handed a copy to Meredith. "Take it and abide by it," he told him.[132]

Kennedy then turned up the heat by citing Ole Miss's three top administrators for contempt of court. In court the administrators agreed to allow Meredith to be admitted. Although Barnett was still recalcitrant, telling Kennedy he was going to only "obey the laws of Mississippi," the attorney general surmised that for political reasons Barnett was looking to play the victim. The next day, Justice attorneys obtained a restraining order enjoining Barnett from preventing Meredith's registration. Led by former Kennedy political operative James McShane, federal marshals brought Meredith to the campus. Again Barnett and a noisy mob barred their way. Kennedy and Barnett spoke later that evening. "It's best for him not to go to Ole Miss," Barnett said. "But he likes Ole Miss," Kennedy replied softly.[133] On September 28, the Justice Department mobilized some four hundred deputy marshals and border patrol personnel at the Memphis naval station to airlift them into Oxford. Kennedy additionally ordered army units to go on alert that afternoon at the naval station.[134]

The contest was now all over the national news. Barnett's defiance of the federal court order coincided with the national celebration of the centennial of the Emancipation Proclamation. The president's message to a gathering at the Lincoln Memorial on September 22 was eloquent, but no one was really listening. The issue was James Meredith. Martin Luther King Jr., James Farmer, and other black leaders were calling for armed enforcement of the court order. Klansmen all over the South were rallying with rhetoric as well as arms to the cause of Mississippi's rights. "THOUSANDS READY TO FIGHT FOR MISSISSIPPI," cried the *Jackson Daily News*.[135] In Dallas, General Edwin A. Walker, who had commanded the U.S. Army detachment that had intervened in the Little Rock, Arkansas, crisis of 1957 but was later relieved of his command in West Germany in June 1961 for publicly calling for war with the Soviet Union, promised guns and volunteers: "Barnett, yes. Castro, no," he said on radio. FBI intelligence from several states did in fact reveal that weapons and racist volunteers were heading for Oxford.

Whether because he was duplicitous, desperate, or demented (he had been struck in the head by an airplane propeller earlier that summer), Barnett proved completely unreliable. At one point he proposed to Kennedy that when the marshals brought Meredith on campus they should draw their sidearms and arrest Barnett himself. In another exchange, he suggested that he and other Mississippians would raise money to send Meredith to college outside the state. Kennedy continued to try to talk him down, but to no avail. Meredith, even with his escort of marshals, was turned back a third time. As Kennedy later explained, it was obvious that what Barnett was "trying to accomplish was the avoidance of integration at the University of Mississippi, number one, and, if he couldn't do that, to be forced to do it by our heavy hand; and his preference was with troops."[136]

With racist gunmen and provocateurs now on the Ole Miss campus, and with the newspapers and radios ringing with revolt, the attorney general asked his brother to intercede with Barnett. A conversation between the president and Barnett was scheduled for Saturday afternoon, September 29. Presidential special assistant Arthur Schlesinger attended the strategy session that preceded the telephone conversation. When the phone rang, the president, "as if rehearsing to himself," said before picking it up: "Governor, this is the president of the United States — not Bobby, not Teddy, not

Princess Radziwill." Once on the phone, Kennedy was matter-of-fact: "I am concerned about this matter as I know you must be. . . . Here's my problem, Governor. I don't know Mr. Meredith, and I didn't put him in there. But under the Constitution I have to carry out the law. I want your help in doing it." Barnett said that his attorney had a new plan and was coming to Washington to work it out with the attorney general. The president pressed him: there was a court order that gave the governor until Tuesday to permit Meredith to be admitted. Barnett claimed the new plan would address that. The president promised to call the governor back after the attorney general had conferred with Barnett's attorney, Tom Watkins.[137]

That Saturday the Kennedy brothers spoke to Barnett twice. The president demanded to know "whether you will maintain law and order — prevent the gathering of a mob and action taken by a mob. Can you stop that?" In reply, Barnett said he would do his best but had another idea: to register Meredith in secret in Jackson, Mississippi. The president accepted the deal, but three hours later, Barnett phoned the attorney general to tell him it wouldn't work. It was at this point that Jack gave the order to federalize the National Guard and to move army troops into Memphis. He decided to make a statement on national television the following night. Burke Marshall then put the president's requests to Barnett in writing, asking him to state once and for all whether he would honor the court order and, above all, whether he would use state law enforcement officials to stop the mobs from collecting in Oxford and especially on the campus. The president asked for his reply in writing by that evening.[138] There was no reply.

The next day — Sunday the thirtieth — a deal was worked out between the attorney general and Barnett. In their twenty-third phone exchange, Bobby told him that the president was going on TV and effectively informing the country that "you broke your word to him." Barnett seemed overcome at this: "Don't say that. Please don't mention it . . . please let us treat what we say as confidential. . . . Let's agree to it now and forget it. I won't want the president saying I broke my word. . . . We will cooperate with you." The agreement was that Meredith would be flown in from Memphis by helicopter, brought on campus, and placed in a dormitory for his safety. The marshals would take their places in front of the Lyceum (the campus's main building). Barnett would thereafter issue a statement informing Mississippians of these facts and announcing that state law enforcement officials were under orders to prevent any disturbances.[139] The statement that the governor's mansion later released did set forth those two items of information, but added some incendiary touches of its own: "To the officials of the federal government, I say: Gentlemen, you are trampling on the sovereignty of this great state and depriving it of every vestige of honor and respect as a member of the Union of States. You are destroying the Constitution of this great nation. May God have mercy on your souls."

The attorney general had meanwhile dispatched Katzenbach to manage the move on the ground. With his usual dark humor he told Katzenbach as he was leaving, "If things get rough, don't worry about yourself. The president needs a moral issue."[140] But Bobby Kennedy was in fact very worried.

In the early afternoon, as planned, Katzenbach, Ed Guthman, and the marshals escorted Meredith onto the campus and put him in a dormitory. Later, the large contingent of state troopers took up positions near the Lyceum but did nothing to otherwise secure the area. As the raucous crowd grew to over 2,500, shouting racist obscenities, throwing rocks, bottles, and in one instance a firebomb, the marshals stood impassively, holding their line. A tall figure in a white ten-gallon hat — former general Walker, with his contingent of gunmen from Dallas — was seen walking through the mob, which was now within an ax handle's distance of the line of marshals. Suddenly, the state troopers withdrew. Katzenbach telephoned an immediate protest to the governor's office. Shortly before the president went on the air, there was a volley of rifle fire. The attorney general called down to Ole Miss from the Oval Office and managed to reach Guthman, a decorated veteran of World War Two, who told him that all hell had broken loose. "It's getting like the Alamo," he said. There was a pause and then Bobby said wryly, "Well, you know what happened to those guys, don't you?"[141] Katzenbach, Guthman, and the rest of the federal contingent asked that army units be flown in immediately. If the mob found Meredith in his dormitory, they would kill him.

President Kennedy immediately called Deputy Secretary of the Army Cyrus Vance, who was acting as liaison between the army and the Justice Department, and asked him to move troops from Memphis with all possible dispatch. Vance relayed the order, but the units in Memphis had gone off alert after hearing the president's televised statement. Then it was discovered that they were armed only with nightsticks. General Creighton Abrams ordered the soldiers to be equipped with full combat gear. Two hours went by. Katzenbach put in a desperate call to the Oval Office from a pay phone — sniper fire audible in the background — to find out why the army had not arrived.

Bobby Kennedy remembered:

That happened six, eight, ten times during the course of the evening. "They're leaving in twenty minutes." We'd call twenty minutes later and they hadn't even arrived to get ready to leave. "They're ready to go now," and they hadn't been called out of their barracks to get into the helicopters yet. "They're in the helicopters now." They were just forming up. "The first helicopter's leaving and will be there in forty minutes." The first helicopter went in the air and then circled and waited for the rest of the helicopters.

The president uncharacteristically went white-hot, blistering General Abrams and Vance with profane abuse. But still no troops. There were two more conversations with Barnett. The Kennedys demanded that he order the state troopers back to the campus. Privately, Jack and Bobby rued their decision to base the effort to enroll Meredith on the assurances of a prevaricator like Barnett. But what choice had they had? If he resorted to full rhetorical rebellion, the chances of a bloodbath would only be enhanced. And so they waited. Midnight. 1 A.M. 2 A.M. For Jack, the situation was another Bay of Pigs — only this time on American soil. He and his brother had based their policy on the best-possible scenario and now were dealing with the worst. They had accepted the tidy assurances of the experts only to discover, as before, an astonishing level of incompetence. Bobby felt that he himself was responsible for "botching things up": "[W]e could just visualize another great disaster, like the Bay of Pigs, and a lot of marshals being killed or James Meredith being strung up. How do we explain that? I don't care what excuses you have; the troops didn't arrive."[142]

Having landed at 3:45 A.M. at the Oxford airport, a half-mile from the campus, the commanding officer waited for the entire battalion to disembark and fall in before proceeding. The president had by now lost all patience, wiring the officer in charge: "People are dying in Oxford. This is the worst thing I've seen in forty-five years. I want the military police battalion to enter the action."[143] In all it took the troops five hours to reach the campus. The army had formally assured the attorney general it would take two. When the army troops (and Mississippi National Guardsmen) finally made it to the campus, the fighting had all but ceased, and there was an eerie and tense calm. Later that morning, Meredith was registered. A fellow student shouted: "Was it worth two lives, nigger?" Throughout the ordeal, Meredith was unflinching. For weeks he was protected by five hundred troops. For months he was accompanied to classes and activities by an escort of marshals. He was to graduate from Ole Miss in August 1963.

As for General Walker, who made no effort to leave Oxford, he was arrested by federal authorities on four counts, including insurrection, and flown to the Medical Center for Federal Prisoners at Springfield, Missouri, for psychiatric observation. The John Birch Society and other far-right groups immediately heralded this as an example of the "Kennedy police state." Congressman Bruce Alger of Texas telephoned the attorney general, demanding to know on what psychiatric grounds Walker was being held. Kennedy replied that it was out of his hands. "I do not have anyone on the line," Alger assured Kennedy, "no secretary or anything."[144] The attorney general, however, did and said nothing further to Alger. Henceforth, the practice of either taping or transcribing sensitive exchanges would become widespread in the Kennedy administration.

Critics of the administration, then and later, would charge that the whole crisis could have been averted if the federal government had moved the army in before the Klansmen had the marshals in their gunsights. The accusation relies essentially on hindsight. As Burke Marshall has commented, from both a legal and political standpoint the federal government had to deal with the state government in the person of Governor Barnett as long as there was the prospect that the state government would assist federal authorities in maintaining order.[145] Bobby Kennedy's exchanges with Barnett from September 15 to September 30 suggested that the government of Mississippi would play such a role. Had federal troops arrived earlier, they might have touched off an even more destructive result. The failure in the end was not one of planning but of execution.

President Kennedy remained outraged at the army's incompetence. The day after Meredith registered, he summoned army general Earle G. Wheeler and informed him and Defense Secretary Robert McNamara that he wanted an investigation.[146] His previous opinion of the "fucking brass hats" had dropped one rung lower: they were worse than arrogant — they were incompetent. This judgment would prove consequential in the Cuban missile crisis.

The president still seemed to tack cautiously on civil rights thereafter. He continued to "equivocate" (the word is Wofford's) on the executive order that was to desegregate federal housing "with the stroke of a pen." Finally, as he and the country were preparing for the long Thanksgiving weekend on the night of November 20, the White House issued a statement that the order had been signed. It was "deliberately sandwiched," in the recollection of Theodore Sorensen, between two important foreign policy statements.[147]

Bobby, on the other hand, had moved further out on the civil rights frontier. His statement the day after the battle of Oxford, praising the federal marshals, the seven Ole Miss staff and administrators who had bravely assisted the marshals, Dr. L. G. Hopkins (an Oxford physician who had treated the wounded during the battle), and several Ole Miss students, was direct and strong. The following Saturday, he went even further in a widely publicized speech in Milwaukee: "We live in a time when the individual's opportunity to meet his responsibilities appears circumscribed by impersonal powers beyond his responsibility. . . . But even today there is so much that a single person can do with faith and courage. . . . James Meredith brought to a head and lent his name to another chapter in the mightiest internal struggle of our time."[148] This was the statement about civil rights that the Kennedy brothers had up to then scrupulously avoided making — to frame the issue as a matter of personal courage, and to place it in a national context. Whenever Robert Kennedy identified public policy in moral terms, he was a difficult man to stop.

There was another consequence to the battle of Oxford. At no previous time had the Kennedy brothers deliberated and collaborated so closely in a crisis. Their techniques in communication and the use of personnel, their incrementalist style of process negotiation, their outrage at the military, even their emotional commiseration over the long night of September 30 and October 1 bound them more tightly together than ever before. Little did they know that within two weeks of the resolution of the Ole Miss crisis, Mississippi would again be the staging ground — this time for divisions of troops, squadrons of aircraft, and fleets of ships in anticipation of an invasion of Cuba to stop the Soviet Union from emplacing offensive nuclear missiles on the island.

October 1, 1962

Washington, D.C.

At first federal attorneys in Louisiana couldn't believe what they were hearing — that Jimmy Hoffa had spoken in detail about murdering Bobby Kennedy. The source was Edward G. Partin, the secretary-treasurer of Teamsters Local 5 in Baton Rouge, who secretly approached Walter Sheridan, Kennedy's top investigator into Hoffa's activities, on September 30 to report that in June 1962 at the Teamsters Union's headquarters in Washington a highly agitated Hoffa had taken him aside. "I've got to do something about that sonofabitch Bobby Kennedy," he declared. "He's got to go. Somebody needs to bump that sonofabitch off. . . . I've got a rundown on him. His house is here, like this, and it's not guarded." Hoffa then diagrammed the location of Hickory Hill with his fingers and said, "He drives alone in a convertible and swims by himself. I've got a .270 rifle with a high-power scope on it that shoots a long way without dropping any. It would be easy to get him with that. But I'm leery of it; it's too obvious." According to Partin, Hoffa also discussed getting someone to throw a bomb into Kennedy's house "so the place'll burn down after it blows up." Partin told Sheridan he was willing to take a lie detector test to prove his truthfulness.[149]

Why had Hoffa brought Partin into his confidence about killing the attorney general? Partin later said, "Hoffa always just assumed that since I was from Louisiana, I was in [Carlos] Marcello's hip pocket."[150]

Sheridan flew back to Washington the next day, October 1, to alert Kennedy. He knew that the attorney general had worked through the night with the president, trying to resolve the bloody standoff at Ole Miss, but the danger, he felt, was real. Hoffa was a man practiced in murder, and Kennedy's investigative dragnet was closing in on him. A grand jury in Nashville had indicted Hoffa for fraud under the Taft-Hartley Act and the trial was to begin in a matter of days.

That afternoon Sheridan caught up with Kennedy as he was coming out of the Justice Department building on his way home. He related Partin's story to Kennedy, who reacted calmly to the report. "What if that fellow passes the test?" he inquired with a wry smile. Sheridan replied he probably would. Kennedy shrugged, climbed into his car, and drove off.[151] In the days that followed, the attorney general took no extra precautions about his safety, despite the urgings of his staff. He refused to accept a security detail.[152] In his war against Hoffa, Kennedy was ready to use every weapon at his disposal, but having learned of Hoffa's determination to kill him, Kennedy himself was content to remain unprotected. He would dare the fates.

In Bobby's view, winning meant taking risks and sticking to your plan of battle. A security detail might tip off the enemy to a leak in his camp. When Jack himself leaked the Partin story to Ben Bradlee — and another one in which Hoffa had tried to silence a witness by poisoning him with arsenic — Bobby refused to confirm the Partin story and successfully pleaded with Bradlee not to print the second one. It would so terrify potential anti-Hoffa witnesses, Bobby told Bradlee, that the anti-Hoffa cause would collapse.[153]

Bobby Kennedy was determined, even desperate, to nail Hoffa. Although the Justice Department had committed thirty-five FBI agents, sixteen federal attorneys, and summoned thirteen grand juries, the Teamsters leader had escaped indictment.[154] Bobby Kennedy took this failure personally. When a *Time* reporter asked him about it, the attorney general became "livid."[155] In 1962, Justice Department lawyers deliberated at length with Kennedy regarding which Hoffa investigations might produce convictions. Two seemed most promising: Hoffa's fraudulent diversion of Central States' pension fund into a Florida real-estate venture known as Sun Valley, a case the Eisenhower administration had dropped as a result of Hoffa's intimacy with Richard Nixon; and the Test Fleet Corporation, a truck-leasing firm that Hoffa had incorporated in Tennessee in 1948 under, among others, his wife's maiden name after he settled a Teamsters Union strike in favor of the trucking company. After betraying the Teamsters local — in violation of the Taft-Hartley Act — Hoffa profited to the tune of hundreds of thousands dollars in the sweetheart arrangement. In the Test Fleet case, assistant attorney general James Neal got a grand jury indictment against Hoffa, and a trial in Nashville was scheduled for October.[156]

Hoffa, meanwhile, was crisscrossing the country, attacking Bobby Kennedy as "a little hoodlum," "the Boston bully boy," who was spending millions of dollars of public money and "wiretapping me left, right, and center" to put him behind bars. The Teamsters Union leadership was going all out to stop the federal investigation. Hoffa had heard some of the mob tapes of Bobby Kennedy's trysts with Marilyn Monroe, at least according to Hoffa attorney William Bufalino.[157] But if this were so, the FBI's cover-up in the aftermath of the actress's death removed corroborating evidence of the relationship and thereby reduced the value of that material. In September, Teamsters' lobbyists touched off a congressional protest from eleven congressmen as well as Senators Homer Capehart and Hiram Fong against the government's persecution of Hoffa. Two weeks before the trial was to start, two of Hoffa's "improvers"— men who fixed jurors through bribery or terror — showed up in Nashville.[158] Shortly thereafter, Partin dropped his bombshell.

As shocking as the story was, it was a logical result of Kennedy's assault against organized crime, which in 1962 went into overdrive. Armed with five new racketeering laws, he targeted no fewer than 991 suspects via Special Prosecution Units, using Justice's Central Intelligence Unit. Kennedy traveled throughout the country, forging personal links between the twenty-five federal investigative agencies, Justice Department strike teams, and local law enforcement departments. The effect on the Mafia was devastating. In 1962 alone indictments numbered over 350, convictions 138; the following year, 615 were indicted, 266 convicted.[159] The critical element was that these prosecutions were aimed, through capo-level informants and plea bargains with street *soldati* — wise guys — at the nation's top gangsters. The Patriarca family in Rhode Island and the De Cavalcante mob in New Jersey were prosecuted out of business. When Joseph Valachi, a member of the Genovese family then in prison, murdered a Mafia inmate he thought had a contract to kill him, federal agents moved in quickly. They offered Valachi life instead of the death penalty if he would talk. He did talk — for days, it turned out — naming names, detailing hits, and exposing the cruel underside of the rackets. He also employed the term La Cosa Nostra to describe the nationwide mob network in which discipline was enforced through an ancient Sicilian code of conduct. When the *Saturday Evening Post* published Valachi's confessions, it caused a collective national shudder. Some huge and unseen enemy was lurking in America. FBI bugs revealed that Mafia chieftains across the country were in a state of fury and foreboding due to the Valachi revelations.[160]

By the summer of 1962, Bobby's favorite United States district attorney, Robert Morgenthau, had gotten indictments on all but two of the *capi di tutti capi* in the New York City area. In Chicago, despite the increase in FBI agents placed on the Mafia detail — from five in 1960 to some seventy by the end of 1961 — and the bugs installed in two Outfit meeting places, prosecutions came more slowly. Corrupt Cook County judges, the deep mob penetration in both the Chicago police department and the Cook County Sheriff's Office, not to mention congressional friends, threw up a barrier of sorts against the feds.[161] But Giancana was rattled, as the altercation the previous summer at O'Hare Airport had demonstrated. The attorney general's personal attention to the war — whether in trips to the field or in seeding his best young attorneys — seemed essential to maintain the pressure. In cities of lesser size like Dallas and Miami, Hoover's policy of tactical coexistence with local mob forces remained the order of the day.

In March 1962, the attorney general flew to Los Angeles to address a conference on crime prevention. In his speech, Kennedy detailed the extraordinary results produced by the cross-fertilization of local, state, and national investigation and intelligence sharing: fifty-seven indictments in California; the conviction of Rosselli lieutenant Frankie Carbo for extortion (an investigation developed initially by the LAPD); and the indictment of Johnny Rosselli's old rival Mickey Cohen for tax evasion.[162] Rosselli was not mentioned in the speech and was probably in Florida at the time doing the CIA's business. But two critical areas of federal action directly affected Rosselli, who was still the Mafia's preeminent ambassador-at-large. The first was Kennedy's new racketeering laws, which targeted interstate trafficking in numbers, wagers, equipment, and "interstate travel to promote or engage in illegal business enterprises." This was the essence of Rosselli's role among the nation's mob families as well as the Teamsters Union, and the new laws made him vulnerable to federal attack. The second was tax investigation and indictment — a proven winner for the "G." Sixty percent of the federal cases against Mafia figures related to tax evasion. Internal Revenue Service commissioner Mortimer Caplin made no secret of the fact that he regarded the IRS as an arm of law enforcement. "The Attorney General," he wrote, "has requested the Service to give top priority to the investigation of the tax affairs of major racketeers," who would be subjected to "'saturation type' investigation. . . . Full use will be made of available electronic equipment and other technical aids."[163] When an IRS regional director refused to allow a Justice Department attorney to view a file, he was removed. On another occasion the attorney general assembled all the regional directors in a lecture hall and told them that if he thought they were doing a good job, he wouldn't have put them in a lecture hall.[164]

Former attorney general (and later Supreme Court justice) Robert Jackson summarized the most dangerous power of the prosecutor: "That he pick people he thinks he should get rather than pick cases that need to be prosecuted." This is precisely what Kennedy and his assistant attorney generals were doing — picking individuals, not cases — and it was a clear breach of procedural separation between Justice and the IRS as well as individual liberties. It was nonetheless effective.[165]

The IRS had launched an audit of Rosselli's tax records in February 1962. Soon the FBI's Mafia detail in L.A. reported that Rosselli was closeted with his tax attorney, Emmanuel Rothman, for hours on end each week, devising, no doubt, defensive measures against the audit. Federal agents were actually coming at him on two fronts — from the IRS Special Investigation Unit, which requested access to all of Rosselli's tax-related files, and from the FBI detail, which secretly scrutinized all his banking and stock transactions (obtained through informants). The FBI had gotten their hands on the records of Monte Prosser Productions, a company owned by Rosselli that booked entertainment talent and owned several nightclubs. As FBI telexes revealed, the strategy was simple: to compare what Rosselli was reporting to the IRS and what the FBI's surreptitious investigation revealed and, if there was a discrepancy, to indict him.[166] The admissibility of the FBI's evidence under the Fourth Amendment did not seem to be of particular concern.

Rosselli, normally a man of icy self-discipline who tended to play things light, grew openly bitter. "Jesus," he told Rothman in July 1962, "I'm being run right into the ground — it's terrible." At around the same time, Rosselli told Joseph Shaw, brother of the former mayor of Los Angeles, "They are looking into me all the time — and threatening people and looking for enemies and looking for friends."[167] The FBI was all over Judy Campbell, Rosselli's friend and Jack's former paramour, tracing her calls, detailing all her bills, and monitoring the balance in her bank account, which averaged $24. The FBI had staked out her apartment and periodically broke in, apparently under orders from Hoover himself.[168]

Rosselli's status as a government agent earned him no quarter. During a plane trip back to Washington in 1962, he again voiced his frustration to an associate. This time he specifically referenced the "screwing" he was getting from Bobby Kennedy. "Here I am helping the government, helping the country, and that little son of a bitch is breaking my balls."[169] But there was little he could do on his own. He would need the authorization from a godfather to retaliate violently against the Kennedys. The same month Partin told his story about Hoffa's threat to kill Bobby Kennedy, there were two other ominous encounters.

At the Scott Bryan Hotel in Miami, José Aleman Jr., a Cuban exile who was in debt, had a meeting with Santos Trafficante, who, Aleman said, owed his cousin a favor. Trafficante agreed to help Aleman by arranging a loan from Jimmy Hoffa. According to Aleman, in the course of a conversation about "democracy and civil liberties," Trafficante suddenly made highly negative comments about President Kennedy: "Have you seen how his brother is hitting Hoffa, a man who is a worker, who is not a millionaire, a friend to the blue collars? He doesn't know that this kind of encounter is very delicate. Mark my words, this man Kennedy is in trouble, and he will get what is coming to him." When Aleman said that he thought

Kennedy would get reelected, Trafficante was more specific: "No, José. Kennedy's not going to make it to the election. He is going to be hit." Aleman later maintained that he reported this comment to two Miami FBI agents, George Davis and Paul Scranton, though it seems clear that had he done so, they would have forwarded it to the FBI director for his urgent consideration.[170] If the FBI director did receive it, he alerted neither the Secret Service nor the attorney general.

Louisiana mob boss Carlos Marcello made the same threat, only this time the logic of murdering the president to stop the attorney general was made clear. By 1962 Marcello was a wounded animal. After being thrown out of the country in April 1961, he made it back only to be indicted for perjury and for falsifying a birth certificate. Additionally, the IRS had assessed him for over $835,000. Finally, adding insult to injury, both Marcello and his brother Joe had been subpoenaed to testify before the McClellan Committee, where they demonstrated a vulgar contempt for the proceedings.

One afternoon in September 1962, at his enormous swampland estate at Churchill Farms, Louisiana, Marcello expressed his vendetta in unmistakable language. The source of the account was Ed Becker, a private investigator from Las Vegas who had once done public relations at the Riviera Casino. Becker had come to New Orleans to meet with Marcello. After introductions and an interlude during which Marcello made some calls to check Becker out (interrupting, Becker later said, a story he was busy telling about his friend Johnny Rosselli), Marcello invited him out to Churchill Farms. They drove out along a narrow dirt road through the vast oozing bayou, with its mud-brown ponds and moss-hung gray cypresses. At the simple farmhouse, Marcello started pouring liberal rounds of Scotch for the party of four (which included two of his henchmen) as they listened to Connie Francis's Italian songs and made small talk about sex and business. At some point, Becker expressed his distaste for Bobby Kennedy. Marcello suddenly erupted, leaping to his feet and shouting in Sicilian: *"Livarsi 'na pietra di la scarpa!* [Take the stone out of my shoe!]." Then he continued in English. "Don't worry about that Bobby son of a bitch. He's going to be taken care of." When Becker replied that that would get him into "a hell of a lot of trouble," Marcello was unmoved. "You know what they say in Sicily," he told Becker, "If you want to kill a dog, you don't cut off its tail, you cut off the head." Still red-faced and fuming, Marcello said they would do it in a way to conceal their hand. He had already thought up a way to set up a "nut" to take the heat. "The way they do in Sicily," he added.[171]

October 16, 1962

Washington, D.C.

A t around 8:30 A.M., President Kennedy and Dave Powers walked from the family quarters in the White House to the second-story Oval Room for breakfast. The weather was unusually warm for late October — 66 degrees. Reports indicated that the radioactivity in the earth's atmosphere was eleven micromercuries, one full unit increase from the day before.

Kennedy sat down at the breakfast table with Powers and scanned the four daily newspapers stacked on the table. (He even looked over the *New York Herald-Tribune*, twenty-two subscriptions of which had been canceled by the president because of the paper's supposed editorial bias.) Powers was reading the sports page, which featured coverage of the seventh game of the World Series. He predicted to the president (correctly, as it turned out) that the Yankees would beat the San Francisco Giants and win the series later that afternoon. Jack's interest in the outcome reflected a more fundamental concern: when the World Series ended, the fall elections began.[172] One issue in electoral question was the administration's foreign policy. All the papers that morning ran the story that former president Eisenhower had criticized the Kennedy administration's foreign policy as weak. Senator Keating was continuing his assault on Kennedy's Cuba policy, claiming that he now had "100 percent proof" that the Soviets had placed nuclear missiles in Cuba. Asked the previous month what he was going to do about Cuba at a press conference, the president had quipped: "I'm not for invading Cuba — at this time."[173] There was laughter, but not in Havana or Moscow.

Sometime around 9 A.M., McGeorge Bundy appeared at the

door and the president, standing up, invited him in. It was illustrative of Kennedy's management style that though he knew Bundy had requested to see him about an "urgent matter," he had made no effort to inquire what it was. As they stood before the pale yellow sofa in the room, Bundy gave him the news: the Joint Photo Interpretation Unit (directed by the CIA) had concluded, after hours of analysis of aerial reconnaissance photos, that the Russians were building offensive nuclear missile sites in Cuba.[174]

The president immediately asked Bundy to get the attorney general on the phone. They spoke briefly. The president told Bobby that there was "great trouble" and asked him to come to the White House immediately.[175] As with so many of their conversations, there is no record of the exchange. Interviews done for this history with four of the principals involved indicate that at the start of the missile crisis the president and his brother determined they faced two challenges: to get the Russian missiles out of Cuba and to contain the war impulses of their own generals and admirals as well as their followers on Capitol Hill. Bobby became the chief executor of this most delicate and dangerous strategy.[176]

At 11:45 that morning, Bobby and several other senior defense and foreign policy officials selected by the president received a full briefing, complete with blown-up photographs and charts. The president later described his reaction as one of "stunned surprise."[177] But Bundy had written him a top-secret memo on August 31 regarding the establishment of "surface-to-surface nuclear missiles which could reach the United States from Cuba."[178] Bobby had worried about the same thing: "Cuba obtaining (nuclear) missiles from the Soviet Union would create a major political problem here."[179] Anticipating just such a contingency for almost six weeks, American U-2 spy planes had photographically scoured Cuba for evidence of missiles. During September, however, the U-2 cameras had been blocked by a succession of heavy weather fronts, which had thrown up huge masses of dark cumulus between the planes and their intended targets. Scattered Cuban refugee reports had indicated that long crates were being transported along Cuban roads, and these are what had touched off the voluble Senator Keating. Air Force intelligence had moreover recently reported that at least six hundred Soviet ships (loaded with crates on deck that looked like those used to move Ilyushin bombers) were steaming in the general direction of Cuba.[180]

What in fact stunned the president and other senior officials was Khrushchev's deliberate and repeated deception about his intentions. In early September, Khrushchev had put a new Russian ambassador in Washington, Anatoly Dobrynin. Dobrynin personally assured Bobby on September 4 that no offensive weapons would be stationed in Cuba. Bobby's back-channel Soviet contact in Washington, Georgi Bolshakov, was even more specific: citing his recent discussion with Mikoyan, he told Kennedy point-blank that the only missiles Castro would be getting were defensive antiaircraft missiles.[181]

At precisely this time, however, work was beginning on the launching pads for the sixty-six medium and intermediate-range missiles then being shipped to Cuba. If the cloud cover had not lifted for another two weeks, or if Soviet rocket general S. I. Biryuzov had properly camouflaged the sites (he was later described by Mikoyan's son, Sergo, as "a fool"), Khrushchev's October gamble would have turned into a November coup. Nuclear-tipped Russian rockets, trigger-ready, would have been aimed at American cities.[182] As it was, the Kennedy administration initially believed that it had a matter of days to get them out.

The other reason for the sensation of "stunned surprise" was domestic. The administration was on the political defensive in the fall of 1962. Eisenhower's description of Kennedy's foreign policy as weak was not merely partisan. The price of engagement in the Third World was mounting, and there were no discernible signs of success, much less victory. The U.S.-financed and costly UN peacekeeping operation in the Congo had bogged down. Secessionist Katanga was still on the loose. The Alliance for Progress had foundered, in the view of many, because the regimes of Latin America receiving foreign aid would not accept conditions of political and social reform. In Vietnam, the dispatch of American military advisors was neither containing the Viet Cong nor strengthening Diem's ability to restrain his vicious in-laws, the Nhus.

But in a political sense, Cuba represented the biggest headache. Operation Mongoose, because it was top secret, provided the administration no anticommunist credits. Throughout the late summer of 1962, while the Soviet Union was shipping MIG fighters, heavy tanks, and patrol boats, as well as forty thousand troops, the administration, in the words of its critics, did little more than maintain that it did not object to "defensive weapons." But to the imperious rulers of the Time-Life empire, Henry and Clare Booth Luce, this was mere appeasement. *Time, Life,* and even *Reader's Digest* made plain their belief that a military showdown with Castro was required.[183]

The president's problems, however, went deeper than the press and Republican criticism. The American military, shamed by Kennedy's order to stand down in the Bay of Pigs, was oiling up its war machine. As early as October 1961, the Joint Chiefs had approved an invasion plan called Operation X in which 100,000 troops would land in Cuba accompanied by heavy aerial bombardment. In August 1962, the Pentagon announced that the armed forces were going to conduct large-scale military exercises dubbed Philbriglex-62 in the Caribbean. The marines were going to invade the mythical Republic of Vieques and liquidate a mythical dictator named Ortsac (Castro spelled backwards).[184] In the first days of the missile crisis, the Joint Chiefs immediately began scrambling fighter-bomber and naval craft under the rubric of war games, before Secretary McNamara pointedly reminded them that this was no game and that there was civilian rule in the American system of government.

Edmund Wilson had once likened men at war to "a school of fish, which will swerve, simultaneously and apparently without leadership, when the shadow of the enemy appears." As the American military swerved and darted toward war, the role of the secretary of defense became critical. To maintain a firm chain of command, McNamara began living in his office.[185] As George Ball later commented, had the occupant of that office been someone like Reagan defense secretary Caspar Weinberger, the missile crisis may well have ended in a shooting war.[186]

At the first meeting to deal with the crisis, Bobby initially seemed interested in a pretext to attack Cuba, suggesting the United States might "sink the *Maine* or something."[187] Kenny O'Donnell (who attended this first meeting) remembered that Bobby stood, arms crossed, about three feet behind the far end of the table, mostly listening and walking back and forth. Everyone else was sitting. The view of about two-thirds of the group (that came to be known as Ex Comm) was to launch an immediate air strike. According to O'Donnell, Bobby studied his brother's face as various members spoke. Suddenly, he walked forward to the table and scribbled a note on a piece of paper, folded it, and walked over and gave it to Ted Sorensen.[188] (In RFK's memoir of the crisis, *Thirteen Days*, he states that he gave this note directly to the president.) The note read: "I now know how Tojo felt when he was planning Pearl Harbor."

Secretary Rusk later said in an interview that writing and passing a note during such a meeting was "wholly inappropriate . . . the gravest question, that included the fate of the world, the most consequential measures, were before us. . . . But, of course, this was Bobby Kennedy — couldn't wait, wouldn't accept the chain of command . . . and, of course, everyone was wondering: 'What the hell did [the note] say?'"[189]

George Ball saw it differently: "To place a rational template on an act of pure instinct," he said in an interview,

> is like trying to explain the movement of an athlete. At the time, I'm not sure I knew what it meant, but later it became clearer to me. First, Bobby was saying to his brother: "I can turn this group around for you." Second, it reminded everyone how strong and seamless the relationship between the brothers was. Third, it totally denigrated the air strike option by likening it to Japan's sneak attack — an act of pure infamy. Dean Acheson later wrote that it was a false analogy. And it was. But that's also a rational reaction to the Tojo remark. In a nonrational way, Bobby spiked all the moral and operational tidiness of the surgical strike.[190]

After that first meeting, the attorney general walked back to the White House with his brother, who, according to Bobby, "decided that he would not attend all the meetings of our committee." Bobby later explained that the purpose of this was to "keep discussions from being inhibited. . . . Personalities change when the president is present."[191] But the tactic was more far-reaching than this. First, with the president absent, Ex Comm could deliberate without entering what is called the "decisional chute." The move, in short, bought time. Second, the president did not have to react on the record to proposed courses of action, as he had so prematurely in the Bay of Pigs crisis. He could choose his shots and slowly build his votes through his brother, Sorensen, and McNamara. Kennedy may have been exaggerating when he said that Congress would impeach him if he did nothing, but he understood that congressional leaders (and opinion makers at large) wouldn't buy the idea of a blockade if Ex Comm and the Joint Chiefs weren't behind it, at least officially. As James Blight and David Welch have concluded, there was a collision of worldviews between the hawks and doves. "The hawks' Cuban missile crisis was relatively understandable, predictable, controllable, and safe. The doves', on the other hand, was inexplicable, unpredictable, uncontrollable, and above all, dangerous. The doves felt enormous anxiety throughout, while the hawks felt virtually none."[192] The Kennedy brothers would have to bring these worlds together.

For six days, the Ex Comm communed with open candor but in total secrecy. The interlude, as George Ball commented later, proved critical to the outcome for it bled down emotion and enhanced caution. As McNamara later commented, "In every crisis you will never know what you need to know, and therefore you should behave cautiously." The idea of the doves was to "turn the screw" slowly — to start with the blockade (now called a quarantine) and then slowly increase the pressure on the Soviets. Above all, there should be no irrevocable actions.[193]

To preserve an appearance of business as usual, the president flew to New Haven on Wednesday the seventeenth to give a speech at Yale, where he was booed by students protesting for a tougher Cuba policy.[194] Late Wednesday afternoon, also to preserve cover, Kennedy met with Soviet foreign minister Andrei Gromyko at the White House. Because the Russians had lied about the missiles, and because his administration had not yet resolved what to do in response, Kennedy chose not to confront him. (At a conference held in 1991, Russian scholars and policymakers suggested that had Kennedy confronted Gromyko, it might have provided an opening to engage the Soviet Union diplomatically.)[195] Instead, Kennedy listened, somewhat astonished, as Gromyko reiterated Russia's

The Kennedy brothers bear down on a Teamsters official at the McClellan
Committee hearings in May 1957.
Courtesy of the John F. Kennedy Library/Look Photo Collection.

"He's always there for you," Jackie said of Bobby. Here they are—with Jack and
daughter Caroline—sailing off Hyannis Port in August 1959.
Courtesy of the John F. Kennedy Library/Look Photo Collection.

In the West Virginia primary in May 1960, Jack—as always—managed to conceal the fact that he was in pain. *Courtesy of the John F. Kennedy Library/Look Photo Collection.*

On election night, November 8, 1960, Bobby has a word with aide Pierre Salinger as Eunice Kennedy Shriver listens.
Courtesy of the John F. Kennedy Library/Look Photo Collection.

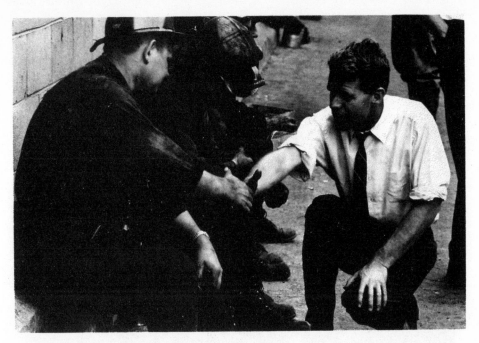

Bobby worked night and day in the West Virginia primary, but in the end it was Joe Kennedy's money that bought the election.
Courtesy of the John F. Kennedy Library/Look Photo Collection.

Here the two couples—Jack and Jackie, Bobby and Ethel—are pictured in Palm Beach, 1958. *Courtesy of the John F. Kennedy Library/Look Photo Collection.*

Jack may have been a wayward husband, but he was also a doting father.
Courtesy of the John F. Kennedy Library/Look Photo Collection.

The dark glasses were part of her silent statement—Jackie (here pictured at Hickory Hill in 1958) detested politics and its impact on her marriage.
Courtesy of the John F. Kennedy Library/Look Photo Collection.

J. Edgar Hoover, with secrets about Jack's philandering and Joe Senior's connections with the mob, was able to blackmail the Kennedys.
Courtesy of the John F. Kennedy Library/Look Photo Collection.

Johnny Rosselli, friend of Joe Kennedy and alleged conspirator in the assassination of President Kennedy. *Courtesy of the author.*

Chicago Outfit boss Sam Giancana. Hoover first learned of his contributions to the Kennedy for President campaign via an FBI bug in Giancana's office in the Armory Lounge. *Courtesy of CORBIS/Bettmann.*

A full year before JFK's assassination, Carlos Marcello, shown here leaving one of his many court appearances, vowed violent revenge against the Kennedys at his swampland estate in Louisiana.

Florida-based godfather Santos Trafficante Jr. maintained his innocence in the plot to kill the president, but his association with Jack Ruby and Johnny Rosselli, among others, suggested otherwise.

Deputy Attorney General Nicholas Katzenbach listens as Alabama governor George Wallace proclaims his defiance of the desegregation order of the University of Alabama. "Dismiss him," Bobby advised Katzenbach, "as a sort of second-rate figure."

The author on Point Mary, Key Largo, where "Colonel" Johnny Rosselli trained his Cuban sniper unit in the summer of 1962. *Courtesy of the author.*

Within days of the Rosselli-CIA meeting in September 1960 to plan the murder of Cuban premier Fidel Castro, this embrace confirmed the Americans' worst fear. *Courtesy of the John F. Kennedy Library/ Look Photo Collection.*

"[T]here is a possibility that an impostor is using Oswald's birth certificate," FBI director Hoover wrote on June 3, 1960, to the State Department. This was an early indication that Oswald's identity was being manipulated.

Former Soviet officials later wondered why President Kennedy did not confront
Soviet Foreign Minister Andrei Gromyko with evidence of Soviet missiles in Cuba in
October 1963, instead of issuing a public ultimatum that pushed the superpowers to
the brink of war. *Courtesy of the John F. Kennedy Library/Look Photo Collection.*

Former anti-Castro underground leader Jorge Recarey Garcia-Vieta, here pictured on his graduation day in April 1963 as an officer of the U.S. Army.
Courtesy of Jorge Recarey Garcia-Vieta.

Jack Ruby, shown here with three of his strippers, met with Johnny Rosselli twice in Miami in early October 1963.
Courtesy of CORBIS/Bettmann.

Their golden year was 1963. Here newly elected senator Edward Kennedy poses outside the Oval Office with his older brothers.
Courtesy of the John F. Kennedy Library/Look Photo Collection.

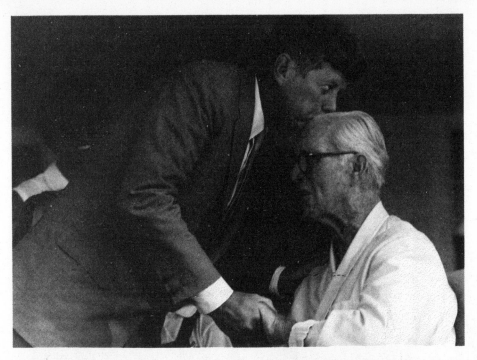

The president visits his stricken father in Hyannis Port, a rare public display of affection. *Courtesy of the John F. Kennedy Library/Look Photo Collection.*

Ambassador William Mahoney, the author's father, discusses the 1964 elections with President Kennedy on November 19, 1963. *Courtesy of William Mahoney.*

LBJ thought JFK's assassination was "divine retribution."
Photo by Yoichi R. Okamoto, courtesy of the Lyndon Baines Johnson Library.

January 1964: a wounded
and bewildered man.
*Photo by Yoichi R. Okamoto,
courtesy of the Lyndon Baines
Johnson Library.*

BELOW: Bobby joins Cesar
Chavez at the Mass of
Thanksgiving held in March
1968 in Delano, California,
to celebrate the end of the
labor leader's fast. For all
their differences of wealth
and power, they were
much alike.

"So far he's run with the ghost of his brother," Senator Eugene McCarthy said about Bobby's run for the presidency. "Now we're going to make him run against it. It's purely Greek: he either has to kill him or be killed by him."

peaceful intentions vis-à-vis Cuba. All weapons being shipped there, he told the president, were defensive. Kennedy then had an aide bring him his statement of September 4 regarding the consequences of placing offensive weapons in Cuba and read it to Gromyko.

The next day, Thursday, new photographic evidence brought bad news: between sixteen and thirty-two missile sites were now under construction and estimates were that some would be ready to fire their missiles within a week. The hawks, now led by the grand old man of containment, former secretary of state Dean Acheson, pressed Kennedy hard. The blockade, they argued, would not "remove the missiles and would not even stop the work from going ahead on the missile sites themselves. [A]ll we would be doing with a blockade would be closing the door after the horse had left the barn." If we blockaded Cuba, the hawks argued, the Soviets would blockade Berlin where their conventional forces were overwhelmingly superior. The place to stop aggression was where it started, where our conventional power was preeminent. A surprise attack could knock out the missiles before they could be armed with warheads.[196] (Soviet and Cuban principals later revealed that there were in fact warheads on the island during the crisis.)

Bobby, who was informally chairing the meeting in his brother's absence, termed this a "Pearl Harbor in reverse" and later explained the gravamen of his belief: "I could not accept the idea that the United States would rain bombs on Cuba, killing thousands and thousands of civilians in a surprise attack. Maybe the alternatives were not very palatable, but I simply did not see how we could accept that course of action for our country."[197] Acheson was contemptuous of this and mocked the attorney general, asking whether it was necessary "to adopt the early nineteenth-century methods of having a man with a red flag walk before a steam engine to warn cattle and people to stay out of the way." Acheson was sufficiently exercised by the younger Kennedy's "moralizing" that he asked to see the president alone that evening. When Jack himself brought up the Pearl Harbor analogy, Acheson told him it was a "silly" way to analyze the problem: "It is unworthy of you to talk that way."[198]

By October 18, Ex Comm appeared more or less split between the blockade and the air strike. But the next day, with the president in Chicago on what was being called a fund-raising trip, Bundy made a determined run at pushing through the air strike. He said that he had spoken to the president that morning, intimating that Kennedy was now leaning toward an air strike. After Bundy finished, Acheson weighed in. Then the other hawks, Dillon, McCone, and Taylor, ticked off their support of the strike. Bobby, now sitting, noted with a grin that he too had talked to the president that morning and that "it would be very, very difficult indeed for the president if the decision were to be for an air strike, with all the memory of Pearl Harbor and with all the implications this would have for us in whatever world there would be afterward. For 175 years we had not been that kind of country. A sneak attack was not in our traditions."[199]

The implicit message in what he said could not be mistaken. Bobby was speaking for his brother, and his brother would not accept an air strike. If there was to be an air strike, it would come later, not sooner. But there was something about the way he made the statement that also impressed his audience, something that Douglas Dillon later called his "quiet and intense passion." "I felt I was at a real turning point in history," Dillon said. "The way Bobby Kennedy spoke was totally convincing to me." It was as if his simplicity of communication and the intensity of the emotion behind his words imparted a special power to them.

Bobby later wrote that "pressure does strange things to a human being, even to brilliant, self-confident, mature, experienced men. For some it brings out characteristics and strengths that perhaps they never knew they had, and for others the pressure is too overwhelming."[200] But if this were true of the other men meeting around the clock (Rusk had suffered something of a mental collapse), the effect of pressure on Bobby was known, especially by his brother. At every crisis point in his life — the McClellan Committee hearings, Jack's campaigns in 1952 and 1960, the successive civil rights crises of 1961 and 1962 — he drew strength from the storm, remaining razor-alert and indefatigable.[201]

By October 18, Ex Comm was ready with its recommendation to the president, who flew home from Chicago. Back in the White House, Bobby sat by the side of the pool and watched his brother do laps for a half hour. While Jack did the breast-stroke, they talked.

Later, they walked over together for a full-dress, two-hour meeting of the National Security Council.

McNamara presented the arguments for a blockade, Taylor for the air strike. (Acheson did not attend, protesting what he regarded as a foreordained decision). The president had indeed decided on the blockade, but not before carefully canvassing the more egomaniacal members of the Joint Chiefs. When General Curtis LeMay took on the president over the advisability of the blockade, Kennedy coldly cut him off. Afterward, Jack said to O'Donnell: "These brass hats had one great advantage in their favor. If we do what they want us to do, no one of us will be alive later to tell them they were wrong."202

After the meeting, which had taken place in the Oval Room, the president walked out onto the small, second-story porch, sun-lit and cool in the late October afternoon. Sorensen and Bobby joined him there, as did a few others from time to time. As he gazed out at the autumn panorama, Jack talked, as Sorensen later wrote, "as he almost never talked," of life and death. He calculated the odds of nuclear war, which he thought were about one in three, and about the killing of children if this were to pass. "If it weren't for them, for those who haven't even lived yet, these decisions would be easier." Then in his abrupt way, he turned to Sorensen. "I hope you realize that there's not enough room for everyone in the White House bomb shelter." Jack, Bobby, and Sorensen joked about who was on the list of invitees and who wasn't.203

The crisis revealed the essence of Jack Kennedy: his sense of theater, his astringent realism and distaste for the moral posture, his profound reservations about the military, his view of history as a march of folly toward war, and, most of all, his profound dependence on his brother.

That evening, the president went to dinner at the home of journalist Joe Alsop in Georgetown. Another guest was Charles Bohlen, former ambassador to the Soviet Union, who was en route to Paris to serve as American ambassador. Kennedy took Bohlen out into the garden and spoke with him for about twenty-five minutes. Later, over dinner, the president asked Bohlen what the Russians had done in the past when backed into a corner. Susan Alsop was to remember Kennedy asking that question twice. After going to bed, she said to her husband, "Darling, there's something going on. I may be crazy but there's something going on." "I think you're crazy," Alsop replied.[204]

An hour before going on television on Monday, October 22, the president met with senior congressional leaders. Senators Richard Russell and J. William Fulbright, both Democrats, expressed their opposition to the blockade, advocating the air strike instead. As he had predicted, Kennedy couldn't hold his own party at this critical juncture. He told Russell and Fulbright that millions of Americans might lose their lives if a shooting war erupted between the superpowers, and therefore he was determined to exhaust all possibilities before taking irrevocable steps.[205] Moments before the speech, Secretary Rusk delivered the text along with a letter to Khrushchev to a stupefied Dobrynin.

In his statement, Kennedy justified the showdown in terms of his conclusion that "this sudden, clandestine decision to station strategic weapons for the first time outside the Soviet Union represents a deliberately provocative and unjustified change in the status quo." As Sorensen, who drafted the speech, later commented: "[JFK] was indeed worried that the world would say, 'What's the difference between Soviet missiles ninety miles away from Florida and American missiles right next door to the Soviet Union in Turkey?' It was precisely for that reason that there was so much emphasis on the *sudden* and *deceptive*. . . . Look at that speech very carefully. We relied heavily on words such as these to make sure that the world didn't focus on the questions of symmetry."[206]

In the days that followed, the Americans launched an inspired diplomatic offensive, complete with the photo blowups and a chronology of Soviet perfidy. During a session of the Security Council in New York, United Nations ambassador Stevenson cross-examined the Soviet ambassador in riveting style, and in far-off Conakry, Guinea, Ambassador Bill Attwood persuaded Guinean president Ahmed Sekou Touré to deny Ilyushin bombers refueling rights in his country. But the American case was thin. As Georgi Shaknazarov later commented, "You speak of deception. . . . But according to international law, we had *no* reason to inform you beforehand."[207]

Khrushchev's reaction to Kennedy's speech was immediate and

unambiguous: "The United States has openly taken the path of grossly violating the United Nations Charter, the path of violating international norms of freedom of navigation of the high seas, the path of aggressive actions both against Cuba and against the Soviet Union." America was pushing mankind "to the abyss of a world missile-nuclear war," he thundered. According to Russian historian Roy Medvedev, Khrushchev then ordered his generals to finish construction of the missile silos and the captains of the Soviet ships to hold course and run the blockade.

The next day, after the Organization of American States approved the American quarantine, Kennedy sent a letter to Khrushchev. He assured Khruschchev that the United States did not want to fire on any ships of the Soviet Union: "I am concerned that we both show prudence and do nothing to allow events to make the situation more difficult than it is." "The great danger and risk in all of this is a miscalculation — a mistake in judgment," he told Bobby, Sorensen, and O'Donnell. They discussed Barbara Tuchman's *The Guns of August* and the "tumble into war" by European nations in 1914 through the toxic combination of overreaction and patriotic vanity. Afterward, Jack asked Bobby to approach Dobrynin.[208]

Bobby met with Dobrynin at 9:30 P.M. that Tuesday for about forty-five minutes on the third floor of the Russian embassy. Kennedy reiterated that Russian deception was the cause of this dangerous reckoning and explained why, in response to Dobrynin's question, the president had not confronted Gromyko with the American position. Back in the White House, Jack joined his brother and British ambassador David Ormsby-Gore, who strongly recommended that the U.S. Navy pull its line of interception back from 800 miles off the coast of Cuba to 500 miles, to give Khrushchev more time.[209] The president agreed. He called McNamara to relay the order. Did the navy actually obey the president's order to move the blockade line closer? Subsequent scholarship by Graham Allison, among others, revealed that it did not.[210]

To maintain control over the generals and admirals, McNamara remained on watch around the clock in his Pentagon office during the crisis. His concern was justified: at a meeting the day before the first Russian ship reached the American blockade, he asked

Admiral George Anderson what would happen when a Soviet ship reached the line.

"We'll hail it," the admiral replied.

"In what language — English or Russian?" McNamara asked.

"How the hell do I know?" Anderson answered, irritated.

"What will you do if they don't understand?"

"I suppose we'll use flags."

"Well, what if they don't stop?"

"We'll send a shot across the bow."

"What if that doesn't work?"

"Then we'll fire into the rudder." The admiral was now angry.

McNamara brought him up short: "You're not going to fire a single shot without my express permission, is that clear?"

Anderson shot back that the navy had been running blockades since the days of John Paul Jones, and that if the secretary would leave them alone they would run this one successfully as well.

McNamara got to his feet and started walking out of the room, then he turned and told Anderson that this was not a blockade but a "means of communication between President Kennedy and Khrushchev."

No force would be applied without the president's permission, McNamara told the admiral. Was that understood? he demanded to know.

The unhappy answer was, "Yes."[211]

By this time south Florida had fully mobilized for the expected invasion. JM/WAVE was distributing road maps of Cuba to Special Forces units. The anti-Castro fighters believed that their hour of deliverance had come at last. If the nation and the world shuddered at the imminence of warfare between the superpowers over Cuba, for the exiles it was nothing less than Gideon's trumpet. According to Cuban Revolutionary Council leader Miro Cardona, Pentagon officials were calling for the "massive enlistment of all Cubans of military age."

The next day, Wednesday, October 24, American warships at the quarantine line sighted two Russian ships. Sonar then revealed a disturbing development: a Russian submarine had moved into position between them. The carrier *Essex*, under the president's orders, scrambled a squadron of helicopters armed with small-explosive depth charges over the submarine while the carrier signaled it to surface. In the Cabinet Room, the members of Ex Comm waited in silence. The president brought his hand up to his face and covered his mouth. He opened and closed his fist. He stared at his brother across the table.

Bobby later wrote about Jack: "Inexplicably, I thought of when he was ill and almost died; when he lost his child; when we learned that our oldest brother had been killed; of personal times of strain and hurt." The voices droned on until finally Bobby heard his brother say, "Isn't there some way we can avoid having our first exchange with a Russian submarine — almost anything but that?" McNamara replied that for the safety of the American ship there was no alternative course of action. At 10:25 A.M., a messenger brought in a note for the CIA director: The Russian ships had stopped dead in the water. Seven minutes later, another report came in. Some of the ships had reversed course. Bobby remembered that instant: "For a moment the world had stood still, and now it was going around again."212

The next problem was getting the Russians to remove the missiles already inside Cuba. Reconnaissance flights revealed that the launching sites were being constructed at breakneck pace and nearing completion. Ex Comm could only guess whether any Russian warheads were on the island. On Friday morning the president told Ex Comm, "We are going to have to face the fact that, if we do invade, by the time we get to these sites, after a very bloody fight, they will be pointed at us. And we must further accept the possibility that when military hostilities first begin, those missiles will be fired."

Suddenly — again — there was a break. At 6 P.M. Khrushchev, in a rambling letter of what looked to be his own composition, stated: "If assurances were given that the president of the United States would not participate in an attack on Cuba and the blockade lifted, then the question of the removal or the destruction of the missile sites in Cuba would then be an entirely different one." His appeal to Kennedy was personal:

> If you have not lost your self-control and sensibly conceive what this might lead to, then, Mr. President, we and you ought not to pull on the ends of the rope in which you have tied the knot

of war, because the more the two of us pull, the tighter the knot will be tied. And a moment may come when that knot will be tied so tight that even he who tied it will not have the strength to untie it, and then it will be necessary to cut that knot, and that would doom the world to the catastrophe of thermonuclear war. [213]

The next day, Saturday, October 27, Khrushchev sent Kennedy yet another letter. This time the tone was formal. Khrushchev added a new condition — the withdrawal of American Jupiter missiles from Turkey. There was the darkest irony in the entirely reasonable request: Kennedy had been demanding the removal of these obsolete missiles from Turkey for the better part of a year, but the State Department had reported that it was unable to get the Turks to agree. The Joint Chiefs of Staff chairman, General Taylor, warned the president that to acquiesce to such blackmail would undermine NATO. The Joint Chiefs recommended an air strike take place that Monday, followed by an invasion, particularly since it was probable that the Soviet missiles in Cuba were not yet loaded with warheads. The president was furious: "I'm not going to war over any damned useless missiles in Turkey," he told Bundy. But that afternoon Ex Comm was informed that an American U-2 spy plane, piloted by Major Rudolf Anderson Jr., had been shot down over Cuba. George Ball recalled his sensation of the beckoning abyss of war. And Bobby wrote later, "The noose was tightening on all of us . . . and the bridges to escape were crumbling."[214]

"My impression was that military operations looked like they were becoming increasingly necessary," Secretary Dillon remembered. "We were drifting without wanting to into becoming victims of a fait accompli. . . . By Saturday the 27th, there was a clear majority in the Ex Comm in favor of taking military action."[215] McNamara, in his recollection of the same day, was to note simply, "There was tremendous pressure . . . for military action." The military recommended that the SAM sites be taken out immediately, but the president pulled everyone back. "It isn't the first step that concerns me," he said, "but both sides escalating to the fourth and fifth step — and we don't go to the sixth because there is no one around to do so." There would be no attack tomorrow, the president said. In Cuba, Castro suggested to the Soviets that in order to "prevent our own missiles from being destroyed, we should launch a preemptive attack against the United States." Although Castro later denied that he had ever proposed this, both he and Che Guevara seemed fatalistically prepared for a catastrophic deluge.[216]

At the Ex Comm meeting that afternoon, Bobby proposed that Jack ignore Khrushchev's second letter and agree to his initial offer to withdraw the missiles in exchange for a no-invasion-of-Cuba pledge. The tactical simplicity of the idea was ingenious; so was the fact that it bought some time.[217] Jack went along with his brother's proposal, and Sorensen and Bobby immediately set to work on a draft. Before Ex Comm reconvened at 9 P.M. that Saturday night, the president undertook another secret maneuver to avoid war: he asked Secretary Rusk to open a channel through the UN secretary general to arrange, if necessary, a public trade of the American Jupiters in Turkey for the Russian missiles in Cuba. That night Jack told his brother that he was going to do everything possible to avert catastrophe. "The thought that disturbed him most, and that made the prospect of war more fearful than it would have otherwise been, was the specter of death of the children of this country and all the world — the young people who had no role, who had no say, who knew nothing even of the confrontation, but whose lives would be snuffed out like everyone else's."[218]

Jack asked Bobby to approach Ambassador Dobrynin again — an idea that had been briefly discussed at the previous Ex Comm meeting. Bobby and Dobrynin met at the attorney general's at 7:45 that evening. According to both his account and Dobrynin's, Bobby said the situation was getting out of control — the accelerated construction of the missile sites, the downing of the U-2, and the fact that United States military "hotheads" were spoiling for a fight. Dobrynin asked about the missiles in Turkey. Bobby replied that the United States intended to remove them "within a short time" but would agree to no quid pro quo made under a Soviet threat.

Bobby then delivered what the Soviets regarded as an ultimatum: if the Soviet Union didn't pull out the missiles, "we would remove them." The president wanted an immediate answer from the Soviet Union.[219] After the meeting, Bobby went back to the White

House and relayed the details of the exchange to his brother. They were not hopeful. The president ordered twenty-four troop-carrier squadrons of the Air Force Reserve to active duty in anticipation of an invasion.

Early the next morning, Bobby took his daughters to a horse-jumping competition at the Washington Armory. In Moscow, "near-panic" had seized Khrushchev and his small group of advisors huddled at the premier's home. "Everyone agreed," Khrushchev aide Oleg Troyanovsky later remembered, "that Kennedy intended to declare war, to launch an attack." They feverishly composed a brief reply in the light of Kennedy's "deadline," rushed the copy to Radio Moscow, and took a specially secure elevator to the sixth floor of the building to make sure it was immediately broadcast word for word. At around 10 A.M., Bobby received a call at the horse show from Rusk. The Russians had publicly agreed to remove their missiles from Cuba. The crisis was over. Castro, who had not been informed of the Russian decision to stand down prior to the broadcast, exploded with anger when he heard the news.

Bobby went over to the White House around noon and had a long talk with his brother. When Bobby got up to leave, Jack said, "This is the night I should go to the theater," apparently referring to the Ford Theater where Lincoln was assassinated. "If you go, I want to go with you," Bobby replied.[220] At their moment of triumph, it was as if Jack, fey and intuitive as always, felt the shadow of a coming event.

December 29, 1962

Miami, Florida

During the height of the Cuban missile crisis, Bobby Kennedy had instructed CIA director John McCone to halt all covert operations aimed at Cuba. When Kennedy discovered a few days later that ZR/RIFLE chief Bill Harvey, with the approval of the Joint Chiefs of Staff, had already dispatched three commando teams into Cuba to prepare for the invasion, he angrily summoned Harvey to the Pentagon and told him to countermand these sorties: "You're dealing with people's lives in a half-assed operation." When Harvey replied that some of his teams were beyond recall, Kennedy stormed out of the room. "Harvey has destroyed himself today," McCone observed.[221] Harvey was relieved of his command of ZR/RIFLE several weeks after the conclusion of the crisis. On October 30, Ex Comm terminated "all sabotage operations" against Cuba. Consistent with the president's secret commitment not to invade Cuba, Operation Mongoose and the executive body that ran it, Special Group (Augmented), were disbanded.

News of Harvey's dismissal and the non-invasion pledge spread like a deadly epidemic among anti-Castro forces in south Florida. One prominent exile wrote: "For hundreds of thousands of Cubans eager to stake their lives to liberate their native land, it was a soul-shattering blow."[222] Suddenly, under Bobby Kennedy's own order, there was a crackdown on the training camps, guerrilla bases, and commando sorties that had been the ramrod of the war against Castro. General Lansdale himself was sent down to Miami to make sure the anti-Castro Cubans and their CIA handlers obeyed the order. On December 4, United States Customs officers detained twelve anti-Castro guerrillas at No Name Key as they were about to embark on a raid to Cuba. Some, like JM/WAVE station chief

215

Shackley, made the best of the bitter business of standing down. But others, like David Phillips, David Morales, and Frank Sturgis, now stripped of all legitimacy, surrounded by enraged Cubans, were moved to seditious resolve against the Kennedys.[223] It was a package programmed to explode — and Johnny Rosselli, once again, was in the middle of it.

David Phillips, under the cover name Maurice Bishop, was already operating independently of the CIA station in Miami. A handsome man in his mid-forties, six feet two inches tall, two hundred pounds, with dark hair and blue eyes, Bishop had served as a CIA agent in Havana before Castro's revolution. There he had become acquainted with Antonio Veciana, an accountant working at the Banco Financiero. Veciana later turned violently against Castro and attempted, with Bishop's guidance, to assassinate the Cuban leader in Havana in October 1961. The attempt failed and Veciana escaped to Miami, where he resumed his partnership with Bishop and, along with an anti-Castro Spaniard named Eloy Gutierrez Menoyo, formed a strike force called Alpha 66. In September 1962, the strike force began launching raids. On October 10, Alpha 66 commandos landed on the Cuban island of Isabela de Sagua and attacked and killed twenty people, including several Russians. On October 15, Alpha 66 struck again, sinking a Cuban patrol boat. Despite the order from Washington to cease all paramilitary activity after the missile crisis, Bishop, according to Veciana, "kept saying Kennedy would have to be forced to make a decision, and the only way was to put him up against the wall."[224] This meant attacking Russian ships and military personnel to provoke a new confrontation between the two superpowers. The situation was explosive, and it seemed imperative, after all the mixed signals the administration had sent to the anti-Castro Cubans, to avoid doing anything that might reignite all the bitter and unresolved passions.

Within three weeks of the Cuban missile crisis, however, Bobby Kennedy dedicated the administration to a new, and seemingly impossible, objective — to liberate the 1,113 captured Bay of Pigs fighters from Castro's jails and recruit them into the American armed forces. It was an extraordinary notion, given the cruel and dangerous odyssey of Cuban-American relations to date. But Bobby felt deep remorse about the fate of these hapless men. Theodore

White once characterized Robert Kennedy as "a moralist" in whom the "motor reflexes are predominant." Once engaged, those "motor reflexes" made him indifferent to questions of risk and proportion. The rescue of the men of Brigade 2506 triggered a motor reflex.

On November 24, having viewed the prisoners in Cuba, Alvaro Sanchez Jr. of the Cuban Families Committee told Bobby: "I'm a cattleman, Mr. Attorney General, and these men look like animals who are going to die. If you are going to rescue these men, this is the time because if you wait you will be liberating corpses." Kennedy turned to his aide Ed Guthman. "We put them there and we're going to get them out — by Christmas," he told him. Guthman said it was not possible. "We will," Kennedy replied.[225] Christmas was one month away.

For the year and a half since the Bay of Pigs, negotiations between Castro and the United States had bogged down in recrimination. Castro's original proposal was to trade the prisoners for either 500 tractors or $28 million in cash. After the captured men were convicted in March of 1962, Roberto San Roman (the brother of 2506's captured commander, Pepe San Roman) then appealed directly to Bobby; it was "like talking to a Brigade man," he said. Bobby pledged his support. He told San Roman to call him ten times a day if necessary. At Kennedy's instigation, the administration offered $28 million in foodstuffs for the prisoners. In April, Castro countered by asking for $62 million. Later that month, as a sign of good faith, Castro released sixty sick and wounded prisoners for $2.9 million, "on credit."

At the airport in Miami, San Roman introduced Kennedy by phone to a former member of his heavy gun battalion, Enrique Ruiz-Williams. Williams, a geologist who had graduated from the Colorado School of Mines, had fought bravely in the Bay of Pigs. *"Un bicho malo nunca muere!* [A son of a bitch never dies!]" he had reportedly shouted after being hit in several places by shrapnel. Before being captured by Castro's forces, he hid a pistol, which in near-delirium he tried to use the next day to shoot Castro. Castro calmly took it away from him. Within minutes of arriving at Miami International, San Roman called Bobby Kennedy and handed the phone over to Ruiz-Williams, who introduced himself to the attorney general as Harry.226 It was the beginning of a close friend-ship. At a face-to-face meeting later that month, Kennedy asked Williams if he could convince his fellow Bay of Pigs veterans to en-list in the U.S. Army. "First, of course, we'll need to get them out," Kennedy remarked with a smile. Williams pledged his help in that cause as well.

Throughout the summer, amid Republican flak for attempting a trade with the enemy as well as quieter entreaties from the State Department to drop the whole thing, Kennedy worked intermit-tently with Williams, San Roman, and Sanchez to get the talks with Castro going again. At Bobby's suggestion, the exiled Cubans hired James B. Donovan, former general counsel to the OSS who had re-cently acted as a go-between in the deal to exchange Soviet spy Rudolf Abel for U-2 pilot Francis Gary Powers. What initial progress Donovan was able to make in his first visit to Cuba in Au-gust 1962 was swept away by the missile crisis of October. Surpris-ingly, Castro still seemed open to the trade and appeared to appreciate Donovan's jocular characterization of the situation: "You can't shoot them [the prisoners]," he told Castro. "If you do, you'll go down as one of the greatest butchers in world his-tory. . . . If you want to get rid of them, if you're going to sell them, you've got to sell them to me. There's no world market for prison-ers."227

Once Bobby had decided to get the men home by Christmas, he immediately committed his already overworked staff to an around-the-clock push. Katzenbach and Oberdorfer headed the ef-fort. Kennedy loyalist and Washington lawyer John E. Nolan Jr. as-sisted Donovan in his negotiations with Castro. Barrett Prettyman, another attorney and former campaign lieutenant, took on the for-midable task of transportation. Kennedy himself took the lead in fund-raising and soliciting in-kind donations to meet Castro's ran-som. He held meetings with pharmaceutical medical supply execu-tives to gather the $11 million worth of drugs and medical goods required. Oberdorfer's office soon took on the feel of a campaign headquarters, with phones ringing, rushed conversations, ad hoc meetings, and so forth. As the donations and commitments steadily mounted, Donovan and Nolan left for Cuba. At their first meeting on December 18, Castro demanded the $2.9 million in cash in exchange for the sixty wounded prisoners he had previously released. Donovan assured him he would get it. Donovan and Nolan remained in Cuba for three days, drafting the specifics of a plan to exchange the prisoners for the cash and supplies.

President Kennedy was most interested in Donovan and Nolan's estimate of Castro's character and state of mind, particularly in the wake of the missile crisis. They reported him to be cunning, charming, and personable, a marathon talker and listener (he would materialize at their quarters late in the evening and converse all night), and reliable in terms of his commitments. To their surprise, they found Castro confident about his personal security. Nolan later described the fluid and masterful security detail that moved around Castro with drill-like precision. On the highway, two heavily armed vehicles weaved back and forth around his Jeep. Castro personally gave the two men a guided tour of the Bay of Pigs battlefield, then invited them to join him scuba diving. "What do you think?" Bobby later asked Nolan. "Can we do business with that fellow?" Nolan's answer was a qualified yes.[228]

On December 23, on the eve of the exchange, the $2.9 million in cash had still not been raised. Bobby appealed to Cardinal Cushing, an old friend of the family, who raised $1 million in a few hours. General Lucius Clay, who had served on the original committee to negotiate the release of the prisoners, contributed the balance. The next day the airlift began, and by the afternoon of Christmas Eve the beleaguered men of Brigade 2506 were back in south Florida. As they stumbled off the planes, journalist Haynes Johnson described them as "earnest, bewildered, still in a state of shock at their sudden liberation, still nursing a bitter sense of betrayal at the manner in which they were sent ashore and abandoned, still torn between trust and cynicism, still in awe at the power of an American government that could . . . pluck them out of the darkest dungeons in Havana and on the Isle of Pines and deposit them back in Florida with their families by Christmas Eve."

The president was enormously pleased and greatly impressed by the herculean effort of his brother and his lieutenants. Bobby spoke with Jack on Christmas Day and encouraged him to go down to Miami to greet the released men in the Orange Bowl. Everyone else in the administration was against the idea. Rusk argued it would only complicate U.S.-Soviet relations; O'Donnell was far more forceful: "Don't go there," he told the president. He tried to convince Kennedy that it would "look as if you're planning to back them in another invasion of Cuba."[229]

The president concurred. "You're absolutely right. I shouldn't do it."

But Bobby insisted. He proposed that Jack first meet with brigade leaders in Palm Beach, and then at least consider welcoming the men at the stadium. Two days after Christmas, Jack spent an hour in Palm Beach with brigade leaders Manuel Artime, Pepe San Roman, Enrique Ruiz-Williams, and a half-dozen others. They invited the president to attend the Orange Bowl rally and to review the troops. Kennedy changed his mind and agreed. Kenny O'Donnell would later write that the president attended in order to ease his "sense of guilt," but it probably went beyond that. He had always respected men who had endured combat. Moreover, Bobby had asked him to go.[230]

From a security standpoint, the appearance was problematic — the Secret Service had no more than two days to perform a security check. There were 40,000 spectators in the Orange Bowl that day. According to two interviews done for this history, there was also an assassin.[231] In his duffel bag was a disassembled, scoped rifle. The Secret Service and the Miami Police Department were tipped off about his presence. They later got wind of the plot and tried unsuccessfully to pick up "A Cuban male, 25 yrs. 5'4", 135–155 lbs, strong muscular build, known only as CHINO" for questioning.[232]

Down on the field, the president reviewed the lines of proud, emaciated men of Brigade 2506 and spoke to several of them before accepting the brigade's flag. With the president and Mrs. Kennedy standing alongside, Manuel Artime told the cheering crowd: "Our plan is to return to Cuba. We will come back — when or where I cannot say — but we will return." The crowd chanted, "Guerra! Guerra!" as the president stepped in front of the microphone. In the heat of the moment, he put aside his prepared text and spoke extemporaneously. "Your conduct and valor are proof that although Castro and his fellow dictators may rule nations, they do not rule people; that they may imprison bodies, but they do not imprison spirits; that they may destroy the exercise of liberty, but they cannot eliminate the determination to be free. I can assure you that this flag will be returned to this brigade in a free Havana." The crowd stood and roared its approval. Many in the brigade began weeping openly. Then Jackie Kennedy took the microphone and made some remarks in her remarkably good Spanish. Referring to her son, John-John, she said: "He's still too young to realize what has happened here but I will make it my business to tell him the story of your courage as he grows up. It is my wish and hope that someday he may be a man at least half as brave as the members of Brigade 2506."[233]

Arthur Schlesinger was probably right in observing later that "both the Brigade and Castro received the wrong message."[234] But in another way, the spectacle summarized the beautiful and dangerous ambition of the Kennedys — their drive to take matters to the edge and beyond. The bright and swirling rage of the Cubans. The assassin seeded among the celebrants. Jack's brave words and consummately theatrical touch. And, most of all, Bobby. His arrogance and overbrimming passion had brought his brother to this place — the bastard city, the habitat of killers.

And now Rosselli and the other murderers began circling, wolflike, for the kill.

Rendezvous

1963

April 9, 1963

Washington, D.C.

If there was one man in the long list of Joe Kennedy's enemies whose ascent to fame had coincided with his descent into disgrace, it was Sir Winston S. Churchill. On the afternoon of April 9, from his wheelchair, the former ambassador looked out from a second-story window of the White House and watched as his son Jack made the former British prime minister an honorary American citizen at a ceremony held in the Rose Garden. Churchill's son Randolph accepted the honor on behalf of his father, who was watching the ceremony on closed-circuit television in Great Britain.

Perhaps if his stroke had not robbed him of his voice or his ability to walk, Joe might have stopped it, or at least given Jack a piece of his mind. Then again, perhaps not. Joe Kennedy had long understood the trade: the vengeance of his enemies had required him to fade from public view and work his deals from the shadows. All for Jack. Now, bent over and drooling, he was a wreck of a man imprisoned in a wheelchair. He was vanishing. But his son was president. His son carried his name. The only sign left of his titanic will were those flashing blue eyes and his frequent screams of "No! No! No!"

That evening, at a small family dinner, the president teased his father about the ceremony for Churchill. "All your good friends showed up, didn't they, Dad?" Jack then went down the list of Joe Kennedy's enemies who had attended that day. "Bernard Baruch . . . Dean Acheson . . . he's on both offense and defense, isn't he, Dad?"[1] The teasing was meant to engage him, distract him, and in the habitat of the Kennedys, it was the truest sign of affection.

Jackie was far gentler with her father-in-law. She took pains to introduce Ben Bradlee, who also attended the ceremony, as "Beebo" Bradlee's son, reminding Joe Sr. that he had once coached a baseball team at Harvard on which Bradlee's father had played. "You remember your friend Beebo," Jackie said. "You said how much better looking he was than Ben." "No! No! No!" was the response.[2]

Jackie and Kennedy cousin Ann Gargan had taken on the difficult chore of helping the old man walk to dinner — something he resolutely demanded to do. With Jackie supporting him on one side and Gargan on the other, kicking his right leg forward between steps, they managed to get him to the table. Bradlee later wrote, "The evening was most moving — sad and joyous at the same time, as the old man's children tried to involve him, while he could only react with the sparkle of his eyes and a crooked smile."

Bobby suggested that he and Teddy sing a two-part harp harmony, which they did. The ambassador tilted his head back to get a better look at them. Then Teddy provided an encore with his imitation of John Fitzgerald, Honey Fitz, Rose Kennedy's father and the former mayor of Boston, "bearing down on the distinctive lisp to much applause." When John-John knocked a drink into his grandfather's lap, Ann Gargan cleaned it up as deftly and quickly as she did the drool that streamed down the right side of his mouth.

The usual place the Kennedys gathered to celebrate and cheer up their father was Hyannis Port. There, amid a chaos of grandchildren, the old man would sit on the front-room couch and listen to his children sing his favorite songs, such as "When Irish Eyes Are Smiling." In his explosive frustration, Joe seemed only to be pacified when there were as many family members around him as possible. It said something about the Kennedys that, in spite of their wealth and obligations, they kept their father within their family, visiting him constantly, rather than consigning him to a clinic or rest home. Perhaps now that he could no longer overpower them and dominate every scene, they could express their love. Even Jack, who avoided public displays of touching, would kiss his father on his forehead. The old man would beam.

Joe Kennedy may have been a shell, but even the fading reflection of his influence seemed to keep them together. He had once rescued Jackie from a failing marriage and then stayed beside her.

He had once critically surveyed Steve Smith, Peter Lawford, and Sargent Shriver as prospective sons-in-law, but once the consecration had been made, he had actively incorporated them into the family circle. For all his faults, his family had always been his prize. He had not justly earned all the wealth that he had accumulated, but this he had — and the family's repayment was vital to him.

April 25, 1963

New Orleans

Early that morning, Lee Harvey Oswald, an unemployed twenty-four-year-old former defector to the Soviet Union, arrived in New Orleans after an overnight bus ride from Dallas. What Oswald did that summer of 1963 — whom he associated with and why — remains at the heart of the controversy of whether or not he was part of a conspiracy to kill President Kennedy.

When he first got to New Orleans, Oswald moved in with the family of Charles "Dutz" Murret, a bookmaker in the Marcello syndicate. Murret had been a surrogate father to Oswald during his troubled youth. Marcello himself was in desperate legal straits during this period. In May the United States Supreme Court declined to review his appeal against the deportation order banishing him from the country. He had one avenue left to save himself: to beat the charges of perjury and conspiracy that Robert Kennedy had brought against him regarding his illegal reentry into the United States in June 1961. The trial date was set for November 1963. In addition to the government's legal assault on Marcello, the attorney general had ordered FBI director Hoover in January to do more to penetrate the Louisiana syndicate and bring down Marcello.

Oswald the "loner," as he was later described, was anything but alone that summer. Many of his associations contradicted his professed sympathies for the cause of Castro's Cuba. He got a job at the W. J. Reily coffee company, known for its anti-Castro position, and later was seen passing out pro-Castro leaflets that bore the stamped address of Guy Banister's violently anti-Castro organization, whose offices were located at 544 Camp Street. On another occasion, after repeatedly offering his services to anti-Castro militant Carlos Bringuier, Oswald initiated a fistfight with Bringuier's group that landed him in the papers and in jail. Emile Bruneau, a liquor store owner with ties to the Marcello family, bailed him out. Oswald was also seen in the company of Banister and David Ferrie, the bizarre, hairless former Eastern Airlines pilot who had once commanded the teenage Oswald in the Civil Air Patrol.[3] Ferrie, a trained hypnotist with a mail-order doctorate in psychology, was then working as a strategist and researcher in Marcello's case against deportation. Ferrie was, despite his checkered employment history, a man of singular talent and savage will, who admitted to FBI investigators in November and December 1963 that he had spoken violently against President Kennedy. Six witnesses confirm seeing Ferrie and Oswald together in Louisiana in the summer of 1963.[4]

Other evidence exists of Oswald's associations with anti-Castro characters. When a man identifying himself as Lee Harvey Oswald applied for and received a Mexican tourist card (FM 824085) in New Orleans on September 17, the individual who received the tourist card with the previous number (FM 824084) was William George Gaudet, the right-wing editor and publisher of *Latin American Report*, who had close ties to the local office of the CIA. Gaudet later admitted under oath that he had seen Oswald one day "in deep conversation with [Banister] on Camp Street right by the post office box. They were leaning over and talking and it was an earnest conversation."[5] Gaudet said his impression was that Banister was asking Oswald to do something for him.[6] Years later, Guy Banister's secretary, Delphine Roberts, remembered a visitor to their office in the weeks before the assassination: Johnny Rosselli.[7] Washington attorney Tom Wadden, a longtime friend and attorney of Rosselli's, subsequently confirmed Rosselli's role in plotting to kill the president.[8] The conclusion, although ultimately based on circumstantial evidence, is that Marcello had his "nut" and the men who could operate him.

By the last week in September 1963, Lee Harvey Oswald was appearing in two places at once. When he was supposed to be in New Orleans about to take a bus to Mexico City, a man calling himself Harvey Oswald petitioned the office of the Selective Service in Austin, Texas, for a revocation of his dishonorable discharge from the Marines. The next day, when Oswald was spotted on the bus to Mexico City, "Leon Oswald" showed up at the Dallas apartment of

Silvia Odio in the company of two Latins, one of whom later called Odio to tell her that Oswald was "an expert marksman . . . kind of loco." In Mexico City, Oswald called the Soviet embassy and was tape-recorded by a CIA tap. The CIA station then reported that the man spoke "broken Russian," though the real Oswald was relatively fluent. CIA surveillance of the Soviet and Cuban embassies later took a picture of a man who was described in a secret cable as "apparent age 35, athletic build, circa 6 feet, receding hairline, balding top." Oswald was in fact 24, 5 foot 9 inches, with no bald spot.[9]

Carlos Marcello was not the only Mafia chieftain vowing vengeance against the Kennedys. The nearly eighty electronic bugs the FBI had placed in the inner sancta of gangster families revealed panic and murderous loathing toward the Kennedys. In Philadelphia, mob capo Willie Weisberg, swore, "With Kennedy, a guy should take a knife . . . and stab and kill that fucker. . . . Somebody's got to get rid of that fucker."[10] But nothing in the record indicates that Bobby Kennedy was ever made aware of these threats. The FBI bureaucratically reasoned that, as always, the highest imperative was to protect sources, especially illegal ones.

In 1963 no fewer than 318 gangsters were indicted. IRS investigations, such as the one launched on Rosselli, numbered over two thousand that year.[11] Benefiting from electronically derived knowledge of the Chicago Outfit, the FBI had adopted face-to-face confrontation with the mafiosi. In April, Washington approved the field office's proposal to initiate round-the-clock "lockstep surveillance" of Sam Giancana and others. Roemer, Rutland, and seven other agents began tailing Giancana by a matter of a few feet, following him in three or four cars, and sometimes blockading him when he tried to leave his home or parking lots. Roemer later described the technique:

> We *literally* lockstepped him. We used nine men on each twelve-hour shift, twenty-four hours a day. If he went to dinner, we went with him. If I was on the shift and he got up from the table to go to the men's room, I'd get up and be at the next urinal. I found that really bugged him. He had shy kidneys. He couldn't do it when I was right there.[12]

At times Giancana, drawing on his old skills as a Capone wheelman, broke away from the tail at high speed. But the special agents would always catch up, snickering and laughing at him. On the golf course, the FBI foursome, playing behind Giancana and compatriots, would often drive their balls in and around the Giancana party. The lockstep exercise completely disrupted the Chicago Outfit's effort to establish casinos in the Dominican Republic by making it impossible for Giancanca to meet with his top gambling experts. When Giancana, a wedding-and-funeral Catholic, attended mass at St. Bernadine's one Sunday, the FBI detail, all practicing Catholics, located in the pew behind, offered guidance: "Kneel down, asshole." Giancana was soon reduced to a ranting spectacle.

Against the advice of his lieutenants, Giancana filed suit against the United States Government in federal court on June 27, claiming that he had been "harassed . . . humiliated . . . [and] embarrassed" and asking for an injunction to protect his civil rights. Giancana himself was the star witness, detailing the alleged harassment and offering as evidence a five-minute color video of Roemer and company in action. Roemer later thought that Giancana's testimony provided the opportunity to cross-examine him on his role as godfather of the rackets and the execution of certain individuals. But under instruction from the attorney general, the government offered no defense, claiming simply that the court lacked jurisdiction. When FBI Special Agent in Charge (SAC) Marlin Johnson took the stand, he refused to respond thirteen times: "I respectfully decline to answer the questions based on instructions from the United States attorney general." For this, Johnson was held in contempt and fined $500. The court also ordered that the FBI maintain specified distances between its agents and Giancana. The Circuit Court of Appeals reversed the lower court's injunction two weeks later, but the outcome coincided with a leak "from Justice Department sources" (almost certainly J. Edgar Hoover) to *Chicago Sun-Times* reporter Sandy Smith that Sam Giancana had done work for the CIA.

Elsewhere the FBI lockstep encountered violent resistance. In April 1963, at the Brooklyn funeral of the father of one of Carlo Gambino's Brooklyn *capo regime,* Special Agent John P. Foley entered Immaculate Heart Church with a camera in hand to film the attendees. Suddenly, he was grabbed, thrown out of the church, and pistol-whipped with his own revolver. The attorney general telephoned Foley in his hospital room to express his concern and thanks.[13] Later, one of Gambino's men was beaten and dumped in a garbage can, apparently by FBI agents. Mafiosi raged in private against the government. An FBI bug picked up Stefano Magaddino suggesting that the Mafia "should kill the whole [Kennedy] family."[14]

Brave as many FBI agents proved themselves in the war against the Mafia, their director conspired to slow down the assault. On May 16, 1963, Hoover formally delivered to the Justice Department a single copy of a two-volume document titled "The Skimming Report," which detailed the inner mechanics of the Mafia's massive and untaxed diversion of gambling profits in Las Vegas. This report was largely based on two years of electronic surveillance of the homes and hotel offices of some twenty-five mafiosi in the Las Vegas area. Three days after the report was handed to Justice, however, someone gave a copy to the Mafia. All over the country, FBI bugs began picking up commentary among gangsters that revealed that the government had been compromised. The FBI promptly pointed at William Hundley, the head of Kennedy's Organized Crime division at Justice, as the one responsible for the leak. It noted that Hundley had taken the report with him on a flight to the University of Notre Dame to give a speech. Someone might have seen it.[15]

Hoover, who was strongly opposed to revealing FBI sources and was himself compromised by the mob, had the motive as well as the means to leak highly charged materials.[16] Hundley did not.

The attorney general ordered that the bugging of Mafia offices and homes in Las Vegas be stopped, but the damage was done: the mob now knew the government had sown its offices and phones with electronic devices, and further, that the information derived from this illegal invasion could never be used in court. Indeed, the Mafia could now sue the government. The leak of The Skimming Report, moreover, may well have kept the FBI from detecting evidence of a plot to murder the president.[17]

That summer Kennedy used the shattering testimony of Joseph Valachi — the attorney general told the nation it was "the greatest intelligence breakthrough in the history of organized crime in America"— to propose a battery of new laws that would enable the government to offer immunity from prosecution to witnesses and broaden the federal right to wiretap. One mafiosi who would read about the testimony of Valachi and Kennedy before Congress was Jack Ruby. A copy of the *New York Daily Mirror* of September 8, 1963, was found in his possession after his arrest for the murder of Oswald.[18]

The publication of an inside account of mob-controlled Las Vegas titled *The Green Felt Jungle* further fractured the mystique of *omerta*. The book also blew Johnny Rosselli's cover. In a telling portrait he was etched as the sophisticated and glamorous don, "soft-spoken and polite," a man of gourmet taste and perfect clothes who "owns no property, has no visible interests in any hotel-casino, and is unemployed. . . . The rough edges of the old torpedo days have been polished to a fine patina of masculine gentility. Gorgeous showgirls hover about him like pigeons waiting for a crumb of bread."[19]

The government was meanwhile closing in on Jimmy Hoffa. By June 1963 over two hundred Teamsters Union officials had been indicted. Ed Partin, the erstwhile Teamsters boss in Baton Rouge, had offered Justice Department lawyers details about Hoffa's role in jury-tampering. One Justice attorney recalled the day Partin walked into the court to testify at Hoffa's trial on the charge: "You could see the blood come up in Hoffa's face."[20] Partin took the stand and for five days underwent a withering cross-examination by eight of Hoffa's attorneys. He held up under the attack. Hoffa was heard snarling at one of his attorneys: "That son of a bitch is killing us." Exiting from an elevator in the court building, Hoffa ran into a federal prosecutor and spat in his face.

Tampa-based attorney Frank Ragano, who represented Santos Trafficante and Hoffa, later recounted that the Teamsters president was furiously demanding that the president be assassinated. On July 23, 1963, Ragano said that he and Hoffa were at Teamsters headquarters deliberating on cases when Hoffa instructed him to tell Trafficante and Marcello when next he saw them, "Something has to be done. The time has come for your friend and Carlos to get rid of him, kill that son of a bitch John Kennedy. This has got to be done. Be sure to tell them what I said. No more fucking around. We're running out of time — something has to be done."

Ragano claimed that when he conveyed Hoffa's message to Trafficante and Marcello, "They looked at each other in a way that scared me. They took it seriously."[21] The House Assassinations Committee concluded in 1979: "There is solid evidence that Hoffa, Marcello, and Trafficante — three of the most important targets for criminal prosecution by the Kennedy administration — had discussions with their subordinates about murdering President Kennedy. Associates of Hoffa, Trafficante, and Marcello were in direct contact with Jack Ruby, the Dallas nightclub owner who killed the 'lone assassin' of the president."[22]

April 26, 1963

Williamsburg, Virginia

It was Bobby's idea but Jack would get the credit: the Kennedy administration would create a domestic peace corps, drawing on the enthusiasm and energy of young Americans to serve the poor and forgotten here at home. The president appointed his brother to chair a cabinet committee to study the idea. As usual Bobby transformed the responsibility into a mission. He broke away from his schedule one Friday afternoon in April 1963 and drove to Virginia's Eastern State facility for the mentally ill. He was revolted by what he saw:

> The children were inside, standing in a room which was bare but for a few benches. The floor was covered with urine. Severely retarded patients were left naked in their cubicles, which suggested kennels, made of an elevated mattress enclosed on three sides by high marble sides and covered on the fourth side by wire mesh so thick you could barely see through it. Patients were washed by a device resembling a carwash — a spraying mechanism through which patients could be directed without the need of anyone to touch them.

In May 1963, in testimony before the Labor Subcommittee of the House Education and Labor Committee, Kennedy described in stark language the cruelty of life for the disadvantaged in America.[23] He told the congressmen about a family of eleven he had encountered that had been living in their car for three months. Two of the children slept in the trunk. Their mother was seriously ill and their father was out of work. Young Americans, Kennedy said, should be asked to invest a year of their lives in serving their fellow citizens: "We are convinced that Americans are equally willing to take on the toughest jobs in this country, whether in a city slum, an Indian reservation, or a mining town. . . . Every sixth citizen needs our help; and there are five of us who should help him."[24]

The triumph of the Cuban missile crisis seemed to allow each of the Kennedy brothers to go his own way in 1963, and to project a more humane form of power. Jack, the political gamesman, elected to risk his political standing for the cause of peace. Bobby, the enforcer, increasingly entered his life's calling as a champion of the abused and neglected.

Paul O'Neil of *Life* had once suggested that Bobby Kennedy was two different men. One was the dry, hyperprocessing attorney general whose face, O'Neil wrote, looked at you "like a miller sizing up a log he was about to cut."[25] He was blunt and ungracious, all results and no reflection. The other man was someone who could suddenly pick up a visiting black schoolchild and sit him on a table, then answer his questions for twenty minutes in language perfectly calibrated to the youth. In the streets of Harlem and Cleveland, visiting the Indian reservations and the state hospitals, and around his Hickory Hill pool with orphans, he could help underdogs, touch them, and maybe give them the courage to change their lives. He could be like his childhood heroes, the saints, performing works of mercy and challenging those in power. There were others in America who had spoken for the forgotten. But Bobby's intensely personal dedication to change the lot of the poor and the brutalized coupled with his political power was unique, and served to quicken the cast of conscience in America.

As always, he was drawn to this mission by his wide array of friendships. His prep school friend David Hackett, then serving as the executive director of the president's Committee on Juvenile Delinquency and Youth Crime (with Bobby as chairman), persuaded him that "delinquency" was nothing more than a code word for the real problem — poverty. Another friend was Representative Edith Green, an Oregonian who had been a Kennedy organizer in 1960. His sister Eunice had worked with delinquents in Chicago and joined Bobby in recommending to Jack the creation of a domestic peace corps to enlist dislocated, antisocial teens into the cause of social recovery.

The attorney general's inquiry into the need for a domestic peace corps led him to the plight of the county's 400,000 migratory workers; 90,000 of these worked fewer than twenty-five days a year. Kennedy's relationship with California farmworker organizers Cesar Chavez and Dolores Huerta, whose acquaintance he had made in the 1960 campaign, would later mature into a friendship that changed Kennedy's public life.[26]

Of all the invisible Americans consigned by race and circumstance to deprivation, none were so invisible in 1963 as the American Indian. They didn't vote, didn't protest, didn't integrate, and mostly remained within their distant and impoverished reservations as part of the vast federal archipelago of colonialism. Americans generally regarded them as pathetic souls, somewhere between simpletons and drunkards. Beginning in February 1963 the attorney general began traveling to reservations. By August, he began speaking publicly about Indians, and the language he used was shocking to those in government. In Bismarck, North Dakota, on September 13, 1963, he spoke to the National Congress of American Indians. After fifteen or so minutes of describing what de Tocqueville called the "natural genius" of America's native peoples, Kennedy turned to their current state:

> Adult Indians today have half as much education as other Americans. Their annual incomes are between one-fourth and one-third as large, and their rate of unemployment is between six and seven times the national average. Their health is so poor that their rate of infant mortality is nearly twice that of any other racial group in the country.

He called this a "national disgrace" and cited the central reason for their plight — racism.[27] This was now his shining cause, and nowhere did it shine so consequentially as in the war for justice for black Americans.

Jack admired Bobby's compassion, but it was his brother's decisiveness that he relied on. "With Bobby," he once remarked, "I have been witness to the testing of his judgment a hundred times. My confidence in him had emerged over years of watching him make decisions under great pressure without ever letting the pressure affect the outcome."[28] Listening to the low-fidelity recordings from the Oval Office in 1963 as the president, the attorney general, and others discussed civil rights, one notes a formal tone to their exchanges. Only the humor, sudden and sometimes sharp, conveys the nature of the bond that existed between them.[29]

It was Jack's belief that his brother, in addition to all his other contributions, had transformed the Department of Justice into the best department in the federal regime. At work in his office, Bobby was all motion and decision, whiplashing his associates, descending abruptly into the ranks of his six hundred attorneys, crossing swords with his key lieutenants on points of strategy, battling the tendency toward group-think by his questioning of himself and others in the course of strategy sessions. The moods came and went — "rain and sunshine," one subordinate termed them. On a good day, he would summon a junior attorney without warning and take him out to lunch at Hickory Hill; on a bad day, he would return scores of calls, demanding to know the reason for the call and settling the matter with a decision, an assurance, or a cold dismissal. At times he would barge into meetings late, remain standing for a period of minutes, bark out a decision, and walk out. He knew he was feared, and he used it.

As Larry O'Brien recalled, he was especially effective because, first, he dispensed with the usual bonhomie and punctilio; second, traded only with the most powerful, when he had to; third, was the equivalent of the president in tone, look, and manner — "only he wasn't, so the president's prerogative was preserved."[30] His drive, his demand for action — even his moods — delivered a singular charge of energy and rigor into his own department and other areas of government.

His management style was to swarm over a problem from a variety of directions. He summoned and deployed his lieutenants at will, according to need and ability, not job description. Thus, Lou Oberdorfer, head of the Tax Division, was the leader of the Cuban prisoner exchange; Ramsey Clark, the head of Lands, found himself in Mississippi, as did Harold Reis, a career attorney in the Office of Legal Counsel who had stuck his head into the attorney general's office one Saturday afternoon in October 1962 and was aboard a plane heading south thirty minutes later. Not long after he took a job as the Kennedys' special assistant, John E. Nolan Jr., the Washington attorney who had assisted William Donovan in the release of the Bay of Pigs prisoners, went to work for Kennedy. Bobby told him to go down to Gadsden, Alabama, to settle some racial trouble, which

Nolan did. After a few days, he called Kennedy and told him things were okay, whereupon Kennedy invited him out to Hickory Hill.[31]

The range of Bobby's decision-making and crisis management would not have been possible — and could well have miscarried in the extreme — were it not for his top lieutenants. Of the Kennedy administration's recruitment of the "best and the brightest," these were arguably the best — superbly trained at Yale and Harvard, tempered by war service (Katzenbach and Guthman were decorated heroes), profoundly dedicated to the constructive use of legal power, and fanatically loyal to their commanding officer. Their fearlessness about physical engagement — Seigenthaler and Doar beaten bloody in Birmingham, Guthman and Katzenbach standing among the dead and wounded at Oxford, Sheridan braving Hoffa's thugs in Nashville, and Roemer and company shadowing the Chicago Outfit — was extraordinary.

But no one could match Bobby in pure physical stamina. When Jack dusted off a Teddy Roosevelt challenge to walk fifty miles, the question arose of who in the administration was up to it. (Certainly not Jack, who told Dave Powers that he preferred to confine his movement to walking to the refrigerator to get another Heineken.)[32] So of course it fell to Bobby, who after a sixteen-hour Friday decided he would attempt it the next morning. At 5 A.M. Kennedy met up with his deputies Jim Symington, Lou Oberdorfer, and Ed Guthman as well as his prep school friend (and star athlete at Milton) Dave Hackett on the Chesapeake and Ohio canal. The idea was to walk to Camp David. It was twenty degrees, and the towpath was covered with ice and snow. Slipping and sliding on the frozen surface, they set out. Symington remembered that he, Guthman, and Oberdorfer, with their World War II experience marching long distances, were wearing sturdy walking shoes with heavy socks. Bobby had loafers on. Several hours later, one by one — exhausted, feet freezing — Hackett, Oberdorfer, Symington, and finally, Guthman dropped out. Kennedy kept trudging on, commenting to Guthman when he quit, "You're lucky, your brother isn't president of the United States."[33] By the time he got to Camp David, completing his fifty miles, Bobby was hobbling painfully. The next day he left on a fact-finding trip to investigate firsthand how the poor and the mentally ill lived in America.

June 11, 1963

Tuscaloosa, Alabama, and Washington, D.C.

Early in the afternoon of June 11 the president gave the go-ahead: he would speak on national television that same evening on civil rights. The fact that no speech had yet been drafted was not the only reason his key advisors opposed the idea. The administration had provisionally reserved the spot for a telecast, expecting to announce that federal troops had taken over the campus of the University of Alabama to enforce the admission of black students, or possibly that Governor George Wallace had been arrested for physically blocking their entry. But the tense standoff had been resolved peacefully. Why give a speech, his advisors asked, when polling showed that the majority of white Americans felt that the president was moving too fast on civil rights? That afternoon Jack called Bobby and said he would do it anyway.

The attorney general and assistant attorney general Burke Marshall showed up at the White House at around seven and sat down with the president in the Cabinet Room. Jack scribbled notes on the back of an envelope in preparation for his remarks. Shortly before airtime Sorensen produced a draft, but it had no concluding section. The president read the draft, wrote in some changes, then got up and walked into the next room. He would conclude his address extemporaneously, something he had never done before in a speech on national television. On so explosive a subject as civil rights, it seemed risky to speak off the cuff, but Kennedy seemed to have reached a personal synthesis regarding the historical moment at hand. As he would tell a friend shortly before his trip to Dallas, there was "no going back."[34]

The issue, Kennedy told the nation, was primarily a moral one,

"as old as the Scriptures and as clear as the American Constitution."
It could not be resolved by "repressive police action":

> The heart of the question is whether all Americans are to be af-
> forded equal rights and equal opportunities, whether we are
> going to treat our fellow Americans as we want to be treated. If
> an American, because his skin is dark, cannot eat lunch in a
> restaurant open to the public, if he cannot send his children to
> the best public school available, if he cannot vote for the public
> officials to represent him, if, in short, he cannot enjoy the full
> and free life which all of us want, then who among us would be
> content to have the color of his skin changed?

Kennedy went on to depict discrimination in terms of the average
black baby — who had half as much chance to complete high school
as his white counterpart, would earn half as much in wages with
twice the chance to be unemployed, and whose life would be seven
years shorter. For seven minutes on prime time, he asked what no
president before or since has asked white Americans — to put themselves in the position of African Americans. Then he turned to the
matter of moral hypocrisy before the world community:

> We preach freedom around the world, and we mean it, and we
> cherish our freedom here at home, but are we to say to the world,
> and much more importantly, to each other that this is the land
> of the free except for the Negroes; that we have no second-class
> citizens except for Negroes; that we have no class or cast system,
> no ghettoes, no master race except with respect to Negroes.

In the coming week he would ask Congress "to make a commitment it has not fully made in this country to the proposition that
race has no place in American life or law."

Bobby watched as his brother paused, placed his hands on the
speech text, and extemporaneously concluded his remarks. It was —
and remains — a statement of unusual eloquence and passion, a *personal* communication that swept away the denials and pierced
through to the heart of racism in America. Reaction from Africa and
black America was thunderously positive; from the white South,
widespread anger. A Gallup poll found that most white Americans
thought their president had gone too far.[35]

Several hours after Kennedy's speech, a white gunman murdered Medgar Evers, the head of the Mississippi NAACP, in front of his home in Jackson. Bobby went to Evers's funeral at Arlington Cemetery. "Bobby sat with me during the funeral and consoled me," Charles Evers, Medgar's brother, said. "The president carried Mrs. Medgar and I and the children back to the White House. We stayed there for the rest of the day."[36]

By 1963 Jack was at the forefront of change. And Bobby had brought him there, against the better judgment of all of his brother's advisors. Just as Jack had subscribed to his brother's passionate attack on the Mafia in 1957, and his opposition to the air strike on Cuba during the missile crisis the previous year, he now found in Bobby the moral compass that would direct them forward.

They had come a long way in just one year. The year 1962 may have been the year of triumph for the Kennedys, but it was, in the view of Martin Luther King Jr., a year of loss and delay and deep frustration for the cause of civil rights. Bobby's maxim to "keep Negroes off the street and in the courts" conveyed the administration's basic tactic. As King noted, "a sweeping revolutionary force is pressed into a narrow tunnel." And as King predicted, it would break out unless something dramatic was done. "The essence of Kennedy's civil rights strategy since inauguration," Theodore Sorensen later wrote, "had been to keep at all times at least one step ahead of the evolving pressures, never to be caught dead in the water, always to have something new."[37] Thus, when there was violence in the South, the attorney general would dispatch John Doar or Burke Marshall or Joe Dolan to search for common ground between the disputing parties. Only in one area — voting — did the administration mount a concerted attack on the pillars of segregation. The thinking was that the vote would eventually vindicate African-American rights in other areas. On a progress report submitted to him, the president jotted: "Keep pushing those cases" at the top. The Justice Department did, bringing thirty in Mississippi alone.[38] But progress was slow and often violent. No less a racist than Georgia's senior senator Richard Russell had predicted in 1957 that the passage of a civil rights bill allowing the Justice Department to investigate voting rights violations would "confine the Federal invasion of the South to the field of voting and keep the withering hand of the Federal Government out of our schools." It was his "sweetest victory" in his twenty-five years as senator.[39]

The FBI's pace of investigation proved glacial, compromised as it usually was by attachments to local law enforcement. "It was unbelievable," one civil rights worker wrote. "They would interrogate a black and scare him out of his pants. They'd interrogate a white sheriff and then report his version straight-faced without 'evaluating' it."[40] "The FBI comes in here every day and we have coffee every day. We're good friends," remarked Chief of Police Collins of Clarksdale, Mississippi, a man who regularly employed intimidation and brutality against civil rights voter registrars.[41] When civil rights workers and local black activists were beaten, harassed, chased away, and even shot, Justice attorneys, with their limited mandate of keeping the peace while advancing their cases, stood silently by. Never, as Victor Navasky has noted, did the attorney general demand that southern FBI agents be reassigned, or that black agents be recruited and assigned to these areas, or that the widespread sweetheart arrangement between special agents and local law enforcement be investigated. Part of the problem, no doubt, was Hoover — a racist practiced at tying attorneys general into bureaucratic knots. But part of the problem, too, was Bobby, who sought to contain the cause of civil rights as much as to advance it.

In February 1963, the administration sent its first civil rights bill up to Capitol Hill. The bill contained a feeble array of token measures that were abandoned almost as soon as it arrived. The president also rejected the proposal made by Martin Luther King and other civil rights leaders to issue a second emancipation proclamation on the 100th anniversary of the first, declaring segregation a violation of human rights. Instead Kennedy threw a party at the White House for one thousand black and civil rights leaders. It was a huge success and dominated African-American media for weeks. The pictures of Harry Belafonte, Lena Horne, and Roy Wilkins celebrating in the White House conveyed an impression that no proposed law could — namely, that blacks were making it. Some black leaders, such as Harvard professor Bayard Rustin, wanted none of it. He charged that the president was a smart, two-faced politician busy getting it both ways. According to Rustin, Kennedy would say to Negro leaders, "I want to help you get money so Negroes can vote," and then be someone who "turns and bows to the Dixiecrats and gives them southern racist judges who make certain that the money the Negro gets will not achieve its purpose."

There was truth to this. By deferring to Judiciary Committee chairman James O. Eastland on federal judicial appointments, Kennedy permitted racists like William Harold Cox to be appointed to the bench in Mississippi. Although Bobby had pressed Cox in an interview about upholding federal civil rights and had received the answers he wanted, Cox did precisely the opposite when he got on the bench. In voting rights litigation in Mississippi, Cox referred to the plaintiffs in court as a "bunch of niggers."

There were, however, some good appointments: Griffin Bell to the Georgia bench, and the already legendary NAACP attorney Thurgood Marshall to the Federal Court of Appeals (one of eleven black judges appointed). But this was institutional progress, not racial change.

It wasn't just a case of appeasing the Dixiecrats. Federal efforts on voting rights for blacks, educational investment, and fair housing were all hostage to state and local governments. Since Reconstruction, these entities had perfected a system of apartheid in which federal money and administrative attention was diverted into the hands of corrupt and conniving local white officials. When blacks were threatened or beaten or shot, local law enforcement would look the other way, or if necessary impanel racist juries. In the major southern cities, FBI offices were deeply infected by racist preferences and practices and could be counted on to side with the locals. After all, the ultimate G-man himself, J. Edgar Hoover, believed that blacks had smaller brains than whites.

The president's own thinking was slowly changing. Prior to the Oxford race riot Jack had regarded Reconstruction as a "black nightmare." "No state suffered more from carpetbag rule than Mississippi," he had written.[42] At one Hickory Hill seminar, which was held in the White House because Bobby was in Asia, historian David Donald found that the president had not progressed very far in his concept of the postwar South.[43] But Oxford had opened the president's eyes to the incontinent fury of southern officeholders, their crude rhetorical replay of the War Between the States, and what he regarded as minimal compliance with a federal court order. On the night of the Oxford riot, Jack had asked Bobby if there would be "any more like this one coming up soon." Bobby replied that a lawsuit to desegregate the University of Alabama was already in the works and would reach the enforcement stage sometime in the spring of 1963. "Let's be ready," the president said.

In February 1963, Reverend King huddled with his advisors to plan a campaign in Birmingham. The plan was to organize sit-ins at segregated lunch counters and to boycott Jim Crow businesses. It was called Operation C, the C standing for confrontation.[44] Birmingham, Alabama's largest city, had possibly the worst history of racism in the South. In 1956, singer Nat King Cole had been beaten on stage during a concert. On Labor Day 1957, a carload of drunken whites had grabbed a black man off a street corner, taken him to a country shack, and castrated him. In May 1961, Reverend King and the Freedom Riders had come close to losing their lives at the hands of a howling mob of Klansmen. King and his deputy Ralph Abernathy put out the word and traveled the country, raising money for the expected bail of the jailed protesters. The attorney general tried to stop the protest. Kennedy's redoubtable deputy Burke Marshall made a personal appeal to King to leave Birmingham, at least until the newly elected mayor, Albert Boutwell, a moderate segregationist, took office. King refused.

On April 6, 1963, the Southern Christian Leadership Conference began its demonstrations and sit-ins. Theophilus Eugene "Bull" Connor, Birmingham's commissioner of public safety, moved immediately on the demonstrators, using nightsticks and paddy wagons to get them off the streets. After two days of violence, Alabama circuit court judge W. A. Jenkins Jr. issued a court order enjoining 133 civil rights leaders from continuing the protests. In Room 30 of the Gaston Hotel, which was serving as the SCLC's headquarters, there was uncertainty. Reverend King was supposed to subject himself to arrest on Good Friday, April 12. But the jails were full, the SCLC was out of money for bail, and there was the threat of increased violence by the Birmingham police. King went into his bedroom alone. When he emerged, he told his staff: "Look, I don't know what to do. I just know something has to change in Birmingham. I don't know whether I can raise money to get people out of jail. I do know that I can go into jail with them."[45] The next day, King went out into the street and was arrested before a crowd of press. Eight white clergymen in Birmingham took out a full-page ad denouncing King, who composed his reply on toilet paper and in the margins of the local newspaper. "For years now, I have heard the word 'Wait.' It rings in the ears of every Negro with piercing familiarity. This 'Wait' has almost always meant 'Never.' "[46]

The Kennedys meanwhile were dealing with another front in the civil rights war. As Bobby had predicted, Governor George Wallace had announced his refusal to allow two black applicants to be admitted to the Huntsville branch of the University of Alabama. "I'm gonna make race the basis of politics in this state," he told legislators the day he was sworn in as governor, "and I'm gonna make race the basis of politics in this country." Wallace, a former boxer with roundhouse racist rhetoric, was no Barnett. He *wanted* a confrontation.

On April 25, Bobby flew down to Montgomery with Burke Marshall and Ed Guthman to meet Wallace face to face. They drove up to the capitol, to find six hundred state troopers encircling the building. One trooper took his billy club and jabbed it in the attorney general's stomach. "The point," Kennedy later said, "was to try to show that my life was in danger in coming to Alabama because people hated me so much."[47] Wallace greeted them by turning on a tape recorder and proceeded to try to extract a vow from the attorney general that he would not move federal troops into Alabama. Kennedy stuck to his Ole Miss line about how his duty was to enforce a court order. He tried to get Wallace to join him in a search for a peaceful solution. "I have a responsibility that goes beyond integration or segregation to enforce the law of the land," he told Wallace, "and to insure that court orders are obeyed. As I said yesterday when I was here, I think if you were in my position, you would do the same thing."[48] Wallace didn't think so, and after an hour-long harangue on states' rights, Negro "agitation," etc., the meeting adjourned. The Kennedy style of negotiation was again evident: frame the exchange in terms of the most irreducible matter of principle and common sense and then slowly tighten the screw of federal power.

On May 18, the president made an attempt to court Wallace.

At a Tennessee Valley Authority commemoration ceremony in Muscle Shoals, Alabama, Kennedy rolled a barrel of pork in Wallace's direction. This too brought no progress. During a helicopter ride, the governor firmly rejected Kennedy's complaisant view of Dr. King, who, he told Kennedy, competed with Ralph Abernathy to see "who could go to bed with the most nigger women and white and red women too."

By this time, there were rumors that the Klan was going to harm the imprisoned Reverend King. His wife, Coretta, called the White House to appeal to the president to protect her husband. Bobby returned her call, explaining that the president was with his father, who was ill, and promising to check into the situation. The next day President Kennedy called Mrs. King to tell her that her husband was safe and would call her shortly, which he did. Eight days after his jailing, Reverend King was released. The Birmingham campaign pushed on. On May 2, he sent six thousand Negro schoolchildren, marching and singing, through Birmingham's streets. Bull Connor responded by firing on them with high-pressure hoses whose force sent some of the children flying into parked cars and curbs. Connor arrested 959 children that day. Despite Bobby's plea to stop using children in the protests, King sent two thousand more children into the streets as well as his SCLC followers. This time Connor unleashed his police dogs on the demonstrators in full view of the cameras. The next day, images of snarling and biting dogs tearing at the arms and legs of the protesters appeared all over the country and the world. The effect was devastating.

Fearing a full-blown race riot, the attorney general sent Burke Marshall and Joe Dolan to negotiate a cease-fire between the parties. They found angry divisions within the white community. Race-baiters like Connor, Klan activists, and Governor Wallace wanted more of the same, but Birmingham's white merchants feared their businesses would be ransacked or burned if the violence escalated. Thousands of blacks were now massing in the streets. King was demanding full integration of Birmingham, not just of lunch counters and downtown stores. Burke Marshall, in his subdued, probing way, proved superbly adept in calming things down. With his indefatigably correct demeanor, he jawboned the white merchants and local press into accepting most of King's demands.

Bobby met with a group of Alabama newspaper editors at the White House to urge them, among other things, to drop their demand that King be federally prosecuted: "You have to understand this about Martin Luther King. If he loses his effort to keep the Negroes nonviolent, the result could be disastrous not only in Birmingham but all over the country. Remember, it was King who went around the pool halls and door to door collecting knives. . . . If King loses, worse leaders are going to take his place. Look at the black Muslims."[49]

By May 9, Marshall and Dolan had brokered a deal that provided a measure of desegregation of eating establishments as well as promises to increase black employment. The night after the accord was announced, however, the Ku Klux Klan rallied outside the city, burning crosses and threatening whites who consorted with blacks with bloody reprisal. Two hours later, a bomb blew up the home of Martin Luther King's brother. Then the Gaston Hotel, where King and his key leaders were staying, exploded. Blacks emptied into the streets and began rioting. Hours later, just when the Birmingham police had the rioting fairly contained, state troopers sent by Governor Wallace moved in and began attacking the protesters with rifle butts and clubs. Seven stores were set ablaze by enraged blacks and the battle went on into the night.

The next day, May 12, the attorney general, Katzenbach, and Marshall met at length with the president, Secretary McNamara, and General Wheeler. Bobby described the situation as dangerous — one death and there would be "chaos." He recommended that the administration send in federal troops. The president was not so sure. Wouldn't this just play into Wallace's hands? he wondered. What if the governor, in the name of states' rights, rejected the federal presence and even proposed armed resistance? Jack thought that the idea was to "get the Negroes off the streets" and the "agreement back in place." He thought it preferable to move the troops to bases in the Birmingham area, which would communicate resolve without risking federal-state polarization. The tape recording from that meeting catches the president's exasperated reaction to General Wheeler's suggestion to send a "battle group" to

Birmingham from Fort Benning in Georgia. Kennedy then ordered the general to airlift — "immediately" — troops to Fort McClellan for possible deployment the following day.[50]

The discussion revealed a critical difference between the Kennedy brothers when it came to framing a public statement about the crisis. The president wanted to make an appeal to restore order and get a resolution. The attorney general wanted an appeal to the hearts and minds of Americans. He believed that the president should first point to the "long abuse" blacks had suffered. Circumspection carried the day. The message dwelt on upholding order. Marshall went back down to Birmingham, shuttled between the disputants, and patched the agreement back together. The new mayor and council took their seats with an expression of reconciliation. But not the outgoing mayor of Birmingham: "I hope that every drop of blood that spills [Robert Kennedy] tastes in his throat, and I hope he chokes on it."

Birmingham had shown the world that there was something new in black protest, which for so long had been muted and tentative. The new element was rage. Despite King's blandishments, blacks had struck back in violence. In northern ghettos, Black Muslim leaders like Elijah Muhammed and his fiery disciple Malcolm X struck at the Christian ethos of forgiveness, calling it the expression of white hypocrisy and black delusion. America was a criminal place; black people were its victims. There was a turning as well among black intellectuals, who habitually had consorted with white liberals and now were echoing the despair and calls for violent separatism. Novelist James Baldwin claimed that "for the horrors of the American Negro's life, there has been almost no language."

Bobby not only read of despair and rage among African Americans, he felt it. On a trip to New York City to persuade chain store executives to desegregate voluntarily (during which several of the executives hid downstairs at the Waldorf-Astoria Hotel to avoid being seen discussing civil rights on camera with the attorney general), Bobby dropped by the Kennedy family apartment to meet with fourteen black entertainers, activists, and leaders.[51] The meeting turned into what black psychologist Kenneth Clark called "one of the most violent, emotional verbal assaults and attacks that I had ever witnessed." A young CORE field organizer, Jerome Smith, touched off the explosion by saying he was nauseated by the necessity of having to be in the same room as the attorney general and plead for the rights of Negroes. James Baldwin asked him whether he would take up arms to defend the United States and Smith said no. Kennedy was shocked. He spoke of the administration's civil rights efforts and accomplishments. Kenneth Clark recalled:

> Bobby became more silent and tense, and he sat immobile in the chair. He no longer continued to defend himself. He just sat, and you could see the tension and the pressure building in him. . . . And it went on for about three hours of this kind of searing, emotional interaction and confrontation. The point we were trying to put over was: Look. The Kennedys have a tremendous amount of credit with the American people. This credit must be used by them. You and your brother must use this credit to lead the American people.[52]

Before he left, Kennedy heard privately from Belafonte and Clarence Jones, King's attorney, about the great job the administration had done in Birmingham. Why, Kennedy asked, had they not said this to the others? Because, Belafonte said, the rest would have thought he had "gone over to the other side." Bobby was furious and later disgustedly told Schlesinger, "It was all emotion, hysteria. They stood up and orated. They cursed. Some of them wept and walked out of the room."[53]

But Kennedy had sat through it, and at a basic level it affected him — much as the Alabama state trooper's club to his gut had communicated the hate of white segregationists. Justice William O. Douglas, who had known and observed Bobby from early childhood, had said his central gift was his "unique capacity for growth." But to grow, Bobby had to feel with his hands and see with his eyes and hear with his ears. This process was often jarring, but its effect was deep and telling.

By the summer of 1963, probably more than anyone in the American power structure, Bobby was absorbing the furious emotions, dark fears, and distant waves of longing that made up the political culture of civil rights. He communicated these to Jack, who, however detached, had never lost his ability to learn from his brother. Bobby's message was that there was no easy way out. One day in the summer of 1963, the president concluded his remarks to his cabinet with Blanche of Castile's speech from *King John:*

> The sun's o'ercast with blood; fair day, adieu!
> Which is the side that I must go withal?
> I am with both; each army hath a hand;
> And in their rage, I having hold of both,
> They whirl asunder and dismember me.

The administration had by this time mounted a massive effort to convince business executives in Alabama to pressure their governor to permit two Negro students to register at the University of Alabama in Tuscaloosa. Burke Marshall had distributed a list of 375 business leaders to cabinet members and agency heads, requesting that they telephone anyone they knew on the list. George Wallace broke off contact with the administration, and by early June nobody was really sure what would happen next. Some FBI reports suggested that Wallace would deploy the state police to stop the black students from registering; other reports claimed that Wallace would rhetorically raise the flag of states' rights and "segregation forever" and then beat a tactical retreat. Unlike Ole Miss, the University of Alabama's leadership was fully in favor of a peaceful admission of the students. Bobby stayed in active touch with Dr. Frank A. Rose, an old friend and president of the university. Reports from the university's trustees about Wallace's behavior at their meetings were discouraging. "They always reported that he was crazy, that he was scared; inevitably they'd say he was acting like a raving lunatic," Kennedy recalled.[54]

As registration day drew close, the Kennedys tightened the vice on Wallace. He was informed that the government would federalize the Alabama National Guard and that it would integrate its peacekeeping role with American army troops from Fort Benning. Chief Judge Seyborn H. Lynne of the Northern District of Alabama signed an order commanding Wallace to comply with federal law; in chambers, Lynne let the attorneys for both parties know that violation of the order would result in Wallace's being sentenced to six months in prison.

On June 11, at a little before 11 A.M., Deputy Attorney General Nick Katzenbach got out of his car at the edge of the Tuscaloosa campus and began to make the long walk to the registration building. Following a plan he worked out with Bobby, he left the two black students back in the car. "Dismiss Wallace," Kennedy had said, "as a sort of second-rate figure." Wallace was waiting for him at the entry to the building in front of a bank of TV cameras, a microphone draped around his neck. Katzenbach read the presidential proclamation, advising the governor to cease and desist from obstruction. Wallace then read from his own statement, decrying federal occupation. They remained there for some minutes, Katzenbach repeating his warning and Wallace, at least rhetorically, having none of it. They then both turned away, Wallace into the auditorium and Katzenbach back to the car. The students were then escorted to their dormitory rooms and registered later that afternoon. There was no violence and little disruption. Wallace had done his theatrical bit and raised the tattered flag of segregation. But the Kennedys had outmaneuvered him with a series of flanking actions that made the registration of the students possible.

July 25, 1963

Moscow and Washington, D.C.

Jack Kennedy rarely indulged in open elation, but when Ambassador Averell Harriman called him from Moscow to tell him that Khrushchev would sign the test ban treaty, Kennedy's voice rose. "Good," he said. "Damn good."[55] During ten days of exchanges in Moscow, the president had personally directed the American negotiation, conferring with Harriman on the phone each day, shaping and reshaping the American strategy and reassuring the congressional leaders who had intimated they were opposed to "a secret deal with Khrushchev." On July 25, the treaty was initialed in Moscow. The next evening the president went on television and told the American people, "Yesterday a shaft of light cut through the darkness. . . . This treaty is not the millennium. . . . But it is an important first step — a step toward peace, a step toward reason, a step away from war."

For nearly seven months, Kennedy had tried to find some basis for negotiation. "I am haunted by the feeling that by 1970," he said in March, "unless we are successful, there may be ten nuclear powers instead of four, and by 1975, fifteen or twenty." After receiving Khrushchev's reply in May to his letter outlining the American wish for a test ban treaty, the president had noted wearily, "I am not hopeful. I am not hopeful." But he had persisted and it had paid off. Still, the breakthrough in Moscow would mean nothing unless the Senate ratified the treaty, and to get that Kennedy knew he would have to rally the American people and put his political future on the line. There was, once again, no going back.

Washington columnist Joseph Kraft wrote that JFK's political motto might have been: "No enemies to the right."[56] That might have summarized his first two years in office, but not the final one.

The missile crisis had brought home to him the prospect of mass slaughter if the superpowers failed to change their dangerous game. It had also fortified Kennedy's deep-seated skepticism about the overwrought pretensions of anticommunism. By 1963 he had changed and was willing to take political risks to find peace.[57]

During the Cuban missile crisis, the president had expected the generals and admirals to recommend war, but he had not expected the same conclusion from congressional leaders. Moments before he went on television to announce the "quarantine" of Cuba, he briefed leaders of the House and Senate, who, practically to a man, rejected the idea of a blockade. The chairman of the Senate Armed Services Committee, Senator Richard Russell of Georgia, told Kennedy war was "our destiny": "The time is going to come, Mr. President, when we're going to have to take this step for Berlin and Korea and Washington, D.C., and Winder, Georgia, for the nuclear war. . . . We've got to take a chance somewhere, sometime, if we're going to retain our position as a great world power. . . . A war, our destiny, will hinge on it. But it's coming someday, Mr. President. Will it ever be under more auspicious circumstances?"[58] Kennedy was appalled.

For all the "eyeball-to-eyeball" talk in the wake of the crisis, the deal cut with Khrushchev was a diplomatic compromise. Kennedy and McNamara had kept a tight rein on military movements. The president had allowed several Soviet ships to pass through the blockade to give Khrushchev more time. He had also refused to retaliate against the downing of an American U-2 plane by a Russian surface-to-air missile.[59] Air force general Curtis LeMay was not the only member of the Joint Chiefs disaffected by the "sell-out."[60] In January 1963, after Kennedy had conferred three times with senior advisors about relaunching negotiations to ban nuclear testing, and had approached Prime Minister Harold Macmillan to develop a joint Anglo-American approach to the Soviets, there was a barrage of criticism from both inside and outside the administration about the futility of trusting the Russians. Perhaps to deflect this criticism as much as to protect America's huge strategic lead, the United States resumed testing in the Pacific in April. In true FDR style, the president developed two tracks — one diplomatic disengagement, the other anticommunist retrenchment — to keep his options open.

Nonetheless, the breach between Kennedy and the right wing was widening.

The administration's efforts to reverse the antinationalist tendency of American policy in the Third World began to succeed. In January 1963, the UN's peacekeeping operation in the Congo — the most expensive in United Nations history — came to a successful conclusion when UN units overran secessionist Katanga. Kennedy's determination in the wake of Premier Lumumba's assassination to "keep the Cold War out of the Congo by keeping the UN in the Congo" had finally paid off. The effort, he wrote one of his advisors, had been "extraordinarily difficult" and they were all entitled to "a little sense of pride."[61] Elsewhere in Africa there was evidence the administration had decided to side with African nationalists and not the European colonial powers, despite criticism that such a policy would only strengthen communist subversion. The United States followed through on its commitment to fund the mercurial Kwame Nkrumah's Volta Dam project, strengthened ties with the Algerian revolutionary leadership, and continued to pressure NATO ally Portugal into freeing its African colonies. When Deputy Assistant Secretary of State for African Affairs Wayne Fredericks called Bobby, suggesting he meet Mozambiquan nationalist Eduardo Mondlane at a non-official location, Kennedy instead insisted that Mondlane be brought to his office at Justice. Mondlane thereafter received covert support from the United States.[62] "The strongest force in the world is the desire for national independence," President Kennedy remarked to Finnish president Urho K. Kekkonen. "That is why I am eager that the United States back nationalist movements even though it embroils us with our friends in Europe."[63]

The American right wing appraised these accommodations to nationalist reality in terms of treason. No place, it seemed, was so grossly chauvinist in its conception of America as Texas. At a White House luncheon for some of the nation's newspaper publishers, the chairman of the board of the *Dallas Morning News*, E. M. Dealey, a rotund man with green-tinted glasses, called Kennedy a weakling to his face. "We need a man on horseback to lead this nation, and many in Texas and the Southwest think that you are riding Caroline's bicycle." Kennedy confined himself to an icy reply. When the or of the *Dallas Times Herald,* the city's afternoon paper, later wrote the president that Dealey wasn't speaking for all Texans, Kennedy added a postscript to his reply: "I'm sure the people of Dallas are glad when afternoon comes." On a trip to the West, Kennedy decried those who call for "a man on horseback because they do not trust the people. They find treason in our churches, in our highest court, in our treatment of water." Earlier, in Seattle, Kennedy had said that the choice was not simply between "appeasement or war, suicide or surrender, humiliation or holocaust, to be either Red or dead. Let our patriotism be reflected in the creation of confidence in one another, rather than in crusades of suspicion."[64]

If anything, these statements fueled the suspicions of the John Birch Society, the Christian Crusade, and the Minutemen, who loaded their guns and raged about treason. There were no fewer than thirty-four threats against Kennedy's life in Texas from November 1961 to November 1963. When anti-Castro paramilitary organizer Gerry Patrick Hemming visited Texas on a fund-raising mission and briefed the rich men in attendance on his plan to murder Castro, one of them said, "Screw Castro, let's get his boss."

"Who's that?" someone asked.

"Smilin' Jack," was the reply.[65]

Perhaps the most sociopathic of all these brave Texas men were oil billionaire H. L. Hunt and his son Lamar. Shortly before Kennedy arrived in Dallas in the third week of November, H. L. Hunt commented to several people that there was "no way to get these traitors out of government except by shooting them out."[66] Kennedy now had enemies to the right — and he was going to take them on.

Though at times openly angry at the talk of treason, Jack Kennedy was usually philosophical. He attributed the destructive instincts in men as having been "implanted in us growing out of the dust." Arthur Schlesinger was later to describe the source of Kennedy's fatalism as "an acute and anguished sense of the fragility of the membranes of civilization, stretched so thin over a nation so disparate in its composition, so tense in its interior relationships, so cunningly enmeshed in underground fears and antagonisms, so entrapped by history in the ethos of violence."[67] The president feared that the "total victory" patriotism of General LeMay and Senator Goldwater exaggerated the evil of the other side and miscast the capacity of the United States to alter human destiny. It created a psychosis of siege and suspicion. The cruel invective of anticommunism, Kennedy felt, made a nuclear Armageddon a "moral imperative" and excused America in the name of national emergency from addressing the scarred and inhuman corners of its own society.[68] Why is it, he asked Kenny O'Donnell one day, that being a warmonger enables you to be a complete racist?[69]

As the president struggled to get negotiations back on track with the Soviet Union to ban nuclear testing, he came to recognize that the brute logic of hatred could only be broken by an unusual overture for peace. In late May Kennedy told McGeorge Bundy that he wanted to make a major statement on the subject of peace. Sorensen produced a draft and Bundy, Schlesinger, and Carl Kaysen took turns editing it. In the course of a long trip home from Hawaii, where he had addressed American mayors on the subject of civil rights, Kennedy reworked the speech draft. He arrived dead tired at Andrews Air Force Base Monday morning, June 10. He proceeded to the White House to change his clothes and then went directly to the sweltering amphitheater at American University. He was scheduled to give the commencement speech. Sweating in the humid 90-degree heat and struggling again with his aggravated back, he gave what the *Manchester Guardian* called "one of the greatest state papers of American history."

Too many Americans, the president said, regarded peace as impossible and war inevitable. "We need not accept that view. Our problems are manmade — therefore, they can be solved by man." Rivalries between states did not last forever. "[T]he tide of time and events will often bring surprising changes in the relations between nations." Kennedy asked the American people to "reexamine our own attitude — as individuals and as a nation." We ought not to, he said,

> fall into the same trap as the Soviets, not to see only a distorted and desperate view of the other side, not to see conflict as inevitable, accommodation as impossible, and communication as nothing more than an exchange of threats. No government or

social system is so evil that its people must be considered as lacking in virtue. . . . No nation in the history of battle ever suffered more than the Soviet Union suffered in the course of the Second World War. We are both caught up in a vicious and dangerous cycle in which suspicion on one side breeds suspicion on the other, and new weapons beget counterweapons.

Kennedy concluded with a call for a treaty to end nuclear testing. "If we cannot end now all of our differences, at least we can help make the world safe for diversity. For in the final analysis, our most basic common link is that we all inhabit this small planet. We all breathe the same air. We all cherish our children's future. And we are all mortal." Premier Khrushchev later told Harriman that it was the greatest speech by an American president since Roosevelt. On July 2, Soviet-American talks to ban atmospheric testing resumed.

Kennedy had meanwhile traveled to Europe to strengthen Allied relations. Détente with the Russians would only be possible, he believed, if NATO, with its exposed eastern flank, was strong. In late June, following French president de Gaulle's public conclusion that America ultimately would fail to defend Europe and his refusal to support the test ban treaty with the Soviets, the president flew to Europe. In Frankfurt, from the towering chamber of Paulskirche, Kennedy set forth the terms of America's commitment: "The United States will risk its cities to defend yours because we need your freedom to protect ours." The next stop was Berlin, where over a million Germans had turned out to greet him. As Air Force One was taxiing in, the president asked O'Donnell, "What was the proud boast of the Romans? *Civis Romanus sum?* Send Bundy here. He'll know how to say it in German." Bundy came and translated this as *Ich bin ein Berliner,* which Kennedy wrote down and then asked, "Now tell me how to say in German: 'Let them come to Berlin.'" The president was first taken to the Berlin Wall and looked out over the mined and wired no-man's land that had cost the lives of hundreds and the freedom of thousands. The sight seemed to incense him. The wildly emotional reception of the 500,000 Berliners who were packed into the Rudolph Wilde Platz only seemed to fuel this sensation. Kennedy gave one of the greatest speeches of his life, the crowd roaring with each ringing phrase. "We'll never have another day like this one," he remarked after it was over. On the world stage, the president's demeanor and mastery of symbol had never seemed so sure. He was tacking smoothly among the currents of his time, shaping them with his own view of history, his romantic sense of self, and his passion for peace.

The entourage then flew to Ireland, where Kennedy, with his unending store of affectionate satire, teased and charmed his way through a sentimental journey. He made a point of quoting the once-banned James Joyce in a speech in the Dail. When his hosts made perhaps a bit too much of his antecedents in New Ross, Kennedy referred in his remarks to a huge ugly building bearing the sign, Albatross Fertilizer Plant. "If my great-grandfather had not left New Ross," he said, pointing to the building, "I would be working today over there at the Albatross Company." "Shoveling shit," he added in a low voice for those alongside him.

Fortunately for Jack, that particular job in his administration had fallen to Bobby. As the president dined with Prime Minister Macmillan on the evening of June 29, he was interrupted by an urgent call from his brother. The *New York Journal-American* that day carried a story with the headline: HIGH U.S. AIDE IMPLICATED IN V-GIRL SCANDAL. The lead read: "One of the biggest names in American politics — a man who holds a 'very high' elective office —has been injected into Britain's vice-security scandal." The article did not name the individual but it became obvious that it was President Kennedy himself.

At the time, the so-called Profumo Affair, in which the British minister of war, John Profumo, had shared the favor of a prostitute with the Soviet naval attaché in London, was about to bring down the Macmillan government. The problem for President Kennedy was that a woman he had had sex with several times in 1960, an Anglo-Czech prostitute named Maria Novotny, was allegedly linked to a Soviet vice ring at the UN, and kept appearing in the investigation of the Profumo scandal. As Bobby Kennedy moved to batten the hatches, forcing the *Journal-American* to drop the story or face an antitrust suit, Hoover was busy prying them back open. The FBI observed and recorded the attorney general's confrontation with the Hearst newspaper and later independently confirmed the truth of the story via an investigation by its London office.[70]

The president had meanwhile taken the case for the test ban treaty to Capitol Hill. The prospects for passage by the required two-thirds majority looked unlikely. The generals were restless; some were angry. The former chairman of the Joint Chiefs, Admiral Arthur Radford, called the treaty "a dangerous mistake." General LeMay commented that he would have opposed the treaty were it not for the fact that it had already been signed.[71] Senior Southern Democrats like Senator Richard Russell (of "war is our destiny" fame) indicated that they would not support the treaty unless the administration gave ground on its civil rights bill. The attorney general, who was leading the legislative charge on the civil rights bill, let Russell, Fulbright, Ervin, and other senators know privately that there could be no linkage between the issues. The White House formed a bipartisan group of prominent Americans and, under the personal direction of the president, began running TV ads and lobbying individual senators. One by one the senators fell in line. By the middle of September, Larry O'Brien was confident that the administration could muster two-thirds of the senate. On September 24, by a vote of 80 to 19, Jack Kennedy won his greatest legislative victory.

Years later, Ambassador Harriman remembered his visit to Hyannis Port shortly after returning from Moscow, where he had initialed the test ban treaty. The president had been his usual brisk self, looking ahead to the fight on Capitol Hill. As Harriman was leaving, JFK invited him to say hello to his father, who was sitting alone on the porch of his house. As Jack briefly explained to him what Harriman had just achieved, the old man looked sharply at Harriman. How different they were, thought Harriman — the old man a reactionary; his son "a genuine statesman."[72]

August 7, 1963

Boston

Jackie had been through this before. Seven months pregnant. Alone. Her husband off in Europe or working round the clock in Washington. Rumors of his infidelity swirling around them. She had spent most of July on Squaw Island off Cape Cod in a rented oceanfront property. Although she had had serious difficulty in previous pregnancies, she continued to smoke and, according to one account, receive intermittent injections of vitamins and amphetamines from Dr. Max Jacobson.[73]

Behind closed doors, Jackie remained a mercurial character. Exuberant one hour and cold silent the next, she could be wistful and satiric in the same sentence. She had an impressive gift of mimicry — the pious, corny LBJ was but one voice — and off camera would often dress with unkempt abandon. As a public persona, however, her discipline and brilliant self-concept as the ultimate American woman were paying off. Everywhere she went, whether on shopping trips to New York or on state visits to foreign countries, she was drawing big crowds. Jack was the first to see it. Her soigné beauty, the Cassini and Halston dresses, the pillbox hats, and her fabulous sense of scene created an aura for the first couple that was nearly royal. Her talent went well beyond fashion, however. It was she who designed and helped execute the huge, glittering ball for Ayub Khan on the grounds of Mount Vernon, the intimate and elegant dinners for Malraux and Agnelli, as well as the White House performance of Pablo Casals. In 1963 Jack may have been a popular president, but Jackie had emerged as a star.

At Jackie's core was an iron will. She coldly accepted Jack's philandering (even with Pamela Turnure, her press secretary), continued to fox-hunt despite a dangerous fall, and cultivated close and constant friendships with the painter William Walton and Roswell Gilpatric, the deputy secretary of defense. Her love for her husband, despite the bruises and the distances, never failed her. The presidency became their relationship and then their locus of new love. They teased each other constantly. A painting entitled *Arab in Desert Seated on Carpet with Tiger,* which hung in the West Sitting Room of the White House, became an in-joke. On the reverse of the painting was a biblical inscription: "It is better to dwell in the wilderness than with a contentious and angry woman." Jack or Jackie would look knowingly at the painting to make the point.[74] There was no great conversion of her wayward husband to a loyal mate, but Kenny O'Donnell's schedule in 1963 reveals them spending hours alone together in the family quarters in the late afternoon.

That summer was a triumphant time for Jack Kennedy. His civil rights legislation was moving slowly through the Congress, a testament to his tenacious negotiations with its leaders.[75] He had been greeted in Europe as the West's conquering hero, and in early August the Partial Test Ban Treaty was signed in Moscow — a signal victory for the administration. Two days later, the president received word that Jackie had gone into labor. On August 7 she delivered her baby five weeks prematurely at the Otis Air Force Base hospital. Patrick Bouvier Kennedy, as he was christened, immediately developed a lung infection that often afflicts premature infants. At first, the infection was not regarded as serious, and Jack, after flying up from Washington, was able to wheel the baby into Jackie's room. When the infection persisted, Patrick was moved to Children's Hospital in Boston and then to Harvard's School of Public Health when his condition worsened.

The president moved into an empty hospital room at the School of Public Health where the infant was convalescing in a high-pressure oxygen chamber. Jack would sit in a straight high-backed chair just outside the chamber, occasionally getting up to peek through the small porthole window in the door.

On the evening of August 8, Bobby flew up from Washington to join his brother. At around four the next morning, the president was awakened. After thirty-nine hours of life, the child's heart had failed and he had died. Bobby waited with Dave Powers while Jack walked back into his empty hospital room and sat down on the bed and cried for a long time.[76] Then they walked out of the hospital together and flew to Otis Air Force Base, where Jackie was recovering. Bobby again waited outside while Jack went in to see Jackie. As they held each other, she sobbed, "Oh, Jack. There's only one thing I could not bear now — if I ever lost you."[77]

At the funeral mass celebrated by Cardinal Cushing, Jack was disconsolate, crying openly during the service. No one had ever seen him like this. When it was over, he was the last to leave and put his hands around the tiny casket. Cushing walked over to him and whispered, "Come on, Jack, let's go. God is good." Patrick was buried in Brookline, not far from where his father was born.

But this was one tragedy he didn't seem to shake, occasionally talking to Powers in the weeks that followed about his memories of the baby. One Saturday in early October, the president, Powers, and O'Donnell went to Harvard Stadium to watch Harvard play Columbia. Toward the end of the first half, Jack said he wanted to go visit his son's gravesite. Eluding the press, they drove out to the cemetery. The president stood before the grave and looked at the headstone with the inscription KENNEDY on it and said, "He seems so alone here."[78]

September 7, 1963

Havana, Cuba

At a reception at the Brazilian embassy in Havana, Fidel Castro approached AP reporter Dennis Harker to deliver a warning about American "plans to assassinate Cuban leaders." Eyes ablaze, Castro told the startled Harker, "United States leaders should think that if they assist in terrorist plans to eliminate Cuban leaders, they themselves will not be safe."[79] At the same time Castro issued this warning, the Kennedy administration was preparing to launch a secret mission led by UN ambassador Bill Attwood to explore the possibility of coexistence with Castro. President Kennedy's preference for a truce with Castro was finally taking precedence over his brother's preference to eliminate him.

It was, however, too late. The Kennedys had lost control of the murder train in south Florida, and Johnny Rosselli and others were pursuing a new imperative — the killing of a president. The plot to kill Castro and his threatened retaliation would be their cover.

At the beginning of 1963, there were good reasons to terminate the policy of violence against Cuba.[80] The get-Castro approach had failed. Moreover, American nonaggression against Cuba had been a Soviet condition for the withdrawal of nuclear missiles from the island. On January 4, 1963, McGeorge Bundy, reflecting the president's judgment, reported, "There is well nigh universal agreement that Mongoose is at a dead end."[81]

But if this was the prevailing sentiment at the White House and State Department, and even among the upper reaches of the CIA, it did not include the attorney general, who was continuing to plot Castro's undoing. Here was the tribal aspect to Bobby's hubris, based on personal loyalty to the anti-Castro Cubans. His friendship with Enrique Ruiz-Williams and Roberto San Roman brought in its wake a close collaboration with Dr. Manuel Artime, the political chieftain of Brigade 2506. In January, the attorney general invited Artime to join him and his wife on a skiing trip in New Hampshire. Artime thereafter went on a $1,500-per-month CIA retainer and, thanks to a directive from the attorney general, relaunched his movement with ample Agency funding.[82] As a condition for such support, Artime and Ruiz supported the Kennedy plan to integrate the Bay of Pigs veterans into the U.S. armed forces. Nearly half the brigade members signed up for a special army training program at Fort Jackson, South Carolina. Three hundred others, including former 2506 frogman Blas Casares and underground organizer Jorge Recarey, achieved officer rank after completion of the Special Officers' Training Program at Fort Benning, Georgia, in March 1963.[83]

Bobby's role went beyond this entirely constructive move to pacify and professionalize the returned fighters. At the April 18 meeting of the "Standing Group," Kennedy pushed hard for more "sabotage and harassment, plus support of exile groups."[84] He also made commitments to both Artime and Ruiz-Williams to open up new anti-Castro fronts in third countries — Ruiz-Williams's group in the Dominican Republic and Artime's in Nicaragua, under the patronage of the son of Central America's most sanguinary dictator, Anastasio Somoza.[85] By early summer 1963, Luis Somoza was in Miami, meeting with exiled leaders and paramilitaries and discussing his plan to open up a new anti-Castro base from Nicaragua. The FBI reported that Somoza claimed that he had conferred with Secretary of State Dean Rusk in Washington and that he had even spoken by telephone with the president.

On July 15, 1963, *Miami News* Latin America editor Hal Hendrix broke the story under the headline "Backstage with Bobby," detailing Kennedy's role as the architect of the Nicaragua-based front against Castro.[86] Artime's revived movement would prove a complete and corrupt bust, but it would give the Somozas a welcome reprieve from Washington for their extraordinarily (even by Central American standards) brutal regime. It was the hell of good anticommunist intentions.

The president was tired, even disgusted, with the entire scene. After a March NSC meeting that dealt among other things with

Castro's lending military assistance to revolutionary movements outside Cuba, Bobby sent his brother a red-blooded memo urging more action. When there was no reply, Bobby sent a second memo. "Do you think there is any merit to my last memo?" he asked.[87] Again Jack made no reply.

The situation meanwhile among the anti-Castro exiles in south Florida was taking on the character of an undeclared rebellion against the official cease-and-desist policy of the Kennedy administration. On March 18, Alpha 66, with the guidance of the CIA's David Phillips, launched an attack on the island of Isabela de Sagua, wounding twelve Soviet soldiers and damaging the Russian freighter *Lvov*.[88] Later that month, exiled Cuban fighters in Commandos L group blew up and sank the Russian merchantman *Baku* off the coast of Cuba. The Soviet Union delivered an angry protest to the United States. Washington assured Moscow it would control the raids. In a press conference, the president noted that such sorties could renew hostilities between the superpowers if they were not stopped.[89]

His exasperation was not shared by others in Washington. By this time the cause of liberating Cuba from Castro had become the grail of the Republican right. *Life* magazine editorially adopted the cause of the exiles as its own, with photo essays on the raids. Clare Booth Luce, the powerful wife of *Life* publisher Henry R. Luce and herself a former congresswoman and United States ambassador, helped finance an anti-Castro platoon — an action that years later pulled her into the investigation of the conspiracy to kill President Kennedy.[90]

Life's full-throttle opposition to Kennedy "appeasement" was a problem for the administration. Along with *Time*, also published by Luce, it was one of the two or three most influential magazines in the country. In April, the president had invited the publisher and his very political wife to lunch at the White House. The Kennedy charm did nothing to deter or otherwise disarm them. The Luces walked out of the lunch to protest the president's warning to cool it on Cuba.[91]

With the president unwilling or unable to put his foot down, Cuba policy swung from nominal consideration of rapprochement with Castro, to plans to blow the man up as he was scuba-diving.

Early in April of 1963, Washington terminated CIA assistance to the Cuban Revolutionary Council. CRC president Miro Cardona accused the Kennedys of treason. In July, William Donovan negotiated the release of an additional 10,000 imprisoned Americans and anti-Castro Cubans from Cuban jails. Castro let it be known through an interview with ABC's Lisa Howard that some sort of entente with the United States was a possibility. But by this time the Standing Group, the reconstituted interagency task force charged with covert operations, had veered back toward sabotage. Bobby admitted on paper that the United States "must do something against Castro, even though we do not believe our actions would bring him down."[92] On June 19, the president, against his better judgment, acceded to the wishes of Bobby and CIA director John McCone and approved a major program of sabotage, including the bombing of refineries, ports, bridges, and power facilities.

It was a fateful decision for which Bobby must bear most of the responsibility. He wouldn't stop. He continued to talk to members of the exile leadership, as phone logs from the attorney general's papers demonstrate, and he shared their violent antipathy to Castro. Moreover, paramilitary activities continued to fascinate him. Captain Ayers, then serving as a CIA trainer of small-team tactics units, would later describe the attorney general turning up in October 1963 at a top-secret CIA outpost deep in the Everglades. In a clearing of the Waloos Glades Hunting Camp, Kennedy walked out of a Quonset hut and into the light of a campfire, shook Ayer's hand, and wished him well on his mission to blow up Cuban ships.[93]

Within this chaos of policy, paramilitary ventures, and right-wing charges of Kennedy betrayal, certain mafiosi began moving their personnel, or "assets." Although Bobby did not know it, the situation in south Florida among the exiles was white-hot. By April, the Miami Police Intelligence Unit was picking up reports that "all violence hitherto directed toward Castro's Cuba will now be directed toward various governmental agencies in the United States." This included the bombing of federal agencies. On April 18, a flyer signed by "a Texan" was circulating around the Cuban community. It read: "Only through one development will you Cuban patriots ever live again in your homeland as freemen . . . if an inspired Act of God should place in the White House within weeks a Texan known to be a friend of all Latin Americans. Though Johnson must now bow to these crafty and cunning Communist-hatching Jews, yet did an Act of God suddenly elevate him into the top position."[94]

It wasn't just exiled Cubans who were spinning out of control. Bill Harvey, the ZR/RIFLE spymaster Bobby had relieved of his role in the war against Castro, was back in touch with Johnny Rosselli. On February 13, 1963, Harvey and Rosselli had drinks together in Los Angeles. According to Harvey's later testimony, they agreed to put the assassination plotting on hold but leave the bounty on Castro of $150,000 where it was.[95] Under the klieg lights of the Church Committee investigation in 1975, this put a nice final punctuation point to the CIA-Mafia conspiracy, but there is evidence that Harvey's collaboration with Rosselli continued.

In April, Harvey submitted an expense sheet to CIA administrators covering the period April 13 to 21. A hotel receipt indicated that Harvey had paid the bill of a "Mr. John A. Wallston" at a Miami hotel. Rosselli's CIA alias was variously "John A. Ralston" or "John Ralston." The entry also gave the client's address as "56510 Wilshire Boulevard, Los Angeles." Further, Harvey chartered a boat at Islamorada, Florida (Key Largo), which he also charged to the Agency after the fact.[96] With a veritable navy of CIA craft in the vicinity, renting a boat seems a curious choice.

On June 20, Rosselli flew into Dulles airport in Washington and was picked up there by Bill Harvey. The FBI surveilled the two as they drove back into the District, picked up Harvey's wife, and went out to dinner at Tino's Continental Restaurant in northwest Washington. After dinner, Rosselli accompanied the Harveys to their home, where he spent the night.[97]

Harvey was later to characterize the meeting as social, but one old Rosselli retainer, D.C. police inspector Joe Shimon, thought the overnight stay at Harvey's home "unlike Johnny unless, of course, they were doing business."[98] For Harvey the entire encounter was risky and he faced immediate trouble from the CIA brass after the meeting.[99] But from Rosselli's standpoint, the relationship was far more critical. JM/WAVE was a rich source of murderous assets and Harvey was still the key to Rosselli's continued access to them. Under the CIA penumbra, Rosselli could move guns and assassins in relative secrecy. All experienced murderers seek cover. By putting the Agency's fingerprints on operations, the mob could anticipate that the CIA would cooperate in the cover-up.

Twelve years later, in 1975, the Church Committee catalogued Harvey's ZR/RIFLE files and found the dossier of one Harold Meltzer, whom Harvey had described as "a resident of Los Angeles with a long criminal record."[100] What the ZR/RIFLE memo did not say was that Meltzer was a longtime collaborator and sometime shooter for Rosselli.[101] Who, if not Rosselli, would have introduced him and vouched for him to Harvey? It was yet another indication that the alliance between Harvey and Rosselli went far deeper than the one-shot joint venture to kill Castro. What sealed their relationship was a venomous hatred of the Kennedys, and their collaboration in the sensitive art of murder. For all of their differences of style — the pale, rotund Harvey with his lumpy countenance and the tanned, slender Rosselli with his husky sotto voce — these were men with the scent of blood in their nostrils and the taste of killing in their mouths.

Rosselli's old friend Inspector Joe Shimon told the author (and the FBI, shortly after Rosselli's murder) about a "little problem Johnny took to Bill Harvey." One of Rosselli's old flames, the wife of a newspaper publisher, had called him in 1973 to say that her husband had put out a contract on her. Could Rosselli help? According to the story Rosselli told Shimon, he turned to Harvey, who did the job himself. The husband died of a massive (and induced, Rosselli said) heart attack.[102] Whether the story is true or not, here was Rosselli ten years later claiming that he and Bill Harvey were still trafficking in murder.

Beginning in April 1963, the Mafia began arming and organizing the Cuban exile movement to relaunch the anti-Castro cause. But was it Castro the Mafia was really after? In April, Dr. Paulino Sierra Martinez, a Cuban attorney from Chicago known to almost no one in the exile community in Miami, surfaced in south Florida to form a united front called the Junta de Gobierno en Exilio. The tall, dapper Sierra, who taught judo and spoke four languages, was accompanied to Florida by a curious character from Dallas named William Trull, an entertainer known to Texas rightwing millionaires like the Klebergs of the King Ranch. FBI reports reveal clearly that the two men scarcely knew each other and offered conflicting versions of why they had teamed up.[103] In May, the *Miami News* reported in an article titled "Gamblers Pop Out of Exile Grab Bag" that Chicago-based gangsters were behind the government-in-exile move.[104] One of the promoters of a united front meeting in Miami in May was George Franci, a Trafficante asset.

By June the question of whose money and muscle were behind Sierra became clearer when the FBI field office heard reports that gambling interests had offered up to $14 million in exchange for a 50 percent interest in gambling concessions in Cuba post-Fidel.[105] The organization supposedly behind Sierra (which employed him), the Union Tank Car Company of Chicago, had no business interests in Cuba. Still, the company's general counsel William Browder (later head of the Chicago Crime Commission) told FBI agents that although he didn't know who was putting up all the money, it was "considerable" and he was managing it.[106] So what was up?

The answer became obvious in late August, when Sierra went on a shopping spree for weapons that included ordering a two-man submarine from California. Rich Lauchli, a prominent Illinois arms dealer and Minuteman supporter, was one of the vendors.[107] The FBI field office in Chicago spoke with Richard Cain, the talkative Mafia *capo regime* then serving as chief investigator for the sheriff of Cook County and who had earlier been implicated in the 1960–61 attempted Mafia hit on Castro. "Johnny's involved," Cain reported.[108] He also said that Giancana and Humphreys, Ambassador Kennedy's one-time luncheon guests with Rosselli, had been two of four underworld figures who had recently contributed $200,000 to the movement.[109] In addition Sierra started making payments to the raider groups — MAPA, Alpha 66, Commandos L — and giving checks to proven sluggers like Tony Cuesta and Aldo Vera Serafin.[110] There was talk of opening up chapters of the Junta de Gobierno en Exilio in cities like Los Angeles and Dallas. The "Government-in-Exile" was laying a wide network of arms and operatives and accumulating the payroll to go with it. Most of all, from the standpoint of Johnny Rosselli, it was creating an alibi that involved the secret recesses of the United States Government.[111]

On July 31, the FBI, acting on a tip, raided a resort cottage near Lake Pontchartrain, Louisiana, and confiscated more than a ton of dynamite, bomb fuses, striker assemblies, and Nuodex (from which napalm is made). Eleven men were arrested, including Mafia fixer Sam Benton, Rich Lauchli, and several Cuban exiles. Despite the apparent commission of at least three felonies, they were released by the FBI without charges the next day. Someone very powerful in the FBI or CIA had obviously interceded. Later the FBI reported that Michael McLaney, a Meyer Lansky partner in Miami, had supplied the explosives as well as the cottage, which was owned by his brother, William.[112] Whatever the purpose of the cache, the raid did reveal a criminal communion among certain Mafia leaders, Cuban exiles, and the violent right wing — and one the FBI backed off from prosecuting.

By November, the CIA's Chicago office still wasn't sure what was brewing but came close when it reported: "Perhaps his [Sierra's] mysterious backers are providing him with sufficient funds to keep the pot boiling."[113] On November 21 in Chicago, a Cuban exile, Homer Echevarria, commented in a meeting of exile activists that he was about to make an arms purchase "as soon as we take care of Kennedy."

In addition to the Mafia role in spreading guns and exiled activists throughout the country, the Mafia also played a role in the so-called Bayo-Pawley mission, which was launched in June 1963. Shortly after the missile crisis, a letter was delivered to the Cuban exile community claiming that two or perhaps four Soviet army colonels wanted to defect to the United States These officers were said to know the location of Soviet nuclear missiles on the island, missiles that had never been removed by the Soviet Union despite its commitment to do so. The fact that a veteran anti-Castro raider, Eduardo Perez (whose nickname Eddie Bayo derived from the legendary guerrilla general who had trained Fidel and Che in Mexico) was determined to lead a sortie into Cuba to liberate the Russian officers lent a certain weight to this otherwise outrageous claim. Bayo was now an adherent of Alpha 66, the renegade outfit advised by the CIA's David Phillips.

The other instigator of the rescue mission was John V. Martino, a Cuban-American released from a Castro prison in October 1962. Before his arrest he had installed security systems at Mafia casinos in Havana. After returning to Miami, Martino joined up with Rosselli, working out of his hotel in Key Biscayne. Within weeks of coming back, right-wing ghostwriter Nathaniel Weyl received a commission to write the memoir of Martino's three-year incarceration, which was later published under the title *I Was Castro's Prisoner.* Weyl was also assisting multimillionaire William D. Pawley — anti-Castro activist, former ambassador under Eisenhower, and founder of the Flying Tigers — with his memoirs.

After having shilled the project around reactionary circles in Florida, Martino and Bayo pitched the idea to Pawley, who in turn took it to JM/WAVE chief Ted Shackley. Pawley told Shackley that he had gotten a call from the chief counsel to the Senate Internal Subcommittee, Jay Sourwine, promising that chairman James O. Eastland of Mississippi would launch hearings if the Soviet officers were sprung. When Shackley learned from Pawley that Martino was involved, he was not pleased. He called Martino a "lowlife." Shackley nonetheless signed on. The operation was a long shot but, if it panned out, a career maker. It might also serve to rehabilitate Shackley's demoted mentor, Bill Harvey. CIA headquarters at first balked at the proposal, having been sufficiently embarrassed by renegade heroics by the Cuban exiles. Then Senator Eastland telephoned Ambassador Pawley to inform him, incredibly enough, that John Martino, a Mafia operative, had personally briefed him on the mission, called Operation Red Cross. The CIA gave Shackley the go-ahead.

It is possible Rosselli and Martino actually believed in the Bayo-Pawley mission. It is equally possible that they were developing an elaborate alibi for another murderous contingency. On June 4, the day before the mission was to be launched, Martino and Bayo told an astounded Pawley that they had agreed to let *Life* magazine cover the raid in exchange for $15,000. Loren Hall, a Trafficante associate later investigated for his contact with Oswald in Dallas, claimed that the Mafia, not *Life,* had in fact put up the $15,000.[114]

On June 5, Pawley's yacht, the *Flying Tiger II,* towing a smaller craft, set sail for its rendezvous point off the coast of Oriente province. Three days later, Pawley himself, accompanied by the ever-ready Rip Robertson, a *Life* photographer, Bayo, and nine other raiders boarded a CIA flying boat. (Pawley was so suspicious about the intentions of Bayo and his raiders that he locked them in the center cabin during the flight.) Off Baracoa, Cuba, they joined up with the yacht. Robertson passed out a full complement of arms to the fighters before they piled into the 22-foot craft and headed for the Cuban shore. The plan was to meet up with the *Flying Tiger II* two days later with the Soviet officers in hand. But Bayo and his comrades were never heard from again. Station chief Shackley later determined that the Soviet defection story had been cover for a "free-lance strike" by Bayo and the others.[115] A review of Cuban army documents relating to the capture or killing of anti-Castro raiders, research done in June 1997, revealed no record of Bayo.

But the Bayo-Pawley mission fit nicely with Rosselli's later claim that President Kennedy was assassinated by an anti-Castro sniper team sent in to murder Castro, captured by the Cubans, tortured, and redeployed in Dallas. Through the handiwork of Rosselli's assistant, John Martino, the CIA, *Life,* Pawley, and Senator Eastland were all variously implicated.

On September 13, 1963, the *Dallas Morning News* confirmed that President Kennedy would be visiting Dallas on November 21 or 22. Several days later, Jack Ruby began telephoning Mafia and Teamsters Union operatives and hitmen all over the country, and made trips to New Orleans, Miami, and Las Vegas.[116] According to the FBI, during his trip to Miami in early October Ruby met twice at different hotels with Johnny Rosselli.[117] We do not know the nature of their exchange, only that subsequent to the Kennedy assassination, Ruby, a man described by Rosselli himself as "one of our boys," stalked, murdered, and thereby silenced Oswald. This act shines out like a neon sign through the fog of controversy surrounding the president's death. Jack Ruby, a wiseguy in training, had met with no less a figure in the Mafia than Johnny Rosselli, who was still communing with renegade elements of the CIA.

October 26, 1963

Amherst, Massachusetts

In May 1963, the president was invited to attend the October groundbreaking for the Robert Frost Library at Amherst College and accepted the invitation. He subsequently asked special assistant Arthur Schlesinger to prepare a draft on the theme of poetry and power that Frost had raised at the Inaugural. The president repeated one of Frost's lines to Schlesinger: "'I am one acquainted with the night.' What a terrific line."[118]

For most of their acquaintanceship, the relationship between the poet and the president had developed into an affectionate joust. Frost had come to the White House on four occasions (enjoining Kennedy at one point to "be more Irish than Harvard") and been awarded the Presidential Medal on his eighty-eighth birthday. Frost and fellow poet Archibald MacLeish strongly urged the attorney general to push for the release of Ezra Pound from an Italian prison.[119]

In September 1962 the relationship had soured. Frost, returning from a trip to the Soviet Union during which he had seen Khrushchev, got off the plane in New York and told the press that the Soviet leader thought Kennedy "too liberal to fight." The next day the quote was featured on the front pages of the nation's newspapers. Kennedy was stung. "Why did he have to say that?" he asked Interior Secretary Stewart Udall.[120] All went silent until the old man died the following January. Udall would later write that the trip to Amherst in October may have been an atonement of sorts on Kennedy's part for not reaching out at the end. "We just didn't know he was so ill," Jack said to Frost's secretary, Kay Morrison.[121]

Joining the president on Air Force One that Saturday morning were Udall, Schlesinger, and James Reed, an Amherst graduate and

274

Jack's former PT-109 buddy, who was then serving at Treasury. Udall told the president that he feared a woman he knew who was fanatically anti-Kennedy might appear and try to disrupt the ceremony. "So if you see me in the crowd struggling with a woman and rolling on the ground, you will know what is going on," he told the president. "In any case, Stewart," Kennedy replied, "we'll give you the benefit of the doubt."[122] They landed at Westover Air Force Base outside of Springfield, Massachusetts. Their motorcade to Amherst wound through the Berkshires, swathed in gold and auburn at the height of Indian summer. At one point they passed by the Amherst hillside where Emily Dickinson had lived out her brief life.[123]

Kennedy by this time had reworked Schlesinger's text, sharpening it and adding phrases of his own.[124] At the ceremony, Archibald MacLeish welcomed the president as one who had "lived half a biblical lifetime" in the "soft, lovely hills" of western Massachusetts. He described Frost in terms of one who had a "lovers' quarrel with the world" — as a poet who "made his finest music out of manhood." MacLeish likened Frost to Oedipus, King of Athens:

> We do not live, I know, in Athens. We live now in an insignificant, remote small suburb of the universe. . . . Homer's heroic world, where men could face their destinies and die, becomes to us, with our more comprehensive information, the absurd world of Sartre, where men can only die. And yet, though all the facts are changed, nothing has changed in fact: we still live lives. And lives still lead to death. And those who live a life that leads to death still need the gift that Oedipus gave to Athens — the gift of self, of beaten self, of wandering, defeated, exiled self that can survive, endure, turn upon the dark pursuers, face its unintelligible destiny with blinded eyes and make a meaning of it: self, above all else, without self-pity.[125]

Kennedy was clearly moved by MacLeish's words and warmly shook his hand. John J. McCloy, president of Chase Manhattan Bank, then introduced the president. Kennedy described Frost as preeminently two things: "an artist and an American":

> A nation reveals itself, not only by the men it produces, but by the men it honors. . . . The men who create power make an

indispensable contribution to a nation's greatness. But the men who question power make a contribution that is just as indispensable — for they determine whether we use power or power uses us. Our national strength matters — but the spirit which informs and controls our strength matters just as much. This was the special significance of Robert Frost. . . . His sense of the human tragedy fortified him against the self-deception and cheap consolation. "I have been," he wrote, "one acquainted with the night."

It is hardly an accident that Frost coupled poetry and power; for he saw poetry as the means of saving power from itself. When power leads a man toward arrogance, poetry reminds him of his limitations. When power narrows the area of man's concern, poetry reminds him of the richness and diversity of his existence. Where power corrupts — poetry cleanses.[126]

Back in Washington the "corruptive" quality of power seemed especially in evidence on that very day. A front-page story in the *Des Moines Register* alleged that certain "prominent New Frontiersmen" had availed themselves of the sexual services of Ellen Rometsch, a beautiful refugee from East Germany who had been deported in August 1963 amid rumors of compromising dalliances, including several with the president. The article, written by Bobby's old friend Clark Mollenhoff, raised the FBI concern that "her activity might be connected with espionage." Bobby tried to close the breach by spiking the source of the story — the FBI — to prevent it from being republished in other papers. When that failed, he dispatched his old McClellan Committee lieutenant LaVerne Duffy to Germany to convince Ms. Rometsch to close her mouth. But Senator John Williams of Delaware now had the account and, according to the *Register* article, was planning to bring it before the Senate Rules Committee the following Tuesday.[127] The administration was now in real danger.

What had prompted Hoover to move from his normal mode of blackmail to open political assault? Bobby's intimation that the FBI director would be retired in Jack's second term was undoubtedly one stimulus. Another could well have been Bobby's interest in exposing the corruption of his other enemy, Lyndon Johnson. Thanks to an impending Senate investigation of Johnson's former aide

Bobby Baker — the so-called 101st senator — on charges of corruption, the vice president's own career was now on the firing line.

Bobby later denied that he had ever targeted the vice president or Bobby Baker, but he said this in 1964, when he was trying to co-exist with Johnson. Given Johnson's nearly pathological level of paranoia, it's possible he imagined that the attorney general was gunning for him when in fact he wasn't. Whatever the case, in October 1963, Johnson felt he had cause to counterattack. On October 18, longtime Johnson protégé Fred Korth, who had taken John Connally's place as navy secretary, was forced to resign. The Justice Department had revealed "indiscreet use" of navy stationery by Korth but Korth's misdeeds definitely went beyond this.[128] Bobby Kennedy's former boss Senator John McClellan was threatening to hold Senate hearings on Korth's conflict of interest with regard to the development of a new fighter, the TFX, by Texas-based General Dynamics.[129] Further, there were reports of secret payoffs (which Donald Reynolds, one of Bobby Baker's associates, later told the Congress amounted to $100,000) to get the contract.[130] The vice president, with the support of Secretary McNamara, appealed to the president to keep Korth, but the attorney general prevailed. Within days of Korth's resignation, the hearings to investigate Baker were scheduled. The problem for Vice President Johnson — and Texas governor Connally — was that if Baker were drawn and quartered over his ties to the Mafia and Texas oil interests they both might go down with him.

Declassified FBI files from the period reveal that certain Texas interests had been busy accumulating dirt on President Kennedy. According to a top-secret FBI document, two men broke into Judy Campbell's apartment in August 1962.[131] One of the men, according to the account, bore "an identical resemblance" to the son of former FBI Special Agent I. B. Hale, who was then in charge of security for General Dynamics (the would-be manufacturer of the TFX) and indeed had driven away in a Chevrolet Corvette registered to I. B. Hale. Hale's son Bobby had been married to John Connally's daughter, a marriage that had come to an end when Connally's daughter died from a shotgun blast to her head. A Texas grand jury had exonerated Hale of any complicity in what it ruled was a suicide.

Whether or not Johnson or Connally had any foreknowledge about the break-in is unknown. From the files it is evident that Hoover was pushing his Los Angeles office hard to link Campbell in some documented way (checks, expense receipts) to the president and to her friend "West Coast hoodlum" Johnny Rosselli. On November 4, for example, a memo to Hoover from his Special Investigation Division informed him that Judy Campbell was back in "telephonic contact" with the president's secretary, Evelyn Lincoln, as well as with Rosselli and Giancana.[132] The information was apparently derived from an FBI bug.

For the Kennedys, the time had come for an emergency ceasefire with their enemies — starting with J. Edgar Hoover. According to Anthony Summers, the attorney general placed an early morning call to the FBI director at his home on Monday, October 28. The idea, as Bobby later admitted, was to protect his brother by confronting senators and congressmen with FBI surveillance of their own sexual escapades: "I put together the information regarding all the girls and the members of Congress and the Senate who had been associated with the girls — and it got to be large numbers in both ways," he told Anthony Lewis.[133] The president approved of the plan, but it was Hoover who made it stick. In a secret meeting in Senate Majority Leader Mike Mansfield's apartment at noon that day, Hoover briefed both Mansfield and Senate Minority Leader Everett Dirksen on the extent of his evidence of Capitol Hill philandering. That put a lid on it. There was no more private discussion, much less public debate, of the Rometsch affair by the "world's greatest deliberative body." But Hoover had a high price for his service: assurance from both the attorney general and the president (with whom he lunched on October 31) that he would be confirmed in his position as director. Further, he exacted from Bobby approval for four new wiretaps on Martin Luther King Jr., a man both Kennedys, but particularly Bobby, had come to admire and respect.[134]

At precisely the same time as the Kennedys were mounting this ugly little rearguard action, they were desperately trying to manage a battle among senior policymakers over what to do in Vietnam. After nearly three years of advising and arming South Vietnam's Ngo Dinh Diem — and increasing the number of American advisors from 685, which was what it was when Kennedy took office in 1961, to 16,732 by October 1963 — the administration was considering abandoning him. Diem had failed to take the fight to the Communist Viet Cong and instead had allowed his brother-in-law, Ngo Dinh Nhu, to harass and murder Buddhist monks protesting his rule. Throughout the summer and fall of 1963, the debate of what to do about Diem — to discipline him or to effect his removal — turned bitter. On August 24, a top-secret cable (cleared by the president) was sent to Ambassador Henry Cabot Lodge, giving a green light to the generals plotting Diem's elimination. The cable had not been cleared, despite what the president apparently thought, with Secretary McNamara or General Taylor, much less with Vice President Johnson (who was fond of Diem). They all remonstrated furiously at the next meeting against the pro-coup trio of Ambassador Harriman, Under Secretary Ball, and Assistant Secretary of State Hilsman.[135] "My God," the president said to Charles Bartlett at one point, "my government's coming apart."[136] It was time to bring in Bobby.

Bobby initially sided with those who wanted Diem gone. "If we have concluded that we are going to lose Diem, why do we not grasp the nettle now?" he asked. Later he seemed to abide the president's view that a phased withdrawal from Vietnam and a Laos-like political solution was the way to go. Diem, if he survived, could be counted on to push the United States out. At the September 6 National Security Council meeting, Bobby openly spoke of withdrawal: "The first question was whether a Communist takeover could be successfully resisted with any government," he wrote later. "If it could not, now was the time to get out of Vietnam entirely, rather than waiting."[137] The president himself had expressed a similar sentiment in April 1962 when he told his aides to "seize upon any favorable moment to reduce our involvement" in Vietnam.[138]

However, in the view of the Kennedys in 1963, this could not be attempted before they won a second term. Truman had lost his presidency over the "loss of China," which in turn had touched off the anticommunist witch hunts by Senator Joseph McCarthy. Troubled as Kennedy was about slipping into an Asian land war, he temporized on the method of disengagement. He wanted out, but ı't know how to get out. And so he kept two policy tracks open — one military, the other political. In this instance, Dean Acheson's essential criticism of JFK seems apt: he avoided decision.[139] The preference to "keep options open" put events — not decisions — "in the saddle," as George Ball later wrote.[140]

But beyond all questions of the president's indecision regarding Diem was the greater strategic dilemma inherent in anticommunist containment. As General Douglas MacArthur had told the president in April 1961, "The chickens are coming home to roost and you are in the chicken coop." The meaning behind the metaphor, which Kennedy repeated to his generals and policymakers, was that try as the president might, and should, to avoid an Asian land war, the consequences of a decade of anticommunist drum-beating made disengagement extremely difficult. Walter Lippmann had made the same point shortly after Truman enunciated the policy of containment in February 1947. It could only be attempted by "recruiting, subsidizing, and directing a heterogeneous array of satellites, dependents, puppets which will be prey to internal insurrection that they will beseech the United States to quell in the name of anticommunism. Confronted with such demands, the United States will have to abandon its puppets, which will be tantamount to appeasement, or support them at an incalculable cost with an unforeseen issue."[141] As Bobby put it in an interview in 1964, "Diem was corrupt and a bad leader. It would have been much better that we didn't have him. But we inherited him . . . so what do you do?"[142]

Kennedy's Vietnam policy drifted. Toward September, under pressure from the American mission in Saigon, the president veered uncertainly toward a decision about Diem: the United States would diplomatically wash its hands of any responsibility for Diem's fate, silently countenancing his removal by the plotting generals. Early in the morning of November 2, the generals moved, overthrowing the regime and murdering Diem. General Taylor was in the room when Kennedy received word. "[The president] leaped to his feet and rushed from the room with a look of shock and dismay on his face which I had never seen before."[143] The reaction seemed reminiscent of Kennedy's horror at receiving the news of Lumumba's murder in February 1961.[144] The difference was that with Lumumba it was regret; with Diem, guilt. The unease the president had so strongly felt about killing Castro — "If we get into that kind of thing, we'll all be targets"— was turning into a darker premonition. He had not stopped capital murder as an instrument of the state. This was not the America he had promised at Amherst — "an America . . . of moral restraint . . . which commands respect throughout the world not only for its strength but for its civilization as well."

National Security Council staffer Samuel E. Belk III remembered a foreign policy exchange that took place that fall in the Rose Garden. He, Bundy, and six others sat on folding chairs in the late morning sun while Jackie Kennedy exercised a horse nearby. The briefing drifted on — Vietnam, the Congo, Soviet relations. Suddenly, five-year-old Caroline appeared and approached her father, saying that she wanted to tell him something. He told her to go watch her mother ride. She persisted. With a smile her father said, "Go ahead." She began to recite a verse, looking directly at him:

> It may be that he will take me by the hand
> And lead me into his dark land
> And close my eyes and quench my breath —
> It may be I shall pass him still.
> I have a rendezvous with death. . . .
> At midnight in some flaming town,
> When spring trips north again this year,
> And I to my pledged word am true,
> I shall not fail that rendezvous.

Jack smiled. It was the same verse by Alan Seeger he had recited for Jackie after they returned from their honeymoon and Jackie, in turn, had learned it by heart to recite it to him.[145] Belk recalled how momentarily mystified, even shocked, the rest of them were. It was if there was "an inner music" he was trying to teach her.[146] Perhaps, as well, this was a part of poetry's "cleansing" powers he had spoken of on that October day in Amherst.

November 17 – 20, 1963

Palm Beach, Florida; Washington, D.C.; Havana, Cuba

Despite the dark turn of events in Vietnam and his near-miss in the Capitol Hill sex scandal, Jack remained serene. He spent the last weekend of his life in Florida, at his father's house in Palm Beach. With him were his best friends Dave Powers and Torbert Macdonald, his former Harvard roommate and now a U.S. congressman.[147] Aside from a trip to Cape Canaveral to watch the firing of a Polaris missile, they spent the weekend hanging around the house and watching football games on television. Powers recalled how relaxed Jack was, almost grateful to be a loafer.[148] Jack bet on Navy in its game with Duke, giving Powers and Macdonald ten points. Navy won 38 to 25 on the passing and running of Roger Staubach, and Jack immediately collected. Sunday he bet on the Bears over Green Bay and won again. That evening the three watched a private screening of the movie *Tom Jones*, with Albert Finney, Susanna York, and lots of amorous rampage. Jack of course loved it. Before going to bed, he sang a song in his uneven voice:

> Oh it's a long long while from May to December
> But the days grow short when you reach September
> When autumn weather turns the leaves to flame
> One hasn't got time for the waiting game.
>
> Oh, the days dwindle down to a precious few
> September, November!
> And these precious days I'll spend with you
> These precious days I'll spend with you.

As serene as Jack may have been, Bobby continued to place himself at the storm's center. As his brother's enforcer on Capitol Hill and the scourge of White House journalists deemed "un-

282

friendly," Bobby thought the administration's enemies had never seemed so numerous or open in their contempt. In August 1963, *Look* writer Fletcher Knebel, an erstwhile ally of the administration, did a harsh portrait of the hectoring style with which the Kennedys handled the press, a style that included threats of legal action and going over reporters' heads to bring them in line.[149] Bobby served as the point man on other apparently minor matters as well. On November 4, the attorney general had received a letter from Byron Skelton, the Democratic national committeeman in Texas, who was a leading attorney in the state and a strong Kennedy ally. Skelton wrote bluntly that the president's safety would be compromised if he went to Dallas. Skelton copied the letter to Walter Jenkins of Vice President Johnson's staff and then flew to Washington to press his case. Bobby Kennedy reacted strongly enough to the letter to forward it to O'Donnell on November 8.

The president himself sensed the trip would be ugly. In early November he told two of his aides that he wished he could cancel it. A month earlier, Ambassador Adlai Stevenson had been spat and set upon in Dallas by a right-wing rabbler after a speech about the United Nations. ("I believe in the forgiveness of sin and the redemption of ignorance," Stevenson had observed as he wiped the spit from his face.) In the weeks before departure, when the trip to Texas was in its final scheduling phase, there were repeated appeals to cancel the visit to Dallas. During a flight to Little Rock, Senator J. William Fulbright plaintively advised the president that Dallas was "a very dangerous place. I wouldn't go there. Don't *you* go." Reverend Billy Graham, through an intermediary, attempted to convey the same message, as did Texas tycoon Stanley Marcus.[150]

Politically, however, Kennedy had no choice. He had won Texas narrowly in the 1960 election — by no more than 46,233 votes — even with favorite son Lyndon Johnson on the ballot. In the 1964 contest, Texas promised to be anything but a political given for the president. For one thing Johnson had become a forgotten figure in the state; for another Kennedy's stand on civil rights had roused Dixiecrat disaffection; and third, there was a highly public dispute between the two leading Democrats in the state — Governor John Connally, a conservative, and Senator Ralph Yarborough, a liberal.

On Monday, November 18, the last week of the trial to deport Carlos Marcello for good began. Bobby was monitoring it closely. Marcello had spent that weekend at Churchill Farms closeted with Lee Harvey Oswald's associate and Cuban exile activist David Ferrie.[151] Ostensibly, the two were discussing defense strategy for Marcello's final week in federal court. Strangely, Marcello's attorneys were not present. Meanwhile, Jack Ruby continued to make calls all over the United States — to Mafia and Teamsters Union henchmen such as Barney Baker (recently released from federal prison), Lenny Patrick, Irwin S. Weiner (of the Chicago Outfit), Alex Gruber, and others who had "worked closely" with Johnny Rosselli.[152]

During the weekend of November 17–18, Rosselli flew to Phoenix. He booked the flight in his own name, something unusual for him. He normally bought his ticket in cash and boarded the plane at the last minute, which kept his name off flight manifests. He also booked reservations in his name at the Phoenix resort known as Mountain Shadows for himself and his rich friend Maury Friedman. They were accompanied by two women, Dina Stephens and Arlene Miller, whom the FBI described as call girls (another uncharacteristic practice for Rosselli, who habitually traveled solo). The FBI also learned that Rosselli was on his way to Washington to see a congressman.[153] All these shreds of fleece left on FBI hedges suggest that Rosselli was developing an alibi. The two couples arrived in Phoenix on November 16 and were immediately tailed by four FBI agents. They described in detail the sartorial getup of Rosselli — now famous in FBI circles as the Mafia's glass of fashion and mold of form: "blue pants, light blue shirt, black sweater, black shoes, dark glasses."

Although the hotel operator at Mountain Shadows had been instructed by the FBI to take note of all incoming or outgoing calls, she only took down one: a call to Los Angeles November 17 at 3:05 A.M. On November 18, Rosselli, apparently canceling his plans to go to Washington, left instead for Las Vegas, where he could make calls and conduct meetings free from FBI surveillance. He checked into a hotel he had helped develop, the New Frontier.

Back in Washington the president moved through his appointments. On Tuesday, November 19, William Mahoney, United States ambassador to Ghana and former Kennedy campaign leader in Arizona, dropped by to see the president. Mahoney had been appointed to handle the vagaries — if this were possible — of Ghana's nonaligned leader, Kwame Nkrumah, a task of particular interest to Kennedy since he had authorized over $150 million in loans and loan guarantees to build Ghana's Volta Dam. The conversation soon turned to the president's dramatic statement on civil rights, which had drawn singular acclaim in black Africa. Kennedy expressed worry over what effect his position on civil rights would have on his reelection prospects. He got up from his rocking chair to show Mahoney poll results from swing precincts in Iowa, where white voters had now turned against him. He asked Mahoney to come home for the 1964 campaign against the probable Republican nominee, Arizona senator Barry M. Goldwater. The president then mentioned another initiative he was contemplating — the recognition of Red China. He told the ambassador that Assistant Secretary of State Roger Hilsman was raising a trial balloon of sorts in a speech about China to the Commonwealth Club of San Francisco. As they parted, Kennedy mentioned his upcoming trip to Texas. Jackie was accompanying him, he told Mahoney. "And she's going all the way with me in '64," he added with a smile.

To 1960 campaign veterans like Mahoney, news that Jackie Kennedy was rallying to her husband's political side was welcome. It suggested that a reconciliation between the two had occurred. Jack's idea to send Jackie on a cruise aboard Aristotle Onassis's yacht in October to take her mind off the loss of their child had worked. She had returned, according to Ben Bradlee, "with stars in her eyes —Greek stars." Jack asked her to join him on a political swing through Texas. "Sure I will, Jack," she had said. "I'll campaign with you anywhere you want." Flipping open her appointment book, she wrote "Texas" across November 21, 22, and 23.[154]

That same Tuesday, November 19, the attorney general called Kenny O'Donnell to see if he could squeeze CIA deputy director Richard Helms into the president's schedule. The CIA was claiming that it had hard evidence of Castro's attempt to overthrow the government of Venezuela. A half hour later, Helms and Bobby Kennedy walked into the Oval Office carrying a submachine gun. On the stock of the gun, which had been recovered from an arms cache in Venezuela, was the official seal of Cuba. Helms apologized for bringing such a "mean-looking weapon" into the president's office. "Yes, it gives me a feeling of confidence," was Jack's's sarcastic reply.[155]

At the time, the president was considering the prospect of a modus vivendi with Castro, and a key condition from the American standpoint was the cessation of all subversive Cuban activities in Latin America. Helms's visit was meant to torpedo any notion of entente. Moreover, within days of a discussion designed to start a negotiated solution between Ambassador William Attwood and the Cuban ambassador to the United Nations, Carlos Lechuga, the CIA's operational wing (DDP) launched a new operation to murder Castro.

Rolando Cubela Secades, a hero of the Castro revolution and an official in the Castro regime, told CIA officers in Brazil in September 1963 that he could perform "an inside job" on Castro's life. His conditions were that the Americans supply the weapons and that he meet personally with Robert Kennedy. Cubela's wide-open approach and his apparent freedom to travel raised suspicions that he was operating under orders from Castro. Furthermore, Cubela was an alcoholic, usually drunk by nine and verbally incontinent thereafter. Nevertheless, Helms authorized a meeting between his deputy Desmond Fitzgerald, masquerading as Robert Kennedy's "personal representative," and Cubela to take place in Paris at the end of October. Helms later conceded in testimony before the Church Committee that he had never sought or received the attorney general's approval, much less that of his own director.[156] It was an extraordinary stretch for a career spymaster. Cubela (code-named AMLASH) and Fitzgerald met — with CIA case officer Nestor Sanchez doing the translating — on October 29. They discussed Cubela's plan to kill Castro. Fitzgerald promised to supply the arms. They arranged for a second meeting on November 22.[157] In an interview conducted in Havana in May 1997, National Assembly president Ricardo Alarcon allowed that Cubela may have been a Castro plant.[158] At the very time the Kennedy administration was considering normalizing relations with the Castro regime, certain CIA officials were assiduously undermining that possibility. In their incompetence, they had allowed themselves to be set up by Castro, a man whom they regarded as a Latin hysteric.

President Kennedy was meanwhile using a back channel to communicate with Castro. Ben Bradlee of *Newsweek* had encouraged Kennedy to have a conversation with the French journalist Jean Daniel before Daniel's trip to Havana. The two sat down in late afternoon of October 24. It was evident from the start that the president wanted to use Daniel as a conduit to Castro. Kennedy told Daniel that he "understood the Cubans. I approved the proclamation which Fidel Castro made in the Sierra Maestra. . . . I will go even further: to some extent it is as though Batista was the incarnation of a number of sins on the part of the United States. Now we shall have to pay for those sins." The problem, Kennedy said, was that Castro had betrayed his promises and agreed to become "a Soviet agent in Latin America." This the United States would not accept, nor his intrusion into the affairs of other countries. Kennedy encouraged Daniel to give him a report on his return from Cuba. "Castro's reactions interest me."[159]

Three weeks later Daniel met with Castro, talking until four in the morning in Daniel's Havana hotel room. Daniel later described Castro as listening with "devouring and passionate interest," stroking his beard, "making me the target of a thousand malicious sparks cast by his deep-sunk lively eyes." He made Daniel repeat three times Kennedy's indictment of Batista and then labeled Kennedy "a realist" and "an intimate enemy." "Personally, I consider him to be responsible for everything," Castro continued, "but I will say this: he has come to understand many things over the past few months."

The day before the president was to leave for Texas, two police officers in downtown Dallas drove though Dealey Plaza on patrol. They noticed several men standing behind a wooden fence on a grassy knoll on one side of the plaza, engaged in what looked to be "target practice" with rifles. When the officers approached the men, they hastened away. The Dallas police gave the officers' report to the FBI, which, in turn, issued its own report of the incident on November 26, 1963. The FBI report was never part of the Warren Commission's investigation. It resurfaced as a result of a Freedom of Information Act request in 1978.[160]

On Wednesday evening, November 20, there was the annual judiciary reception in the East Room, and afterward a birthday party for Bobby, his thirty-eighth, at Hickory Hill. Earlier that day, staff members at Justice had thrown a party for their boss and had given him a joke gift — a Monopoly board game with spaces altered to read with things like "Land on White House." Kennedy was clearly anxious to move on and had even begun to refer to his tenure as attorney general in the past tense.[161] The surprise party was "miserable," in the words of his deputy John Douglas. Bobby was in a bad mood. He stood up on his desk and delivered a sarcastic toast to himself for having assured the president's reelection with all of his "popular actions"— civil rights, wiretapping, Hoffa.

After the reception, Bobby went upstairs to talk to Jackie. Jack joined them. They chatted briefly about the trip to Texas before Ethel came up to remind him of his own party that evening at Hickory Hill. Perhaps because Jackie was there, Bobby did not convey his concern to Jack about the letter Byron Skelton had sent urging him to convince the president to avoid Dallas. The fact that Bobby immediately raised this subject with Kenny O'Donnell at the birthday party at Hickory Hill later that evening reveals that it was very much on his mind. O'Donnell replied that showing the letter to the president would have been "a waste of time."[162] Kennedy would never go to Texas and skip Dallas.

On Thursday morning, November 21, the president woke up alone in his bed. After showering, he strapped on his back brace with valet George Thomas's help, dressed himself, and had Thomas tie his shoes, the left one with a quarter-inch lift to ease the anatomic seesaw in his lower back. Despite the cortisone he took orally each day and the intermittent injections of uppers, he was in the best shape of his beleaguered life. The daily regimen of swimming and stretching had had salutary effect. After breakfast, he walked over to the Oval Office to do some last-minute paperwork. The president summoned Sorensen for some tweaking of the Texas speeches.

Kennedy was not going to let up in his attack on the right and its equation of peacemaking with treason. The speech at the Dallas Trade Mart was going to take on the right wing for "expressing opposition without alternatives, finding fault but never favor, perceiving gloom on every side and seeking influence without responsibility . . . [finding] vituperation as good as victory and peace as a sign of weakness." The president read it over as Sorensen waited. At points, the text seemed especially sharp: "We cannot hope that everyone, to use a phrase from a decade ago, will "talk sense to the American people." But we can hope that fewer people will listen to nonsense." Finished reading it, Kennedy said, "Good," then asked Sorensen to come up with a joke or two. Reading an advance copy of the speech the following morning, Robert MacNeil of NBC News "felt a warm surge of the intellectual power and rational force that he represented. I felt warmed by it and was looking forward to the moment when he would release his barrage on the citizenry of Dallas."[163]

Saying good-bye to those on his staff who were staying behind, Jack walked out to the helicopter pad with his son. Together they boarded a brown, double-rotored army helicopter, one of the three that would airlift the White House party to Andrews Air Force Base. It drizzled as they waited for Jackie to board. At Andrews, the Kennedys boarded Air Force One, leaving John-John, crying, in the hands of a Secret Service agent. As William Manchester and others later reported, Kennedy's mood was upbeat. Jackie was along and, as she busied herself in one of the forward cabins, O'Donnell conferred with the president alone about some details concerning the trip. O'Donnell would later recount that he was "a little surprised" when Kennedy suddenly brought up the subject of assassination. "If anybody really wanted to shoot the president," Kennedy remarked to O'Donnell, "it was not a very difficult job — all one had to do was get on a high building someday with a telescopic rifle, and there was nothing anybody could do to defend against such an attempt."[164]

November 22, 1963

Washington, D. C.; Dallas; and Havana

The schedule on November 22 called for a breakfast at the Chamber of Commerce in Fort Worth, and then it was on to Dallas. It was raining. The president got up before Jackie, shaved, and scanned the *Dallas Morning News.* On the front page were stories about the rift between Connally and Yarborough as well as the prediction of former vice president Nixon that LBJ would be dropped from the ticket in 1964. Inside the first section was a black-bordered, full-page ad taken out by "The American Fact-Finding Committee" that accused the Kennedy administration of selling out to the communists. Jack told Dave Powers to make sure the paper wasn't around when Jackie got up. After breakfast, however, he must have had second thoughts, for he showed her the paper. As she read the ad, he observed, "We're entering nut country today. But, Jackie, if somebody wants to shoot me from a window with a rifle, nobody can stop it, so why worry about it?"[165] He walked over to where she was sitting, "Last night would have been a hell of a night to assassinate a president," he continued. "I mean it — the rain and the night and we were all getting jostled."[166]

During the thirteen-minute flight from Fort Worth to Dallas, the weather began to clear. By the time the door of Air Force One cracked open at 11:38 at Love Field, the sun shone brilliantly. After the motorcade departed from Love Field, Jackie put on her dark glasses. Jack asked her to take them off; the crowd had come to see her, he told her. As the presidential party threaded its way through the cluster of downtown buildings on Live Oak Street, heading toward Main, the crowds grew to ten to twelve deep on the sidewalks. The shouting was deafening. "Jackie!" "Jackie!" could be heard over the din. Meanwhile in Dealey Plaza, Lee Bowers, a Dallas railroad veteran who was standing atop a train tower, saw three cars cruising around the railroad lot contiguous to the plaza. The driver of one of the cars was talking into what appeared to be a walkie-talkie. Bowers also later testified that there were two men behind the picket fence that went down the grassy hill toward Elm Street. The distance between them and Elm Street was about thirty-five yards.[167]

In Dealey Plaza, those waiting to see the president could hear the faint drafts of cheering in the distance and the snarl of the motorcycle escort. They were turned expectantly toward the east end of the plaza where the president's car would enter. Overlooking this juncture was the Texas School Book Depository. Bystanders who later gave testimony to the FBI saw variously one or two men on the fifth and sixth floors. Two amateur photographers, Charles Bronson and Robert Hughes, took motion pictures of the building six minutes before the motorcade came into Dealey Plaza.[168] These films show two men moving from window to window on the sixth floor. As the motorcade took a sharp left into the plaza, it slowed to 11.2 miles an hour. It was 12:30. Suddenly, there was a shot. Then another in rapid succession. The president was struck once through the back and neck, a serious but probably not fatal wound. Five seconds ticked by with the Secret Service detail behind the president's car doing nothing. Jackie by this time had turned toward her slumping husband, who "looked puzzled" as he leaned toward her. Powers, watching the president from farther back in the motorcade, told O'Donnell he thought Kennedy had been hit.

Mary Elizabeth Woodward was standing on the Elm Street curb watching the motorcade when, as she later said, "there was a horrible, ear-shattering noise coming from behind us and a little to the right."[169] This was the picket fence area. Lee Bowers, the railroad man atop the tower, saw "a flash of light or smoke" from the same place. Powers and O'Donnell described the impact. "The third shot took the side of his head off. We saw pieces of bone and brain tissue and bits of his reddish hair flying through the air. The impact lifted him and shook him limply, as if he was a rag doll."[170] Jackie had watched "this perfectly clean piece [of skull] detaching itself from his head. Then he slumped in my lap, his blood and brains were in my lap."

Inside the Lincoln, there was mayhem. Connally, wounded seriously, was shouting, "No! No! No!" as his wife tried to shield him. As the limo accelerated, Secret Service agent Clint Hill jumped up on the bumper and Jackie stood on the back seat and pulled him into the car. She then lay on top of her husband as the car headed toward Parkland Memorial Hospital. "Jack, Jack," she said, moaning. "Can you hear me? I love you, Jack."[171]

Bystanders on Elm Street and the motorcycle policemen trailing the motorcade headed immediately toward the grassy hill, from which at least one of the shots had come. When Dallas police officer Joe M. Smith, pistol drawn, accosted a man standing behind the picket fence, the man produced Secret Service credentials — though, according to Secret Service Chief James Rowley, there were no Secret Service agents in that area. Dallas police later found three "tramps" in a railroad area near the grassy hill. They were detained, questioned, and released but a photograph taken reveals that one of them was Charles V. Harrelson, a shooter for the Marcello family who was later convicted of assassinating federal judge John Wood in San Antonio, Texas. At the time of his arrest, Harrelson said he participated in the Kennedy assassination.[172]

Railroad signal supervisor S. M. Holland ran over to the place "where I saw the smoke come from and heard the shot. . . . Well, you know it'd been raining that morning and behind the station wagon from one end of the bumper to the other, I expect you could've counted four or five hundred footprints down there. It looked like a lion pacing a cage."[173] Analyzing a Dallas police recording from a police motorcycle near the presidential limo, acoustical experts concluded in testimony before the House Assassinations Committee that the third shot "with a probability of 95 percent or better" was fired from the grassy knoll.[174]

In Washington, Bobby Kennedy was holding an all-day meeting on organized crime in his Justice Department office. About forty top law enforcement officials had gathered to discuss the state of their battle against the underworld. Shortly after noon Bobby adjourned the meeting. He invited New York district attorney Robert Morgenthau and his assistant, criminal division chief Silvio Mollo, out to Hickory Hill for lunch. Kennedy took a quick swim in the backyard pool, changed into dry shorts and a T-shirt, and joined Ethel and his two guests around a table for a lunch of clam chowder and tuna fish sandwiches. Workmen nearby were finishing construction on a new wing on the far side of the house. Morgenthau remembered watching one of the workmen hanging shutters with one hand and holding a transistor radio with the other.

From his fifth-floor office at Justice, J. Edgar Hoover placed a call to the attorney general's office on the direct line. Angie Novello took the call. Seconds earlier, a UPI dispatch had reached the office, reporting the wounding of the president. Novello told Hoover that he should call the attorney general at home. A White House operator patched the FBI director to extension 163 at Hickory Hill. It was 1:45 P.M. Bobby Kennedy was glancing at his watch and suggesting that Morgenthau and his deputy accompany him back to his office. When the phone rang at one end of the pool, Ethel answered it and was told by the operator that the director was calling.

"The attorney general is at lunch," she replied.

"This is urgent," the operator said.

Ethel motioned to her husband. "It's J. Edgar Hoover," she said.

Bobby took the phone just as the workman with the transistor radio to his ear began walking toward the pool, shouting.

"I have news for you," Hoover said in his high, staccato voice. "The president's been shot."

Kennedy paused, then asked if it were serious.

"I think it's serious," Hoover replied. "I am endeavoring to get details. I'll call you back when I find out more." Kennedy hung up the phone and stared at Ethel and his two guests. He began walking toward them. Suddenly it hit him. He sagged as if every muscle in his body was contorted with horror. "Jack's been shot," he said, clapping his hand to his face.[175] Ethel ran to him and embraced him. They went into the house and Bobby went upstairs to call Kenny O'Donnell at Parkland Memorial Hospital. When no one could locate O'Donnell, Bobby spoke with the person at the hospital who took his call. "And I asked if he [Jack] was conscious and they said he wasn't, and I asked if they had gotten a priest, and they said they had. . . . And I said will you call me back and he said yes." Presently, someone in the presidential party — probably White House attaché Tazwell Shephard — did call Bobby back. "The president's dead," he told him.

Within minutes, all four phones in the house began ringing. Bobby went from one call to the next, asking his brother Teddy to go to Hyannis Port to tell their parents, taking a call from LBJ, who wanted to know who could swear him in, and, most memorably, from Hoover, who coldly told him what he already knew — that his brother was dead. His close friend and press secretary Ed Guthman joined him as he fielded the calls. They then went outside and took a walk. "I thought they'd get one of us," Bobby said to Guthman, "but Jack, after all he'd been through, never worried about it. . . . I thought it would be me."[176]

Between 2 and 2:30 P.M., Bobby took a call from CIA director John McCone, who told him he would drive over from Langley. When McCone arrived, Kennedy went out on the lawn with him. "I asked McCone," Kennedy was to tell his trusted aide Walter Sheridan, "if they had killed my brother, and I asked him in a way that he couldn't lie to me."[177] McCone was one of Bobby's closest friends in the administration, and this extraordinary question revealed a deep and terrible suspicion about the CIA, something born of some knowledge, or at least intuition, and not simply the incontinence of grief. The picture that emerges of Bobby Kennedy during these first minutes and hours after the news of his brother's death is that of a soldier who has taken a direct hit. The endorphins produced by the shock cause a high level of lucidity. The collapse would come later.

At around 4 P.M., Kennedy made a call to the Ebbit Hotel on H Street in Washington. The Ebbit (whose number shows up regularly on the attorney general's phone logs) was used by the CIA to house Cuban operatives. Kennedy spoke first with his friend Enrique Ruiz-Williams, then asked to be passed to journalist Haynes Johnson, then working on a book about the Bay of Pigs. "Robert Kennedy was utterly in control of his emotions when he came on the line," Johnson recalled, "and sounded almost studiedly brisk as he said, 'One of your guys did it.' "[178]

He clearly was referring to embittered Cubans deployed by elements in the CIA. Asking McCone if the CIA was involved in such a way that "he could not lie" suggested that Kennedy thought the CIA operatives were acting at a deniable distance. Perhaps he had heard or read about the shooter in the Orange Bowl. Perhaps his constant communications with the anti-Castro Cubans had revealed to him their bitter despair as well as the ferocity of their CIA handlers. We cannot know for certain.

Within minutes of Lee Harvey Oswald's arrest for the shooting of officer J. D. Tippit (at about 2:10 P.M. Central Standard Time on November 22), Hoover called the attorney general at Hickory Hill. "I told him," his notes from the exchange read, "that I thought we had the man who killed the president down in Dallas . . . a mean-minded individual . . . in the category of a nut who was an ex-Marine who had defected to the Soviet Union."[179]

Bobby left for Andrews Air Force Base at 4:30 the afternoon of the twenty-second, arriving an hour before Air Force One was to land. He walked around aimlessly, avoiding the gathering crowd. Finding a deserted air force truck, he vaulted over the tailgate and sat on the bed in the darkness. When Air Force One finally arrived, Bobby ran up the ramp near the front entrance to the plane, straight past President Johnson and his staff, to the plane's back compartment: "Hi, Jackie," he said putting his arm around her. She replied, "Oh, Bobby." He was always there when you needed him, she later said. But now the opposite was true: he needed her.[180]

Jackie insisted on riding with the body to Bethesda Naval Hospital in the gray ambulance. Bobby joined her. Jackie was still wearing her pink, blood-soaked dress. When someone on the flight home had suggested she change out of it, she had whispered fiercely, "No. Let them see what they have done to him." Leaning on the coffin, she said, "Oh, Bobby. I just can't believe Jack is gone." She then recounted to him the scene of the murder and the noise and blinding light. He sat there for twenty minutes and listened to the horror of Jack's destruction. The ambulance came within sight of the gleaming Capitol. He later recalled reflecting on his and Jack's dramatic days together on the McClellan Committee.[181] This and other memories cut into him but still he could not cry. His "motor reflexes," as Theodore White once expressed it, continued to drive him forward, to seek some order in the chaos.

Kenny O'Donnell later told Bobby about Jack's "premonitions" about assassination on the Texas trip. Unlike Bobby, Jack had been ready to celebrate self "without self-pity," as Archibald MacLeish had described Oedipus on that golden day in Amherst. He had seen something coming and he had accepted it. To be swept away at the glittering summit like Roland or Arthur was the rendezvous Jack had sensed. His youth, in the phrase he had copied down after Joe's death, was now eternal. Jack would never know, Jackie wrote a few weeks later, "age nor stagnation, nor despair, nor crippling illness, nor loss of any more people he loved. His high noon kept all the freshness of the morning."[182]

At about four the next morning, Jackie and Bobby rode back to the White House with Jack's body, now in a flag-draped coffin, for a ceremony in the East Room. The priest blessed the body with Psalm 130: "My soul waits for the Lord more than sentinels wait for the dawn." As Mrs. Kennedy drew away, Bobby asked that the coffin be opened to settle the question of whether there would be an open or closed casket. "I asked everybody to leave and I asked them to open it. . . . When I saw it, I'd made my mind up, I didn't want it open." Others whom Bobby asked to view Jack agreed.

It was almost 5 A.M. when Charles Spalding, one of Jack's oldest friends, walked with Bobby to the Lincoln bedroom. Spalding produced a sleeping pill, which Bobby took. "God, it's so awful," Bobby said. "Everything was really beginning to run so well." Spalding bid him good night and closed the door. As he turned away, he heard Bobby break down — at last — and start to sob: "Why, God?"[183] Stewart Udall spent time with the attorney general the next day, discussing the location of the grave site at Arlington. Udall, who subsequently dropped Kennedy off at Hickory Hill, sensed that Bobby was suffering from something "deeper than grief itself."[184]

For millions of people, John F. Kennedy's death destroyed an illusion of invulnerability. Grief became a sort of unction, each person carrying the memory of the moment when he or she got the news. In a suite of rooms at the Beverly Crest Hotel in Los Angeles, where Johnny Rosselli had put her in the days before the assassination, Judy Campbell was alone when the news reached her. Distraught and frightened by the killing of her former lover, she refused to take any of Rosselli's calls and barricaded herself in her room. Rosselli later showed up at the hotel and persuaded the hotel management to open the locked door. He found Campbell on the verge of complete breakdown. Despite her initial rebuff, "gently, patiently, he persuaded her to join him for dinner."[185]

But for Joe Kennedy, blinking in and out of lucidity in his convalescence in Hyannis Port, there was no such consolation. He had awakened from his nap that afternoon and been told that the television would not work.[186] Teddy arrived and tried to put on a cheery charade, which the old man seemed to see through. He demanded with crippled gestures that the TV be turned on. Teddy then went and pulled out the plug. The old man pointed accusingly at the dangling cord. Teddy knelt and obediently inserted the plug. As the set began to warm up, Teddy tore the wires out of the back of it.

Bobby Alone

1964 – 1968

September 27, 1964

New York City

On September 27, 1964, three weeks after Robert Kennedy resigned the attorney generalship, the Warren Commission released its report on the assassination of President Kennedy. The next day Kennedy, running for the United States senate seat from New York, canceled his campaign schedule and instead remained in his hotel room. Several days later at Columbia University, a student asked him whether he agreed with the commission's finding that Lee Harvey Oswald had acted alone. Kennedy stood there paralyzed for almost five minutes, saying nothing.[1] He turned his back to the audience so they could not see his tears. Finally he said softly that he agreed. Oswald was the sole assassin.

Bobby had dragged himself through the days and months after November 22, 1963, desolate, bewildered, and anguished. Far beyond his loss of power after Jack's death, Bobby had lost himself. He had given everything he had to promote and protect Jack, shouldered the impossible tasks and ingested all the ugly emotions. He had thought, as he told Ed Guthman shortly after he got the news from Dallas, that "they would get one of us, but . . . I thought it would be me."[2] In the end, Jack was the one who had taken the hit and Bobby could only wonder if he himself had been the real target.

Like a widowed spouse, Bobby tried at times to repress the fatal event. He refused to say "November twenty-second" or "Dallas," and referred to Jack's assassin as "Harvey Oswald." If someone said "Jack," he would wince and correct the person — "the president"— as if it were less painful to commit a public figure to history.[3] He took down portraits of his brother and would go from room to room in friends' homes, turning over magazines with Jack's

301

picture.[4] Sometimes he would put on his brother's clothes — an old tweed overcoat and a navy sea jacket from his PT boat days — or would slip into a reverie, his lips moving silently. Kenny O'Donnell at first thought Bobby had taken to talking to himself but then realized he was talking to Jack.[5] There was no exit.

Bobby grimly lockstepped through the cascade of oral tributes, the unending references in his presence to the tragedy and the greatness of his brother, and the renaming of parks, boulevards, and airports in President Kennedy's name. Gradually he learned to speak about Jack in public without breaking down. At a St. Patrick's Day dinner in Wilkes-Barre, Pennsylvania, in 1964, he quoted the lines Jack had often used in reference to Owen Roe O'Neill, an Irish freedom fighter:

> We are sheep without a shepherd,
> When the snow shuts out the sky —
> Oh! Why did you leave us, Owen?
> Why did you die?

Jack was now becoming in death what he had never been in life — a saint — but a saint with a past. Bobby knew that if he challenged Johnson and Hoover, they had the motive and the means to desecrate the Kennedy shrine. Within days of the assassination, Hoover was supplying Johnson with damning material about Bobby's alleged plot to unseat him. It fueled Johnson's worst fears, and he turned demonic. Kennedy aide Ralph Dungan was working late in his office in the West Wing several days after the burial when suddenly he heard a noise at the door. Dungan looked up and there was President Johnson, wearing nothing but a T-shirt and boxer shorts.[6] Johnson said, "Ralph, I want to talk to you," and motioned for Dungan to follow him. The president led Dungan into the Oval Office. Johnson seemed agitated and paced around. Finally he walked over to where Dungan was standing in front of a sofa and put both his hands on Dungan's shoulders and forced him down onto the sofa. He then turned and started to walk away. Suddenly Johnson turned back and said in a low voice: "I want to tell you why Kennedy died." Dungan was stunned and sat there numbly, looking at the floor. Johnson, his face contorted, pointed his finger at Dungan. "Divine retribution," he said grimly. Dungan remembered feeling ill when he heard this. The president said it again: "Divine retribution. He murdered Diem and then he got it himself."

It wasn't long before the president was probing into the Cuban connection. In a conversation with Hoover on November 29, 1963, Johnson — clearly in search of ammunition against Bobby — asked Hoover "whether [Oswald] was connected with the Cuban operation [Mongoose] with money." Hoover was guarded in his reply: "That's what we're trying to nail down now." He pointed out that everything indicated that Oswald's associations were with pro-Castro causes and groups.[7] But Johnson was not persuaded.

Bobby, while sure that Oswald did the shooting, told Arthur Schlesinger Jr. on December 9 that "there was still argument if he had done it himself or as part of a larger plot, whether organized by Castro or by gangsters."[8] As Schlesinger suggests, Kennedy had reached no conclusions, but his instincts led him to consider the likelihood of a conspiracy. If there had been a conspiracy involving gangsters, anti-Castro Cubans, and renegade CIA elements, and if this were revealed, Bobby must have sensed that it would be fatal to the reputation of his beloved brother and to himself. He held his silence. Perhaps the most damningly perceptive observation about Kennedy came from his hated rival Jimmy Hoffa, who told a reporter: "Bobby Kennedy is just another lawyer now."[9]

Bobby became increasingly consumed by his own suspicions. His comment to Schlesinger revealed as much. But he never acted on his suspicions or caused anyone else to. Perhaps his silence stemmed from his paralyzing grief, perhaps from the realization that no investigation would ever bring back his beloved brother. But it also must have been evident to him that any investigation of the violent nexus among the Cubans, their CIA handlers, and the Mafia could well reveal one of the darkest secrets of the Kennedy administration and his own preeminent role in it.

The assassination investigation commissioned by President Johnson was a further agony. When a *Paris Match* reporter asked him for a comment on the work of the Warren Commission, Bobby cut him off.[10] Did Kennedy realize, as Majority Leader and Warren Commission member Representative Hale Boggs put it, that "Hoover lied his eyes out to the Commission, on Oswald, on Ruby, on their friends, the bullets, the gun, you name it?"[11] All we know is that Kennedy asked his old friend and aide Walter Sheridan to look into Jimmy Hoffa's reaction to the murder.

With Hoover back in command (he ordered his secretary to get rid of the phone on his desk that linked him to the attorney general), the organized crime operation came to a halt. As Bill Hundley, head of the Organized Crime Section, put it, "The minute that bullet hit Jack Kennedy's head, it was all over. Right then. The organized crime program just stopped, and Hoover took control back."[12] Marcello had been right: cut the dog's head off and the rest of it would die.

President Johnson meanwhile kept Bobby off balance by blending occasional affirmation with abusive treatment. In January of 1964 he sent the attorney general on a diplomatic mission to Indonesia, but Kennedy heard reports from O'Donnell and others that the president harbored destructive sentiments. Seeing one of his Secret Service detail still wearing a JFK PT-109 tie clasp, Johnson tore it off the agent and threw it to the ground.[13]

For all his fear of the Kennedys, Johnson understood that to win the 1964 presidential election, he had to cast himself as the steward of JFK's unfinished business. He kept on Kennedy's team of advisors and appointees, was solicitous of Jackie, and even dangled the possibility of making Bobby Kennedy his vice presidential running mate. But Johnson recognized that ultimately Bobby was the heir apparent to his martyred brother. He also knew that Kennedy regarded him as a usurper. Beyond their history of "mutual contempt," Johnson saw the Bobby Baker investigation, which had been delayed by the assassination, as a time bomb.[14] As attorney general, Kennedy still had the power to break open the rotten nexus of payoffs, kickbacks, and mob-connected deals surrounding the Baker affair, which could reveal Johnson's own corruption. The fact that such an investigation would also uncover JFK's philandering, both while on the Hill and in the White House, might have calmed Johnson's worries, but, as Bobby Baker himself later noted, Johnson was practically "paranoiac" on the subject of Robert Kennedy. He claimed that the attorney general was holding off-the-record press briefings on the scandal. There was no truth to this but it gave Hoover, who hated Kennedy possibly more than

Johnson did, the opening he needed to send the president concocted reports that Kennedy was conspiring to undermine him.

Knowing that it would get back to him, Johnson likened Bobby to a boy he had once known who had misbehaved, done bad things to other people, and gotten away with them. Then one day, the boy crashed his sled into a tree and become cross-eyed. Johnson found the analogy so much to his liking that he referred to Kennedy as "that cross-eyed boy."[15]

After excluding Bobby as a vice presidential candidate, Johnson did everything in his power to guard against any apparition of the Kennedy magic at the Democratic national convention in Atlantic City in August 1964. The administration deployed FBI agents and surveillance devices to monitor Bobby — by then a candidate in the Democratic primary for the U.S. Senate seat in New York — and rescheduled a televised tribute to President Kennedy to the latest possible point in the convention program. It didn't work.

By the time Bobby reached the podium to introduce the film, the ovation by the delegates on the convention floor had become a roar. When Kennedy made an effort to quiet them, the applause became even more deafening. He looked down, then up. He bit his lip to keep himself from crying. On and on the cheering went, dipping and cresting for twenty-two minutes. The applause finally subsided. Bobby spoke briefly about his brother, concluding with some lines from Shakespeare's *Romeo and Juliet* Jackie had suggested:

> When he shall die
> Take him and cut him out in little stars,
> And he will make the face of heaven so fine
> That all the world will be in love with night,
> And pay no worship to the garish sun.

A week later Bobby received nominations for the Senate seat for New York from both the Democratic and Liberal parties. The Republican incumbent was the popular Kenneth Keating. What began as the foregone conclusion that Kennedy would sweep to the Senate soon began to fall apart. Memories of Jack seemed to waft through Bobby like nerve gas. One moment Bobby was there, another moment he was gone, locked in a deep reverie. When his old political comrade Paul Corbin realized one day that in his Senate campaign Bobby was retracing Jack's 1960 schedule, he called Kennedy. "God damn, Bob, be yourself," he told him. "Get hold of yourself. You're real. Your brother's dead."[16] At the end of a day of campaigning in Buffalo, Ed Guthman commented to Bobby how good the crowds were. "Don't you know?" Kennedy said. "They're for him — they're for him."[17]

The problem for Bobby was that he wanted to be Jack, and wasn't. When people saw him in person or on television, they wanted the same thing — Jack — but instead they saw a small man, possibly unhappy, definitely uneasy, and not nearly as good-looking, a man who spoke in hard-edged fragments and tended to avoid eye contact. The voice was reminiscent of the president's but higher and sort of barky. Television had always been JFK's best friend. For Bobby, it was an enemy that revealed all of his unresolved emotion and the terrible truth that he might not have what it took to live up to his brother's worshiped image.

His campaign for the Senate revealed these infirmities. He was awkward on the stump (sometimes vomiting before speeches out of nervousness), he quoted his brother endlessly, and he seemed un-certain about the issues. The takes for his 30-second TV ads were endless and awful. The *New York Herald Tribune* described Ken-nedy as "an adventurer determined to stay in office as a personal ne-cessity." Ethel thought the campaign slogan should be: "There's only so much you can do for Massachusetts."[18] Bobby arranged to have his father brought up to New York to play a role in the cam-paign, and this too miscarried. Disoriented, the old man could only babble. "I'll make changes, Dad," Bobby cried out to him. "You know I'll make changes. Millions of people need help. My God, they need help."[19] Everything, it seemed, had changed; his father and his brother — the very polestars of his existence — were gone. He was alone, and all was now in question. By the first week in Oc-tober, the fourteen-point lead he had enjoyed over Keating in Au-gust had disappeared entirely, and it looked as if he might lose. Trying to get movement back into the numbers, Steve Smith de-cided to ride President Johnson's coattails for all they were worth.

Suddenly, at Columbia University in the first week of October, there was an interesting development. After his stump speech,

Kennedy spent two hours sparring with a group of antagonistic students who had accused him of opportunism, of running on the Kennedy name in a state where he had never lived. The tape was so good — Bobby laughing at the abuse and razor-sharp in his replies — that the campaign bought a half hour of statewide television on prime time and ran the exchange, later distilling 30-second ads from the tape. During the final weeks before election day, the Kennedy campaign hired a film crew that followed Bobby everywhere, feeding the unedited tape each evening to every TV station in the state.[20] In a business in which control over imagery and sound bite is critical, this seemed like a strange strategy: put your man in an unknown and sometimes explosive crowd scene and watch him go. But because the technique went straight to the character of Robert Kennedy, it worked.

On October 20, in a bid to reverse Kennedy's gains and recapture the Jewish vote, Keating accused him of having made a "deal" as attorney general to turn over General Aniline & Film Company to "front" for I. G. Farben Company, a "huge Nazi cartel." Kennedy repudiated the charge: "If this charge were true, I wouldn't deserve to be elected to public office. The charge isn't true. . . . I lost my brother and brother-in-law to the Germans. The idea that I would turn over money to the Nazis is ridiculous."[21] Once on the attack, Bobby quickly ran up the score against Keating, defeating him by more than 719,000 votes in the November election. The victory celebration that night turned into a mob scene, as if the Restoration were about to take place. Campaign aide Bill Barry finally caught up to the senator-elect to congratulate him. "Well, if my brother was alive," Bobby said to Barry, "I wouldn't be here. I'd rather have it that way."[22]

March 24, 1965

Mount Kennedy, Yukon Territory

Jim Whittaker, the first American to scale Mount Everest, later described it as "an anxious moment." About 500 feet below the 14,000-foot pyramid-shaped summit of Mount Kennedy, named for the late president by the Canadian government, Bobby Kennedy and the other eight climbers prepared to ascend a jagged, windswept 65-degree slope. Whittaker went first, using both his ice ax and crampons to scale the face of the mountain. At the top of the steep slope, he slammed the shaft of his ice ax deep into the snowpack, wrapped and tied his nylon rope around its neck, and bent over the top of the ax with his 200-pound frame to hold it in place.[23]

Kennedy, with Whittaker's rope tied around his waist, was next. He was about 60 feet below Whittaker; beneath Bobby, 6,000-feet down, was the Lowell Glacier. The fact that Bobby had insisted on carrying what everyone else was — a 45-pound pack — didn't help.

"You're on belay," Whittaker yelled down. "Now you climb!"

Kennedy hesitated a moment. Then he struck his ax into the snowpack, gouged a hole for his foot with one crampon as he had been instructed, and hauled himself up a couple of feet. He repeated the procedure again and again. As he talked Kennedy up the slope, Whittaker pulled up the slack in the rope. "Remember to breathe," Whittaker shouted down to Bobby, who was now panting heavily. "You're doing fine. Keep it up."

When Kennedy finally pulled himself over the face, Whittaker pointed out the 150-mile vista, with the bright sun sparkling against the pinnacles, ice falls, and rock cliffs. "What do you think of it?" he asked Bobby. "I don't want to look at anything," Bobby said. "I just want to stay right here." Face drawn, head splitting from the thin air, Kennedy waited until the other climbers joined them. Whittaker then told Bobby to go first to the summit of the never-before-scaled peak. Bobby slowly made his way up the 20-degree spine toward the summit, planting one foot on one side of the ridge and one on the other.

Whittaker watched him make the final steps. Bobby reached back over his shoulder into his backpack and pulled out a pole around which the Kennedy family flag was wrapped. He jammed it into the snow and made the sign of the cross. He stood there a long time, head bowed, watching the flag whip in the wind. Whittaker moved up to him and gave Kennedy a hug. "You did a tremendous job," he told Bobby. "Your brother would be proud of you."

It was the first time Bobby had ever scaled a mountain. His preparation, he said, was to run up the stairs in his Hickory Hill home and shout, "Help!" Between the lines of his and Whittaker's published accounts of their five-day ascent of Mount Kennedy, one senses his fright. He had never been a man with sangfroid — only daring. Skiing at a breakneck pace down expert slopes, shooting Colorado rapids in a kayak, or setting off in a rainstorm at night into an unknown tributary in the Amazon were Bobby's dares with death. Dancing along the edge, he could feel the pulse of life.

The scene in late August 1967 off the coast of Maine was typical. No sooner had Bobby's rented pale-blue yawl pulled out of the harbor of Camden on a three-day sailing venture with friends, than he stripped off his clothes and plunged into near-freezing swells for a swim. Bobby's cruises always seemed to have a madcap quality to them. He never charted a course before setting off, often getting lost miles off the coast in open sea. Friends who knew nothing about sailing usually served as crew. Kay Evans, the wife of journalist Rowland Evans, remembered being unable to sleep one night out of pure fright.[24] She came on deck at 3 or 4 A.M. to find Bobby's friend Dean Markham at the helm. Asked what his course was, Markham could only reply, "I'm steering just a little bit left of the moon." Michael Forrestal remembered coming upon the Kennedy boat in Muscle Ridge, off Rockland, Maine. "It seemed as if there were a circus on board. There were not only a great many people on the boat, some in costume, but also a menagerie of animals." Kennedy shouted across the water at Forrestal's perfectly crewed boat: "I'll bet you rather wish you'd never met us, Forrestal." On that particular trip, there were hardly any provisions and the stove didn't work, so they subsisted on doughnuts. Most everyone by the end of the second day was exhausted; some were seasick. "But Bobby just loved it." Exposed to the natural elements — wind and water, snow and sun — Bobby came alive. Danger was a beckoning, a reminder of the fickleness of life. "Living each day," Bobby often said after Jack's death, "is like Russian roulette."

To brave those odds was what Joe Kennedy had imbued in his sons, but he himself began to have second thoughts. When he saw the TV footage of Bobby in mountain gear, readying himself for the climb of Mount Kennedy, the old man exploded in monosyllabic wrath, "Naaaa!" He tore out newspaper articles about the climb and threw them on the floor. "Bobby didn't know," Lem Billings said, "that his father was trying to stop this thing that had gotten started — this Kennedy thing of daring the gods."[25]

Bobby himself thought it was too late. His fate was set. He plumbed Shakespeare and the Greek tragedies and found an emotional sanctuary in their depiction of the cruelty of life and the price of arrogance. He now saw himself and his family in a tragic light. When the poet Robert Lowell once suggested that Kennedy could be cast as Falstaff, Kennedy said that instead he should be Henry the Fifth. Lowell thought this "trite" and reminded Kennedy of Hal's misadventure: he died young, failed on the battlefield, and his son was murdered. Bobby walked over to a collection of Shakespeare's historical plays and turned to Henry the Fourth's death speech, which he read, including the line, "The canker'd heaps of strange-achieved gold." When he'd finished, Bobby said, "Henry the Fourth. That's my father."[26] Bobby recognized that he was doomed — and this became the basis for his rebirth.

March 15, 1966

Delano, California

Something about the farmworker struggle "touched a nerve" in Bobby Kennedy, as his legislative aide Peter Edelman later put it. In September 1965 over two thousand farmworkers, a low-paid, itinerant, and largely Mexican group of field hands based mostly in California, went on strike. In December, farmworker leader Cesar Chavez called for a boycott of the products of Schenley Industries, a liquor producer with the second-largest grape ranch in the region. The growers struck back, trucking in strikebreakers from Arizona, Texas, and Mexico. The local sheriff of Kern County began making preemptive arrests of anyone distributing pro-strike literature or even using the Spanish word for strike, *huelga*.[27] J. Edgar Hoover suggested that the farmworkers might have communist ties.

The fact that Bobby's old enemy, the Teamsters Union, had moved in with money and muscle to displace Chavez's union with locals amenable to the growers may have also galvanized him. Although Hoffa was now in federal prison in Lewisburg, Pennsylvania, Einar Mohn, former executive assistant to Dave Beck and now director of the Teamsters Western Conference, and several of Kennedy's old nemeses were actively maneuvering against Chavez. So too was Sidney Korshak, an attorney and friend of Johnny Rosselli who represented the Chicago Mafia in Los Angeles as well as the Teamsters and Schenley Industries.[28] Korshak was also the majority owner of the Associated Booking Corporation, whose main office Jack Ruby had visited in New York City on August 5, 1963.

On March 15, 1966, Kennedy flew out west for the hearings of the Senate Subcommittee on Migratory Labor. Chavez and his supporters gave him a tour of the organizing hall, their strike kitchen, and the picket lines around the Di Giorgio grape farm. At the hearings, after Chavez had testified, Kern County sheriff Roy Galyen explained his efforts to keep order, including photographing everyone on the picket line.

> KENNEDY: Do you take pictures of everyone in the city?
>
> GALYEN: Well, if he is on strike, or something like that.
>
> KENNEDY: Is this a preventative measure?
>
> GALYEN: Well, if I have reason to believe that there's going to be a riot started, and somebody tells me that there's going to be trouble if you don't stop them, then it's my duty to stop them.
>
> KENNEDY: You go out there and arrest them?
>
> GALYEN: Absolutely.
>
> KENNEDY: Who told you that they were going to riot?
>
> GALYEN: The men right out there in the field that they were talking to said if you don't get them out of here we're going to cut their hearts out.
>
> KENNEDY: This is a most interesting concept, I think, that you suddenly hear talk about somebody's going to get out of order, perhaps violate the law, and you go in and arrest them, and they haven't done anything wrong. How do you go arrest somebody if they haven't violated the law?
>
> GALYEN: They are ready to violate the law, in other words.
>
> KENNEDY: Could I suggest that in the interim period of time . . . that the sheriff and the district attorney read the Constitution of the United States?[29]

This exchange brought down the farmworker-packed house. At the back of the hall, Chavez supporters waved crudely imprinted placards: "Kennedy for President in '68."[30]

Kennedy took it a step further. He left the hearings and went straight back to Filipino Hall and publicly declared his support for the grape strike. Even Chavez thought it was an unnecessary risk. Finding, as always, concept and purpose in the battle zone, Bobby then accompanied over one hundred pickets to the Di Giorgio Fruit Corporation's 4,400-acre ranch and manned a picket line in front of one of the farm's entrances. Both the growers and the farmworkers were stunned. The next morning, March 17, Chavez and his followers set out on foot to make a *peregrinación,* or pilgrimage, to Sacramento. The distance was 300 miles. The objective was to reach the state capital on Easter Sunday.

Bobby Kennedy had first met Cesar Chavez in late November 1959 in East Los Angeles, where Chavez was executive director of the Community Service Organization (CSO). In the course of his travels with the Stevenson campaign in 1956, Kennedy had noted the growing influence of the Mexican-American vote in states like Texas and California. Chavez remembered the first meeting as involving a vigorous dispute between those advocating a high-profile media blitz to register Mexican-Americans and CSO activists like Chavez, who wanted to continue the door-to-door approach they had perfected in ten years of grass-roots work in the barrios. The meeting went late — until around 3 A.M. — and Kennedy walked in toward the end, saying little and listening. He finally sided with Chavez. "Well, if he's been here for ten years, why can't he do it the way he wants to do it?"[31] He seemed "very young" and "all business," Chavez told the author.[32]

Jack Kennedy lost California by a slim margin to Nixon, but the Hispanic turnout was exceptionally high. In a statement quoted in *Time,* the Kennedy campaign gave credit to established Mexican-American politicians rather than to the CSO. Dolores Huerta, Chavez's two-fisted lieutenant, got Cesar's permission to let Kennedy know about who really got the vote out. She fairly broke into his office with a copy of *Time* in her hand. "Bobby Kennedy was standing there; he was talking to a lot of people. I think he saw this wild-eyed looking person coming toward him, and he threw up his hands, 'I know, I know.'" He promised Huerta he would correct it.[33]

In 1962, Chavez and Huerta had left the CSO and moved to the town of Delano in the San Joaquin Valley to launch a union for farmworkers. Kennedy wasn't much help as attorney general but he was as senator. His office ran interference for Chavez's movement, trying to get green cards for some workers, or pressuring the Texas Rangers to stop trying to break the strike in central Texas. By 1967, the farmworkers made what seemed a breakthrough. Schenley signed, and the largest vintners in the country — Gallo,

Christian Brothers, Almaden, and Paul Masson — all agreed to negotiate with the farmworkers. But the talks soon stalled. The National Farmworkers Association (NFWA) responded by picketing the offices of the corporate giants. When the police arrested the picketers on technical grounds, Dolores Huerta called Senator Kennedy's office. On one occasion in New York, she tracked him down at the Puerto Rican Commonwealth building. "Senator, some of our people are in jail." Kennedy seemed exasperated: "Every time I see you, you have people in jail. They're either in jail in California, or San Francisco, or Texas." "Well, now they're in jail in New York," Huerta replied.[34] Kennedy would always make the call to get them out.

Bobby's adoption of the farmworker cause was just one of a succession of personal breakouts that led to moral growth. In Washington, amid the white noise and maneuvering, the endless postures and compromises, as well as the intermittent savagery of his enemies, Kennedy felt trapped. On the Senate floor or in committee, "you always had the feeling that Bobby might explode," Ted Kennedy's aide Dun Gifford remembered. On one occasion in the course of an endless debate on the floor, Bobby walked up behind Ted Kennedy's chair — Ted had been elected senator from Massachusetts in 1962 — and whispered, "Is this how you become a member of the club, Senator?"[35] Bobby put in long days, manfully performed his duties, but his heart wasn't in it.

His sojourns outside of Washington drew him into the scarred and wasted places in America — Indian reservations, Mississippi shanties, New York City tenements. There his anger and his empathy, his sense of what we were doing to the least of our brethren, would surge up. When he heard that a baby had died on an Indian reservation during his visit he said, "When that baby died, a little bit of me died too." He went into the slums of Harlem, sometimes alone, over thirty times. "I have been in tenements in Harlem in the past several weeks where the smell of rats was so strong it was difficult to stay there for five minutes, and where children slept with lights turned on their feet to discourage attacks."[36]

Ironically, this moral awakening and the brutal directness with which Kennedy communicated it further complicated his relations with the liberals. It was not enough, he said, to go on marches in

Alabama and ignore the race-based decay and terror in the Bronx. Here he was, not calling just for some constitutionally derived vindication of black rights or a raft of new federal programs, but for a conversion of capitalism to a more human-based community of reconstruction. "People like myself can't go around making nice speeches all the time. We can't just keep raising expectations. We have to do some damn hard work, too."[37] He spearheaded a huge project to transform Bedford-Stuyvesant, a black and Puerto Rican community of a half-million people in Brooklyn. The focus was to create jobs and reconstruct housing by attracting business investment, a formula Robert Scheer of *Ramparts* magazine later described as more "reminiscent of Ronald Reagan than Herbert Lehman." With Tom Johnston and Adam Walinsky, staffing the effort, Kennedy brought in leading CEOs to run two nonprofit corporations. The results were slow but impressive. Even William F. Buckley approved.[38]

Liberals, however, who continued to think that government was the right instrument of social improvement, remained suspicious of Kennedy. The drift of "corporate liberalism," as E. J. Dionne has termed it, was toward big labor and big government, not self-help and private investment.[39] Kennedy did not use the right liberal words or say the expected things, unlike Vice President Hubert Humphrey, for example. He seemed far too blunt, even discordant. The other significant liberal group in the country, America's Jewish population, was also skeptical. David Halberstam thought that Bobby Kennedy reminded Jews of a "tough little Irish kid who punched you in the nose."[40] Journalist and political activist Jack Newfield recalled a confrontation with the attorney general in June 1963. He described Kennedy's "hard, Irish face; alert, but without much character, a little like the faces that used to follow me home from Hebrew school, taunting, 'Christ killer.'"[41]

But Kennedy's problem went well beyond his discomfiting demeanor. In a time of prosperity, he was critiquing America the greedy. Racism, he said, was a form of economic abuse anchored in an amoral capitalism. The money culture dehumanized people, made them into economic beings, and cast off the infirm, the black, and the uneducated alike. In one speech Kennedy went so far as to question what material richness had gotten America:

[W]e have a great gross national product, now soaring beyond $800 billion a year. But that counts air pollution, and cigarette advertising, and ambulances to clear out highways of carnage. It counts special locks for our doors, and jails for the people who break them. It counts the destruction of the redwoods and equipment for police to put down riots in our cities. . . . The gross national product does not allow for the health of our children, the quality of their education, or the joy of their play. It is indifferent to the decency of our factories and the safety of our streets alike. It does not include the beauty of our poetry or the strength of our marriages, the intelligence of our public debate or the integrity of our public officials.[42]

The reactionaries, who had always reserved a special hatred for Bobby, regarded such statements as treasonous. The great mass of white Americans, on their way to safety in the suburbs, were simply not listening. But this seemed to have no effect on Kennedy.

At one point Bobby suggested that network television move a camera into the tenement of a single black woman and her family so that Americans could see the violence all around her, the rat bites on her children's faces, and the complete dilapidation of her apartment. But TV was busy beating its path toward its viewership and preferred more happy and simple-minded imagery.

In April 1967, Kennedy went to Mississippi for Senate Labor Subcommittee hearings about the displacement of black labor by reductions in federal subsidies for cotton farming. After a day of hearings, Kennedy asked Charles Evers, who had befriended Bobby after his brother Medgar was shot in 1963, to take him out to the Delta. The next day they visited, as Evers later put it, "one of the worst places I'd ever seen." *Des Moines Register* reporter Nick Kotz, who accompanied them, later described the dark, windowless shack reeking of mildew and urine — the "odor was so bad you could hardly keep the nausea down" — out of which a half-naked woman walked out. When she learned that this was Senator Kennedy, she "just put her arms out and she said, 'Thank God,' and then she just held his hand." When Kennedy went inside the shack, he found a child playing on the floor with pieces of rice. "His tummy was sticking way out just like he was pregnant. Bobby looked down at the child, and then he picked him up and sat down on that dirty bed.

He was rubbing the child's stomach. He said, 'My God, I didn't know this kind of thing existed. How can a country like this allow it?'" He tried to evoke some response from the boy by caressing and tickling him, but the child seemed to be in a trance. "Tears were running down [Kennedy's] cheek and he just sat there and held that little child. Roaches and rats were all over the floor."[43]

Kennedy's sense of outrage, once directed at Mafia thugs, southern sheriffs, and indolent performers in his brother's administration, was now turned upon generic evils — violence, cruelty, poverty, and arrogant indifference to human suffering. He often quoted Camus:

> We are faced with evil. I feel rather like Augustine did before becoming a Christian when he said, "I tried to find out the source of evil and I got nowhere." But it is also true that I and few others know what must be done. . . . Perhaps we cannot prevent this world from being a world in which children are tortured. But we can reduce the number of tortured children.*

Bobby had undergone a transformation whose proportions he could never have imagined in November 1963. "What do you think of Che Guevara?" he asked civil libertarian Roger Baldwin one day. "I think he is a bandit," replied Baldwin. "I think he is a revolutionary hero," Kennedy said. When journalist Stanley Tretrick suggested that maybe Bobby belonged in the hills with Fidel and Che, he replied, "I know it."[44] This from the man who less than four years earlier had spearheaded the move to eliminate these men. Even his attitude toward the now-imprisoned Jimmy Hoffa, about whom he would inquire from time to time, had softened.[45] Bill Hundley thought that one of the first things Bobby would do if he ever became president would be to pardon Hoffa.

The man who had once embodied street-tactics warfare was now opening himself up to a whole different form of engagement — and the sight was puzzling to many. "He's unassimilated, isn't he?" Robert Lowell asked, observing Bobby at a party. The public didn't get him, either. A poll comparing RFK to JFK showed

---

* Shortly before his death, Kennedy used this quotation in an interview with David Frost to express how he hoped to be remembered.

this all too clearly. Only 24 percent of those polled in early 1968 thought that Bobby had "the outstanding qualities of President Kennedy." Compared to his martyred brother, Bobby seemed variously awkward, unpredictable, and extreme. Jack had understood that in the age of mass media, the expression of power should be personal, not simply moral or ideological. Like a great actor responding to the circumstance of the moment, Jack could achieve an equipoise between change and continuity. He could promise change and decisive action while preserving his options. The style was the message.

Joe Kennedy had often observed about Jack that people found it difficult to dislike him. Bobby was just the opposite; he was easy to dislike, even hate. But when people came to know him, including members of the press, they could also become devoted to him. Part of it had to do with the absolute loyalty he required and returned in kind. Part of it was that behind that mask of taut and brusque resolve, people discovered the compassion of a man wholly engaged by life. "A lover," as JFK speechwriter Richard Goodwin put it.[46] He wrote very personal notes to all sorts of people, sat alone petting a dog (his or anyone else's), and spontaneously hugged children. Jack had been a taker; this man was a giver. Bobby had once hardened himself to his father's demands and his older brother's needs. But on his own he refound his acute and tumultuous sensitivities and proceeded through his days in a whirl of polylinear encounter.

June 6, 1966

Cape Town, South Africa

The *Washington Post* thought that Bobby Kennedy's decision to go to South Africa and challenge apartheid was based on his "unnerving compulsion to seek out the excitement of danger." But what good could it do in a police state with a Nazi-like level of control? What was the point in addressing a student group the government considered subversive?

Kennedy himself had similar concerns as he made his way to the University of Cape Town to deliver the Day of Affirmation speech. A crowd of 18,000 was waiting for him when he arrived at the university, and it took him nearly a half hour to get from the car to the stage in Jameson Hall, where he gave what many consider the greatest speech of his public life. It was as elegant in verse and form as any that Jack had ever given, but the melody of pain and solitude belonged to Bobby.

Kennedy's Senate office had received the invitation to give the address from the National Union of South African Students in late November 1965. Kennedy called Wayne Fredericks, the State Department Africanist he most trusted, to get his view. Fredericks, a soft-spoken man then serving as deputy assistant secretary of state for African Affairs, was at heart a liberationist. He advised Kennedy to go. On the basis of Fredericks's recommendation, Kennedy's office accepted the invitation to go to South Africa and applied for visas. Five months went by with no response from the South African government. Finally on March 22, 1966, four visas were delivered to Kennedy's Senate office. They had requested twelve. Tom Johnston, an aide to the senator from his New York office, was assigned to do the advance work and immediately left for South Africa. He was not encouraged by what he found there. Bobby, Johnston later said, was going into "a terribly explosive and delicate situation where the government was completely against him and the largest percentage of the white people were against him; and the blacks were in no position to really have any information, or be for him or against him. The whole trip had the makings of one of the major disasters of his life."[47]

Security was a wide-open issue with the South African government, which had characterized Kennedy's trip as private, refusing to help. If Minister of Justice Balthazar Vorster thought this would scare Kennedy off, he clearly had not been briefed about the senator's November 1965 trip through Latin America. Kennedy had plunged into crowds of screaming and spitting communist students in Chile with a wry smile on his face, walked though Brazilian *favelas* with no security, and dove into a piranha-infested river in the Amazon jungle.[48] But South Africa was more treacherous ground. If blacks were in a majority, they weren't a political majority. Kennedy could endanger their status simply by drawing them out. Were there deaths or mass arrests during his visit, the senator would be blamed. South African students were also enmeshed in a web of informants and secret police. There wouldn't be the huge crowds of young people as in Asia in 1962 or Latin America in 1965, nor opportunities for the sort of inspired exchanges that played into Kennedy's emphasis on youth and idealism. Two weeks before Kennedy was to leave, Ian Robertson, the twenty-one–year-old medical student who had officially invited Kennedy, was "banned" or placed under house arrest by the government.

Bobby called Fredericks. Should he cancel? Fredericks said no, go. The Kennedy staff scrambled to get prepared. Legislative aide Adam Walinsky did the speech drafts and, with Fredericks's help, coordinated briefing sessions for Kennedy at Hickory Hill.[49] Six days before he was to leave came another blow: the South African government announced that it would not give visas for the forty-odd press that had applied for them. Bobby would be alone, with Ethel and three aides. How different this was from Jack's calibrated foray into the subject of the African revolution in his speech in July 1957 on Algeria — a speech given after months of research and drafting and delivered on the floor of an empty Senate chamber. Fortunately, Walinsky in Washington and Johnston in South Africa had worked out a strategy of sorts: the senator would talk about the struggle for racial justice in *America,* a subject he knew deeply. This would disarm the Afrikaners and, at the same time, appeal to white progressives and black South Africans.

The day before he was to leave, Kennedy went to his UN Plaza apartment in New York and called radical activist Allard Lowenstein, who had spent time in southern Africa, to see if he could press him into a last-minute review of the Cape Town speech. Lowenstein delayed his trip to the Dominican Republic long enough to stop by for a look. He immediately pronounced the draft "disastrous, terrible." He thought it too cautious. He telephoned two South Africans who happened to be in New York at the time, Frances Suzman and Treber Coon, and got them to come over to the apartment to give ballast to his view. With Kennedy's agreement, Walinsky and Lowenstein spent that afternoon strengthening the speech.[50] Bobby also got Dick Goodwin, who had accompanied him to Latin America the previous year, to take a final cut at the text. Goodwin added soaring metaphors about courage as well as an existential counterpoint about sacrifice. The result, as the *London Daily Telegraph* later put it, was "perhaps the most fluent and inspiring speech ever given by a foreigner in South Africa."

The senator, Ethel, Angie Novello, and Walinsky landed at 11:40 P.M. at Jan Smuts airport in Johannesburg, where a crowd of 1,500 people was on hand to greet them. Kennedy's first word — *Gooinaand* ("Good evening" in Afrikaans) — did not exactly strike the right note with his English South African audience. ("There's his first mistake," someone said. "I suppose someone told him that there would be lots of Afrikaners here to greet him.")[51] But the effect elsewhere was properly anodyne, particularly when the senator proceeded to speak about his grandfather, Congressman John F. Fitzgerald, who in December 1900 had recommended that the Boers, who were concluding a bloody war against imperial Britain, be allowed to emigrate to the United States. He quoted his grandfather's resolution, describing the good character, self-reliance, and industriousness of the Boers.[52] It was a nice touch and showed up in the Afrikaner press. Seeing a "Yankee Go Home" sign, Kennedy pointed to it and said, "We will not always agree, as we in the United States do not always agree among ourselves. But what is important is that we frankly discuss the problems and prospects of the future, the hopes and the hazards, which we share as inhabitants of the globe." At the conclusion of his remarks, the crowd surged toward Kennedy, cheering and reaching for him. He climbed to the top of the limo — the first of three whose tops he would scratch, the American mission was to note sourly — but not before his cuff links were torn off.[53] It was a sign of things to come.

The next afternoon, Bobby met with four editors of the Afrikaans newspapers (*Die Transvaler, Die Vaderland, Die Beel* and *Dagbreek*). He dispensed with any introductory exchange and instead began asking questions. What did "colored" mean? "Bastard," one editor replied. Kennedy then asked if a child born out of wedlock to a white man and a white woman would be considered colored. They said no.[54] Another editor said "colored" was someone who was neither white nor black. Was a South American "colored"? Kennedy asked. Yes, they said. An Indian? Yes. A Chinese? Yes. A Japanese? No, one replied, "because there are so few of them."[55]

That evening Kennedy had dinner with leading members of South African industry at the Johannesburg Country Club. His host, J. de L. Sorour, remarked that, despite differences about racial policies, South Africa had earned its status as an American ally because of its anticommunism. Kennedy asked another of his jarring questions. "But what does it mean to be against communism if one's own system denies the value of the individual and gives all power to the government — just as the Communists do?" The South African businessmen retorted that South Africa's problem was unique. "Cruelty and hatred anywhere can affect men everywhere," Kennedy said.[56] But you don't understand, they countered, we are beleaguered. But who really was beleaguered? Kennedy asked. Was it his dinner companions "talking easily over cigars and brandy and baked Alaska? Or Robertson and Paton and Luthuli? And the Indian population being evicted from District 6, an area of Cape Town, after living there for decades, its leadership banned for five years for protesting?"

As a result of his own intense preparation for the trip, Kennedy understood apartheid for what it was — a resilient tyranny that carefully matched repression to threat. He later explained its workings in an article in *Look* magazine:

> The minister of justice can deprive a person of his job, his income, his freedom and — if he is black — his family. The minister's word alone can jail any person for up to six months as a "material witness," unspecified as to what. The prisoner has no right to consult a lawyer or his family. Without government permission, it is a criminal offense even to tell anyone he is being detained. He simply disappears, and he may be in solitary confinement for the entire six months. No court can hear his case or order his release.

The next day, after meeting with African journalists and progressive churchmen, the Kennedy party flew to Cape Town for the Day of Affirmation speech. As the airplane banked over the city in the bright sunlight, the view was spectacular — the rocky slopes of the Cape of Good Hope, the blue waters of the Atlantic and Pacific, and Cape Town itself perched in white on the sea. When someone pointed out Robben Island, where two thousand political prisoners, including Nelson Mandela and Walter Sisulu, were living out their lives, the plane went "silent and cold," according to Kennedy. From D. F. Malan airport in Cape Town, where a crowd of three thousand greeted him, Kennedy went directly to the apartment of his now-banned host, Ian Robertson. To avoid putting Robertson in further jeopardy, Bobby asked if he thought he was being bugged. When Robertson responded positively, Kennedy told him to turn on the phonograph. To further drown out the listening devices, Robertson began kicking the floor boards with his foot. Kennedy gave him a copy of *Profiles in Courage* signed by himself and Jackie Kennedy.

From there Bobby proceeded to the university to deliver his address. Enunciating the essential liberties of all human beings — the right to speak freely, the right to be heard, the right to limit government — Kennedy spoke of America's long and imperfect journey toward full human rights, pointing out that "even as my father grew up in Boston, signs told him 'No Irish Need Apply.'"[57] The most important thing, Kennedy said, was to try:

There is discrimination in New York, the racial inequality of apartheid in South Africa, and serfdom in the mountains of Peru. People starve in the streets in India, a former prime minister is summarily executed in the Congo, intellectuals go to jail in Russia, thousands are slaughtered in Indonesia, wealth is lavished on armaments everywhere. These are differing evils — but they are the common works of man. They reflect the imperfections of human justice, the inadequacy of human compassion, the defectiveness of our sensibility toward the sufferings of our fellows. . . . And therefore they call upon common qualities of conscience and of indignation, a shared determination to wipe away the unnecessary sufferings of our fellow human beings.

The only way to salvage hope was to rely on youth:

The cruelties and obstacles of this swiftly changing planet . . . cannot be moved by those who cling to a present which is already dying, who prefer the illusion of security to the excitement and danger which comes with the most peaceful progress. This world demands the qualities of youth: not a time of life but a state of mind, a temper of will, a quality of the imagination, a predominance of courage over timidity, of the appetite of adventure over a love of ease. It is a revolutionary world we live in.

He then spoke of the "dangers" to courage — futility, timidity, and expediency — and encouraged the students never to give up:

A young monk began the Protestant Reformation, a young general extended an empire from Macedonia to the borders of the earth, and a young woman reclaimed the territory of France. It was a young Italian explorer who discovered the New World, and the thirty-two-year-old Thomas Jefferson who proclaimed that all men are created equal. . . . Few will have the greatness to bend history itself, but each of us can work to change a small portion of events, and in the total of all those acts of courage will be written the history of this generation. . . . Each time a man stands up for an ideal, or acts to improve the lot of others, or strikes out against injustice, he sends forth a tiny ripple of hope, and crossing each other from a million different centers of belief and daring, those ripples build a current which can sweep down the mightiest walls of oppression and resistance.

It was late in the evening when he finished, but the crowd went wild, screaming, chanting, and stamping its feet at this small, slump-shouldered man who now in repose looked vulnerable but seconds earlier had literally trembled with fight. The crowd, it seemed, had determined that it would not let him leave. Back in the car, the Kennedy party's euphoria didn't last long. They learned that James Meredith had been shot on his freedom walk in Alabama.

The next day Kennedy visited a far tougher place — the University of Stellenbosch — a fountainhead of Afrikaner racialism. Expecting a hostile reception from the students, Kennedy was surprised when they pounded soup spoons on tables, making a sound he later described "like rolling thunder." The initial invitation to speak from the Current Affairs Club had been withdrawn because of public intimidation, only to be reconveyed by one of the men's residence halls.[58] Kennedy began with the trope Walinsky had developed for the Day of Affirmation speech:

> I come here because of my deep interest and affection for a land settled by the Dutch in the mid-seventeenth century, then taken over by the British, and at last independent; a land in which the native inhabitants were at first subdued, but relations with whom remain a problem to this day; a land which defined itself on a hostile frontier; a land which has tamed rich natural resources through the energetic application of modern technology; a land which once imported slaves, and now must struggle to wipe out the last traces of that former bondage. I refer, of course, to the United States of America. But I am glad to come here to South Africa.

There was laughter and cheering. During the question-and-answer session, the students defended apartheid by saying it would produce two nations, one white, the other black, in the manner of India and Pakistan. Did the black people have a choice? Kennedy asked. They made up 78 percent of the population but owned only 12 percent of the land, with no seaport or major city. How could they live in areas whose soil was already exhausted and which had no industry? And they had no education to prepare them: one in every fourteen white students reaches the university, one in 762 blacks makes it.

The Kennedy party then flew to Durban, where Kennedy met with white and African progressive leaders — the novelist Alan Paton of the outlawed Liberal party, Zulu chief Gatsha Buthelezi, Archbishop Denis Hurley of Durban, and others.[59] That evening he spoke at the University of Natal before a crowd of ten thousand. Buoyed by their extraordinary reception, Kennedy now opened up in his counterpunching style: "Maybe there is a black man outside this room who is brighter than anyone — the chances are that there are many." Incredibly, there was applause. During the question-and-answer period, someone argued that Black Africa was too primitive for self-government, that violence and chaos were part of the fabric of African character. In response, Kennedy said that he deplored such massacres as those that had recently taken place in the Congo but that no race or people were without fault: "Was Stalin black? Was Hitler black? Who killed forty million people just twenty-five years ago? It wasn't black people, it was white."

Another man said that the Dutch Reformed Church taught apartheid as "a moral necessity." The Bible says that the Negro should serve.

"But suppose God is black," Kennedy replied. "What if we go to heaven and we, all our lives, have treated the Negro as an inferior, and God is there, and we look up and he is not white? What then is our response?" There was silence in the hall. Suddenly someone asked Kennedy to lead the singing of "We Shall Overcome," which he did.

Bobby was now in his element. Navigating the hot current of crowd emotion — the anger, the cheering, the heckling, the questions — he seemed to draw out the poison and the adrenalin to produce a group catharsis. The style was all the more effective because it was disjointed. He would often start with dry, self-deprecatory humor, then ask the audience questions, and suddenly begin punching the air in a downward motion with his right hand as he delivered simple and emotional conclusions. Walinsky later described Bobby as an "instinctive dancer."[60] It was as if, caught between hope and melancholy, boldness and despair, Kennedy could not communicate unless he seized hands, gazed into faces, and absorbed the emotion of crowds. He was as they were.

Late on the evening of June 7 Kennedy received word at his

hotel that the South African government would permit him to visit Chief Albert John Luthuli, the 1961 Nobel Peace Prize laureate who had been banned and was confined to his home in Groutville, some forty miles inland from Durban. At dawn the next morning, he and Ethel were flown by helicopter down the Valley of a Thousand Hills. Kennedy later described the visit with Luthuli:

> He is a most impressive man, with a marvelously lined face, strong yet kind. My eyes first went to the white goatee, so familiar in his pictures but then the smile took over, illuminating his whole presence, eyes dancing and sparkling. At the mention of apartheid, however, his eyes went hurt and hard. To talk privately, we walked out under the trees and through the fields. "What are they doing to my country, to my countrymen," he sighed. "Can't they see that men of all races can work together — and that the alternative is a terrible disaster for us all?"[61]

Bobby played the speech Jack had given about civil rights on June 11, 1963, on a portable record player he had brought. The old chief was "deeply moved," Kennedy later wrote. Later that day in the huge, seething township of Soweto, standing atop the limo, he told crowds that he had seen Luthuli and that together they had listened to President Kennedy's message to American whites that summer of 1963. He quoted the passages by heart, his eyes teary at points: "We face a moral crisis as a country and a people. It cannot be met by repressive police action. . . . It cannot be quieted by token moves to talk. It is time to act."

His presence, his bold statement, the sight of him standing on the car, sent a shock wave through the township. Soon a huge cavalcade of Africans were running behind and alongside, shouting, "Master! Master!" Kennedy asked them not to call him that, but it made no difference. Later that afternoon at the American consul-general's reception for Kennedy in Johannesburg, hundreds of black South Africans broke "pass laws" by walking to the house, located in a rich neighborhood, and filling both it and the two-acre backyard. There wasn't much more to say, so Bobby, Ethel, and Tom Johnston, their backs to the fireplace, began singing, "We Shall Overcome."[62]

That evening, before seven thousand people at the University of Witwatersrand, Kennedy turned his rhetoric up another notch. Efficiency had led to Auschwitz, he said. Only love would allow us to climb the hill to the Acropolis. "It was not the black man of Africa who invented and used poisoned gas and the atomic bomb, who sent six million men and women and children to the gas ovens and used their bodies as fertilizer." He spoke of all the excuses given for continuing the subjugation: "Everything that is now said about the Negro was said about Irish Catholics. They were useless, they were worthless, they couldn't learn anything. Why did they settle [in Boston]? Why don't we see if we can't get boats and send them back to Ireland? They obviously aren't equipped for education and they certainly can never rule." Kennedy smiled at this. "I suppose there are still some who might agree with that."

The next morning the Kennedy party left South Africa for Tanzania. The newspapers fairly rang with encomia. The *Rand Daily Mail* wrote, "It is as if a window had been flung open and a gust of fresh air has swept into a room in which the atmosphere has become stale and foetid."[63] The *Johannesburg Star* called the visit "unquestionably one of the most important political events in South Africa for many years."[64] Back home, the *Washington Post* commented that his trip was "serious, free of self-righteousness and finally, revolutionary." *The Nation* thought the trip converted Kennedy into "an international figure. Now, with the continuation of nerve and verve, he is in a position to capitalize on it in United States politics." The Johnson White House fretted and calculated just what the impact of Kennedy's play might be.[65]

But beyond the trip's political impact in the United States and South Africa, it was a personal triumph for Bobby. It was the sort of thing Jack would never have done. The percentages were wrong. Tom Johnston later described Bobby's virtuoso performance:

He was initially in a position of being very much the intruder, the man coming to exploit the South Africa situation for his own short-term political benefit, with a lot of self-righteousness and preaching . . . and yet he came out of it five days later, just terribly close to as popular a person and as widely and warmly acclaimed by all sorts of people in that country as you can imagine.[66]

The *Rand Daily Mail* compiled a pamphlet with articles about the visit and the text of four of Kennedy's speeches. It immediately sold out and was reprinted. Several thousand found their way into white offices and black shanties. In June 1986, twenty years later, in a simple bookcase in the office of Cyril Ramaphosa, the leader of the Congress of South African Trades Unions (COSATU), the author found this same little collection, a parable of a beautiful interlude, or maybe even a foreshadowing of the impossible dream.

In those months, Kennedy was reading and occasionally copying out passages from Camus's *Resistance, Rebellion, and Death.* One such passage quoted Pascal: "A man does not show his greatness by being at one extremity, but rather by touching both at once." Bobby felt he had done this. In response to a question a student asked him at Witwatersrand about how difficult, if not hopeless and fatal, it was to fight against institutionalized evil, Bobby had said: "The only alternative is to give up, to admit that you are beaten. I have never admitted that I am beaten."[67] He had come a long way from the black-and-white days of McCarthy and McClellan, of Castro and Marcello. He carried around a small book Jackie had given him at Easter 1964 — *The Greek Way* by Edith Hamilton. He underlined passages that depicted notions such as "tragic pleasure" and memorized one particular passage from Aeschylus: "God, whose law it is that he who learns must suffer. And even in our sleep, pain that cannot forget, falls drop by drop upon the heart, and in our despair, against our will, comes wisdom through the awful grace of God."[68]

November 2, 1966

New York City

Bobby spent the day campaigning for Frank O'Connor, who was running against incumbent Nelson Rockefeller for the governorship of New York. At the four street corner rallies in Midtown Manhattan that day the crowds were disappointingly small. Kennedy said almost nothing about the merits of O'Connor's candidacy except that he would win. Instead Bobby criticized Rockefeller's program of mandatory treatment for drug offenders, pointing out that California's system of voluntary treatment at community clinics and shelters worked far better. It was not exactly a rallying cry, but at least he had fulfilled a political obligation. At the last rally, Bobby spotted two nurses who had served as volunteers in his 1964 Senate race. He invited them and journalist Jack Newfield back to his UN Plaza apartment for a drink.

Newfield would later describe it as an awkward scene. Bobby would talk to his former volunteers about their jobs, their families, asking them what they thought of the speeches that day, and then turn to Newfield and discuss the St. Louis Cardinals' backfield. The young women soon left. Bobby asked Newfield with some embarrassment if he liked poetry. Newfield said he did.

"Can I read you some poetry by a poet I like very much?" Kennedy asked. He disappeared into the bedroom and returned with a thin, dog-eared volume. Silhouetted against a neon Pepsi-Cola sign in Queens, he began to read a poem by Ralph Waldo Emerson:

> He pays too high a price
> For knowledge and for fame
> Who sells his sinews to be wise,

His teeth and bones to buy a name,
And crawls through life a paralytic
To earn the praise of bard and critic

Were it not better done,
To dine and sleep through forty years;
Be loved by a few; be feared by none;
Laugh life away, have wine for tears;
And take the mortal leap undaunted,
Content that all we asked was granted?

But Fate will not permit
The seed of gods to die
Nor suffer sense to win from wit
Its guerdon in the sky,
Nor let us hide, whate'er our pleasure,
The world's light underneath a measure

Bobby knew the poem's last stanza by heart. His eyes focused on the middle distance as he recited it:

Go then, sad youth, and shine,
Go, sacrifice to Fame;
Put youth, joy, health upon the shrine,
And life to fan the flame;
Being for Seeming bravely barter,
And die to Fame a happy martyr.[69]

February 6, 1967

Washington, D.C.

Lyndon Johnson now had him in his sights. For the first time in two years, he was ahead of Bobby Kennedy in the polls — by no fewer than 22 points. "I'll destroy you and every one of your dove friends," he told Bobby bluntly during a face-to-face meeting. "You'll be dead politically in six months." Johnson accused Kennedy of leaking to the press a "peace feeler" from Hanoi that Bobby had supposedly received while in Paris. Kennedy told the president that the press report wasn't true, he had done no such thing, but Johnson pressed on. Stop talking about a bombing halt, the president said. Kennedy ignored the threat and enjoined Johnson to stop the bombing. "There is not a chance in hell I will do that," the president replied. He added that Bobby and his friends were giving comfort to the enemy. They were encouraging Hanoi to keep on fighting and keep on killing American boys. Bobby, he said, had blood on his hands. Kennedy stood up. "Look, I don't have to take that from you," he snapped.[70]

Johnson was taking Bobby to task not simply because of Kennedy's position on Vietnam but because of questions involving the assassination of President Kennedy. In January 1967 *Washington Post* columnist Drew Pearson had visited Johnson and told him about a story he was working on — that the Kennedy administration tried to kill Castro, and that Castro retaliated by killing Kennedy. This was called the "turnaround theory" and it gave Johnson fresh proof that the "cross-eyed boy" had caused his own brother's assassination. On February 18, President Johnson phoned acting attorney general Ramsey Clark. Pearson, the president told Clark, had spoken of "a man that was involved, that was brought into the CIA with a number of others, and instructed by the CIA and the attorney general to assassinate Castro after the Bay of Pigs." The man Johnson was describing was Johnny Rosselli, the Mafia's man of masks and adventure, who had once golfed with Joseph Kennedy Sr., bagged money for the Kennedy campaign in 1960 — and who had met in secrecy with Jack Ruby several weeks before the assassination in Dallas.[71]

Two days after Johnson's warning to stop criticizing the administration, Kennedy used harsh language in a speech at the University of Chicago to question American policy in Asia. A few days later Johnson — through Pearson — struck back. Pearson's nationally syndicated "Washington Merry-Go-Round" reported that "President Johnson is sitting on a political H-bomb, an unconfirmed report that Sen. Robert Kennedy may have approved an assassination plot which then possibly backfired against his late brother."[72] Arthur Schlesinger saw Bobby not long after this article appeared. "An indefinable sense of depression hung over him," Schlesinger wrote, "as if he felt cornered by circumstance and did not know how to break out."

Bobby's arrogant zeal seemed to reach out from the past and bedevil him. In May 1966 the bugging issue, long smoldering inside the Justice Department and the FBI, ignited publicly. Fred B. Black Jr., a Washington lobbyist and Rosselli intimate who had been convicted for income tax evasion, made an appeal to the Supreme Court, claiming that the FBI had bugged his hotel suite in D.C. in 1963. The Supreme Court took Black's appeal. Senator Kennedy called his former deputy and now newly appointed attorney general Nicholas Katzenbach, and asked him to state in the government's brief that Kennedy had no knowledge of the Black bug or bugging in general. Katzenbach demurred, preferring to leave it vague. Kennedy was furious. Later he called Katzenbach and admitted that he had listened to recordings made by bugs.[73]

"The Skimming Report," which Kennedy had forced the FBI to produce in May 1963 as part of his attack on organized crime, was now being used to block federal prosecution. All over the country Mafia attorneys such as Tom Wadden, Jack Wasserman, and Edward Bennett Williams mounted Fourth Amendment search and seizure defenses for their clients.[74] The attorneys for Bobby Baker, who was charged with tax evasion, theft, and conspiracy, did the same, claiming in federal court that FBI bugs had picked up Baker's conversations with "business associates" at six gambling casinos.

Senator Edward Long of Missouri, a Hoffa loyalist, seized on the government's brief in the Black appeal and called for an investigation. White House aide Bill Moyers told Dick Goodwin, who was now Johnson's chief speechwriter, that the president "is egging [Long] on." On December 10, Hoover let loose, charging that Kennedy had directly approved the electronic surveillance.[75] Contacted by reporters, Kennedy refused comment. Later his office issued a statement denying the charge and issued a letter from Courtney Evans (the FBI's former liaison to the former attorney general) exonerating Kennedy. A file in Kennedy aide Frank Mankiewicz's papers reveals, however, that there was nothing simple about the senator's defense. Essentially, Kennedy's claim was that he should have known but didn't, and had never formally ordered electronic surveillance — an awkward piece of casuistry at best.[76]

The charges and countercharges between Hoover and Kennedy went on for weeks in the press. Edwyn Silberling, the former chief of Kennedy's organized crime section, did not help his former boss's position when he told *New York Times* reporter Leslie Whitten that he distinctly remembered a meeting in 1961 in which Kennedy demanded that the FBI step up its efforts to develop evidence against Cosa Nostra officials: "Everybody at the meeting knew he [Kennedy] was talking about electronic surveillance — parabolic microphones, spike microphones, bugs — that is micro-transmitters — the whole thing."[77]

Kennedy loyalists stuck to the position that Robert Kennedy would not lie. "I am absolutely persuaded that Bobby Kennedy did not know about the FBI buggings," Katzenbach said. "I am also absolutely persuaded that any objective observer would believe that he did."[78]

In December 1966, Jimmy Hoffa's appeal to the Supreme Court to overturn his jury-tampering conviction refocused scrutiny on former attorney general Kennedy's prosecutorial tactics. The Supreme Court upheld the conviction, but in a close vote. Chief Justice Warren and Justice William O. Douglas wrote separate and vigorous opinions, questioning the government's use of evidence from an informer planted inside of Hoffa's leadership.[79]

For many liberals the scandal confirmed their view of Kennedy's questionable record on civil liberties. In his State of the Union address to Congress, President Johnson, a man who routinely perused the salacious fruits of FBI surveillance of certain congressional personae, called for a ban on all forms of electronic eavesdropping except in matters of national security. As the Congress applauded, Kennedy sat there, embarrassed and galled.

At around this same time, Bobby was scourged by intimations and rumors of a far more terrible nature — that Jack had been killed by a conspiracy that Bobby had himself given life to. In the summer of 1966, New Orleans district attorney Jim Garrison launched an investigation of what he later claimed to be a New Orleans–based conspiracy to kill President Kennedy. Central to the investigation was the movement and associations of David Ferrie. In mid-December 1966, Garrison brought Ferrie in for questioning. He also sent two of his investigators to Miami to follow up on a lead that brought Santos Trafficante into the loop of the inquiry.

The Warren Report was drawing new fire from serious scholars. Edward J. Epstein, in his book *Inquest: The Warren Commission and the Establishment of Truth,* demonstrated that the Commission's investigation had been sloppy and never proved that Oswald had acted alone or even was the killer. Dick Goodwin wrote a laudatory review of the book in the *Washington Post's Book Week,* calling for a new investigation by an independent group. A few days later, in a late-night conversation with Bobby at his UN Plaza apartment, Goodwin recounted his doubts about the Warren Commission.

"Bobby listened silently, without objection," Goodwin later wrote, "his inner tension or distaste revealed only by the circling currents of Scotch in the glass he was obsessively rotating between his hands, staring at the floor in a posture of avoidance."

He finally looked up when Goodwin was finished. "I'm sorry, Dick," he said. "I just can't focus on it."

But Goodwin pressed the issue. "I think we should find our own investigator — someone with absolute loyalty and discretion."

"You might try Carmine Bellino. He's the best in the country."

That was as much as Kennedy would say. The conversation

shifted to Vietnam. At 2:30 A.M., they both retired to their bed-rooms. Goodwin later described Bobby as pausing for a moment as he entered his bedroom and then looking toward him: " 'About that other thing.' I knew instantly he meant the conversation about the assassination that had begun that evening. 'I never thought it was the Cubans. If anyone was involved it was organized crime. But there's nothing I can do about it. Not now.' "[80]

Garrison brought Ferrie in for questioning in December 1966. If Ferrie broke, Marcello, with whom Ferrie had been closeted at Churchill Farms in the days before JFK's assassination, stood to be questioned. It was a dangerous time for the conspirators. Either under instruction or by his own initiative, Johnny Rosselli launched a disinformation campaign to neutralize Garrison's investigation. Rosselli's chosen conduit was Edward P. Morgan, a Hoffa attorney who had also done work for Meyer Lansky and had strong contacts with senior officials in the CIA and the FBI. Morgan already knew the first part of what Rosselli told him: that he, Rosselli, had been the go-between in the CIA-Mafia plot to kill Castro. The second part Morgan did not know: that in the course of this operation there had supposedly been a disastrous reversal of fortune. A sniper team sent to Havana in 1963 under order of the attorney general had been captured, tortured, and redeployed back into the United States to assassinate President Kennedy.[81] After accomplishing their mission, two of the snipers had escaped to New Jersey, where they were now in hiding.

The false story threw up four principal barriers against any in-vestigation that might lead to the real killers of President Kennedy:

1) The CIA. It was obvious to Rosselli and anyone in the know that the CIA, in particular Allen Dulles, a Warren Commission member, had covered up the CIA's violent relationship with anti-Castro Cubans and the fact that Oswald, as Senator Richard Schweiker later said, "had the fingerprints of Intelli-gence all over him."[82] The CIA had serious reason to block anything that would expose its sometime partner in capital crime — Santos Trafficante.

2) The FBI. The reason Hoover had lied so extensively while as-sisting the Warren Commission was probably to cover up the

Bureau's gross incompetence. The director had censured no
fewer than seventeen Special Agents after the fact for lapses and
investigative errors. It could be expected that the FBI would
play the same role in shutting down Garrison.

3) Senator Robert F. Kennedy. Kennedy had publicly announced
his support for the Warren Commission's findings. If Garrison
broke anything open, the senator could call for a new federal
investigation. What better way to blackmail him into silence
than by suggesting that Kennedy himself had caused the assassination by conspiring to kill Castro?

4) Lee Harvey Oswald. The turnaround theory, involving the redeployed sniper team, matched Oswald's known profile as a
pro-Castro sympathizer and "explained the ubiquitous presence of Cubans in the Kennedy plots [and] anticipated the possibility that Garrison or another investigator would trace a hit
team back to Trafficante's Miami — where else would Castro's
sharpshooters make their U.S. beachhead?"[83]

Morgan had forwarded Rosselli's story to Drew Pearson via
Pearson's partner, Jack Anderson. Pearson was impressed enough
with the story that he sent it to Chief Justice Earl Warren, who
turned it over to the Secret Service. James Rowley, the head of the
Secret Service, in turn relayed it to Hoover, who buried it: "Consideration was given to furnishing this information to the White
House," the internal FBI memo read, "but since this matter does
not concern, nor is it pertinent to, the current administration, no
letter was sent."[84] In the third week of January, President Johnson
learned about it directly from Pearson.

In New Orleans, Garrison took Ferrie, who now feared for his
life, into protective custody. On February 21, he released Ferrie to
confinement in his own apartment. He was found dead the next
morning. The coroner ruled the cause cerebral hemorrhage, but authorities found two unsigned typewritten suicide notes. Acting
attorney general Clark told the president that the FBI believed that
Ferrie had died of natural causes.[85] Twelve hours later, the body of
the other witness Garrison's investigators were seeking in Miami,
Eladio del Valle, was found in a Miami parking lot. He had been
tortured, his head split open with an ax, and shot through the heart

for extra demonstrative measure.[86] This was *omerta* the old-country way.

Garrison brandished these deaths, particularly del Valle's, as evidence of a conspiracy, and his allegations took on weight. To slow Garrison down, Rosselli now tried to go public with his turnaround story, again through his attorney Edward P. Morgan. Someone, supposedly "from the inside of Garrison's office," leaked another version of the story to Texas Governor John Connally, who immediately called the president. On the evening of March 2, he told Johnson that his "secret report" revealed that "Castro and his people heard the whole story" about the CIA's scheme to kill the Cuban leader from the assassination teams that had been captured. Castro had also learned, Connally said, that "President Kennedy did not give the order to the CIA, but that some other person extremely close to President Kennedy did. They did not name names, but the inference was very clear. The inference was that it was his brother."[87] The president, who was in a raging mood over a speech Bobby Kennedy had given that morning attacking America's war in Vietnam, briefed Connally on the impact of that speech in the Congress. The next day Pearson published his extraordinary claim that Robert Kennedy had approved an assassination plot that backfired on his brother.

Through his aides, Johnson demanded on March 17 that the FBI interview Morgan. The FBI's Cartha DeLoach resisted, saying that Morgan didn't want to be interviewed and that the FBI did not want to encourage "publicity seeker" Garrison. The White House finally ordered the FBI to comply.

On March 20, FBI agents spoke with Morgan for two hours in his Washington office at 300 Farragut Building. Morgan, who was already well known in FBI circles, immediately set the ground rules: "He [Morgan] was not stating or implying his clients were either directly or indirectly involved in the death of the president or could be prosecuted in that regard — the Statute of Limitations has not run out on conspiracy to kill."[88] Morgan said that "if he were a government investigator assigned to unravel all facets of the assassination of President Kennedy he would first concern himself with the topic of the Castro plot." He did not mention the attorney general's role in particular, only that the project to kill Castro had "the highest governmental approval." He then took the agents through the process by which the plot to kill Castro had rebounded on President Kennedy.

Morgan described Rosselli, without naming him, as "a high type individual of the Catholic faith whose conscience bothered him." According to Morgan, the client, "when hearing the statement that Lee Harvey Oswald was the sole assassin of President Kennedy, laughs with tears in his eyes." It was an unusual moment — a Mafia murderer confirming that there had been a conspiracy to kill the president in order to force the federal government, its own hands dirty, to cover up that very assassination by neutralizing Garrison. Morgan avowed his client would not deal with Garrison and found it "inconceivable that an agency of the government which conducts intelligence-type investigations outside the United States has not come forth to make this most important data available to the Warren Commission." President Johnson then demanded that the CIA do just that — brief him on its role in the Castro plots. He later charged that the Kennedys had been running "a damn Murder Incorporated in the Caribbean."[89] Now the CIA was on the chopping block.

Garrison's own investigation had by this time undergone a bewildering shift, consistent with the maneuvering going on in Washington. Garrison dropped his inquiry into the Mafia and, on March 1, 1967, arrested businessman Clay Shaw on charges that he conspired to kill President Kennedy. Named in the subsequent indictment were fourteen CIA officials who had allegedly co-conspired with Shaw, including a former deputy director of the CIA, General Charles Cabell. Why this complete change of direction? Many contend that Carlos Marcello had gotten to Garrison, underwriting construction of an expensive home and picking up gambling debts. For good measure, Rosselli met with Garrison in Las Vegas, further compromising him. (Garrison, later under fire for his mob connections, vehemently denied that the meeting ever took place.)[90]

CIA officials understood the game Rosselli was playing and commented in a top-secret internal memo: "The Rosselli-Garrison contact in Las Vegas is particularly disturbing. It lends substance to reports that Castro had something to do with the Kennedy assassination in retaliation for American's attempts on Castro's life. We do *not* know that Castro actually tried to retaliate, but we do know there were plots against Castro. Unhappily, it now appears that Garrison may also know this" (emphasis in original).[91] Rosselli's legend had molded itself perfectly to the confederacy of bureaucratic self-interest in Washington. In the end, Johnson's hatred for Robert Kennedy was not enough to pry open the rotten trunk of the Warren Commission.

As Marcello's operatives rolled over Garrison, a farcical denouement was taking place. Mafia front men, in order to spring Hoffa, moved on the man who had once been Bobby's star witness against Hoffa, Ed Partin. The first effort was to bribe Partin to recant his testimony in exchange for a $1 million payment from Marcello *consiglieri* D'Alton Smith, but this did not work. In June the demoralized and desperate Garrison made a sensational claim: that Ed Partin, the man who in 1962 had warned Bobby Kennedy that Hoffa was conspiring to kill him, was himself involved in the assassination of President Kennedy.[92] Facing an eight-year sentence in the federal penitentiary, Hoffa launched into a last-ditch effort for a Supreme Court rehearing. It was denied.

By the spring of 1967 Lyndon Johnson's war against Bobby Kennedy had taken its toll. For the first time, as we've seen, he moved ahead of Bobby Kennedy in national polls as the preferred Democrat for president in 1968. The bugging scandal, the Kennedys' dispute with historian William Manchester over his authorized book, *Death of a President* — a dispute involving control over the transcripts of interviews a grief-stricken Jackie had given Manchester — as well as the reprise of controversy about the Kennedy assassination had eroded his popular standing. Kennedy now understood that Johnson would give him no quarter. According to Kenny O'Donnell, it was a time of pain and doubt for Bobby: Hoover and Johnson were trying to destroy him — and sully the memory of Jack — and they had the goods to do it. What they were trying to exact from him was silence. Silence on civil rights. Silence on Vietnam.[93] Once again he turned to Camus for solace and guidance: "Smiling despair. No solution, but constantly exercising an authority over myself that I know is useless. The essential thing is not to lose oneself, and not to lose the part of oneself that lies sleeping in the world."

Despite his South Africa speech, despite his work as a senator, Bobby felt that the self that had lain sleeping in these bitter years after Jack's death was Bobby the combatant, the crusader. With 500,000 American soldiers now in Vietnam — 100 each week coming home in body bags — and President Johnson accusing antiwar critics of perfidy, the only thing left for Bobby to do was to throw caution to the wind, to run against Johnson and the war, to run beyond the shadow of Jack.

He was back on the boat off Nantucket on that long-ago summer day in 1929.

March 16, 1968

Washington, D.C.

Bobby looked unhappy, nervous, and, above all, unready for what he was about to do. "I am announcing today my candidacy for the presidency of the United States," he began. "I do not run for the presidency merely to oppose any man" — as he paused, someone giggled — "but to propose new policies." He stumbled on through the lame counterpoint: paying tribute to Johnson, but not his policies, congratulating Senator Eugene McCarthy in his near-upset of the president in the New Hampshire primary, suggesting that they run "in harmony" (whatever that meant). He was entering late, so late that he would not qualify for the ballot in some primary states. He had no campaign staff and no strategy for a national campaign. But he was John F. Kennedy's brother and, therefore, the heir apparent.

When he concluded his statement, he called for questions. Most were hostile. One reporter asked him how his candidacy was not "opportunism on your part. . . . McCarthy had the courage to go into New Hampshire while you hesitated."[94] Kennedy's reply was awkward and unconvincing. Still, his timing may have been terrible, but at least he was entering the fray — his native habitat.

If there was one reason why Bobby was running, it was to end America's war in Vietnam. In a speech in the Senate a year earlier he had broken dramatically with the Johnson administration regarding the war. At that point, it seemed axiomatic that if the war widened, he would be pushed into running against President Johnson in the 1968 election. Politically, however, this looked self-destructive. A substantial majority of Americans supported the president's policy. The antiwar movement, though a significant new factor in American politics, was not yet a defining factor. The war

342

itself conduced to self-deception. There were no set-piece battles, no certain terrain to be won or lost, but rather a slow hemorrhage of ambushes and infiltrations by the communists, followed by massive stanching actions by American forces.

The United States had become consumed with the tactic of the war — strategic hamlets, free-fire zones, body counts, bombing defoliation — not one of which would win the battle in the field, and all of which incrementally drew American forces deeper. Like a half-mad captain on a burning deck, Secretary McNamara would dash to the White House with his new numbers and paper Congress with his charts and graphs. In the spring of 1967, President Johnson let it be known that the war would probably be won by "June or July."

The safer route for Kennedy would have been to reiterate the critique of the war set forth by Under Secretary George Ball within the administration and J. William Fulbright in the Senate. Vietnam was, as Ball put it, an "aberration" from America's containment policy that undermined other security interests. The contest was essentially a civil war in which North Vietnam was stronger. The corrupt elite in Saigon was at war with its own people as much as with the communists. To the extent there was a solution, it was political, not military. "For a guerrilla to win, it is only necessary for him not to lose," Ball wrote, quoting Mao Zedong.[95]

This was the reasoned discourse of policy debate — that Vietnam was faulty statecraft — but it was not the tack Bobby took. Rising on the Senate floor on March 2, 1967, he began with a pro forma defense of America's presence in Vietnam. Then, in an abrupt shift, Kennedy went on to describe the horror of war from the standpoint of the Vietnamese. The Vietnam War, he said, had become:

> The vacant moment of amazed fear as a mother and child watch death by fire fall down from an improbable machine sent by a country they hardly comprehend . . . a land deadened by an unending crescendo of violence, hatred, and savage fury. . . . Although the world's imperfection may call forth the act of war, righteousness cannot obscure the agony and pain those acts bring to a single child. It is we who live in abundance and send our young men out to die. It is our chemicals that scorch the children and our bombs that level the villages. We are all participants.

Johnson did everything he could to upstage and discredit the statement in public. He unleashed that Drew Pearson story about Bobby's role in bringing about his brother's assassination. Had Johnson been able to force the CIA to reveal Bobby's association with the Castro murder plots, or had he persuaded Hoover to re-open the investigation of President Kennedy's assassination, the damage would have been considerable. But these agencies and the men who led them, as Rosselli had calculated, had the motive and capacity to block any serious inquiry.

Beyond the disposition of these secrets, Kennedy faced a continuing predicament: if he took issue with Johnson administration policy or even distanced himself from the president, the press played it as the ambitious Bobby Kennedy starting to make his move. Article after article used that scarlet adjective dating back to McClellan Committee — "ruthless" — and it stung Kennedy to silence.

On November 26, 1967, Kennedy appeared on CBS's *Face the Nation*. The issue, it seemed the only issue, the press queried him on in those days was whether he would run against President Johnson. In response to a question by Tom Wicker, Kennedy wearily said, "No matter what I do, I am in difficulty. . . . I don't know what I can do except perhaps try to get off the earth in some way." But how could he oppose the war, Wicker asked, and not run against Johnson? Bobby's reaction was an emotional outpouring:

> We're going in there and we're killing South Vietnamese, we're killing children, we're killing women, we're killing innocent people because we don't want a war fought on American soil, or because [the Viet Cong are] 12,000 miles away and they might get 11,000 miles away. Do we have the right, here in the United States, to say we're going to kill tens of thousands, make millions of people, as we have, millions of people refugees, killing women and children, as we have?[96]

The idea of taking on Johnson seemed foolhardy. Sorensen, O'Donnell, O'Brien, Smith, Salinger, and even Bobby's brother Ted all told him not to. Johnson couldn't be beaten, they said; it would ruin the party and elect Richard Nixon; it would finish Bobby's chances in 1972 and would even undermine the reason why Bobby said he wanted to run — to stop the war in Vietnam. Ted thought their father would have said, "Don't do it." And what would Jack have said? Dick Goodwin asked Ted. "Jack would have probably cautioned him against it, but he might have done it himself."

But Bobby was not Jack. He was not a percentage player. As hard-bitten a political veteran as he was, he was essentially running on emotion. He hated the war, hated Lyndon Johnson, and feared that Vietnam and racial division were killing America. To be president was not a personal ambition so much as a moral ambition. It would have to be a crusade, not a campaign. The people Bobby increasingly looked to for guidance were his key staffers Walinsky and Edelman, journalists like Jack Newfield and Pete Hamill, and liberal activists like Allard Lowenstein. They all believed that he should take on Johnson. The problem was, in O'Donnell's words, "Bobby had no Bobby. And Joe and Jack were gone." And so he remained paralyzed in indecision.

Ethel was urging him to run, and her recommendation was critical. She and Bobby remained inseparable. There was no one whose company he sought and enjoyed so much. In 1951, he had sent her a note containing his paraphrase of the biblical Book of Ruth: "And Ruth said, "Entreat me not to leave thee, or to return from following after Thee, for whither Thou goeth I will go; and whither Thou lodgest I will lodge; Thy people shall be my people and Thy God my God. When Thou diest then I will die and we will be together forever."[97] Ethel was hypercompetitive and instinctual. Tanned, athletic, and beaming, she wore skirts with hemlines three inches above the knee onstage. Offstage she was a constant cut-up. She was also one of the best campaigners in the entire Kennedy family.[98] She shared the Kennedys' tribal view of the world, referring to Johnson, for example, as "Huckleberry Capone." Without Ethel, Bobby would never have braved his troubled odyssey.

On January 19, 1968, over dinner with Steve and Jean Smith and Pat Lawford, Bobby said he thought he would run. "This is going to cost you a lot of money," he added and laughed.[99] Publicly, however, he was still reticent. Eleven days after the dinner, he released a statement to the press that "I have told friends and supporters who are urging me to run that I would not oppose Lyndon Johnson under any foreseeable circumstances." Walinsky was so upset by this that he threatened to resign. Meanwhile, Senator Eugene McCarthy announced his candidacy for president and began mounting what looked to be a hapless challenge to Johnson in New Hampshire. Bobby watched, undecided and tormented, while old friends such as Goodwin, Lowenstein, and John Kenneth Galbraith signed on with McCarthy. Kennedy clearly underestimated McCarthy, thinking him lazy and diffident, not recognizing that beyond the antiwar posture, McCarthy's cool, distanced demeanor offered an attractive counterpoint to the hot and ugly emotions of the day.

In early February, the North Vietnamese and Viet Cong unleashed a surprise attack on Saigon during the Tet holiday. Suddenly the war spilled into the living rooms of America though television images of people being shot dead in the streets of Saigon and the American embassy under siege. On February 8, in Chicago, Kennedy denounced in sweeping language American policy in Vietnam. He had now moved into open confrontation to Johnson, but was still uncertain about jumping in. Seeing McCarthy's numbers rise in New Hampshire, Goodwin advised him: "Declare now."

In the midst of a furious debate among his lieutenants about whether he should run, Bobby received an unusual request. Embattled farmworker leader Cesar Chavez, in his fourth week without food to protest violence in the vineyards of California, wanted Kennedy to fly out to the San Joaquin Valley to celebrate his fast over mass. His advisors, with the exception of Edelman, were opposed. The idea of a potential presidential candidate attending mass with a starving Mexican labor leader seemed needlessly provocative. When Ed Guthman questioned the idea, Bobby said, "I know, but I like Cesar."[100]

In California the Teamsters had unleashed their usual battery of assault troops — lawyers in the courts, lobbyists with checks in hand in the state capitals, and goon squads in the fields. Threats and violence by the growers and Teamsters began to force farmworkers into armed resistance and sabotage despite Chavez's insistence on nonviolence. Fields and sheds were set afire and water pumps blown up. The NFWA tried to confiscate guns from union members. "No union movement is worth the death of one farmworker or his child or one grower and his child," Chavez told his followers. "I despise exploitation and I want change, but I'm willing to pay the price in terms of time."[101] But given the level of anger and frustration among his followers, that old Mexican saying — *Hay más tiempo que vida* (there is more time than life) — didn't seem true anymore.

Another issue ripping apart the Hispanic community was the Vietnam War. Each week, scores of body bags containing the remains of Mexican-American soldiers killed in Vietnam were coming home to the barrios of southern California. The American dream seemed like a treacherous fraud. In an interview, Chavez remembers his followers saying to him, "Hey, we've got to burn these sons of bitches down. We've got to kill a few of them."[102] Like Martin Luther King Jr., Cesar Chavez was being bypassed by the disciples of violence.

On February 19, 1968, out of desperation more than some vision of renewal, Chavez told his amazed followers that he would not take one more bite of food until the violence stopped. With this he left them at Filipino Hall and started walking down the garbage-strewn highway toward his small windowless room at Forty Acres. No one liked the idea. His wife told him he was crazy. Saul Alinsky, his mentor, was disgusted to hear the news; he thought it too Catholic. Even his fiery deputy Dolores Huerta begged him to stop. But Chavez was unmoved.[103]

At first glance, Chavez didn't seem the hero type. He had, as his friend Jim Drake said, a bad back and too many children. Most of the time when he spoke he could scarcely make himself heard. He was uneducated, having never started high school. But in his capacity for sacrifice — traveling all night to join strikers at a picket, walking 300 miles to Sacramento, or even simply finding someone a job — he was matchless. This power of sacrifice, writer Peter Matthiesen said, derived from the complete simplicity and transparency of the man. His voice "comes as naturally as bird song — it is a pleasure to watch him move. He has what the Japanese call, *hara,* or 'belly' — that is, he is centered in himself."[104] Arthur Schlesinger thought that for all their differences Chavez and Kennedy were rather alike: "Both short, shy, familial, devout, opponents of violence, with a strong vein of melancholy and fatalism."[105] They shared a love for Saint Francis of Assisi, that most gentle of saints, and believed that acts of faith could change the world.

On the thirteenth day of his fast, Chavez left his cot to travel to Bakersfield to contest a contempt charge in Kern County Superior Court. As attorney Jerry Cohen helped him into a waiting car, they could see through the early morning fog the lights of hundreds of farmworker cars waiting to accompany them. In and around the court building later that morning, some four thousand farmworkers knelt and prayed as the hearing began. The judge ordered the contempt charges against Chavez dropped. The scene made national news. Senator Kennedy sent Chavez a telex. "He asked me to consider the consequences of what would happen if my health failed," Chavez recalled.[106]

When Chavez returned to his cot that afternoon, he had to make his way through a mass of supporters who had gathered at the Forty Acres. Along the roads leading into Delano came a steady stream of people, some walking, others in cars or the backs of trucks. The compound filled with tents. Crosses and Virgin of Guadalupe statues were erected. Priests wore vestments cut from union flags and offered mass with union wine. Prayer rallies continued well into the night. Having failed to contain violence in his ceaseless travels, much less organize anything more than a fraction of the farms of California, Chavez had succeeded by the example of his courage and vulnerability in rallying his followers.

By the twentieth day of his fast, Chavez's body began breaking down. He lost consciousness at points. His weight, normally about 150 pounds, was down to 120. He had fasted longer than Mohandas Gandhi had during his hunger strike of 1924. But his gentle sense of humor remained. Unable now to talk to the people who wanted to see him, he instructed one of his followers to tell those who knocked at the door: "Don't bother him. He's eating right now." In his moments of lucidity, Chavez reflected on the dilemma before him. If he died, the fast would have been fruitless. But if he was to break the fast, how?[107] Dolores Huerta, then in New York, had the answer: Bobby Kennedy. He would come back to Delano and at a mass of thanksgiving break bread with Cesar. There wasn't much time. Most of Kennedy's staff thought it was a terrible idea. So of course Bobby went.

Kennedy flew from Iowa, where he had given a jumbled speech in favor of Governor Harold Hughes, who was running for the Senate, to Los Angeles, and then in a smaller plane to Delano. With him were Ed Guthman and John Seigenthaler, who had accompanied him that December 1960 morning when he tried to tell Jack he wanted out.

The news of his arrival swelled the crowds to six or seven thousand around Forty Acres. Chavez waited in a happy blur, "getting minute-by-minute details," as he later remembered, and blessing God for Dolores Huerta. Then the shouts of "Viva Kennedy!" as the car carrying Bobby pulled up.[108] Before walking into Chavez's room, Bobby said to his aide, "What do you say to a guy who's on a fast?" They didn't say much, as it turned out, looking and smiling at each other and nodding their heads.[109]

When they emerged, with Chavez being supported by two aides, Kennedy remarked to the press, motioning toward Chavez: "This is one of the heroic figures of our time." When Kennedy arrived at the county park for the mass, the crowd of several thousand went crazy. Dolores Huerta remembered:

> People were coming up to him, and they would grab him and hug him and kiss him on the mouth! And, you know, *un gran hombre* — great man, Kennedy — *un gran hombre*. People would grab him, and his hands were all scratched up. When he sat down in front of me, his hands were all bloodied.[110]

The mass was celebrated on the back of a flat-bed truck. Kennedy and Chavez sat side by side, flanked by Chavez's wife, Helen Fabela, and his mother Juana.

"Well, how goes the boycott, Cesar?"

"How goes running for president, Bob?" Chavez replied, and both men laughed.

At the conclusion of the service, Kennedy took a homemade Mexican bread loaf called *semita,* broke off a piece and gave it to Chavez. The ABC cameraman did not get the shot and said to Kennedy: "Senator, this is perhaps the most ridiculous remark I've ever made in my life. Would you mind giving Cesar another piece of bread so we can get a picture?" Kennedy declined.[111]

Reverend Jim Drake then read a statement written by Chavez, too weak to read it himself, first in Spanish, then in English:

> Our struggle is not easy. Those who oppose our cause are rich and powerful, and they have many allies in high places. We are poor. Our allies are few. But we have something the rich do not own. We have our bodies and spirits and the justice of our cause as our weapons. When we are really honest with ourselves, we must admit that our lives are all that really belong to us. So it is how we use our lives that determines what kind of men we are. It is my deepest belief that only by giving our lives do we find life. I am convinced that the truest act of courage, the strongest act of manliness is to sacrifice ourselves for others in a totally non-violent struggle for justice. To be a man is to suffer for others. God help us be men![112]

Kennedy then stood up and briefly spoke, with Huerta providing the interpretation:

> I am here out of respect for one of the heroic figures of our time — Cesar Chavez. I congratulate all of you who are locked with Cesar in the struggle for justice for the farm worker, and in the struggle for justice for Spanish-speaking Americans. . . . There are those of you who question the principle of nonviolence. Let me say to you that violence is no answer.[113]

Bobby then attempted two phrases in Spanish. The result was impenetrable. "Am I murdering the language?" he asked Chavez, who was laughing. "Yes. Go ahead."[114] The effect was nonetheless thunderous approval. When Kennedy finished speaking, the crowd surged toward him. As his chair was knocked forward, Chavez, still dazed and dizzy, said to Kennedy, "We're pretty lousy in controlling crowds."[115] Dolores Huerta noticed that the senator was staring at a man standing at the edge of the circle. The man was wearing blue jeans and a blue-jeans jacket. His hair and eyes were gray.[116]

"Who is that man?" Kennedy asked her. She said she didn't

know and approached the man, asking him in Spanish if he were a member of the union. It was evident from his reaction that he didn't understand what she was saying. As Kennedy tried to make his way back to the car, he was again mobbed by well-wishers. Mack Lyons, a black union leader who was trying to escort the senator through the crowd, remembered Kennedy saying to him, "That man is trying to kill me." He was referring to the man Huerta had approached.[117] Chavez meanwhile had been carried back by supporters to a station wagon and placed on a mattress in the back. He could hear the crowd cheering and shouting to Bobby in Spanish, "Run! Run!" as he dozed off.

When he got into the car, Kennedy turned to Jim Drake. "Well, I might just do that." Suddenly Bobby jumped out of the car, climbed up on the roof, and shouted to the crowd: *"Viva la Causa!"*[118] By the time he got on the plane, he was more emphatic about running for president. "Yes, I'm going to do it."[119] He called Ethel and she, in turn, called Arthur Schlesinger with jubilation in her voice to relay the news.

March 16 galvanized Bobby Kennedy. It had had everything: the giving of hope to the forgotten; the act of touching, even to be bloodied by, people who needed him; the beatification of his hero at the mass; and the premonition of martyrdom — in the figure of the man with the gray eyes. The sacrifice, Chavez later thought, was to be consumed by love. By crossing a line "you very seldom cross," Bobby had entered "a closeness that creates tearing him to pieces, little by little, just wanting him all for you."[120]

A few days after the announcement, Schlesinger encountered Jackie Kennedy at a dinner party in New York. She took him aside: "Do you know what I think will happen to Bobby?" Schlesinger replied that he didn't. "The same thing that happened to Jack."[121]

Several weeks later, an informant for the FBI told his overseeing agent that there was a Mafia contract of several hundred thousand dollars to assassinate Kennedy "in the event it appeared he might receive the Democratic nomination."[122] Presidential candidates in those days received no protection from the Secret Service. As a federal elected officer, Senator Kennedy would have received the benefit of the FBI's existing surveillance in major American cities, were it to pick up any indication of a plot to kill him. But

Hoover had made it clear that Kennedy was a man the FBI would do nothing to protect. Startling his colleagues at an executive staff meeting, Clyde Tolson, Hoover's office factotum and live-in partner, expressed a darker wish: "I hope someone shoots and kills that son of a bitch."[123]

June 5, 1968

Los Angeles

Dolores Huerta would remember the ride down the elevator that night at the Ambassador Hotel. How she had told Bobby Kennedy that several Mexican precincts had voted 100 percent for him that day. How he had given her a hug and how she had hugged him back. She would remember asking herself why he had no security, the way Cesar did. Perhaps she should say something. How Bobby had first waved at the kitchen staff as he got out of the elevator on the first floor and then walked over to shake their hands. Again the thought: no security. She would remember the roar and crush in the ballroom as he entered to accept victory.[124]

In Bobby Kennedy's 85-day run for president, the end, it seemed, was always near. The theologian Michael Novak saw "a very fragile, vulnerable person who was absolutely certain he was going to die. I just couldn't escape the feeling in his eyes." Novak thought that like Thomas à Becket in T. S. Eliot's play *Murder in the Cathedral,* Bobby struggled between "his commitment to the pragmatic and the concrete" and "his need to give witness." In speeches endorsing Kennedy's candidacy Novak would tell his listeners: "You people just won't understand Robert Kennedy unless you understand that he doesn't know if he's going to live tomorrow. And therefore, he's got to do it today — he's just got to act because he can't care about the consequences."[125]

Kennedy became like a soldier in combat: alert, feeding off intuition, and operating freely in a space somewhere between life and death. Jack had looked at his fate and the prospect of glory coldly, but the man a young Mormon student named Kit Christofferson saw at close range in the Joseph Smith Fieldhouse at Brigham Young University on the morning of May 27 was anything but certain.

"His eyes were going this way and that, up and down. He looked trapped and wary, not what I expected, until they introduced him. Then he drew up and before long everyone — and these were Mormon Republicans — was screaming."[126]

On the ninth day of Bobby's extraordinary two-week, fifteen-state barnstorm across the country in March 1968, *Los Angeles Times* reporter Robert J. Donovan wrote that "the Kennedy blitz is a spectacle without parallel in the American experience."[127] The strategy was to do what supposedly could not be done — win the nomination "in the streets." In part, the move across the country was born of desperation. Kennedy was months late in announcing his candidacy. Whatever Johnson's infirmities, he had a solid lock on many delegations and the support of nearly all the party bosses. Thus, the strategy of stampede. The other crippling problem for Kennedy's candidacy was the press. His announcement had been greeted with furious denunciations by editorial boards, columnists, and reporters, including those who had once supported him and considered themselves personal friends. Murray Kempton of the *New York Post,* in a column entitled "Farewell Senator Kennedy," wrote that only a "coward" would come "down from the hills to shoot the wounded . . . he has managed to confirm the worst things his enemies have ever said about him." Another erstwhile Kennedy supporter, Mary McGrory, raised an old theme: "Kennedy thinks that American youth belongs to him at the bequest of his brother. Seeing the romance flower between them and McCarthy, he moved with the ruthlessness of a Victorian father whose daughter has fallen in love with a dustman."[128] The *Washington Post* cruelly observed that even the men Kennedy had named three of his children after — Maxwell Taylor, Averell Harriman, and Douglas Dillon — refused to support him. Kennedy may have left Washington to take his candidacy to the people, but he also left simply to stop getting hit.

A schedule was thrown together as Kennedy loyalists converged on Washington with chaotic results. One such loyalist, Arthur Schlesinger, summarized the state of things in a memo with the capitalized inquiry: "IS ANYONE IN CHARGE OF ANYTHING, ANY-WHERE?"[129] On May 17, Kennedy flew to Kansas for appearances at the two major universities in the state. The next morning, before 14,000 students in Kansas State University's Ahearn Fieldhouse,

Kennedy began reading his speech, stammering at points, his right leg shaking behind the lectern. When he read a quote from William Allen White about the imperative of youth to rebel, even riot, for their beliefs, the "wholesome, corn-fed prairie faces," Jack Newfield wrote, "let out a happy roar."[130] The intensity of the response seemed to stir him to a new level of projection. He acknowledged his own responsibility for the American presence in Vietnam: "I am willing to bear my share of responsibility, before history and before my fellow citizens. But past error is no excuse for its perpetuation. Tragedy is a tool for the living — as in the Antigone of Sophocles: 'All men make mistakes, but a good man yields when he knows his course is wrong, and repairs the evil. The only sin is pride.'"[131] Suddenly — as earlier in South Africa — the crowd sensed in this slight intense figure with his jagged delivery the voice of authentic emotion. The response in the field house was deafening.

Over the next fourteen days through fifteen states, Kennedy spoke to or greeted 250,000 Americans in person and reached several million more on television. Except for Alabama and Arizona, where the crowds were merely positive, the reaction, as one reporter termed it, was "explosive, uproarious, shrieking, and frenzied" everywhere he went.[132] The reception in California was the most intense of all. Bobby was literally besieged by supporters in Los Angeles, his clothes torn, his motorcade waylaid for an hour. The *Los Angeles Times* described Kennedy's speeches as hitting a "live nerve" of revulsion over the war and fear about racial strife, as well as stirring "the ashes of Dallas" that brought back memories of the beloved president. Everywhere he went, Kennedy spoke of the horror of Vietnam and the suffering of the poor and the forgotten. At the Greek Theatre in Los Angeles he opened up on President Johnson, accusing him of "calling upon the darker impulses of the American spirit."[133]

But Bobby himself was also stirring up poisonous emotions. The hatred his candidacy inspired in many corners of the country was "practically chemical," in the phrase of James Reston. The aspect of personal risk was obvious and troubling. The comedian Alan King told Bobby on one occasion, "They're going to hurt you." Kennedy replied, "Well, so many people hate me that I've got to give the people that love me a chance to get at me."[134] Only Bill

Barry, a burly former FBI agent, provided a small semblance of security for the candidate. When Kennedy stood in the back seat in motorcades, Barry would simply hang on to his waist to prevent him from being pulled completely out of the car. "They're here because they care for us and want to show us," he told Barry at one point. But it was Bobby as much as the rampaging crowds that wanted it this way. There was much about public life he dreaded or did badly, but this he loved. Stung and repudiated in Washington, awkward and uneven in interviews and prepared remarks, he could touch and be touched by those who, like him, were searching for something. In Kansas Jimmy Breslin asked him if he could see the faces. "I saw them," Kennedy replied. "I saw every one in the building."

Lyndon Johnson, bedeviled once more by the myth of the invincible Kennedys, watched all this with a mounting sense of dread. He elected initially to go toe to toe with Kennedy, and delivered a podium-pounding, finger-jabbing declaration on March 18 against "surrender and cowardice" at the National Farmers Union in Minneapolis. The reaction was muted.[135] A few days later came more bad news for the president: a Gallup poll placed Kennedy ahead of Johnson and indicated that Johnson would probably be beaten by Eugene McCarthy in Wisconsin on April 2. LBJ told presidential intern Doris Kearns that he had had a dream in which he was all alone sitting in a straight-back chair in a vast plain, cattle stampeding toward him, unable to move. He fretted about his health, particularly his heart. Both awake and asleep, he imagined himself paralyzed, lying conscious but stricken like Woodrow Wilson. At times, drenched with sweat, he would get up from his bed to walk downstairs with a flashlight and touch Wilson's portrait.[136] In the third week of March, the White House announced that the president would address the nation on the evening of March 31.

For all the energy and electricity of its first days, the Kennedy campaign had serious weaknesses. The surfeit of campaign leadership, without job titles or rank order at Bobby's insistence, imperiled quick and authoritative decision making. "The worst problem I'm going to have," Kennedy predicted, "is putting together the men who were with my brother with the men who have been with me."[137] It was actually more complex than that. There were the JFK men — Sorensen, O'Donnell, Ted Kennedy, Schlesinger,

Salinger, Smith, Bruno, and later Goodwin and O'Brien; the former attorney general's lieutenants — Marshall, Nolan, Oberdorfer; Kennedy's Senate staffers — Edelman, Dolan, Walinsky, Mankiewicz, Jeff Greenfield, and Bobby's indispensable secretary Angie Novello; and a cohort of Ted Kennedy aides and advisors — Richard Drayne, Dun Gifford, and Milton Gwirtzman.[138] On the flights and in the campaign appearances a steady stream of personalities came and went simply on the basis of their friendship with the senator. They included journalists-cum-activists such as Pete Hamill and Jack Newfield, an assortment of Kennedy family members, athletes such as Rafer Johnson and Rosey Grier, the occasional crooner (Andy Williams), an astronaut (John Glenn), and an Irish cocker spaniel called Freckles. The most important new member of the traveling team was Fred Dutton, who had worked in the Kennedy White House and been a key aide to California governor Pat Brown. Dutton became to Bobby what Kenny O'Donnell had been for JFK, the close-at-hand strategist and scheduler who remained constantly at his side.

Several of the senior staff members, Sorensen and Gwirtzman to name two, thought the "win it in the streets" strategy made Bobby's candidacy, with its mob scenes and wild motorcades, look like a "mobile riot" to people watching on TV.[139] A lot of the so-called jumpers and screamers who enlivened these appearances were not even voters. Many of Kennedy's advisors, moreover, thought his message needed to be broadened beyond Vietnam and the poor and targeted more toward the white middle class. In his first national swing, Bobby nonetheless resisted any change in his message and consistently vetoed image-driven campaigning. He continued going to where his heart was, spending over half his time during a two-day visit to Arizona and New Mexico on the Navajo Indian reservation.

In Albuquerque on March 29, Kennedy visited a Native American boarding school and, in remarks that brought the normally taciturn Indians to their feet, blasted the U.S. Bureau of Indian Affairs for spending 22 cents a meal on the children. "When I was attorney general," he said, looking at school superintendent Dr. Solon Ayers, "we spent more than that on the prisoners in Alcatraz."[140] Later that night in Window Rock, Arizona, the Navajo capital, Kennedy took leave of his prepared text and cut loose with an even stronger attack on the BIA, claiming that it was a form of "American colonialism." The idea, he said, of sending five-, six-, and seven-year-old children thousands of miles away to school was barbaric. "You have your culture. You have your history. You have your language," Kennedy said. The Navajos responded with war whoops and ear-rending applause. On his way out of the Navajo tribal hogan, William P. Mahoney, who was leading the Arizona effort for Kennedy and who had grown up near the reservation, was stopped by a Navajo, who told him, "I have waited all my life for a white man to say that." When Bobby heard this, he was deeply moved.[141] The next day, Kennedy presided over several hours of a hearing of the Senate Subcommittee on Indian Education, which was being held in Flagstaff. Back in Washington senior staff members complained that Bobby was wasting time with people who were politically irrelevant. "You sons of bitches, " Kennedy said when he learned about the complaint, "you don't really care about suffering."[142]

The succession of eighteen-hour days, and his practice of plowing the fullest measure of emotion into the campaign, started to take a noticeable toll on Bobby. He flew into Tucson, Arizona, dead-tired, his voice hoarse, his skin burned and peeling in places. Moments before he was to speak, he got up from his seat, hurried to a bathroom, and threw up. During his speech, he stumbled twice over the same word and said, "God, it's been a long, long day."[143] The next evening in Phoenix at the Arizona Biltmore Hotel he stammered his way through a speech he had given many times before.[144] Utterly spent, he left for New York the next morning and, shortly after arriving at La Guardia Airport on March 31, he was informed that Johnson had announced that he was withdrawing from the race.

Some in the Kennedy entourage wanted to celebrate. Bobby didn't, sensing that he had lost his target, Johnson, and possibly his issue, the war. The next morning James Stevenson of *The New Yorker* rode in a car with the man who would be president:

> When a traffic light changes to green, Kennedy's fingers twitch an instant before Frank Bilotti can accelerate the car. Bill Barry's eyes close; he is exhausted. He dozes. Kennedy was up until

three o'clock. Carter Burden asks, "Are you tired?" Kennedy shakes his head, murmurs no, no — brushing it off as if the question is not worth consideration. On the East River Drive, a taxi-driver recognizes Kennedy and yells, "Give it to 'em, Bobby!" Kennedy waves, then stares ahead again. He is deeply preoccupied now, at his most private. (When Barry wakes and offers everyone chewing gum, Kennedy does not hear him.) He abandons, piece by piece, the outside world — he puts away the magazines, the cigar is forgotten, the offer of gum is unheard, and he is utterly alone. His silence is not passive; it is intense. His face, close up, is structurally hard; there is nothing wasted, nothing left over and not put to use; everything has been enlisted in the cause, whatever it may be. His features look dug out, jammed together, scraped away. There is an impression of almost too much going on in too many directions in too little space; the nose hooks outward, the teeth protrude, the lower lip sticks forward, the hair hangs down, the ears go up and out, the chin juts, the eyelids push down, slanting toward the cheekbones, almost covering the eyes (a surprising blue). His expression is tough, but the toughness seems largely directed toward himself, inward — a contempt for self-indulgence, for weakness. The sadness in his face, by the same token, is not sentimental sadness, which would imply self-pity, but rather, at some level, a resident, melancholy bleakness.[145]

Kennedy tried to suture his relationship with Johnson. They met on April 3 at the White House. Bobby asked the president if he would stay neutral in the race. "I'm no king maker and don't want to be," Johnson replied.[146] But there was little Johnson could do, or wanted to do, to stop Vice President Humphrey from entering the race and picking up the thousand-plus delegates either pledged or leaning to LBJ.[147] As David Halberstam put it, Humphrey, a figure of parody as Johnson's Man Friday, suddenly became the "man of reconciliation" who could bring together the key power bases of the party, all of which opposed Bobby's candidacy to a greater or lesser degree — the labor unions, the southern governors, the Jews, and the big-city bosses.[148] Kennedy was left to fight it out in the primaries with Gene McCarthy, who had just scored an impressive, though largely uncontested, win in Wisconsin.

The Kennedy-McCarthy contest with Johnson in the race had been characterized by a sort of forced mutual tolerance. It quickly polarized after the president's withdrawal. McCarthy's essential insight into Kennedy, which he sowed first in encounters with the press and later more openly, was that Bobby was a parvenu, trading on his name and money, and that he had a great deal more ambition than ability. Kennedy regarded the Minnesota senator, on the other hand, as a sort of lazy poseur who had gotten lucky doing the right thing. McCarthy's odd style made him a figure of fun in Kennedy circles. On one occasion McCarthy arrived early to give a speech to his supporters, delivered it to an empty hall, and walked out as his supporters were filing in. On another occasion, addressing dairy farmers in Wisconsin, McCarthy quoted the ancient Irish bard Caduc the Wise at length. His preferred traveling companion was the poet Robert Lowell. As aides would desperately try to brief or otherwise engage McCarthy with the business at hand, the two men would discuss how the Guelphs and Ghibelines in fourteenth-century Florence might see the race.[149] The press at points featured their arcane exchanges, such as this one about deferments from the draft to boost the volunteer ranks:

LOWELL: Can they draft monks?
MCCARTHY: No.
LOWELL: Well, that's a loophole.
MCCARTHY: Do you suppose we could get some bishop to give all our student supporters minor orders?

Whatever his self-indulgences, McCarthy proved tough and resourceful. First against Johnson and then Kennedy, he mastered the guerrilla strategy of underplaying his chances, waiting for his opponent to make a mistake, and then basing his appeal as much on contrast as on message. In a divisive and disordered time, his cool juxtaposed Bobby's pure heat. Tom Wicker thought that it was McCarthy, not Kennedy, who "had broken with the past" and who represented the "new politics."[150] His aloof disposition, his tart treatment of the press, his communication that Washington had betrayed the people — this was the beginning of anti-politics. In the face of Kennedy money and organization, the McCarthy tactic was to dodge in and out of the primary states in search of high ground. In Oregon he was to find it.

Within a few days of LBJ's announcement, another hammer-blow struck the country: the assassination of Martin Luther King Jr. Kennedy got the news that King had been shot as he flew from Terre Haute to Indianapolis. After the plane landed, he was informed that King was dead. He seemed "to shrink back as if struck physically," gasping, "Oh, God. When is this violence going to stop?" He was scheduled to go to a rally in the black section of Indianapolis but several people in the campaign, including the usually indomitable Ethel, thought they should all go immediately to the hotel. Bobby decided he would go, despite a warning from the chief of police that it would not be safe. As Kennedy's car entered the ghetto, the motorcycle escort pulled off.[151] When the car reached the large, unpaved parking lot where the rally was to take place, it was clear that the crowd had not heard the news. Kennedy climbed up onto the flat-bed truck that served as a dais and grasped a portable microphone: "I have some terrible news for you. Martin Luther King has been shot." A gasp went up from the crowd as Kennedy, "hunched in his black overcoat, his face gaunt and distressed and full of anguish," continued:

Martin Luther King dedicated his life to love and to justice for his fellow human beings, and he died because of that effort. In this difficult day, in this difficult time for the United States, it is perhaps well to ask what kind of a nation we are and what direction we want to move in. For those of you who are black — considering the evidence . . . that there were white people who were responsible — you can be filled with bitterness, with hatred, and a desire for revenge. . . . Or we can make an effort, as Martin Luther King did, to understand and to comprehend, and to replace that stain of bloodshed that has spread across our land, with an effort to understand with compassion and love. For those of you who are black and are tempted to be filled with hatred and distrust at the injustice of such an act, against all white people, I can only say that I feel in my own heart the same kind of feeling. I had a member of my family killed . . .

What we need in the United States is not division; what we need in the United States is not hatred; what we need in the

United States is not violence or lawlessness, but love and wisdom, and compassion toward one another, and a feeling of justice toward those who still suffer within our country, whether they be white or they be black. . . . Let us dedicate ourselves to what the Greeks wrote so many years ago: to tame the savageness in man and to make gentle the life of this world. Let us dedicate ourselves to that, and say a prayer for our country and our people.[152]

At King's funeral at the Ebenezer Baptist Church in Atlanta on a hot spring day, Kennedy and McCarthy sat in pews one behind the other, part of a scattering of other white politicians and progressives amid a vast crowd of poor southern blacks. Allard Lowenstein remembered the singing of the hymn, "Earnestly, Tenderly Jesus Is Calling," which concluded with the words, "Come home, come home, ye who are weary, come home, come home."[153]

In the pall of shock and grief surrounding the assassination, every presidential candidate except Kennedy waited for the temperature to cool down before dealing with the rage caused by King's death. The day after the murder, Bobby spoke to a largely white audience in Cleveland and delivered what would become his essential message for the balance of his campaign. He decried not only America's dark habit of political and social violence, but spoke of:

another kind of violence, slower but just as deadly, destructive as the shot or bomb in the night. This is the violence of institutions; indifference and inaction and slow decay. This is the violence that afflicts the poor, that poisons relations between men because their skin has different colors. This is the slow destruction of a child by hunger, and schools without books and homes without heat in the winter. This is the breaking of a man's spirit by denying him the chance to stand as a father and as a man among men.

Kennedy asked Americans to recognize "in our own hearts . . . the terrible truths of our existence," truths that could not be vanquished with a program or a resolution. "[P]erhaps we can remember — even if only for a short time — that those who live with us are our brothers, that they share with us the same short move-ment of life, that they seek — as we do — nothing but the chance to live out their lives in purpose and happiness, winning what satis-faction and fulfillment they can."[154]

Bobby had already sensed the shadow of his own fate. King's murder only quickened this sensation and sharpened his outrage at the bitter plight of millions of Americans. He had always had a deep need to find definition by contending with evil. It no longer mat-tered that the country wasn't ready or wouldn't listen. He would strike the bell.

As the Kennedy campaign headed into the primaries in Indiana and Nebraska, the exhausted candidate would fly home and spend Sunday with his family at Hickory Hill. A reporter observed him one such day in the dining room, eating a sandwich as he listened to a briefing on hog prices. Each time one of his various children would wander by, Bobby would reach out, his eyes never leaving the face of his interlocutor, and squeeze the child's hand. After lunch he played with each of his children. At times, he openly won-dered at the path he had taken, commenting to a reporter: "I think — I think — I would make this one effort and if it fails I would go back to my children. If you bring children into the world, you should stay with them, see them through."[155]

Gene McCarthy thought he saw a new counterpoint in the race for the nomination. "It's narrowed down to Bobby and me," he re-marked. "So far he's run *with* the ghost of his brother. Now we're going to make him run *against* it. It's purely Greek: he either has to kill him or be killed by him. We'll make him run against Jack. And I'm Jack."[156] Whether McCarthy was Jack or not, Bobby's candidacy, as Victor Navasky wrote during this period, was bump-ing into "a ghost, a shadow, an image, and a specter. The ghost is the idealized memory of his brother, President John F. Kennedy. The shadow, cast by the ghost, is what gets in the way of the voter trying to see Robert as a man rather than as a Kennedy. The image of Robert's ruthlessness is at least partly a legacy of his service to his brother. And the specter is of a Kennedy dynasty."[157]

Bobby was facing the same old problem. The more people saw of him, the less he looked like Jack — and Jack was what people wanted to see. In this sense, McCarthy was right: the ghost Bobby wanted to run with would always be against him. John F. Kennedy, now gloriously ensconced in the Camelot myth, could never be beaten. At the same time the press, fueling expectations of how Bobby would have to perform in primaries to win, also criticized him for his constant references to his brother in his speeches. By the second week of May, Bobby stopped quoting Jack altogether. In private, however, he reminisced more openly than ever about him, as if, Louis Oberdorfer later said, "he could see Jack and wanted to be with him."[158]

As in JFK's do-or-die effort in West Virginia in May 1960, Bobby needed a primary win and took the gamble of entering the Indiana contest. With both McCarthy and popular Indiana governor Roger Branigan on the ballot, Kennedy risked the real possibility of coming in second. The Kennedy message of social and racial reconstruction was potentially too radical for the largely white conservative electorate. The strategy that emerged in the Indiana campaign was the one Kennedy forces had perfected in 1960: divide the state into districts that represented key parts of the electorate and bring in out-of-state coordinators to run those districts; distribute several million flyers; schedule appearances by local officials and celebrities supportive of the senator, along with Kennedy family members and national celebrities, to boost visibility and persuasion; outhustle the opposition; by doubling the number of appearances by the candidate via tight scheduling and fifteen to eighteen hours a day campaigning; spend as much as you had to.

Bobby's first days on the campaign trail in Indiana went dismally. In a state known for its phlegmatic reserve, people would show up at the rallies to heckle him. The characteristic reaction to his message of racial and economic justice was cold indifference. Bobby sensed he was hitting a brick wall, telling David Brinkley on one occasion, "They *hate* me in Kokomo."[159] On another occasion, he told reporters with his brutal candor, "So far in Indiana, they seem to want to see me as a member of the black race." One woman who came to a small airport gathering where Kennedy spoke about his farm program was openly scornful, as television correspondent Charles Quinn later told some Kennedy staffers. Bobby overheard the report.

"What did she say?" he asked Quinn.

"I can't tell you what she said, Senator. It's kind of embarrassing."

"Tell me what she said," he repeated.

"All right," Quinn agreed. "I'll tell you what she said. She said, 'Hmmph. The only reason I came down here is to find out if he looked like Bugs Bunny, and he does.'"

Kennedy laughed loud and long at this, finally throwing himself into his seat, exhausted. "You know what? I *feel* like Bugs Bunny too!"[160]

At points there were sustained confrontations between Bobby and his audiences. On April 26, at the Indiana University Medical Center, medical students openly scorned his proposals to help the elderly and the poor. One student asked, "Where are we going to get the money to pay for all these new programs you're proposing?"

"From you," Kennedy replied icily. "I look around this room and I don't see many black faces who will become doctors. Part of civilized society is to let people go to medical school who come from ghettos. I don't see many people coming here from slums, or off of Indian reservations. You are the privileged ones here. It's easy for you to sit back and say it's the fault of the Federal Government. But it's our responsibility too. It's our society too. . . . It's the poor who carry the major burden of the struggle in Vietnam. You sit here as white medical students, while black people carry the burden of the fighting in Vietnam." There was hissing and booing.[161] Earlier that year the pollster Richard Scammon had warned Bobby that if he was perceived as an extremist he would get "a one-way ticket to oblivion." He didn't seem to care.

Such angry exchanges may have defied every known precept in the art of the possible, but they also sealed the growing regard for Bobby among the fifty or so press traveling with the candidate. The stories they filed depicted Kennedy's honesty, his self-deprecating humor, and his fantastic drive. An incident in tiny Mishawaka, Indiana — in which cheering youth hurled Kennedy against the side of his car, chipping his front tooth and splitting his lip — actually cost him the votes of most adults in attendance, but in the press it became another instance of "Bobby fever."[162]

The candidate and his campaign moved slowly, very slowly, into a winning groove in Indiana. On April 23, the Kennedy entourage boarded a train in north central Indiana on the old Wabash line. At each stop the band would play "The Wabash Cannonball," before the senator would introduce his wife and speak off the back platform. The press on the train composed their own, seven-stanza version called "The Ruthless Cannonball" and sang it to the candidate at the end of the day:

> Now good clean Gene McCarthy came down the other track
> A thousand Radcliffe dropouts all massed for the attack.
> But Bobby's bought the right-of-way from here back to St. Paul,
> 'Cause money is no object on the Ruthless Cannonball.

Kennedy listened to this rendition with his usual deadpan expression, observing at its conclusion, "As George Bernard Shaw once said" — the reporters began to laugh — "as George Bernard Shaw once said," he continued, "'the same to you, buddy!'"[163]

Kennedy became effective at loosening up Indiana crowds, often employing a sort of comic antiphony.

"Will you vote for me?" he would ask the crowd.

"Yes!" the crowd would respond.

"Will you get your friends to vote for me?"

"Yes!"

"When people say something bad about me, will you say it isn't true?

"Yes!"

"Have you read my book?"

"Yes!"

"You lie."

In the final days of the campaign, Kennedy went to his only real area of strength in Indiana, the industrial north. A nine-hour motorcade that began in South Bend took him through cheering crowds in thirteen smaller cities and towns. At the Gary city line, two men got in the back seat to stand with Kennedy — former middleweight champion Tony Zale from Gary and the new black mayor of Gary, Richard Hatcher. There they stood, arms around each other, waving at a city that had been on the brink of a race war. In Miller, six-year-old Sam Vagenas, whose mother was a Kennedy volunteer, felt an electric emotion sweep through the crowd as

Kennedy waded into the throng.[164] It confirmed his entry into a life of political action.

It was in the blue-collar neighborhoods of Lake County that Kennedy for the first time bridged the distance between black powerlessness and white ethnic fear: "This is your country. You have a right to work, to be cared for. And I'm not going to let them take it away." Dick Goodwin felt Bobby had found his message at long last: "His inner urge toward defiance — of unjust privilege, indifferent power, concentrated wealth — which provoked so much fear and even hatred among some, was also the source of his greatest strength, arousing the hopes and expectations of millions who felt themselves victimized."[165]

On election day in Indiana, Kennedy seemed possessed by a strange, cathartic joy. Out on the lawn of the Indianapolis Holiday Inn he played a full-contact game of touch football, in which two men left the field injured. He spoke to reporters about his deep respect for the authenticity of the tens of thousands of Hoosiers he had met, contrasting them with the "neurotic, hypocritical" people in New York and Washington. By nine that evening it was obvious he had won impressively — by a margin of 42 percent to Branigan's 31 and McCarthy's 27 percent. Before there was time to savor the victory, however, the television networks converted the result into Kennedy doing less well than expected. He was furious. When Walter Cronkite asked him, with McCarthy on the other side of the split screen, about the level of his campaign expenditures, Bobby attacked the networks, saying they made enough profits to give all the candidates free airtime.[166] It was the sort of impolitic dismissal that had always cost him dearly and reminded the high priests of the press of the old accusation — ruthlessness.[167]

Kennedy and McCarthy moved on to Nebraska, while Humphrey zigzagged across the country locking down former Johnson delegates. Benefiting from the statewide organization of Phil C. Sorensen (the former lieutenant governor of Nebraska who had run unsuccessfully for governor in 1966) and deep local organizing, Kennedy gained an early lead. He kept up the level of banter. In Tecumseh, when the wind tore a scrap of paper from his hand, Kennedy quipped, "That's my farm program. Give it back quickly." Low on money and still searching for higher ground,

McCarthy abandoned the state after a single visit, giving Kennedy a win, although one that gained him little national momentum.

The candidate who was really winning in these Kennedy-McCarthy battles was Hubert Humphrey, who had not entered a single primary. By the third week of May, *Newsweek* reported that Humphrey was already within striking distance of the nomination, with 1,280 "committed or leaning" delegates out of the 1,312 needed to win. If Bobby could not knock McCarthy out of the race and pick up his delegates, and then subsequently stampede some of Humphrey's "leaners," his race for the presidency would be over.

In Oregon McCarthy, perhaps sensing that Kennedy could not afford to retaliate without losing McCarthy voters and delegates later in the campaign, stepped up his attacks. He brought up Bobby's role in getting America into Vietnam to bait him to deny or even denounce his own brother's policy. But Kennedy refused to respond — or to accept McCarthy's challenge to debate him. The result was disastrous. Kennedy never found his message, lecturing white suburbanites outside Portland on the horrors of Native American life and sparring with gun patriots in Roseburg.

J. Edgar Hoover did his part to trip Kennedy up. He leaked a report to Drew Pearson and Jack Anderson that the former attorney general had authorized the FBI to wiretap Martin Luther King in 1963. For a critical period of days, the charge, and Bobby's half-hearted denial, swirled around in the press, reinforcing that old accusation of ruthlessness and dulling his final run of media in Oregon.[168] Four days before his defeat in Oregon, Bobby suggested to Jack Newfield that he would not make it as the nominee: "I can accept the fact that I may not be nominated now. If that happens, I will just go back to the Senate, and say what I believe, and not try in '72. Somebody has to speak up for the Negroes and Indians and Mexicans and poor whites. Maybe that's what I do best. Maybe my personality just isn't built for this."[169]

The near-hopelessness now of the race seemed to release Bobby from any constraint, and his campaign became even more spontaneous and freewheeling. But behind it was still a fear of the past. There was a surprise birthday party for bodyguard Bill Barry on-board the plane with Barry and Kennedy's faces painted in frosting on the cake. Champagne was being served all around when suddenly a balloon popped loudly. Kennedy's hand rose slowly to his face, covering his eyes, and the gaiety stopped cold for ten seconds. Then the party resumed. In Los Angeles Bobby got off the plane for a rally, leaving most members of the press and his staff behind to continue to party with Ethel. Reporters soon began singing all the songs they knew — folk songs, patriotic marches, and Christian hymns, including "What a Friend We Have in Bobby."

Kennedy got back on the plane at around 2 A.M. and Ethel told him excitedly, "Oh, Bobby. You don't know what you have missed." She told him about their singing for three hours — "Battle Hymn of the Republic," "Onward Christian Soldiers," and so on.

Bobby, who liked to sing himself, tried to lead the group — with dissonant results. *Washington Post* reporter Richard Harwood stopped Bobby and told him he would have to listen for a change. After that the reporters sang "Battle Hymn of the Republic" in harmony. Kennedy seemed moved in a sad way. They also sang, "I Come to the Garden Alone" and "Softly, Earnestly, Jesus Is Calling." Kennedy asked them to sing, "Where Have All the Flowers Gone?" And then asked them to do it again and again. They sang all the way to Portland, producer Sylvia Wright remembered:

> Bobby was sitting down, and some of us were sitting on the floor around him, and we were all kind of huddled together. And then pretty soon, it sort of vaguely started to get light out, and it was about a quarter to five and we all just fell asleep together, huddled up there in the front of the plane. All these great big guys! All the seats were empty in the back of the plane. We all fell asleep lying across each other and huddled up together. Then Bobby got up and snapped the lights off over his shoulder and went off to sleep with the dog in the front.[170]

The journey, so rude and bitter at the start, was now blessed by song and friendship — and the sense that somehow it wouldn't last. On May 28, McCarthy defeated Kennedy in Oregon by 6 percent. Bobby's concession statement had a quiet and easy grace to it. Defeat brought release, and a chance for redirection and new self-discovery. He was now an underdog. In Los Angeles the next morning Kennedy went on a two-hour motorcade and, to his surprise and gratification, the response was thunderous and undiminished. He declared Los Angeles his "Resurrection City."[171]

On June 1, he debated Senator McCarthy on national television in San Francisco. The debate turned out to be something of a non-event, with the candidates trading complaints over campaign materials and quibbling over the means to bring a coalition government to Saigon. But the debate served Kennedy well by stemming the slide toward McCarthy in California, and removing the issue of his refusal to debate. With four days to go before election day, there was another marathon dash up and down the state in search of crowds.

After one motorcade, reporter John J. Lindsay saw Kennedy get back on the plane — his tie gone, his cuff links and tie-clip torn off, his shirt stuck with sweat to his chest, limping, with one shoe gone. He said, "Don't tell me people in this country don't love me." Then he paused. "On the other hand, perhaps all they wanted was a shoe."[172]

With its huge black and Hispanic communities, California was natural territory for Bobby — if the minorities would turn out. Chavez and his farmworkers by this time had registered in excess of the 100,000 voters they had promised. In the final days they regrouped to get out the vote, moving in groups of three hundred through the endless barrios of East Los Angeles, and in smaller teams through the little towns in the San Joaquin, Imperial, Central and Coachella valleys. The communication was simple, "Cesar wants you to tell everyone to vote for Kennedy," along with a printed statement detailing Kennedy's loyalty. It was entitled *"Hechos Son Amor"* (Actions Are Love).[173]

The off-moments of the final days found a motley humor in the entourage. Freckles the dog had by this time become an important member of the campaign. He slept next to the senator between the seats of the airplane, rode with him in all the motorcades, and gave Bobby the excuse to break off and go for walks. Kennedy drew much pleasure from generalizing about Freckles's reactions to campaigning. If the crowd was small, the dog would go to sleep and Kennedy would summon Jerry Bruno or Dick Tuck: "The dog's pretty upset with this crowd. You didn't do much of a job getting this crowd together." Tuck pointed out that the dog would only go to sleep *during* his speeches. In Fresno, Bobby asked someone to walk Freckles. Tuck, always the jester, replied: "Ambassadorship to Rome?" Kennedy said yes. Later, when Tuck couldn't find Freckles, someone said, "You know, it's just a dog," to which Tuck responded, "To you it's a dog. To me it's an ambassadorship."

But again there were intimations of disaster. In San Francisco's Chinatown the day before the primary, as Bobby's motorcade inched through the choked streets, firecrackers went off in sharp bursts of purple smoke. Kennedy's face froze in a half-smile and a shudder went through his body.[174] Perhaps it was scenes such as these or something related to the sunny nightmare of California with all its warring voices and its legions of rootless, gun-angry people, but some around Bobby began to talk openly about the inevitable. French novelist Romain Gary, then living in Los Angeles, told Pierre Salinger, "Your candidate is going to get killed." When Jimmy Breslin asked several reporters around a table whether they thought Bobby had "the stuff to go all the way," John J. Lindsay replied, "Yes, of course, he has the stuff to go all the way, but he's not going to go all the way. The reason is that somebody is going to shoot him. I know it and you know it, just as sure as we're sitting here. He's out there waiting for him."[175]

One man out there waiting for him was Palestinian immigrant Sirhan Sirhan. Sirhan had worked at both the Santa Anita and Del Mar racetracks, popular meeting grounds for mafiosi. At Santa Anita in 1966, Sirhan had become acquainted with Frank Donneroummas, alias Henry Ramistella, who later had gotten him a job at the Corona Breeding Farm, where the two saw each other frequently. Donneroummas's rap sheet included several arrests in New York and Miami. He was a wiseguy. Sirhan's notebooks would later show that their relationship was also based on gambling and debt: "happiness hppiness [*sic*] Dona Donaruma Donaruma Frank Donaruma pl please ple please pay to 5 please pay to the order of Sirhan Sirhan the amount of 5."[176] The FBI had been picking up unconfirmed reports of a conspiracy that included an overheard conversation between Hoffa and his cronies in the Lewisburg penitentiary about "a contract to kill Bob Kennedy."[177]

Bobby spent election day in Malibu at the beachfront home of John Frankenheimer. He body-surfed with his children (fishing his son David out of an undertow) and napped off and on throughout the day. In the evening, just as the returns were coming in, he went to his suite on the fifth floor of the Ambassador Hotel. Kennedy watched the returns in his own room with Ethel and his close advisors, while in Room 516 across the hall journalists and politicians gathered in an exuberant mood. At around 8 P.M., Bobby stuck his head out of his room and asked if anyone wanted to hear about how the Indians had voted in South Dakota (which was also holding its primary that day). He announced that the returns from an Indian precinct were 878 for Kennedy, 9 for the Humphrey-Johnson slate, and 2 for McCarthy.[178] (He won South Dakota's 24 delegates with 50 percent of the vote.)

The evening drifted on. More heartfelt congratulations from the Kennedy entourage of activists, advisors, and newsmen. More interviews that both heralded the obvious victory in California and the difficulty of winning the nomination, given Humphrey's lead in delegates. Smoking a small cigar, at points going back to his own room to talk with Ethel, Walinsky, or Sorensen, Bobby seemed uncharacteristically settled. Richard Goodwin noticed "an easy grace, a strength that was unafraid of softness. For the first time since he had announced his candidacy, Robert Kennedy reminded me of his slain brother. If he looks like that for the rest of the campaign, we might win, I thought."[179]

In the final count the margin over McCarthy, 46.3 percent to 41.8 percent, was more narrow than expected, an indication of continued electoral resistance among educated whites, particularly Jews, to Bobby's candidacy. The victory did confirm, however, that Kennedy was attempting something unprecedented (and perhaps unachievable) in modern American political history — not simply to base his run for the presidency on the poor and the minorities, but also to make of their ascendancy the new moral basis for political power. At the hour of his greatest victory, as if to underscore this fact, he kept asking people if they had seen Cesar Chavez so they might go down to the ballroom together and accept victory.

The campaign, in the end, was not a campaign; it was a crusade. It proposed to do what Norman Mailer had once thought Jack capable of doing — linking the "two rivers" that had coursed through the country's history and deepest consciousness, one of material power and military imposition and the other of myth and moral awakening. JFK had embodied the possibility of that linkage, but it was RFK who consciously proposed his life for it. He recognized "the terrible truths of existence," as he put it the day after King's death, but there was the always the adventure "to sail beyond the Western stars until I die," as he had said so often, quoting Tennyson. To America, the bourgeois imperium, he embodied something very different — what Nietzsche called "tragic pleasure." He had lived "in the face of death" and found joy in his affirmation of human tragedy.

Around midnight, Bobby decided to go downstairs to the packed ballroom. He asked once again for Chavez to walk with him, but Chavez could not be found, so instead Bobby asked Dolores Huerta to join him. On the way down the elevator, she told him that in several Mexican precincts that day the turnout had been 100 percent. He reached out and gave her a hug and then she returned it.[180] They went first to the kitchen, where Kennedy shook everyone's hand, including that of Juan Romero, a busboy, and then proceeded to the ballroom, where he mounted the podium. The crowd roared. As Bobby was thanking a list of supporters that included Freckles, Pete Hamill saw a young man try to get onto the platform through the drapes, but Barry shooed him off. Was it Sirhan? Hamill was later uncertain. Kennedy, uncharacteristically relaxed and smiling, now switched from his wry recognitions to the reason for his cause:

> What I think is quite clear is that we can work together in the last analysis, and that what has been going on in the United States over the last three years — the division, the violence, the disenchantment with our society; the divisions, whether it's between blacks and whites, between the poor and the more affluent, or between age groups or on the war in Vietnam — is that we can start to work together. We are a great country, an unselfish country and a compassionate country. I intend to make that my basis for running.

As the crowd cheered, there was a brief discussion about how to get to a press conference in the Colonial Room. Someone proposed a shorter route through the kitchen. As Kennedy made his way through the crush of people, both Barry and Ethel were pushed several feet behind him. Security guard Thane Eugene Cesar got hold of Bobby's right elbow to escort him through the serving pantry when Sirhan opened fire. He had been standing more or less in front of Kennedy. The shots wounded Kennedy and five other people. According to eyewitnesses, the muzzle of Sirhan's .22 caliber gun was never less than two feet from Kennedy. The fatal bullet, according to Los Angeles County coroner Thomas Noguchi, was fired "less than one inch from his [Kennedy's] head" and from behind the senator.[181] The precise manner of his death would never be firmly established.

Kennedy was visibly conscious for a period of seconds, as he lay face up on the gummy pantry floor, blood pooling around his head. "I'm hurt," he whispered. "I'm hurt." And then, "No, no, no." As several men rushed to subdue Sirhan, Juan Romero, the busboy whose hand Kennedy had earlier shaken, knelt next to him and looked up pleadingly. Someone put some rosary beads in Bobby's hand. He gripped them tightly. As Ethel struggled to get through the crowd to him, a friend saw his lips moving, leaned down next to him, and heard him say, "Jack. Jack."[182]

Epilogue

After Jack was killed, Jackie Kennedy said that she had once thought of history as something that "bitter old men" wrote. "Then I realized history made Jack what he was. You must think of him as this little boy, sick so much of the time, reading the *Knights of the Round Table,* reading Marlborough. For Jack, history was full of heroes. . . . Men are such a combination of good and bad."

Jack was that combination of good and bad, but always with the heroic pose. His was not the Catholic view of the hero — one engaged in sacrificial penance, struggling in a moral kinesis. His was, rather, the Greek view of the hero, celebrating the possibilities of self as an aesthetic pursuit. JFK's pose was egocentric, but he found balance in the ironic. If he could take it over the edge, as he did at the Orange Bowl on that dangerous day in December 1962, or at the Berlin Wall the following summer in his instant of histrionic glory, he could also mock his pretense for the heroic. "This is the night I should go to the theater," he had said to Bobby at their moment of triumph in the missile crisis (referring, as we have seen, to Lincoln's assassination at the Ford Theater). Bobby had replied, of course, "If you go, I want to go with you."

Jack Kennedy could never have been the hero that he wanted to be, or celebrate himself in so dramatic and imaginative a way, were it not for his soldier-brother — advising him, protecting him, and imparting discipline in the ranks. Asked in his final press conference how he regarded the presidency, JFK replied, "I have given before to this group the definition of happiness of the Greeks, and I will define it again: it is the full use of your powers along the lines of excellence. I find, therefore, the presidency affords some happiness." But Jack wanted more than that: not just mastery of the presidency during the day but the Dionysian interlude at night; and

Bobby, like a sleepless watchman on the rampart, made this possible too.

To be heroic in the Greek view was to die willingly. Jack had always been romanced by death. He read about it, talked about it, had visions of it, and coolly went into it. "His high noon kept all the freshness of the morning," as Jackie had written a few days after his assassination. Death preserved his youth.

It was for Bobby to contemplate their murderous reversal of fortune and recognize his place in it. In his desperate search for some reference point, he underlined a passage from Aeschylus: "All arrogance will reap a harvest rich in tears. God calls men to a heavy reckoning for overweening pride." The book Jackie gave him at Easter 1964, *The Greek Way,* became his guide through the wilderness. He could not admit, and probably did not know, just where his family had paid the blood price for this harvest rich in tears. Was it his father's dealings with the underworld? Was it his scourge of the Mafia at a time when he had countenanced the use of Rosselli and his confederates in the vendetta against Castro? Was it renegade CIA paramilitaries who he himself had unleashed? Had Jack's hedonism somehow exposed him to retribution? He had no answers and could permit himself no answers. One goes back to that moment when Robert Lowell asked what character in Shakespeare Bobby would choose to be, and Bobby chose Henry the Fifth, then read to Lowell the death speech of Henry the Fourth, whose bitter legacy to his children includes "[T]he cankeréd heaps of strange-achieved gold."

"Henry the Fourth. That's my father," Bobby had said to Lowell. There would be no exit, only further pain and destruction.

Bobby became a man on fire. He would make of his curse a romance. "The fullness of life is in the hazards of life" was a passage from Aeschylus he had underlined. "To the heroic, desperate odds fling a challenge." Archibald MacLeish, on that golden late October day in 1963 in Amherst at the dedication of the Robert Frost Library, had described such a hero, Oedipus. Blinded and alone for his father's sins and his own, he was yet able, as MacLeish put it, to "face his dark pursuers. By embracing his tragic fate, Oedipus had shown us self without self-pity." Bobby Kennedy used his rage to make amends. His presidency would create a new basis for power — the poor and minorities — that would renew our humanity.

Here the Kennedys, with all their romance and irony, finally unite in an aesthetic comparable to the Greeks that they read about and quoted: they were daring and they were doomed, and they knew it and accepted it. They would die and make their deaths into creative acts of history. They would be heroes. And they would give their country an imperishable poignancy in its heart.

Notes

Abbreviations

AA	Assassination Archives
CCC	Chicago Crime Commission Files
HSCA	House Select Committee on Assassinations
JFK	John F. Kennedy
JFKL	John F. Kennedy Library
LBJL	Lyndon B. Johnson Library
NA	National Archives
PPP	Pre-Presidential Papers (John F. Kennedy)
RFK	Robert F. Kennedy
RFKP	Robert F. Kennedy Papers

Crusades: 1951–1959

1 David Halberstam, *The Best and the Brightest* (New York: Random House, 1972), p. 119.

2 Trip file, September–November 1951, PPP, JFKL.

3 Edmund A. Gullion, in an interview, set the scene. At the time, Gullion was second in command in the American legation in Vietnam. In 1962, he became President Kennedy's ambassador to the Congo.

4 Interview, Edmund A. Gullion. See also Norman Sherry, *The Life of Graham Greene,* vol. 2 (New York: Penguin Books, 1994), pp. 359–78.

5 Quoted in Herbert S. Parmet, *Jack: The Struggles of John F. Kennedy* (New York: The Dial Press, 1980), p. 210.

6 Edwin O. Guthman and Jeffrey Shulman, eds., *Robert Kennedy in His Own Words* (New York: Bantam, 1988), p. 436.

7 Characterization of Professor Carl J. Friedrich as quoted in Parmet, *Jack,* pp. 69–70.

8 Oral history of Joseph Spalding, JFKL.

9 Quoted in Parmet, *Jack,* p. 321.

10 Quoted in Arthur M. Schlesinger Jr., *A Thousand Days: John F. Kennedy in the White House* (Boston: Houghton Mifflin, 1965), p. 96.

11 Quoted in Parmet, *Jack*, p. 190.

12 Quoted in Schlesinger, *A Thousand Days*, p. 87.

13 John F. Kennedy, ed., *As We Remember Joe* (privately printed), pp. 3–4.

14 Parmet, *Jack*, p. 56.

15 Robert E. Thompson and Hortense Myers, *Robert Kennedy: The Brother Within* (New York: Macmillan, 1962), pp. 62–63.

16 Arthur Krock, *Memoirs: Sixty Years on the Firing Line* (New York: Funk & Wagnalls, 1968), p. 354.

17 Schlesinger, *Robert Kennedy and His Times* (Boston: Houghton Mifflin, 1978), pp. 68–69.

18 Ibid., p. 69.

19 Interview, David F. Powers.

20 Thompson and Myers, p. 45.

21 RFK, untitled journal, RFKP, JFKL.

22 Guthman and Shulman, eds., *In His Own Words*, p. 439.

23 Ibid., pp. 436–39.

24 Ibid., p. 438.

25 Advance report on his trip to the Middle and Far East by Hon. John F. Kennedy, Mutual Broadcasting Network, 14 November 1951, PPP, JFKL.

26 Sherry, *Life of Graham Greene*, pp. 368–71.

Mon enfant, ma sœur/ Songe à la douceur/ D'aller là-bas vivre ensemble.

(My child, my sister/ Dream of the sweetness/To go down there to live together.)

27 Ibid., pp. 398–434.

28 Interview, Kenneth P. O'Donnell.

29 Interview, O'Donnell. See also Kenneth P. O'Donnell and David F. Powers with Joe McCarthy, *"Johnny, We Hardly Knew Ye": Memories of John Fitzgerald Kennedy* (Boston: Little, Brown, 1972), pp. 92–93. O'Donnell's version of this story is somewhat differently told in Stein and Plimpton, *American Journey: The Times of Robert Kennedy* (New York: Harcourt Brace Jovanovich, 1970) pp. 40–42. Also Helen O'Donnell, *A Common Good, The Friendship of Robert F. Kennedy and Kenneth P. O'Donnell* (New York: William Morrow, 1998), p. 80.

30 Schlesinger, *Robert Kennedy and His Times*, p. 106.

31 *New York Times*, 14 August 1956, p. 2.

32 O'Donnell and Powers, *"Johnny We Hardly Knew Ye,"* p. 133.

33 Sorensen's pre-presidential papers contain copies of JFK's correspondence with his father that summer.

34 Gore Vidal, "Eleanor Roosevelt," *New York Review of Books,* 18 November 1971, p. 13.

35 Interview, O'Donnell.

36 Parmet, *Jack,* p. 372.

37 Interview, O'Donnell. In his book with Dave Powers, O'Donnell observed that Joe Kennedy's "blue language flashed all over the room." *"Johnny We Hardly Knew Ye,"* p. 138.

38 Ibid., p. 139.

39 Anderson, *Jack and Jackie* (New York: William Morrow, 1996), pp. 168–71.

40 Ibid., p. 171.

41 Interview: Francis D. Flanigan. Flanigan later became chief counsel to the Permanent Subcommittee on Investigations.

42 Edwin O. Guthman, *We Band of Brothers: A Memoir of Robert F. Kennedy* (New York: Harper & Row, 1971), p. 17.

43 Thompson and Myers, *The Brother Within,* pp. 105–16.

44 Joseph P. Kennedy to Robert F. Kennedy, 21 July 1955. RFKP, pre-administration personal correspondence, JFKL.

45 Clark Mollenhoff and Thomas B. Morgan, "The Dizzy Descent of Dave Beck," *Look,* 15 April 1957.

46 Robert F. Kennedy, *The Enemy Within* (New York: Harper & Brothers, 1960), p. 8.

47 Arthur Schlesinger quoting Jean Kennedy Smith. See Schlesinger, *Robert Kennedy and His Times,* p. 153.

48 Quoted in Peter Collier and David Horowitz, *The Kennedys: An American Dream* (New York: Summit Books, 1984), p. 220.

49 Kennedy, *The Enemy Within,* p. 17.

50 Interview, Kenneth O'Donnell. The proper name of the McClellan Committee was the Senate Select Committee on Improper Activities in the Labor or Management Field.

51 Quoted in Collier and Horowitz, *The Kennedys,* p. 162.

52 Ralph G. Martin, *Seeds of Destruction: Joe Kennedy and His Sons* (New York: Putnam, 1995), p. 210.

53 Interview, Barry M. Goldwater.

54 Kennedy, *The Enemy Within,* p. 35.

55 Ibid., p. 88. The story was recounted by Scott to Kennedy investigator Walter Sheridan.

56 Schlesinger, *Robert Kennedy and His Times,* p. 179.

57 Hoffa's account is contained in Arthur A. Sloane, *Hoffa* (Cambridge: MIT Press, 1991), p. 28.

58 Nick Thimmesch and William O. Johnson, *Robert Kennedy at Forty* (New York: W. W. Norton, 1965), p. 73.

59 Sloane, *Hoffa,* chap. 11.

60 Quoted in ibid., p. 60.

61 *Newsweek,* 8 April 1957, p. 36.

62 Kennedy, *The Enemy Within,* pp. 74–75.

63 Ibid., p. 62.

64 Schlesinger, *Robert Kennedy and His Times,* p. 173.

65 "The Rise of the Brothers Kennedy," *Look,* 6 August 1957; "The Kennedy Brothers: Off to a Fast Start," *U.S. News and World Report,* 12 April 1957; "Young Crusader: He's Making the Spot Hot," *Newsweek,* 22 July 1957; "Young Man with Tough Questions," *Life,* 1 July 1957.

66 Kennedy had been briefed in preparation for Marcello's testimony by Aaron Kohn, a former FBI agent whose life's work was to track Louisiana's "Little Man."

67 Kennedy, *The Enemy Within,* p. 75.

68 Ibid., pp. 249–50. Gallo and his brother, Lawrence, were credited with no less than seventeen hits by this time. When Kennedy asked him about one in which the victim's face had been shot so many times he was unrecognizable, Joey Gallo simply giggled.

69 Ibid., p. 160.

70 Quoted in Schlesinger, *Robert Kennedy and His Times,* p. 172.

71 Timmesch and Johnson, *Robert Kennedy at Forty,* pp. 24–25.

72 Parmet, *Jack,* pp. 424–37.

73 *Arizona Republic,* 21 January 1983, p. 3.

74 Mahoney, *JFK: Ordeal in Africa* (New York: Oxford University Press, 1983), pp. 20–24.

75 Quoted in Schlesinger, *Robert Kennedy and His Times,* p. 206.

76 Parmet, *Jack,* pp. 417–31.

77 Thompson and Myers, *The Brother Within,* p. 25.

78 Kennedy, *The Enemy Within,* p. 325.

79 Quoted in Ralph G. Martin, *Seeds of Destruction* (New York: 1995), p. 217.

80 Martin, *Hoffa,* p. 142.

81 See p. 171, Kennedy, *The Enemy Within.* Confidential interview: 37. A committee investigator commented that RFK's "recharacterization" of Teitelbaum's offer was very different in its original iteration by the gangster lawyer.

82 Interviews, Goldwater, O'Donnell. Kennedy's account in *The Enemy Within* is on p. 171.

83 Costello and Giancana's relationships with Joseph Kennedy are set forth in the "February 29, 1960, New York City" chapter. Moe Dalitz, a brilliant Jewish gangster from Detroit, was involved with Kennedy in bootlegging during the 1920s and in 1950 opened the Desert Inn in Las Vegas, thereafter becoming one of the most prominent mafiosi in Las Vegas. Interview, Dean Elson, FBI Special Agent in Charge in Las Vegas, 1961–1969.

84 JFK at mass with Battaglia is cited in Anthony Summers, *Official and Confidential: The Secret Life of J. Edgar Hoover* (New York: Putnam, 1993), p. 269. Summers cites FBI files at p. 489 of his book as the source. The Battaglia fund-raiser is cited in the JFKL PPP, 1960 election, Arizona file. Also Joseph Bonanno, *A Man of Honor: The Autobiography of Joseph Bonanno* (New York: Simon and Schuster, 1983), p. 114.

85 Quoted in David E. Scheim, *Contract on America: The Mafia Murders of John and Robert Kennedy* (Silver Spring, MD: Argyle Press, 1983), p. 171. Nixon's Mafia ties were wide-ranging: Bebe Rebozo and James Crosby in south Florida, Carlos Marcello in New Orleans (a heavy Nixon contributor), C. Arnholt Smith and John Alessio in California, as well as Teamster mob chieftains like Anthony Provenzano. The *Los Angeles Times* titled a lead editorial on Nixon's Mafia and Teamster ties during his presidency: "Nixon, the Teamsters, the Mafia," 1 June 1973. Jack Halfen was a prominent Texas gangster until his conviction for income tax fraud in 1954. In prison he talked to U.S. Marshal J. Neal Matthews and told him that the mob had given LBJ $500,000 in cash and campaign contributions while Johnson was in the Senate. Halfen had pictures of himself and Johnson as well as a letter from LBJ to the Texas Board of Paroles. According to LBJ biographer Robert Caro, Johnson as congressman, senator, and vice president received "envelopes stuffed with cash" from lobbyists.

The Campaign: 1960

1 Personal memo from J. Edgar Hoover to the attorney general, 16 August 1962. The memo states: "Before the last presidential election, Joseph P. Kennedy (the father of President John Kennedy) had been visited by many gangsters with gambling interests and a deal was made which resulted in Peter Lawford, Frank Sinatra, Dean Martin and others obtaining a lucrative gambling establishment, the Cal-Neva Hotel, at Lake Tahoe."

2 Charles Rappleye and Ed Becker, *All-American Mafioso: The Johnny Rosselli Story* (New York: Doubleday, 1991), p. 202.

3 Leonard Katz, *Uncle Frank: The Biography of Frank Costello* (New York: Drake Publishers, 1973), pp. 68–69. Costello related details of his relationship with the elder Kennedy to noted journalist Peter Maas, among others.

4 FBI telex LA 92–113, "Background on Hoodlum John Rosselli," July 1961. Rosselli unofficially managed the Tropicana in Las Vegas in the late 1950s, in which Costello had a major interest. See also Sam and Chuck Giancana, *Double Cross* (New York: Warner Books, 1992), pp. 228–29. I am grateful to the Chicago Crime Commission for its assistance in my research.

5 Interview, Mario Brod. In addition to top-secret spot work (such as structuring retainers for defecting Soviet spies in Manhattan), Brod also represented the Teamsters. See Tom Mangold, *Cold Warrior: James Jesus Angleton: The CIA's Master Spy Hunter* (New York: Simon and Schuster, 1991) and Dan E. Moldea, *The Hoffa Wars: Teamsters, Rebels, Politicians, and the Mob* (New York: Paddington Press, 1978). In interview, Brod described himself as "no particular friend of the Kennedys" and did not recall who in particular had invited him to the lunch.

6 Edna Daulyton, a hostess at Young's that day, in an interview with Anthony Summers, recollected a far larger gathering of gangsters, including Carlos Marcello, who is known to have contributed $500,000 to Vice President Richard Nixon in 1960 and supported Senator Lyndon Johnson in the primary against Kennedy. See Summers, *Official and Confidential,* p. 269.

7 Interview, O'Donnell.

8 LBJ's ties to Marcello through Bobby Parker, his chief aide when he was Senate majority leader, went back to the early 1950s. Marcello's Texas "political fixer" Jack Halfen reportedly arranged to siphon off a percentage of the mobster's racing wire and slot machine profits for LBJ's Senate campaigns. Journalist Michael Dorman alleged that in exchange for such contributions, LBJ stopped anti-racketeering legislation. After becoming president, Johnson ordered all FBI bugging (principally of the Mafia) to cease. Part of the reason may have been that a Senate investigation of Bobby Baker's corruption was leading directly to mob connections. Special Agent Willliam F. Roemer Jr., who had been spearheading the attack on the mob in Chicago, concluded: "If you judge a man by his acts, here was a man [LBJ] who did more to hinder the government agency fighting crime than any other president or leader in our history." William F. Roemer Jr., *Roemer: Man Against the Mob* (New York: Ballan-

tine, 1989), p. 218. See Dick Russell, *The Man Who Knew Too Much* (New York: Carroll & Graf, 1992), p. 524. Nixon's friend Bebe Rebozo was a well-known figure in various mob families. Among other things, Rebozo arranged the purchase of Nixon's Key Biscayne property through a corrupt series of financial maneuvers. See Warren Hinckle and William W. Turner, *The Fish Is Red: The Story of the Secret War Against Castro* (New York: Harper & Row, 1981), pp. 296–98.

9 Confidential interview with a former employee in Kennedy's Manhattan office who worked for Steve Smith during the 1960 campaign characterized Joe Kennedy's comment in these words. Regarding Nixon's mob ties, see John H. Davis, *Mafia Kingfish* (New York: McGraw-Hill, 1989), pp. 360–66.

10 See Michael R. Beschloss, *Kennedy and Roosevelt: The Uneasy Alliance* (New York: W. W. Norton, 1980).

11 Truman later said that he had replied: "If you say another word about Roosevelt, I'm going to throw you out the window." See Parmet, *Jack*, p. 141. Also quoted in Merle Miller, *Plain Speaking: An Oral Autobiography of Harry S Truman* (New York: Berkeley Books, 1974), p. 186.

12 Arthur Schlesinger Jr. makes reference to this practice as well in *Robert Kennedy and His Times*, p. 61.

13 Paul Fay, *The Pleasure of His Company* (New York: Harper & Row, 1966), p. 27.

14 Miller, *Plain Speaking*, p. 187.

15 Interview, Kenneth O'Donnell. Kennedy had first recounted the spoof at a Gridiron Club dinner in March 1958. See Box 900, PPP, JFKL.

16 Parmet, *Jack*, p. 511.

17 See Memorandum from Jerrold B. Brown to Inspector General, CIA. Background on Jim Angleton's Call to Senate Committee Counsels, July 1975. Assassination Archives (AA), Church Committee files.

18 For fuller portraits of Accardo and Humphreys, see Roemer, *Roemer: Man Against the Mob*.

19 Seymour M. Hersh, *The Dark Side of Camelot* (New York: Little, Brown, 1997), p. 143.

20 This description of Rosselli draws on the magisterial book by Rappleye and Becker, *All-American Mafioso*.

21 FBI telex 2162, 10 March 1960, at The National Archives in Suitland, Maryland, has a multibox file spanning fourteen years regarding Rosselli.

22 FBI memorandum, THP, "Background on Johnny Rosselli," 19 July 1960, FBI numbered files, AA. Carmen is quoted in Rappleye and Becker, *All-American Mafioso*, p. 209.

23 Peter Collier and David Horowitz, *The Kennedys: An American Drama* (New York: Summit Books, 1984), p. 284. The author's judgment regarding the state of Robert Kennedy's knowledge of his father's and brother's sexual indiscretions is drawn from numerous interviews with family friends.

24 Kennedy interviewed Edmund Notti, then Las Vegas assistant city manager and later assistant clerk of Cook County (Illinois). The testimony of Notti, who later described himself to FBI agents as a friend of Rosselli's, can be found in FBI numbered files, July 1962, AA.

25 See the *World Encyclopedia of Crime*, pp. 1894–97, for background on Lansky. Also Rappleye and Becker, *All-American Mafioso*, pp. 139–40.

26 Interviews: Robert R. Fuesel, former IRS Treasury agent (Criminal Investigation Unit, Chicago) and president, Chicago Crime Commission, and Peter McClennen and Robert Rose (Chicago political consultants). The Chicago Crime Commission granted the author access to its immense files. See also Ovid Demaris, *Captive City: Chicago in Chains* (New York: Buccaneer Books, 1993).

27 Interview, Brod. Humphrey's characterization of the exchange was not entirely accurate. Kennedy asked, after Giancana laughed at one of his questions, if he was "giggling. I thought only little girls did that, Mr. Giancana."

28 This is consistent with Giancana's reported reasoning for supporting JFK in Giancana and Giancana, *Double Cross,* p. 280.

29 According to Kitty Kelley in her unauthorized biography of Frank Sinatra, FBI wiretaps revealed that Skinny D'Amato claimed that he had distributed $50,000 for Jack Kennedy in the West Virginia primary. *His Way* (New York: Bantam Books, 1986), pp. 295, 581. In *The Dark Side of Camelot,* Seymour Hersh disputes this based on his interviews with Milton Rudin, a Los Angeles attorney who represented Sinatra and other entertainment figures. D'Amato moved mob cash from Las Vegas directly to the Kennedy campaign. This conforms with Brod's recollection. According to Hersh's account, D'Amato, bragging about his role in the campaign, was picked up by an FBI bug. He was subsequently indicted on income tax evasion charges by the Justice Department, an action concerning which Rudin approached Steve Smith (pp. 100–101).

30 This account is essentially drawn from interviews with Larry O'Brien and Kenneth O'Donnell as well as Theodore White's *The Making of the President 1960* (New York: Atheneum, 1961), pp. 78–95.

31 Oral history, Charles Spalding, JFKL. O'Donnell, *A Common Good*, p. 184.

32 Schlesinger, *Robert Kennedy and His Times,* p. 212.

33 White, *The Making of the American President 1960,* p. 108.

34 Interview, Raymond Chafin.

35 Quoted in Ronald Kessler, *The Sins of the Father* (New York: Warner Books, 1996), p. 376.

36 Hubert Humphrey, *The Education of a Public Man: My Life and Politics* (Garden City, NY: Doubleday, 1976), p. 217.

37 White, *The Making of the President 1960,* p. 112.

38 O'Donnell and Powers, *"Johnny We Hardly Knew Ye,"* p. 147.

39 See chapter entitled "July 13, 1961, Chicago, Illinois."

40 This is based on review of *Granma,* the Cuban Communist party daily, 1–20 March 1960, as well as an interview in Havana with one of Castro's lieutenants during that period, Ignacio Perez Cerezo.

41 This account is based on a host of sources, the most important of which is Tad Szulc, *Fidel Castro: A Critical Portrait* (New York: Morrow, 1986).

42 In mid-December 1963, the CIA's Florida station known as JM/WAVE launched Operation Duck, in which a crew of exiles infiltrated Cuban waters and placed time-delayed charges under Cuban PT boats. After setting off a small initial charge, the invaders fled. At daybreak the next morning, with a host of Cuban vessels in the vicinity, a second, far larger detonation took place. See David Corn, *Blond Ghost: Ted Shackley and the CIA's Crusades* (New York: Simon and Schuster, 1994), pp. 111–12.

43 As quoted in Szulc, *Fidel Castro,* p. 515.

44 John Pearson, *The Life of Ian Fleming* (New York: McGraw-Hill, 1966), pp. 296–97.

45 See Hinckle and Turner, *The Fish Is Red,* pp. 44–45.

46 Interview, Ricardo Alarcón de Quesada, June 1997. At the time of the interview, Alarcón was serving as Cuban president of the National Congress.

47 Interview, Peter Lawford.

48 Parmet, *Jack,* pp. 191–92. Kennedy had likened his disease, in a conversation with Joe Alsop in the late 1940s, as "slow-motion leukemia." Also James A. Nicholas, Charles L. Busstein et al., "Management of Adrenocortical Insufficiency During Surgery," *Archive of Surgery,* November 1955, p. 736.

49 Oral history of Janet Travell M.D., JFKL.

50 See Carl Rollyson, *The Lives of Norman Mailer: A Biography* (New York: Paragon House, 1991), pp. 134–35.

51 Norman Mailer, "Superman Comes to the Supermarket," *Esquire,* September 1960.

52 Interview, Lawford. Sinatra repeated this phrase incessantly to his friends and associates.

53 Sam Giancana, according to his brother and son, had Sinatra under instruction to "pull out all the stops" to get Kennedy elected president. See Giancana and Giancana, *Double Cross*, p. 281, and passim.

54 Interview, Meredith Harless. She served as Louis B. Mayer's assistant during the 1930s and 1940s. For an in-depth discussion of this incident, see Rappleye and Becker, *All-American Mafioso*, pp. 132–33.

55 Interview, Lawford.

56 Quoted in Christopher Andersen, *Jack and Jackie*, p. 214.

57 Interview, Harless.

58 James Spada, *Peter Lawford: The Man Who Kept the Secrets* (New York: Bantam Books, 1991), pp. 191–93.

59 Interview, Lawford. The author attempted to interview Frank Sinatra on several occasions but Sinatra, through staff, declined.

60 Interview, Berle. I am grateful to Irwin Schaeffer for having made the introduction.

61 Christopher Anderson has written that there had been a party the previous evening, July 15, at the Lawford home in which Marilyn Monroe and Angie Dickinson, among other guests, went skinny-dipping. Anderson, *Jack and Jackie*, p. 214.

62 Otash has since maintained that there were bugs planted in the house prior to the Mafia eavesdropping. Spada, *Peter Lawford*, pp. 310–11.

63 In its wiretap (ELSUR) of Giancana in Chicago, the FBI learned that Rosselli wanted his apartment (the Diplomat) swept for bugs and was trying to get the most recent generation of bugs from the CIA. See LA 92–113 (transcribed conversation between Giancana and Rosselli), as well as FBI field analysis. FBI numbered files, AA.

64 See Richard D. Mahoney, *JFK: Ordeal in Africa*, p. 34.

65 Drawn from the testimony of Maheu, Rosselli, and Jim O'Connell before the Church Committee. Alleged Assassination Plots Involving Foreign Leaders, pp. 75–76.

66 Rappleye and Becker, *All-American Mafioso*, pp. 145–47.

67 As quoted in Szulc, *Fidel*, p. 525.

68 See David Wise and Thomas B. Ross, *The Espionage Establishment* (New York: Random House, 1967), p. 130.

69 See FBI Memorandum on Albert Foley, S.J., FBI numbered files, AA. Rappleye and Becker, *All-American Mafioso*, p. 252.

70 Based on the testimony of Rosselli, O'Connell, Maheu, and Trafficante before the Church Committee in June 1975. Also Hinckle and Turner, *The Fish Is Red*, p. 29.

71 Interview, Jorge Recarey. Recarey's father, trained as an attorney, was one of the largest produce merchants in Cuba.

72 Quoted in Haynes Johnson, *The Bay of Pigs: The Leader's Story of Brigade 2056* (New York: W. W. Norton, 1964), p. 27.

73 Eugenio Martinez was later to achieve Watergate fame as one of the hotel burglars.

74 See Andy Postal Memorandum for the Record Re: Chronology of Events As We Now Know Them, 12 September 1975. AA.

75 Summers, *Official and Confidential,* pp. 237–53.

76 Testimony of Eugene H. Brading, 26 July 1978, HSCA, AA. Brading testified that mob capo Joey Snyder had introduced him to Hoover. He also admitted, under risk of perjury, that he was acquainted with Anthony Spilotro, Marshall Caifano, and Allen Dorfman, all Chicago mob figures. He further testified (p. 45) that, within days of Rosselli's murder in July 1976, he was paged at the Atlanta Marriott. When he answered the phone, he was informed: "You're next." Brading was in Los Angeles, more than 100 miles from his own home, the night of Robert Kennedy's assassination in Los Angeles and was extensively questioned about this by Los Angeles police. See Peter Noyes, *Legacy of Doubt* (New York: Pinnacle Books, 1973) and David Scheim, *Contract on America* (New York: Pinnacle Books, 1983).

77 The FBI ELSUR (electronic surveillance) intercept is quoted in HSCA memorandum "Involvement of Organized Crime in Plots to Assassinate Fidel Castro" (Secret/Declassified), p. 8. Roemer's description of Cain is contained in *Man Against the Mob,* p. 210. The author reviewed the Chicago Crime Commission's entire file on Cain and also interviewed both Jack Mabely (former columnist for the *Chicago Daily News*) and Treasury agent Robert R. Fuesel.

78 Roemer, *Man Against the Mob,* p. 172. This description of Cain is also based on the Chicago Crime Commission (CCC) files.

79 Interview, Jack Mabely.

80 Undated staff memorandum, House Select Committee on Assassinations, AA.

81 White, *The Making of the American President 1960,* p. 12. This account is based on those of White and O'Donnell and Powers in *"Johnny We Hardly Knew Ye."* Also interviews, Dave Powers, Kenneth O'Donnell, Ralph Dungan, and Larry O'Brien.

82 Leo Damore, *The Cape Cod Years of John Fitzgerald Kennedy* (Englewood Cliffs, NJ: Prentice Hall, 1967), pp. 216–23.

83 This is White's judgment, *The Making of the American President 1960,* pp. 9–10.

84 Interview, Larry O'Brien. RFK took extensive notes on an election form that evening. See Personal Correspondence, file folder DNC 1960, RFKP, JFKL.

85 Interview, Dungan. O'Donnell and Powers refer to Kennedy's "sailorish language," *"Johnny We Hardly Knew Ye,"* p. 224.

86 William Manchester, *One Brief Shining Moment: Remembering Kennedy* (Boston: Little, Brown, 1983), p. 121.

87 White, *The Making of the President 1960,* pp. 13–14.

88 Interview, Dungan. The next day, 9 November 1960, JFK quoted Daley as saying, "Mr. President, with a little bit of luck and the help of a few close friends, you're going to carry Illinois." Quoted in Ben Bradlee, *A Good Life: Newspapering and Other Adventures* (New York: Simon and Schuster, 1995), p. 212.

89 Interviews: Doris Mulcahy (whose husband was a "Democratic associate" of Inglese) was one of the women working at the Armory Lounge that night. The Lounge was then owned by Joey Aiuppa, the Outfit's boss in Cicero. Rosselli's fingertip ability with facts and figures was evident fifteen years later, on 24 June 1975, when he testified about the CIA-Mafia plots to kill Castro before the Church Committee:

SENATOR GOLDWATER: Mr. Rosselli, we've had CIA agents, we've had FBI agents, we've had other members of the government here, and all of them came in with their notes and files, and referred to them in answering our questions, and it's remarkable to me how your testimony dovetails with theirs. Tell me, Mr. Rosselli, during the time that all this was going on, were you taking notes?

MR. ROSSELLI: Senator, in my business, we don't take notes.

90 See Roemer, *Man Against the Mob,* p. 145.

91 Ovid Demaris, *Captive City* (New York: L. Stuart, 1969).

92 O'Donnell and Powers, *"Johnny We Hardly Knew Ye,"* p. 224.

93 Ibid., p. 195. Sworn testimony of Donald Pecock before the Illinois Election Laws Commission. See also Mike Royko, chap. 4, "The Machine," in *Boss: Richard J. Daley of Chicago* (New York: Dutton, 1971).

94 Milton L. Rakove, *We Don't Want Nobody Nobody Sent: An Oral History of the Daley Years* (Bloomington: Indiana University Press, 1979).

95 Ibid., p. 106.

96 Manchester, *One Brief Shining Moment,* p. 121.

97 Hersh, *The Dark Side of Camelot,* p. 140.

98 Interview, O'Brien. He later stuck to the story: "There was a degree of hanky-panky in Illinois, but I always felt that whatever it was—and I had no knowledge of it—it happened in the southern part of the state." Quoted in F. Richard Ciccone, *Daley: Power and Presidential Politics*

(Chicago: Contemporary Books, 1996), p. 142. Ethel Kennedy's quote is contained in Thompson and Myers, *The Brother Within*, p. 12.

99 Oral history of John Seigenthaler, JFKL.

100 Ibid. Also Thompson and Myers, *The Brother Within*, p. 21.

101 Oral history of Robert F. Kennedy, JFKL.

102 See Thompson and Myers, *The Brother Within*, pp. 39–40.

103 Oral history, Seigenthaler.

104 This portrait of Robert F. Kennedy is based on several interviews, the most significant of which were with Kenneth O'Donnell, Dave Powers, William P. Mahoney, and Ralph Dungan.

105 Schlesinger, *Robert Kennedy and His Times*, p. 242.

106 Ibid., p. 243.

107 Giancana and Giancana, *Double Cross*, pp. 294–95.

108 *Wall Street Journal*, 19 December 1960.

109 Quoting Harold Gibbons in Steven Brill, *The Teamsters* (New York: Simon and Schuster, 1978), p. 30.

110 Oral history, Seigenthaler.

111 Ibid., p. 243.

Ordeal: 1961

1 Mahoney, *JFK: Ordeal in Africa*, pp. 69–70.

2 John Ranelagh, *The Agency: The Rise and Decline of the CIA* (New York: Simon and Schuster, 1986), pp. 288–96.

3 Mahoney, *JFK: Ordeal in Africa*, p. 59.

4 In *The Dark Side of Camelot*, Seymour Hersh states that "Jack Kennedy knew of and endorsed the CIA's assassination plotting against Lumumba." He offers no evidence of this claim, which is entirely contrary to this author's research. Hersh further states that Lumumba was "murdered during Kennedy's thousand days in the presidency." Lumumba was in fact murdered two days before Kennedy became president. Among Hersh's other claims is that "Jack Kennedy had personally authorized Richard Bissell to set up ZR/RIFLE before his inauguration" (p. 192). ZR/RIFLE was in fact created in early November 1960, two and a half months before Kennedy took office. See HSCA staff Memorandum from Mason Cargill, 21 May 1976. Also Staff Summary, 7 June 1976.

5 See news release, The Fontainebleau Hilton Resort and Towers.

6 Interview, Joe Shimon.

7 House Assassinations Committee staff memorandum, p. 8, AA.

8 Davis, *Mafia Kingfish*, pp. 91–93.

9 Ibid., pp. 97–98.

10 See FBI airtels 92–113, 27 June 1961 and 4 September 1961, FBI numbered files, AA.

11 This investigation is summarized in FBI memorandum to Director (92-3267) from SAC, Los Angeles (92-113), 14 February 1963, FBI numbered files, AA.

12 FBI airtel to Director, 26 March 1961, FBI numbered files, AA. See also Rappleye and Becker, *All-American Mafioso*, p. 201.

13 Richard Nixon, *RN: The Memoirs of Richard Nixon* (New York: Grosset & Dunlap, 1978), p. 596.

14 Interview, O'Donnell.

15 Peter Lawford to Robert F. Kennedy, 7 April 1961, Personal Correspondence, RFKP, JFKL.

16 Oral history of Robert F. Kennedy, JFKL.

17 J. E. Hoover to Robert F. Kennedy, 9 June 1961, Personal Correspondence, RFKP, JFKL.

18 Quoted in Schlesinger, *Robert Kennedy and His Times*, p. 483.

19 See Summers, *Official and Confidential*, pp. 246–66.

20 Ibid., pp. 257–65

21 Ibid., p. 281.

22 Nicholas Katzenbach, Kennedy's chief deputy, later expressed the problem of bugs before the Senate Judiciary Committee: "The practice (of electronic surveillance) is self-defeating . . . a wiretap constitutes a grant of immunity to the subjects through tainted evidence." Testimony of Attorney General Katzenbach, Committee print, 13 July 1965.

23 See Roemer, *Man Against the Mob*, pp. 69–70.

24 Schlesinger, *Robert Kennedy and His Times*, p. 296. Schlesinger believes Kennedy may not have fully realized that he was sanctioning their use.

25 Interview, Fuesel.

26 Victor S. Navasky, *Kennedy Justice* (New York: Atheneum, 1971), pp. 44–46.

27 Edmund G. Brown to Robert F. Kennedy, 12 December 1961, Personal Correspondence, RFKP, JFKL.

28 John C. McWilliams, *The Protectors: Harry S. Anslinger and the Federal Bureau of Narcotics* (Newark, DE: University of Delaware Press, 1990), pp. 215–16.

29 Budd Schulberg, "RFK—Harbinger of Hope," *Playboy*, January 1969.

30 *Variety*, 3 May 1961.

31 See Wald and Schulberg folders, 1961–1963, Personal Correspondence, RFKP, JFKL.

32 Interview, Fuesel.

33 Schlesinger, *Robert Kennedy and His Times,* p. 286.

34 On a late occasion, Rosselli told Las Vegas SAC Dean W. Elson that he had told his new apartment manager that he should get a discount for the FBI detail that would move into the neighborhood and bring down the number of burglaries and street crime. Memorandum to Director (92-3267) from SAC LA (92-113c), 14 March 1963, FBI numbered files, AA.

35 Electronics expert Gordon Novel claimed to have also seen such a shot, shown to him by CIA counterintelligence chief James Angleton: "What I saw was a picture of him [Hoover] giving Clyde Tolson a blow job." See Summers, *Official and Confidential,* pp. 243–45.

36 Roemer, *Man Against the Mob,* p. 206.

37 Ibid., p. 207.

38 Davis in *Mafia Kingfish* states that it was via a Trujillo-provided jet (p. 100). The draft Staff Report of the Select Committee on Assassinations, March 1979, concludes that it was Ferrie, citing a border control report.

39 Ranelagh, *The Agency,* pp. 357–59.

40 As cited in Hugh Thomas, *Cuba: The Pursuit of Freedom* (New York: Harper & Row, 1971), pp. 1372–74.

41 Interview, Recarey.

42 "Did Switch Doom Bay of Pigs?" *Miami Herald,* 5 January 1997.

43 Lucien S. Vandenbroucke, "The Confessions of Allen Dulles: New Evidence on the Bay of Pigs," *Diplomatic History* (Fall 1984). Also Richard M. Bissell Jr., "Response to Lucien Vandenbroucke's 'The Confessions of Allen Dulles,'" *Diplomatic History* (Fall 1984).

44 Hersh, *The Dark Side of Camelot,* p. 207.

45 Judith Exner, *My Story* (New York: Grove Press, 1977); *New York Post,* 22 December 1975; Hersh, *The Dark Side of Camelot,* pp. 306–8.

46 Liz Smith, "Judith Exner's Final Revelation about JFK," *Vanity Fair,* January 1997.

47 Quoted in the Church Committee Report, "Assassination Plots," p. 313.

48 Szulc, *Fidel,* p. 543.

49 Interview, Blas Casares.

50 Schlesinger, *A Thousand Days,* p. 269.

51 Interview, Mario Martinez Malo, Brigade 2506 veteran.

52 Schlesinger, *A Thousand Days,* p. 267.

53 Thomas, *Cuba,* p. 356.

54 Szulc, *Fidel,* p. 547.

55 Oral history, Joseph Spalding, JFKL.

56 Szulc, *Fidel,* pp. 548–49.

57 Interview, Recarey.

58 Peter Wyden, *Bay of Pigs: The Untold Story* (New York: Simon and Schuster, 1979), pp. 210–71.

59 The man who reportedly vomited was Richard Drain, code-named Bill; in David Phillips, *The Night Watch* (New York: Atheneum, 1977), p. 109.

60 Copies of these messages were provided to the author by Blas Casares.

61 Interview, Casares.

62 Oral history, Robert F. Kennedy, JFKL.

63 Schlesinger, *A Thousand Days,* pp. 283–84.

64 Ibid., p. 284.

65 Quoted in Ralph Martin, *Seeds of Destruction,* p. 333.

66 Interview, O'Donnell.

67 Richard Goodwin, *Remembering America: A Voice from the Sixties* (Boston: Little, Brown, 1988), p. 400.

68 Harris Wofford, *Of Kennedys and Kings: Making Sense of the Sixties* (Pittsburgh: University of Pittsburgh Press, 1992), pp. 152–53.

69 Theodore C. Sorensen to Robert F. Kennedy, pre-administration personal correspondence, 14 December 1959.

70 Wofford, *Of Kennedys and Kings,* pp. 103–53.

71 This is drawn from RFK's speech file on the Athens speech, RFKP, JFKL.

72 Address by the Hon. Robert F. Kennedy, University of Georgia Law School, 6 May 1961, Speeches 1961–1964, RFKP, JFKL.

73 Thompson and Myers, *The Brother Within,* p. 152.

74 Wofford, *Of Kennedys and Kings,* p. 153.

75 Thompson and Myers, *The Brother Within,* pp. 169–70.

76 Wofford, *Of Kennedys and Kings,* pp. 157–58.

77 The Cal-Neva opened in April 1962.

78 Personal memo from J. Edgar Hoover to the attorney general, 16 August 1962.

79 This account of the July 13 incident is drawn from Roemer, *Man Against the Mob,* pp. 138–45.

80 Roemer, *Man Against the Mob,* pp. 145–51.

81 Rappleye and Becker, *All-American Mafioso,* pp. 218–19.

82 Rosselli did briefly own a 1961 Chevy Monza, but when a girlfriend cracked it up, he went back to his usual mode.

83 J. Edgar Hoover to Robert F. Kennedy, 15 December 1961, personal correspondence, RFKP, JFKL.

84 Quoted in Davis, *Mafia Kingfish,* p. 136.

85 Tad Szulc, "Cuba on Our Mind," *Esquire,* February 1974.

86 Interview, O'Donnell; Wyden, *Bay of Pigs,* pp. 289–312.

87 Interview, O'Donnell. The president told William Manchester that he had lost "all illusions about the infallibility of the Joint Chiefs" in *One Brief Shining Moment,* p. 137.

88 Mansfield to JFK, 1 May 1961 cited in Schlesinger, *Robert Kennedy and His Times,* p. 509. See RFKP, Cuba 1961, with note from Angela Novello, JFKL.

89 Interview, David Ormsby-Gore.

90 Gore Vidal, "President Kennedy,' *London Sunday Telegraph,* 9 April 1961.

91 Interview, Casares.

92 McNamara quoted in the Church Committee Interim Report, p. 142.

93 Church Committee Interim Report, p. 77.

94 Hoover memo quoted in *Church Committee Interim Report,* p. 127.

95 Hoover memo to RFK (and RFK's notation) quoted in "Assassination Plots," Church Committee Report, pp. 127–28.

96 Schlesinger, *Robert Kennedy and His Times,* pp. 508–9.

97 Interview, George Ball.

98 Interview, Averell Harriman.

99 David Halberstam interview with James Reston, in Martin, *Seeds of Destruction,* p. 352.

100 Schlesinger, *A Thousand Days,* p. 463.

101 Quoted in Heather A. Purcell and James K. Galbraith, "Did the U.S. Military Plan a Nuclear First Strike for 1963?" *American Prospect,* Fall 1994.

102 Oral history, Robert F. Kennedy, JFKL.

103 Matthew Maxwell Taylor Kennedy.

104 Quoted in Norman Sherry, *The Life of Graham Greene,* vol. 2 (New York: Penguin Books, 1990), p. 412.

105 DOD Task #69, 3 August 1962, from Edward Lansdale, AA.

106 Quoted in Ranelagh, *The Agency,* p. 386.

107 Interview, James Symington.

108 Wofford, *Of Kennedys and Kings,* p. 386.

109 Helms is quoted in Ranelagh, *The Agency,* p. 385.

110 Ranelagh, *The Agency,* pp. 385–88. The quarterly *Foreign Affairs* described the book as "the best and most comprehensive history" of its kind.

111 Wofford, *Of Kennedys and Kings,* p. 398.

112 Quoted in Schlesinger, *Robert Kennedy and His Times,* p. 530.

113 Cable 5816, CIA Station (Scott), 19 Nov. 1961 to Base, confirming receipt of Harvey's cable, AA.

114 Collier and Horowitz, *The Kennedys,* pp. 286–87.

115 The description of the president's reaction is from Manchester, *One Brief Shining Moment,* p. 245.

116 See his personal correspondence 1962 file in the weeks and months following. RFKP, JFKL.

117 Quoted in Martin, *Seeds of Destruction,* p. 359.

118 Oral history, Robert F. Kennedy, JFKL.

119 Quoted in Schlesinger, *Robert Kennedy and His Times,* p. 483.

120 Manchester, *One Brief Shining Moment,* pp. 165–66.

121 Interview, O'Donnell.

122 Interview, Lawford.

123 Collier and Horowitz, *The Kennedys,* p. 283.

124 See Bradlee, *A Good Life,* pp. 267–69. Bradlee was married to Mary Meyer's sister, Tony.

125 Mahoney, *JFK: Ordeal in Africa,* pp. 175–79.

126 Manchester, *One Brief Shining Moment,* p. 245.

127 Martin, *Seeds of Destruction,* p. 363.

128 Interview, Powers.

Triumph: 1962

1 See Paul O'Neil, "The No. 2 Man in Washington," *Life,* 26 January 1962, p. 18.

2 *Time,* 16 February 1962, p. 22.

3 Interview, David Ormsby-Gore.

4 Galbraith's comment is on the jacket of Schlesinger, *A Thousand Days.* See also his article in *Washington Post,* 30 November 1963, about JFK.

5 O'Neil, *Life,* 26 January 1962.

6 Undated clipping from March 1962 file, RFKP, General Files, JFKL.

7 Interview, William French.

8 Gore Vidal, "The Best Man, 1968," *Esquire,* 2 March 1963.

9 Interview, Mary McGrory.

10 Typewritten phone message dated 13 December 1961, RFKP, General Files, telephone logs, JFKL.

11 *Time,* 16 February 1962, p. 22.

12 Memo from Angela Novello to the attorney general, 4 November 1963. RFK's handwritten notation is on the bottom of the document, RFKP, JFKL.

13 Bradlee, *A Good Life,* p. 243.

14 Schlesinger, *Robert Kennedy and His Times,* p. 642. The incident, much embellished subsequently, was recorded in Schlesinger's contemporaneous journal.

15 Interview, O'Donnell.

16 *Time,* 16 February 1962.

17 RFK letter to Angier Biddle Duke, 18 July 1961; correspondence file, 1961, RFKP, JFKL.

18 Cuba: 1961, RFKP, JFKL.

19 *Time,* 16 February 1962.

20 Kim Novak to RFK, undated; correspondence file, 1961, RFKP, JFKL.

21 Interview, Lawford.

22 Ibid.

23 *Time,* 16 February 1962.

24 Ibid. See also Schlesinger, *Robert Kennedy and His Times,* pp. 609–10.

25 *Time,* 16 February 1962.

26 *Newsweek,* 12 February 1962.

27 Accompanying him on the trip was his close friend and advisor, John Seigenthaler, who recounts this scene in his oral history at the JFKL.

28 Schlesinger, *Robert Kennedy and His Times,* p. 617.

29 RFK's correspondence file 1962–63, RFKP, JFKL, evidences these communications.

30 Collier and Horowitz, *The Kennedys,* pp. 284–89.

31 Ibid., p. 289.

32 Gore Vidal, who did not himself attend the seminar, made this characterization. Vidal, "The Best Man, 1968," *Esquire,* 2 March 1963.

33 James Brent Clarke to RFK, 10 June 1962; RFK to James Brent Clarke, 14 June 1962.

34 *Time,* 16 February 1962.

35 Ibid.

36 Guthman and Shulman, eds., *In His Own Words,* pp. 332–34.

37 *Christian Science Monitor,* 16 April 1962; *Wall Street Journal,* 19 April 1962; Charles Reich, *The New Republic,* 30 April 1962.

38 Guthman and Shulman, eds., *In His Own Words,* p. 334.

39 Bradlee, *A Good Life,* p. 240. At the White House correspondents' dinner that spring, the president did a civil liberties takeoff on himself and

the administration's handling of the steel crisis. *Robert Kennedy On His Own,* p. 335.

40 Drew Pearson, "Washington Merry-Go-Round," *Washington Post,* 6 January 1962.

41 Memorandum from J. Edgar Hoover to Kenneth O'Donnell, 27 February 1962, no. 92–3267–125.

42 Interview, O'Donnell. The president's schedule indicates the 1 P.M. appointment and contains no other entries for that afternoon. JFKL.

43 Wofford, *Of Kennedys and Kings,* p. 405.

44 At least in terms of the attorney general's telephone logs, the exchanges and messages between RFK and JFK were approximately twice the normal. RFKP, JFKL.

45 Rappleye and Becker, *All-American Mafioso,* pp. 207–8.

46 Memorandum to Mr. Belmont from C. A. Evans, Subject: John Roselli Anti-Racketeering, 29 August 1962, NA.

47 Liz Smith, "The Exner Files," *Vanity Fair,* January 1997. In the article, there is a reprint of the Walter Winchell item.

48 Bradlee, *A Good Life,* pp. 238–39.

49 Hersh, *The Dark Side of Camelot,* pp. 326–47.

50 James Spada, *Peter Lawford,* pp. 292–94.

51 Ibid., pp. 297–98.

52 Anthony Summers reports another version of this comment: "They can't touch me while I'm alive, and after I'm dead, who cares?" *Official and Confidential,* p. 270.

53 Memorandum to the attorney general from Herbert J. Miller, Assistant Attorney General, Criminal Division, Subject: Arthur J. Balletti Wiretap Case, 24 April 1962, NA.

54 Testimony of Lawrence Houston, HSCA, p. 62, NA.

55 Rothman's visit is detailed in HSCA staff memorandum, "Norman 'Roughouse' Rothman," dated 20 January 1975, NA.

56 See Andy Postal Memorandum for the Record, Re: Chronology of Events as We Now Know Them, 12 September 1975, NA.

57 Arthur M. Schlesinger Jr. gives the most detailed case absolving RFK. See *Robert Kennedy and His Times,* pp. 525–32.

58 Andy Postal, Rhett Dawson Memorandum (Top Secret/Declassified) to John Bayly, Charles Kirbow, Mike Madigan. Subject: Relevance of Department of Justice Documents to Awareness of Assassination Plots, 12 August 1975, NA.

59 Andy Postal Memorandum for the Record, Re: Chronology of Events as We Now Know Them, 12 September 1975.

60 Spada describes the now-famous scene in *Peter Lawford,* pp. 303–5.

61 Quoted in Schlesinger, *Robert Kennedy and His Times,* p. 636.

62 Summers, *Official and Confidential,* p. 296.

63 Ibid., pp. 296–99.

64 Schlesinger, *Robert Kennedy and His Times,* p. 637.

65 Marilyn Monroe cable to the attorney general, dated 27 May 1962. RFKP, JFKL.

66 Quoted in Spada, *Peter Lawford,* p. 308.

67 Roemer, *Man Against the Mob,* p. 175.

68 Interview, Lawford.

69 Quoted in Anderson, *Jack and Jackie,* pp. 336–37.

70 Phil Potter to RFK, 7 August 1962. Potter enclosed the AP story quoting the attorney general. Correspondence file, RFKP, JFKL.

71 RFK to Phil Potter, 18 August 1962, correspondence file, RFKP, JFKL.

72 J. Edgar Hoover personal memo to the attorney general, 16 August 1962, FBI Archives.

73 The HSCA internally concluded that the attorney general did not know that the Rosselli connection continued and that it had been "reactivated." Harvey's denial of the Edwards memo is on page 97 of his testimony before the committee on 25 June 1975. Andy Postal Memorandum, Re: Chronology of Events as We Now Know Them, 12 September 1975.

74 Confidential interview 18 with an anti-Castro operative, then twenty-two years old, and currently an attorney in Miami.

75 Bradley Earl Ayers, *The War That Never Was: An Insider's Account of CIA Covert Operations Against Cuba* (Indianapolis: Bobbs-Merrill, 1976), p. 38.

76 Ibid., pp. 38–47.

77 This memorandum is quoted in "Alleged Assassination Plots Against Foreign Leaders," the Church Committee Report, p. 141.

78 E. G. Lansdale Memorandum, Subject: The Cuba Project, 20 February 1962, NA.

79 FBIS, 28 January 1962, Cuba file, 1962, RFKP, JFKL.

80 Interview, Alarcon. See also Jon Lee Anderson, *Che Guevara: A Revolutionary Life* (New York: Grove Press, 1997), pp. 518–20.

81 See Corn, *Blond Ghost,* pp. 65–119. Also, Hinckle and Turner, *The Fish Is Red,* pp. 96–107.

82 CIA Inspector General Report (May 1967), p. 6. The author of the IG report was J. S. Earman, NA.

83 Rappleye and Becker, *All-American Mafioso,* p. 220.

84 Alleged Assassination Plots Against Foreign Leaders, *Church Committee Report,* p. 83.

85 HSCA staff untitled secret memorandum (sanitized and declassified), n.d., NA.

86 It is possible that Rosselli and Morales knew each other previously from their days in Havana. See Rappleye and Becker, *All-American Mafioso,* p. 147.

87 Hinckle and Turner, *The Fish Is Red,* pp. 172–75.

88 Rosselli gave this account to Jack Anderson and Les Whitten, Jimmy Breslin, as well as his attorneys. Bill Harvey and Bradley Ayers among others later confirmed his role in the commando operations. Rappleye and Becker, *All-American Mafioso,* pp. 224–25.

89 The author toured the site, now overgrown with mangrove trees, in November 1996.

90 Director FBI (92–3267) to SAC Los Angeles (92–113), radiogram. Subject: John Roselli (*sic*), 11 May 1962.

91 In his testimony before the HSCA on 25 May 1975, Bill Harvey characterized Rosselli as "honestly motivated by patriotism" with "high marks for personal integrity."

92 Rappleye and Becker, *All-American Mafioso,* pp. 103–5.

93 The attorney general's telephone log and typewritten messages evidence the constancy of this connection. See also RFK's correspondence file, which contains letters from San Roman and other Brigade 2506 leaders.

94 William D. Pawley to Robert F. Kennedy, 2 July 1962, with reference to Goodwin's role. See also Novello message log of call from Goodwin to RFK, 9 July 1962.

95 It is not known whether RFK knew Rosselli was a subscriber. Evidence of this is contained in SAC (LA) to Director, FBI airtel 92–168, 20 August 1962, NA.

96 Background on the Rosselli-Foley relationship is contained in SAC (LA) to Director, FBI airtel 97–881, 20 January 1963, NA.

97 Kennedy and Foley met 8 June 1962. Knebel's message is contained in the telephone message file, RFKP, JFKL.

98 The account is from *Granma,* 16 October 1971.

99 Ibid. Also Hinckle and Turner, *The Fish Is Red,* pp. 106–7.

100 Corn, *Blond Ghost,* pp. 76, 84.

101 HSCA RG 233, JFK Collection, staff memorandum, n.d., inventoried 2 March 1977, NA.

102 Hinckle and Turner, *The Fish Is Red,* p. 175.

103 Wyden, *Bay of Pigs,* p. 326.

104 Robert F. Kennedy, *To Seek a Newer World* (Garden City, NY: Doubleday, 1967), pp. 116–17.

105 Corn, *Blond Ghost,* p. 82.

106 The author's interviews with former Cuban exile operatives reflect the consistent sentiment of approval regarding RFK.

107 Interview, Ball.

108 Interview, Bundy.

109 Corn, *Blond Ghost,* pp. 82–83.

110 RFK Appointments, 5.62, RFKP, JFKL.

111 The HSCA staff compiled profiles of operatives Masferrer, del Valle, Sturgis, and 27 others in the course of its investigation. NA.

112 Quoted in Russell, *The Man Who Knew Too Much,* pp. 508–9.

113 David Aaron Memorandum to Bill Miller, Fritz Schwarz, Curt Smothers, Bill Bader, Subject: Assassinations—Castro, 27 May 1975. HSCA, NA.

114 William Harvey Memorandum to Deputy Director (Plans), Subject: Operation Mongoose, 14 August 1962. In the memorandum, Harvey refers to the phrase "including liquidation of leaders," contained in Lansdale memo.

115 Corn, *Blond Ghost,* p. 87.

116 This is the recollection of Sergo Mikoyan, the son of Soviet first deputy premier Anastas I. Mikoyan. The younger Mikoyan at the time was the editor of *Latinskaya Amerika.* He offered this account at the Cambridge Conference of former Soviet and American foreign policy leaders regarding the Cuban missile crisis. James G. Blight and David A. Welch, *On the Brink: American and Soviets Reexamine the Cuban Missile Crisis* (New York: Hill and Wang, 1992), pp. 238–39.

117 Quoted in Schlesinger, *A Thousand Days,* pp. 798–99.

118 The characterization is Schlesinger's. See *Robert Kennedy and His Times,* p. 543.

119 James G. Blight, Bruce J. Allyn, and David A. Welch, *Cuba on the Brink: Castro, The Missile Crisis and the Soviet Collapse* (New York: Pantheon, 1993), pp. 342–43. In his foreword to the book, Harvard professor Jorge I. Dominguez reaches a similar conclusion: "U.S. decision makers and scholars have typically thought that the Soviet Union deployed ballistic missiles in Cuba in order to redress the strategic imbalance between the United States and the Soviet Union. This book suggests that the deployment may well have had a significant impact of such imbalance had the Soviet Union been able to retain its strategic weapons in Cuba. But this book also makes clear that a comparably important motivation for

the Soviet deployment was the defense of Cuba against U.S. aggression" (p. x).

120 Many of the descriptions of the confrontation at the University of Mississippi are based on those in Walter Lord, *The Past That Would Not Die* (New York: Harper & Row, 1965).

121 Guthman and Shulman, eds., *In His Own Words*, pp. 161–62.

122 Harris Wofford to John F. Kennedy, 30 December 1960, PPP, JFKL; also Wofford, *Of Kennedys and Kings*, p. 133.

123 Wofford's conclusion at pp. 142–43 is supported by the scholarship of Carl M. Brauer, *John F. Kennedy and the Second Reconstruction* (New York: Columbia University Press, 1977), p. 167.

124 William A. Geoghegan (Assistant Deputy Attorney General), memorandum to the attorney general with appended statement, 10 March 1962, RFKP, JFKL.

125 Martin Luther King Jr., "Bold Design for a New South," *The Nation*, 30 March 1963.

126 Quoted in Wofford, *Of Kennedys and Kings*, p. 161.

127 Guthman and Shulman, eds., *In His Own Words*, p. 109.

128 File: James Meredith, n.d. Burke Marshall Papers, RFKP, JFKL.

129 Transcriptions of the 26 telephone conversations between RFK and Barnett and JFK and Barnett are found in the Burke Marshall Papers, JFKL. The dates are 15 through 28 September 1962.

130 Burke Marshall, Professor of Law at Yale Law School, commented on the Kennedy negotiation style in interview with the author. "Process theory" is explicated in Roger Fisher and William Ury, *Getting to Yes* (New York: Penguin, 1988).

131 Transcript of conversation between RFK and Barnett, 25 September 1962. Burke Marshall Papers, JFKL.

132 Lord, *The Past That Would Not Die*, p. 122.

133 Transcript of conversation between RFK and Barnett, 25 September 1962. Burke Marshall Papers, JFKL.

134 William A. Geoghegan, memorandum to the attorney general, 28 September 1962. RFKP, JFKL.

135 Quoted in Lord, *The Past That Would Not Die*, p. 175.

136 Guthman and Shulman, eds., *In His Own Words*, p. 160.

137 Schlesinger, *Robert Kennedy and His Times*, p. 344.

138 Lord, *The Past That Would Not Die*, p. 189.

139 Guthman, *We Band of Brothers*, pp. 200–1.

140 Quoted in Schlesinger, *Robert Kennedy and His Times*, p. 346.

141 Guthman, *We Band of Brothers*, p. 204.

142 Guthman and Shulman, eds., *In His Own Words*, p. 166.

143 The president's communication is quoted in Lord, *The Past That Would Not Die,* pp. 3–4.

144 Transcribed conversation between RFK and Congressman Bruce Alger (R-Tex), 4 October 1962.

145 Interview, Marshall.

146 Guthman and Shulman, eds., *In His Own Words,* p. 164.

147 Quoted in Wofford, *Of Kennedys and Kings,* p. 170.

148 The three drafts of this speech can be found in the Burke Marshall Papers, JFKL.

149 *New York Times,* 12 April 1964; *Life,* 15 May 1964.

150 Dan E. Moldea, *The Hoffa Wars,* p. 149. HSCA, Final Report (HR-951828), p. 88.

151 Walter Sheridan, *The Fall and Rise of Jimmy Hoffa* (New York: Saturday Review Press. 1972), p. 217.

152 Interviews, Novello and French.

153 Bradlee, *A Good Life,* pp. 243–44. *Newsweek* printed neither story.

154 The dispositive account of the war against Hoffa is Sheridan, *The Fall and Rise of Jimmy Hoffa.*

155 *Time,* 16 February 1962.

156 A member of the Justice legal team, William French, was helpful in reminiscence with the author.

157 Summers, *Official and Confidential,* p. 296.

158 Navasky, *Kennedy Justice,* pp. 418–19. Also Sheridan, *The Fall and Rise of Jimmy Hoffa,* p. 283.

159 Organized Crime files 1962 and 1963, RFKP, JFKL.

160 The attorney general initially did not want publicity over Valachi's revelations. When Hoover tried to give the story to the press, with all credit going to the FBI, Kennedy and his press aide Ed Guthman blocked it. Later, when congressional testimony by Valachi was unavoidable, the story was released to Peter Maas.

161 Roemer, *Man Against the Mob,* pp. 105–13, 203–8.

162 Statement by Attorney General Robert F. Kennedy Before Subcommittee No. 5 of the House Committee on the Judiciary H.R. 4616. Also Remarks of the Hon. Robert F. Kennedy before the Conference of Federal, State and Local Law Enforcement Officials, Los Angeles, 21 March 1962.

163 Interview, Mortimer Caplin. IRS oral history interview with Mortimer M. Caplin (provided to the author by Professor Caplin).

164 Navasky, *Kennedy Justice,* p. 61.

165 In an interview, Louis Oberdorfer, the head of the tax division

under Kennedy, insisted that the decisional procedure regarding prosecution followed a separate and disinterested process. With regard to "cross-fertilization of case development" between the Organized Crime division and IRS leadership, this was clearly not the case.

166 See SAC, LA 92–113 to Director, 28 March 1962, NA.

167 Ibid.

168 C. A. Evans to Mr. Belmont, Subject: John Roselli (*sic*), 22 August 1962. Indication that the director himself was monitoring the surveillance is found in 92–3267 Director to SAC LA, 11 May 1962. "FURNISH BUREAU ADDITIONAL INFORMATION REGARDING NECESSITY OF RENTING APARTMENT EIGHT FOUR ONE, FOUNTAIN AVENUE, LOS ANGELES, TO INSURE THIS MATTER MAY BE PROPERLY EVALUATED."

169 Michael Hellerman (with Thomas C. Renner), *Wall Street Swindler* (Garden City, NY: Doubleday, 1977), p. 86.

170 *Washington Post*, 2 May 1976. Interviewed by HSCA investigator Gaeton Fonzi in 1977, Aleman reiterated his story as well as the fact that he had reported Trafficante's statement to the FBI. Trafficante, in testimony before the HSCA in 1978, conceded that he had met Aleman but denied that he had ever said Kennedy was going to get hit: "I might have told him he wasn't going to get reelected." Fonzi later observed that one factor weighing against the veracity of Aleman's allegation was his known association with the FBI during the period and Trafficante's customary discretion in terms of incriminating statements. Fonzi, *The Last Investigation*, pp. 256–57.

171 Davis, *Mafia Kingfish*, pp. 106–12, 209–15.

172 Interview, Powers.

173 Fletcher Knebel, "154 Hours on the Brink of War," *Look*, 12 November 1962.

174 Ibid.

175 Robert F. Kennedy, *Thirteen Days: A Memoir of the Cuban Missile Crisis* (New York: W. W. Norton, 1969), p. 23.

176 Interviews: Rusk, Nitze, Ball, O'Donnell.

177 Kennedy, *Thirteen Days*, p. 24.

178 McGeorge Bundy Memorandum to the President, 31 August 1962, National Security Files, JFKL.

179 RFK Memorandum (for the record), 11 September 1962, RFKP, JFKL.

180 Knebel, "154 Hours on the Brink of War."

181 Reference to Kennedy's exchange with Ambassador Dobrynin is contained on pp. 25–26 of *Thirteen Days*. The RFK-Georgi Bolshakov exchange can be found in Blight and Welch, *On The Brink*, p. 231.

182 Blight and Welch, *On The Brink*, pp. 236–48.

183 Richard Rovere in *The New Yorker* commented that the "war party in Washington" was as active as the jingoists of 1898. Cited in Schlesinger, *Robert Kennedy and His Times*, p. 545.

184 The invasion plan is set forth in Knebel, "154 Hours on the Brink of War."

185 Blight and Welch, *On the Brink*, p. 63.

186 Ibid., p. 49.

187 Cuban Missile Crisis Meetings, 16 October 1962, Presidential Recordings, JFKL.

188 Interview, O'Donnell.

189 Interview, Rusk.

190 Interview, Ball.

191 Kennedy, *Thirteen Days*, p. 33.

192 Blight and Welch, *On The Brink*, p. 201.

193 At the Hawk's Cay Conference, Ball, McNamara, and others discussed these conclusions. Blight and Welch, *On The Brink*, pp. 21–25.

194 Knebel, "154 Hours on the Brink of War."

195 At the Cambridge Conference, Khrushchev's former speech-writer Fyodor Burlatsky posed the question of why JFK did not confront Gromyko directly. The answer that McGeorge Bundy gave was: "We couldn't believe that Gromyko could be trusted to handle a private negotiation without going public on us because he had been assuring us in no uncertain terms for a long time that there were no offensive missiles in Cuba. Theodore Sorensen doubted that such a confrontation would have caused the missiles to be withdrawn." Blight and Welch, *On the Brink*, p. 246.

196 Cuban Missile Crisis Meetings, 17 October 1962, Presidential Recordings, JFKL.

197 Kennedy, *Thirteen Days*, pp. 38–39.

198 Dean Acheson, "Dean Acheson's Version of Robert Kennedy's Version of the Cuban Missile Crisis," *Esquire*, February 1969. Also Douglas Brinkley, *Dean Acheson: The Cold War Years, 1953–71* (New Haven: Yale University Press, 1992), pp. 160–61.

199 Schlesinger, *Robert Kennedy and His Times*, pp. 548–49, quoting Leonard C. Meeker's memorandum of discussion.

200 Kennedy, *Thirteen Days*, p. 44.

201 Schlesinger, *Robert Kennedy and His Times*, pp. 546–47. Ed Guthman's *We Band of Brothers* contains an interesting account of his highly confidential exchanges with RFK, pp. 118–28.

202 O'Donnell and Powers, *"Johnny We Hardly Knew Ye,"* p. 361.

203 Theodore C. Sorensen, *Kennedy,* (New York: Harper & Row, 1965), p. 705.

204 Blight and Welch, *On the Brink,* pp. 406–7.

205 Cuban Missile Crisis Meetings, 22 October 1962, Presidential Recordings, JFKL.

206 Blight and Welch, *On the Brink,* p. 246.

207 Ibid., p. 247. Shaknazarov, a former aide to Mikhail Gorbachev, spoke to several of the Soviet principals in the crisis, including Ambassador Dobrynin.

208 Kennedy, *Thirteen Days,* p. 62.

209 Interview, Harlech.

210 Graham T. Allison, "Conceptual Models and the Cuban Missile Crisis," *American Political Science Review* 63 (September 1969).

211 Quoted in Blight and Welch, *On the Brink,* p. 64.

212 Kennedy, *Thirteen Days,* p. 70.

213 Ibid., pp. 89–90.

214 Ball quoted in Blight and Welch, *On the Brink,* p. 49. Kennedy, *Thirteen Days,* p. 97.

215 Blight and Welch, *On the Brink,* p. 72.

216 Ibid., pp. 360–63.

217 The so-called Trollope Ploy is best discussed in Graham Allison, *Essence of Decision: Explaining the Cuban Missile Crisis* (Boston: Little, Brown, 1971). Also Schlesinger, *Robert Kennedy and His Times.*

218 Kennedy, *Thirteen Days,* p. 106.

219 The delicate balance RFK tried to strike was to confront Dobrynin with: 1) a deadline (9 A.M. Washington time, 3 P.M. Moscow time) along with a recitation of military contingencies that were possible if a commitment to withdraw the missiles was not made by Khrushchev; and 2) no categoric commitment that the United States would attack. The Soviet leadership may well have taken this as an ultimatum, although RFK later characterized it as "a statement of fact." See Blight and Welch, *On the Brink,* p. 264, and Kennedy, *Thirteen Days,* p. 108.

220 Kennedy, *Thirteen Days,* p. 130.

221 Guthman and Shulman, eds., *In His Own Words,* pp. 378–79.

222 Mario Lazo, *Dagger in the Heart: American Policy Failures in Cuba* (New York: Funk & Wagnalls, 1968), p. 378.

223 For a contemporaneous account filed by the FBI field office in Miami, see FBI Memorandum 105–1198, 20 January 1963, NA. Also Hinckle and Turner, *The Fish Is Red,* pp. 154–57.

224 Veciana's testimony, HSCA Report, 18 September 1978, NA.

225 Ibid., p. 132.

226 Hinckle and Turner, *The Fish Is Red*, pp. 15–52.

227 Interview, John Nolan. See also "Cuban Prisoner Release" oral histories of Joseph Dolan, John Nolan, Mitchell Rogovin, John Jones, Louis F. Oberdorfer, JFKL.

228 Interview, Nolan. Also oral history of John E. Nolan Jr., JFKL.

229 Interview, O'Donnell. O'Donnell and Powers, "*Johnny We Hardly Knew Ye*," pp. 312–13.

230 Ibid., p. 313. Guthman, *We Band of Brothers*, p. 136.

231 Confidential interview 11. In the course of the interview, the respondent (currently a Miami attorney) placed a call at the author's request for verification of his assertion that there had been an assassin in the Orange Bowl that day to a fellow veteran of the Bay of Pigs invasion. This individual, serving a twenty-year-sentence for narcotics trafficking, agreed to be interviewed the following day by phone. In the interview, he stated that it was "well-known that there was a hitter in the stadium." When asked if he knew the identity of the man, he said he did not. Confidential interview 19 with a Brigade 2506 veteran, wounded during the invasion and released in May 1962.

232 Miami Police Department, Intelligence Unit, initialed by Mary L. Gilbert, 3 January 1963. "Capt. Napier called this date, and stated that John Marshall of the U.S. Secret Service was anxious to find out some information concerning the following individual: A Cuban male, 25 yrs., 5'4", 135–155 lbs., strong muscular build, known only as CHINO." NA.

233 Quoted in *Time*, 4 January 1963.

234 Schlesinger, *Robert Kennedy and His Times*, p. 580.

Rendezvous: 1963

1 Bradlee, *A Good Life*, pp. 345–46.

2 Ibid., p. 346.

3 In *Case Closed*, Gerald Posner concedes the existence of two photos showing Ferrie and Oswald together at a Civil Air Patrol get-together in the middle 1950s, pp. 142–48.

4 This is the conclusion of the former chief counsel to the House Select Committee on Assassinations, G. Robert Blakey, and his co-author Richard N. Billings in *The Plot to Kill the President* (New York: Times Books, 1981), pp. 345–47.

5 Gaudet draft memo, undated, untitled, from HSCA files (declassified by the CIA), AA.

6 Five days after the assassination, Gaudet would telephone the local office of the FBI in New Orleans and tell Special Agent J. W. Miller that

Jack Ruby, the Mafia operative who had just killed Oswald, had been in New Orleans to purchase some paintings from an art gallery on Royal Street.

7 Summers, *Conspiracy*, p. 579.

8 Wadden indicated Rosselli's role in conversation with his former partner and head of the Justice Department's Organized Crime Division, William Hundley. Interview, Hundley.

9 See Cable 1539, 3 October 1963, describing "Oswald" at the Soviet embassy in Mexico City. HSCA, NA.

10 Quoted in Rappleye and Becker, *All-American Mafioso*, p. 236.

11 Lou Oberdorfer, the head of Justice's Tax Division, later defended the targeting of tax investigations and prosecutions by pointing out that the Tax Division wouldn't prosecute unless there were probability of victory. But in the field, the use of audits and investigations—as well as electronic bugs—against organized crime personalities was wide-ranging. Navasky, *Kennedy Justice*, pp. 58–59.

12 Roemer, *Man Against the Mob*, p. 249.

13 Attorney General's telephone log, 23 April 1963, General Files. RFKP, JFKL.

14 Quoted in Blakey and Billings, *The Plot to Kill the President*, pp. 239–40.

15 Interview, William Hundley. Confidential interviews 38, 42 (former officials in the FBI). Hundley remembered taking the report home and that his deputy Henry Petersen and Jack Miller, the head of the Criminal Division, also viewed copies of the report. He expressed strong doubt that either of them leaked the document and denied ever doing so himself.

16 Navasky, *Kennedy Justice*, p. 80.

17 But in a sense Bobby Kennedy was also to blame. Kennedy had pushed the FBI to use every means at its disposal to attack the mob. According to the testimony of retired agents who served in Chicago, Los Angeles, and Las Vegas, Kennedy had been informed in visits to those cities about electronic surveillance efforts. Although he later denied that he had ever "ordered" their use (and, bureaucratically speaking, he had not), he clearly knew of and countenanced the FBI's campaign to penetrate the mob's inner sanctums. In so doing, he had adopted Hoover's arrangement of "don't ask, don't tell." Victor Navasky has argued "that Robert Kennedy should have known but did not, that he should have asked but did not, that he is therefore chargeable with responsibility for the FBI's illegal privacy invasions."

18 Scheim, *Contract on America*, p. 107.

19 Rosselli was said to be furious at the description, possibly because the report of opulence would further spur the IRS or Kennedy's Justice Department, or perhaps because he sensed that the consequence of press attention would only complicate his multitiered life. Of all the places he worked—L.A., Miami, Chicago, D.C.—Las Vegas was the one that he alone had created; and the Desert Inn was his sanctum of pleasure, fellowship and seamlessly-administered diplomacy:

> Rosselli spends his leisure hours at the Desert Inn Country Club. He has breakfast there in the morning, seated at a table overlooking the eighteenth green. Between golf rounds, meals, steam baths, shaves and trims, Twisting, romancing and drinking, there is time for private little conferences at his favorite table with people seeking his counsel or friendship. It may be a newsman, a local politician, a casino owner, a prostitute, a famous entertainer, a deputy sheriff, a U.S. Senator, or the Governor of Nevada.

Ed Reid and Ovid Demaris, *The Green Felt Jungle* (New York: Trident Press, 1963), p. 191.

20 Interview, French.

21 Frank Ragano, *Mob Lawyer* (New York: Scribners, 1994), p. 144. Anthony and Robbyn Summers have revealed some holes in Ragano's account in "The Ghosts of November," *Vanity Fair*, December 1994, p. 112.

22 HSCA, Final Draft Report, p. 274. AA.

23 RFK also made a four-day trip (11–15 February 1963) to California, Arizona, New Mexico, and Texas, examining the nature of poverty in the United States. *New York Times*, 12 February 1963.

24 Kennedy testified in front of the Subcommittee on Labor of the House Committee on Education and Labor in May 1963. His testimony in the RFKP at JFKL is undated. See Robert F. Kennedy, *The Pursuit of Justice* (New York: Harper & Row, 1964), pp. 30–38.

25 O'Neil, *Life*, 26 January 1962.

26 Interview, Dolores Huerta. Also Schlesinger, *Robert Kennedy and His Times*, p. 852.

27 Remarks by Attorney General Robert F. Kennedy before the National Congress of American Indians, Bismarck, North Dakota, 13 September 1963, RFKP, JFKL.

28 Quoted in Thompson and Myers, *The Brother Within*, p. 24.

29 See Dictabelt Recordings, Civil Rights 1963, JFKL.

30 Interview, O'Brien.

31 Navasky, *Kennedy Justice*, p. 27.

32 Interview, Powers.

33 Guthman, *We Band of Brothers*, p. 232. Interview, Symington.

34 Interview, William P. Mahoney Jr. Mahoney was the American ambassador to Ghana and visited with the president on 19 November 1963.

35 Martin Luther King called the speech "a hallmark in the annals of American history." President Kwame Nkrumah of Ghana read passages of the speech to an aide, his voice breaking. Thirty-six percent of Americans interviewed on 16 June 1963 by the Gallup organization thought President Kennedy was advancing civil rights "too fast"; 32 percent thought "about right"; and 18 percent "not fast enough." From March to June 1963, Kennedy's approval rating in the South fell from 60 percent to 33 percent.

36 Quoted in Schlesinger, *Robert Kennedy and His Times*, p. 370.

37 Sorensen, *Kennedy*, p. 494.

38 Wofford, *Of Kennedys and Kings*, p. 160.

39 Quoted in Carl M. Brauer, *John F. Kennedy and the Second Reconstruction*, p. 10.

40 Quoted in Navasky, *Kennedy Justice*, p. 103.

41 Ibid., p. 107.

42 John F. Kennedy, *Profiles in Courage* (illustrated edition) (New York: Black Dog & Leventhal, 1998), p. 42.

43 Carl M. Brauer, *John F. Kennedy and the Second Reconstruction* (New York: Columbia University Press, 1977), p. 153.

44 Juan Williams, *Eyes on the Prize: America's Civil Rights Years, 1954–1965* (New York: Viking, 1987), pp. 181–82.

45 Ibid., p. 186.

46 See "Letter from a Birmingham Jail," reprinted in Williams, *Eyes on the Prize*, pp. 187–89.

47 Guthman and Shulman, *In His Own Words*, pp. 185–86.

48 See transcript of conversation between Attorney General Robert Kennedy and Governor Wallace, Montgomery, Alabama, 25 September 1963, RFKP, JFKL.

49 Quoted in Navasky, *Kennedy Justice*, p. 218.

50 Taped conversation, 12 May 1963, Participants: JFK, RFK, Marshall, McNamara, Wheeler, Salinger, Katzenbach, "Civil Rights—Birmingham," Item 86.2, JFKL.

51 Guthman and Shulman, *In His Own Words*, p. 181.

52 Stein and Plimpton, *American Journey*, pp. 120–21.

53 Schlesinger, *A Thousand Days*, p. 963.

54 Guthman and Shulman, eds., *In His Own Words*, pp. 189–90.

55 Interview, Harriman. The author also interviewed Carl Kaysen, Bundy's deputy, who was part of the American negotiating team, as well as William R. Tyler, Assistant Secretary of State for European Affairs.

56 Joseph Kraft, *Profiles in Power* (New York: New American Library, 1966), p. 28.

57 This judgment is drawn from interviews with British ambassador Ormsby-Gore as well as Kenny O'Donnell.

58 This exchange took place at the meeting between the president and congressional leaders at 5 P.M. on 22 October 1962. *New York Times*, 5 October 1997.

59 Allison, "Conceptual Models and the Cuban Missile Crisis," *American Political Science Association*, September 1969.

60 Interview, Ormsby-Gore.

61 Mahoney, *JFK: Ordeal in Africa*, p. 156.

62 Interview, J. Wayne Fredericks.

63 Schlesinger, *A Thousand Days*, p. 248.

64 Ibid., pp. 752–53.

65 Hinckle and Turner, *The Fish Is Red*, p. 161.

66 Russell, *The Man Who Knew Too Much*, p. 373

67 Schlesinger, *A Thousand Days*, pp. 724–25.

68 Ambassador Ormsby-Gore's characterization of the president's thinking.

69 Interview, O'Donnell.

70 See Summers, *Official and Confidential*, pp. 306–9.

71 Schlesinger, *A Thousand Days*, p. 911.

72 Interview, Harriman. The former governor requested that this and other comments not be attributed to him "until the appropriate time." He died in 1986.

73 Anderson, *Jack and Jackie*, pp. 347–48.

74 Ibid., p. 326.

75 The Kennedy Library contains 11 hours of White House dictabelt recordings from July through September 1963.

76 Interview, Powers.

77 Anderson, *Jack and Jackie*, p. 353.

78 O'Donnell and Powers, *"Johnny We Hardly Knew Ye,"* pp. 430–31.

79 Quoted in Russell, *The Man Who Knew Too Much*, p. 434.

80 Interview, Bundy.

81 McGeorge Bundy Memorandum for the President, "Further Organization of the Government in Dealing with Cuba," 4 January 1963, NSF, JFKL.

82 Corn, *Blond Ghost*, pp. 96–97.

83 Interviews, Casares, Recarey.

84 "Maximum Covert Action Program," Standing Group Minutes, 18 April 1963, HSCA. Also in attendance were McGeorge Bundy, Maxwell Taylor, John McCone, Roswell Gilpatric, Edward R. Murrow, and Harvey's replacement, Desmond Fitzgerald.

85 See SN Memorandum to the Attorney General, 5 July 1963, RFKP, JFKL.

86 See FBI Memorandum, RE: Anti-Fidel Castro Activities Internal Security, 105–1742, 19 July 1963, HSCA, AA.

87 As quoted in Schlesinger, *Robert Kennedy and His Times*, pp. 580–81.

88 "U.S.-Cuba Relations, 1960–63: Neutrality Enforcement and the Cuban Exiles During the Kennedy Administration," Congressional Research Service, p. 12.

89 Ibid., p. 71.

90 See Gaeton Fonzi, *The Last Investigation* (New York: Thunder's Mouth Press, 1993), pp. 53–59.

91 Hinckle and Turner, *The Fish Is Red*, p. 164.

92 Quoted in Schlesinger, *Robert Kennedy and His Times*, p. 585.

93 Ayers, *The War That Never Was*, pp. 147–48. Arthur Schlesinger Jr. disputes this story on the grounds that the attorney general's schedule book shows no Florida trips between April 27 and November 28, 1963. Kennedy's schedule book, however, represents only a partial record of his appointments and trips.

94 Quoted in Russell, *The Man Who Knew Too Much*, pp. 299–300.

95 Testimony of William Harvey before the HSCA, p. 68. Also see William Harvey, "Short Chronology from the Report of the Inspector General of the CIA," Top Secret, HSCA.

96 Mason Cargill Memorandum to the File, Subject: Project ZR/RIFLE and QJ/WIN, 30 April 1975, Commission on CIA Activities in the United States, HSCA.

97 Report of the Inspector General of the CIA, 1967, HSCA, AA.

98 Interview, Shimon.

99 The FBI's CIA liaison, Sam Papich, reported the meeting to Director Hoover. Harvey contacted Papich to ask that he be informed if Hoover told CIA director McCone. Hoover did not.

100 Mason Cargill Memorandum to the File, Subject: Project ZR/RIFLE and QJ/WIN, 30 April 1975, HSCA.

101 For a description of Harold "Happy" Meltzer, see Ed Reid, *The*

Anatomy of Organized Crime in America: The Grim Reapers (Chicago: Regnery, 1969), pp. 291–92.

102 Joseph W. Shimon, FBI statement, 8 September 1976, Rosselli file, AA; interview, Shimon.

103 This account is drawn from Staff Summary of FBI file for Paulino Sierra Martinez, HSCA. Also HSCA Staff Summary of CIA file, n.d.

104 *Miami News*, 19 May 1963.

105 HSCA Staff Summary of CIA Handbook, Secret.

106 Staff Summary for Carlos Quesada, Ref. FBI Report #105–1210–31, 28 January 1964.

107 FBI memorandum from Miami, 14 November 1963, HSCA.

108 Re: Richard Cain, undated FBI teletype, Chicago Crime Commission files.

109 See HSCA Staff Summary Re: "Richard Cain Information." The $200,000 donation was provided by a "confidential informant" of the FBI in July 1963.

110 See FBI memorandum, 2 November 1963, from Miami. Also Staff Summary of CIA File, HSCA.

111 In the course of its investigation into Paulino Sierra in 1978, the HSCA staff investigated Rogelio Cisneros, who admitted in 1964 that he had visited Silvia Odio, the daughter of a prominent anti-Castro exile in Dallas during the summer of 1963. Odio later told the FBI and the HSCA, in a widely accepted account, that she was visited in September by two Hispanic men and a "Leon Oswald." On that trip, Hall, who had served time with John Martino and Santos Trafficante in La Cabana prison in Cuba, and Lawrence Howard were driving from Los Angeles to Miami with a trailerload of arms that they later said they had to leave in Dallas for lack of a hiding place in Florida.

112 *Times-Picayune*, 1 August 1963. Also, Hinckle and Turner, *The Fish Is Red*, pp. 199–200.

113 HSCA Staff Summary of FBI file as well as the CIA file.

114 See footnote 42, at pp. 340–50, that reports Hall's commentary to authors Hinckle and Turner in *The Fish Is Red*. In 1977, Hall testified on condition of immunity from prosecution. In a taped interview that same year, he stated: "As it stands right now, there's only two of us left alive—that's me and Santos Trafficante. And as far as I am concerned we're both going to stay alive—because I ain't gonna say shit." Quoted in Anthony and Robbyn Sommers, "The Ghosts of November," *Vanity Fair*, December 1994, p. 112.

115 The author's efforts in Cuba in May–June 1997 to determine what happened to Bayo and his fellow raiders turned up nothing but

hearsay reports that they had all been killed in a firefight with Castro forces.

116 Ruby's trips to New Orleans, Miami, and probably Las Vegas and Ruby's long-distance calls to Mafia hitmen like Russell Matthews, Lewis McWillie, and Barney Baker (who also worked for Hoffa), as well as his contacts with Mafia chieftains like Irwin Weiner and Nofio Pecora, are detailed in Scheim, *Contract on America*, pp. 215–30.

117 William Scott Malone, "The Secret Life of Jack Ruby," New Times, 23 January 1978.

118 Schlesinger, *A Thousand Days*, p. 1015.

119 Stewart Udall, unpublished ms., "A Memoir of John F. Kennedy and Robert Frost's Odyssey of Poetry and Power," Udall file on Frost and Amherst dedication.

120 Udall, "Robert Frost's Last Adventure," *New York Times Magazine*, 11 June 1972.

121 Ibid.

122 Schlesinger, *A Thousand Days*, p. 1015.

123 Interview, Udall.

124 A photocopy of the president's reworked text is in Udall's file of the trip.

125 Archibald MacLeish, *A Continuing Journey*, pp. 299–306.

126 President Kennedy, annotated, interlineated speech draft, Udall file on Frost and Amherst dedication.

127 Summers, *Official and Confidential*, pp. 309–12.

128 In an interview for the Kennedy Library in March, April, and May 1964 with John Bartlow Martin, RFK said: "Basically [Korth] had an exchange in correspondence with a bank about taking customers of his out on the *Sequoia* (which is a U.S. Navy boat) in order to help the bank get customers. He was taking an interest in which the bank had an interest." Guthman and Shulman, *In His Own Words*, p. 372. Kennedy then contended that the TFX scandal—involving the awarding of a $6.5 billion contract to the General Dynamic Corporation to build the TFX jet fighter—and Korth's firing were unrelated. For an alternative view, see Russell, *The Man Who Knew Too Much*, p. 523.

129 RFK later said, "John McClellan was looking for a scandal. . . . Our relationship with McClellan deteriorated very badly during this period of time, and I had a bitter exchange with Jerry Adlerman [chief counsel, Senate Permanent Subcommittee on Investigations]." Guthman and Shulman, *In His Own Words*, p. 371.

130 Demaris, *Captive City*, p. 227.

131 See Mr. Belmont to C.A. Evans Memorandum, Subject: John Roselli (*sic*), 22 August 1963.

132 Special Investigation Division, FBI memorandum of 4 November 1963.

133 Guthman and Shulman, *In His Own Words*, p. 130.

134 Summers, *Official and Confidential*, pp. 312–13.

135 Interviews, Harriman, Ball, Bundy, Rusk. Ball's transcribed phone conversations reveal the apparently accurate rumor that Harriman might be demoted by the president, a possibility Robert Kennedy opposed.

136 Schlesinger, *Robert Kennedy and His Times*, p. 770.

137 Quoted in Roger Hilsman, *To Move a Nation* (Garden City, NY: Doubleday, 1967), p. 501.

138 The memorandum, written by Bundy's aide Michael Y. Forrestal, is dated 26 April 1962. *New York Times*, 5 December 1998.

139 See Douglas Brinkley, *Dean Acheson: The Cold War Years, 1953– 71* (New Haven: Yale University Press, 1992), p. 174.

140 George Ball, *The Past Has Another Pattern* (New York: W. W. Norton, 1982), p. 312.

141 Ronald Steel, *Walter Lippmann and the American Century* (Boston: Little, Brown, 1980), p. 280.

142 Guthman and Shulman, *In His Own Words*, p. 404.

143 Maxwell Taylor, *Swords Into Plowshares* (New York: W. W. Norton, 1972), p. 301.

144 See chapter "January 18, 1961, Léopoldville, The Congo."

145 Schlesinger, *A Thousand Days*, p. 98.

146 Interview, Samuel E. Belk III. The date was 5 October 1963. The National Security Council meeting was supposed to adjourn at 10:45 A.M. but the president's scheduled meeting thereafter with U.S. ambassador to France Charles "Chip" Bohlen was canceled and the NSC meeting continued in the Rose Garden.

147 Manchester, *One Brief Shining Moment*, p. 86.

148 Interview, Powers.

149 Fletcher Knebel, "Kennedy vs. the Press," *Look*, 26 August 1962.

150 Manchester, *Death of a President*, pp. 37–39.

151 Davis, *Mafia Kingfish*, pp. 172–73. The HSCA reached a similar conclusion about Marcello's and Ferrie's weekend together.

152 Rappleye and Becker in *All-American Mafioso*, p. 245, detail Rosselli's connections.

153 Rosselli's Phoenix trip is fully set forth in FBI LA telexes to HQs 92–113, 92–446, 21 November 1963.

154 Manchester, *One Brief Shining Moment*, pp. 259–60.

155 Helms, Remarks at Donovan Award Dinner, 24 May 1983. Quoted in Ranelagh, *The Agency*, p. 416.

156 Helms's testimony is found on p. 91 of the Church Committee's Interim Report: "Alleged Assassination Plots Involving Foreign Leaders."

157 Corn, *Blond Ghost*, pp. 105–6.

158 Interview, Ricardo Alarcon.

159 Jean Daniel, *Le Temps Qui Reste* (Paris: Gallimard, 1984), pp. 201–08.

160 Davis, *Mafia Kingfish*, pp. 175–76.

161 Manchester, *Death of a President*, p. 17.

162 O'Donnell and Powers, *"Johnny We Hardly Knew Ye,"* pp. 18–19. Interview, O'Donnell.

163 Robert MacNeil, *The Right Place at the Right Time* (Thorndike, ME: Thorndike Press, 1982), p. 200.

164 Quoting O'Donnell in Blakey and Billings, *The Plot to Kill the President*, p. 7. Interview, O'Donnell.

165 Ibid., p.26.

166 Manchester, *Death of a President*, p. 121.

167 Scheim, *Contract on America*, pp. 22–23.

168 Davis, *Mafia Kingfish*, p. 177.

169 Jim Marrs, *Crossfire: The Plot that Killed Kennedy* (New York: Carroll & Graf, 1989), p. 133.

170 O'Donnell and Powers, *"Johnny We Hardly Knew Ye,"* p. 29.

171 Andersen, *Jack and Jackie*, p. 365.

172 Jim Marrs, *Crossfire*, pp. 333–37. Gerald Posner disputes the claim that Harrelson was one of the tramps in *Case Closed: Lee Harvey Oswald and the Assassination of JFK* (New York: Random House, 1993), p. 465.

173 Josiah Thompson, *Six Seconds in Dallas* (New York: B. Geiss Associates, 1967), p. 122.

174 House Assassination Hearings, U.S. Congress, Select Committee on Assassinations, p. 556.

175 This account is taken from Manchester, *Death of a President*, pp. 195–97.

176 Ibid., p. 259.

177 Oral history of Walter Sheridan, RFKP, JFKL.

178 Summers and Summers, "The Ghosts of November."

179 *Fort Worth Star-Telegram*, 7 December 1977.

180 Ibid., p. 387.

181 Manchester, *Death of a President*, pp. 391–92.

182 Quoted in ibid., p. 646.

183 Oral history of Charles Spalding, JFKL.

184 Interview, Udall.

185 See FBI memorandum to Director 92–113, 28 January 1964, HSCA, AA; Rappleye and Becker, *All-American Mafioso*, pp. 249–50.

186 Manchester, *Death of a President*, p. 372–73.

Bobby Alone: 1964–1968

1 William vanden Heuvel and Milton Gwirtzman, *On His Own: Robert F. Kennedy 1964–68* (Garden City, NY: Doubleday, 1970), pp. 43–44. At Columbia University, Kennedy said, "As I said when I was asked this question in Poland, I agree with the conclusion of the report that the man they identified was the man, that he acted on his own, and that he was not motivated by Communist ideology."

2 Guthman, *We Band of Brothers*, p. 244.

3 Interview, Powers.

4 Collier and Horowitz, *The Kennedys*, p. 315.

5 Interview, O'Donnell.

6 Interview, Dungan.

7 Jeff Shesol, *Mutual Contempt* (New York: W. W. Norton, 1997), p. 131.

8 Schlesinger, *Robert Kennedy and His Times*, p. 664.

9 "A torrent of prejudicial information about Oswald started to flow within hours of the assassination," Anthony and Robbyn Summers have written. ("Ghosts of November"). Clare Boothe Luce got a late-night call on 22 November from one of her anti-Castro Cuban "boys" in New Orleans. He claimed that the DRE (Directorio Revolucionario Estudiantil) had "penetrated" Oswald's organization and had actually tape-recorded Oswald saying he was "the greatest shot in the world with a telescopic rifle." Luce later said that she told him to turn over everything to the FBI. Then there was the matter of linking Oswald to the murder weapon. On 23 November at 4 A.M. CST, executives at Klein's Sporting Goods in Chicago discovered the American Rifleman coupon with which Oswald had allegedly ordered the Mannlicher-Carcano, number C2766. CIA files from the Assassination Archives reveal that the first lead as to the location of the rifle came from the chief investigator of the Cook County Sheriff's Office, Richard Cain, a Rosselli-Giancana confederate who had been involved in the first plot to hit Castro.

According to John V. Martino, Oswald had been "put together" by "anti-Castro types. . . . Oswald didn't know who he was working for. . . . He was to meet his contact at the Texas Theatre [the movie house where he was arrested]. . . . They were to meet Oswald in the theater and get him out of the country, then eliminate him. Oswald made a mistake. There was no way we could get to him. They had Ruby kill him." Martino told his wife after the assassination, "When they went to the theater and got Oswald, they blew it. . . . There was a Cuban in there. They let him come out. They let the guy go, the other trigger." This conforms with what Johnny Rosselli told columnist Jack Anderson in 1967: "When Oswald was picked up, the underworld conspirators feared he would crack and disclose information that might lead to them. This almost certainly would have brought a massive U.S. crackdown on the Mafia. So Jack Ruby was ordered to eliminate Oswald."

But what of the role of certain CIA agents in creating Oswald as a "cut-out"? As Summers and others have demonstrated, the orchestration of Oswald's trip to Mexico, his encounters in the Cuban embassy and over the phone with a top KGB officer in the Russian embassy, his receipt of $5,000 from a "Negro with reddish hair" to kill the president—all false or fabricated contentions—reveal a pattern of manipulation by agents and operatives in the CIA station in Mexico City.

After Oswald's execution on 24 November, the Mexico City CIA cabled something new and explosive to Washington: that one Gilberto Policarpo Lopez, a U.S. passport holder who had crossed into Mexico via Laredo on 23 November, had "a probable role" in the Kennedy assassination. The source for this allegation was a Covert American Source (CAS) in Mexico's *Gobernacion* ministry (which coordinated federal order and internal security). No less than eight cables followed, building up the story. On 27 November, Lopez had supposedly boarded Cubana flight #465 for Havana as the only passenger on the plane. The CIA station had procured a photo of the suspect as well as his passport number—310162—and alleged that Lopez was known in the Los Angeles area as a pro-Castro activist. At a time when everyone in Washington had already settled on the lone assassin theory to bring a quick closure to the Kennedy killing, the CIA shop in Mexico was alleging that a "suspect" had escaped to Cuba. If the story took, the sequel would be either a public or private ultimatum to Castro to hand over Lopez or face American retaliation. It might result in what David Phillips, David Morales, and Bill Harvey and the thousands of anti-Castro fighters in their train had demanded: a second invasion of Cuba, this one led by the United States.

10 The transcript of the interview is in attorney general files, RFKP.

11 Quoted in Summers, *Official and Confidential*, p. 314.

12 Shesol, *Mutual Contempt*, p. 332.

13 Oral history, Milton Gwirtzman, JFKL.

14 Shesol, *Mutual Contempt*.

15 Interview, Pierre Salinger. Salinger, along with Ralph Dungan, was also on the receiving end of the "divine retribution" communication.

16 Quoted in Schlesinger, *Robert Kennedy and His Times*, p. 723.

17 Guthman, *We Band of Brothers*, p. 294.

18 Quoted in Schlesinger, *Robert Kennedy and His Times*, p. 721.

19 Collier and Horowitz, *The Kennedys*, p. 339.

20 Guthman, *We Band of Brothers*, pp. 306–7.

21 Quoted in a compilation of RFK statements, "1964," Mankiewicz Papers, JFKL.

22 Quoted in Stein and Plimpton, *American Journey*, p. 182.

23 This account is based on James W. Whittaker, "The First Ascent," *National Geographic*, July 1967. Besides Whittaker and Kennedy, the other climbers were: Dee Molenaar, William N. Prather, James Craig, George R. Senner, Barry W. Prather, and William A. Allard. See also coverage of the *Whitehorse Star*, 12–26 March 1967.

24 Stein and Plimpton, *American Journey*, pp. 172–75.

25 Collier and Horowitz, *The Kennedys*, pp. 339–40.

26 Stein and Plimpton, *American Journey*, p. 36.

27 See Susan Ferriss and Ricardo Sandoval, *The Fight in the Fields: Cesar Chavez and the Farmworkers Movement* (New York: Harcourt Brace, 1997), pp. 140–49.

28 Jacques Levy, *Cesar Chavez: Autobiography of La Causa* (New York: W. W. Norton, 1975), pp. 215–16.

29 Ferriss and Sandoval, *The Fight in the Fields*, pp. 116–17.

30 Oral history, Cesar Chavez, JFKL.

31 Oral history, Chavez.

32 Interview, Chavez.

33 Interview, Huerta.

34 Stein and Plimpton, *American Journey*, p. 284.

35 Ibid., p. 182.

36 Schlesinger, *Robert Kennedy and His Times*, p. 839.

37 Jack Newfield, *Robert F. Kennedy: A Memoir* (New York: Berkeley, 1978), p. 96.

38 Tom Johnston's papers at the JFKL contain as complete a documentary archive as there is on the Bedford-Stuyvesant project. Also Newfield's chapter in *Robert Kennedy*, pp. 87–109.

39 E. J. Dionne, *Why Americans Hate Politics* (New York: Simon and Schuster, 1991), pp. 31–54.

40 David Halberstam, *The Unfinished Odyssey of Robert Kennedy* (New York: Random House, 1968), p. 177.

41 Newfield, *Robert Kennedy*, p. 22.

42 Quoted in vanden Heuvel and Gwirtzman, *On His Own*, p. 99.

43 Schlesinger, *Robert Kennedy and His Times*, p. 855.

44 Ibid., pp. 861–62.

45 Interview, Novello.

46 Goodwin, *Remembering America*, p. 224.

47 Schlesinger, *Robert Kennedy and His Times*, p. 802.

48 Goodwin, *Remembering America*, p. 442.

49 Oral history, Walinsky. See also Papers of Adam Walinsky, JFKL.

50 Oral history, Allard Lowenstein, JFKL.

51 Quoted in vanden Heuvel and Gwirtzman, *On His Own*, p. 152.

52 The speech text is contained in the Walinsky Papers, JFKL.

53 Telex from Usemb Pretoria 3958, 10 June 1966, National Security Files, LBJL.

54 Robert F. Kennedy, "Suppose God Is Black," *Look*, 23 August 1966.

55 Kennedy later ventured that the Japanese had achieved honorary white status because South Africa traded heavily with Japan.

56 Robert F. Kennedy, "Suppose God Is Black," *Look*, 23 August 1966.

57 Senator Robert F. Kennedy, Day of Affirmation address, University of Cape Town, 6 June 1966, Walinsky Papers, JFKL.

58 Vanden Heuvel and Gwirtzman, *On His Own*, p. 152.

59 Kennedy's South African schedule can be found in the Walinsky Papers, JFKL.

60 Oral history, Walinsky.

61 Kennedy, "Suppose God Is Black."

62 This is the recollection of Lucy Jarvis, NBC producer, in Plimpton and Stein, *American Journey*, p. 156.

63 Quoted in Schlesinger, *Robert Kennedy and His Times*, p. 806.

64 *Johannesburg Star*, 11 June 1966.

65 Shesol, *Mutual Contempt*, p. 302.

66 Plimpton and Stein, *American Journey*, pp. 155–56.

67 vanden Heuvel and Gwirtzman, *On His Own*, p. 160.

68 The Aeschylus quote is from *Agamemnon*. Edith Hamilton, *The Greek Way* (New York: Aeonian Press, 1964), p. 156.

69 *New York Times*, 3 November 1966. The balance of this account is taken from Jack Newfield, *Robert Kennedy: A Memoir*, pp. 25–27.

70 Shesol, *Mutual Contempt*, pp. 365–66.

71 Recordings of Telephone Conversations, JFK Series, Tape K67.02, LBJL. In his account, historian Shesol characterizes Johnson's reference to "a man that was involved (in the JFK assassination)." But it is more probable that Johnson was referring to Rosselli's role in the CIA-Mafia plot against Castro (p. 132).

72 "Washington Merry-Go-Round," *Washington Post*, 3 March 1967.

73 Shesol, *Mutual Contempt*, p. 351.

74 Copies of the complaints and motion filings are contained in the Mankiewicz Papers, JFKL.

75 *New York Times*, 11 December 1966. Also *U.S. News and World Report*, 11 July 1966

76 Mankiewicz's files contain a seven-page internal question-and-answer document designed to get the story straight.

77 *New York Times*, 1 January 1967.

78 Quoted in Shesol, *Mutual Contempt*, p. 352.

79 *Newsweek*, 26 December 1966.

80 Goodwin, *Remembering America*, pp. 403–5.

81 Rappleye and Becker, *All-American Mafioso*, p. 268.

82 Fonzi, *The Last Investigation*, p. 31.

83 Rappleye and Becker, *All-American Mafioso*, p. 269.

84 Shesol, *Mutual Contempt*, p. 132.

85 Ibid., Tape K67.02.

86 Davis, *Mafia Kingfish*, pp. 332–34.

87 Recording of conversation with Gov. John Connally, Tape K67.02, LBJL.

88 FBI Memorandum, Assassination of President John F. Kennedy, 21 March 1967, AA.

89 Leo Janos, "The Last Days of the President," *Atlantic Monthly*, July 1973.

90 Rappleye and Becker, *All-American Mafioso*, p. 272.

91 CIA Inspector General's Report, 1967, quoted in internal memo of HSCA staff investigation, p. 18, AA.

92 Davis, *Mafia Kingfish*, p. 335.

93 Interview, O'Donnell.

94 *New York Times*, 17 March 1968.

95 George Ball, *The Past Has Another Pattern* (New York: W. W.

Norton, 1982); J. William Fulbright, *The Arrogance of Power* (New York: Random House, 1966).

96 Newfield, *Robert Kennedy*, pp. 56–57.

97 vanden Heuvel and Gwirtzman, *On His Own*, p. 180.

98 See Myra MacPherson's portrait of RFK in the *New York Times*, 20 April 1968.

99 Ibid., p. 53.

100 Guthman, *We Band of Brothers*, p. 326.

101 Ferriss and Sandoval, *The Fight in the Fields*, p. 141.

102 Levy, *Cesar Chavez*, p. 272.

103 Ferriss and Sandoval, *The Fight in the Fields*, p. 142; and Levy, *Cesar Chavez*, pp. 272–87.

104 Peter Matthiessen, *Sal Si Puedes: Cesar Chavez and the New American Revolution* (New York: Random House, 1969), p. 173.

105 Schlesinger, *Robert Kennedy and His Times*, p. 852.

106 Levy, *Cesar Chavez*, p. 196.

107 This is Chavez's characterization of his options in conversation with the author in September 1975.

108 Stein and Plimpton, *American Journey*, p. 283.

109 Oral history, Chavez, JFKL.

110 Stein and Plimpton, *American Journey*, p. 282.

111 Ibid., p. 283.

112 Levy, *Cesar Chavez*, pp. 286–87.

113 Quoted in Guthman, *We Band of Brothers*, p. 326.

114 Oral history, Chavez, JFKL.

115 Ibid.

116 Huerta quoted in Stein and Plimpton, *American Journey*, p. 282.

117 Ibid.

118 Levy, *Cesar Chavez*, p. 287.

119 Oral history, Edelman, JFKL.

120 Oral history, Chavez, JFKL.

121 Schlesinger, *Robert Kennedy and His Times*, p. 921.

122 Davis, *Mafia Kingfish*, p. 345.

123 William C. Sullivan, *The Bureau: My Thirty Years in Hoover's FBI* (New York: W. W. Norton, 1979), p. 56.

124 Interview, Huerta. Bill Barry did accompany Kennedy on the way down the elevator that night. Huerta's point was that there was no security detail, ahead of and around Kennedy, and that he moved freely without interposition.

125 Stein and Plimpton, *American Journey*, p. 284.

126 Interview, Kit Christofferson.

127 *Los Angeles Times*, 25 March 1968.

128 See "Reaction to Bobby," *Time*, 5 April 1968.

129 vanden Heuvel and Gwirtzman, *On His Own*, p. 316.

130 Newfield, *Robert Kennedy*, p. 233.

131 *New York Times*, 19 March 1968.

132 *Los Angeles Times*, 25 March 1968.

133 Ibid.

134 Schlesinger, *Robert Kennedy and His Times*, p. 929.

135 *New York Times*, 19 March 1968.

136 Doris Kearns, *Lyndon Johnson and the American Dream* (New York: Harper & Row, 1976), pp. 342–43.

137 vanden Heuvel and Gwirtzman, *On His Own*, p. 318.

138 See the oral history of David Hackett for a commentary on the interaction of the contending groups around RFK, JFKL.

139 Oral history of Milton Gwirtzman, JFKL.

140 *New York Times*, 30 March 1968.

141 Interview, William P. Mahoney Jr. See also the *New York Times*, 30 March 1968.

142 Newfield incorrectly attributes RFK's remark to criticism of local supporters when in fact it was in reaction to national staff. Newfield, *Robert Kennedy*, p. 242.

143 *Los Angeles Times*, 30 March 1968.

144 The author, age sixteen, attended the dinner.

145 The account is in *The New Yorker*, 15 June 1968.

146 Shesol, *Mutual Contempt*, pp. 442–43.

147 *New York Times*, 31 March 1968.

148 Halberstam, *The Unfinished Odyssey of Robert Kennedy*, pp. 166–68.

149 *New York Times*, 29 March 1968. Lowell wrote that he supported McCarthy "because of his lack of negative qualities: lack of excessive charisma, driving ambition, machinelike drive and the too great wish to be President." *New Republic*, 13 April 1968.

150 Stein and Plimpton, *American Journey*, pp. 236–37.

151 Schlesinger, *Robert Kennedy and His Times*, p. 939.

152 The speech is contained in the Mankiewicz Papers, JFKL, Box 22.

153 Stein and Plimpton, *American Journey*, p. 258.

154 The final speech text as well as the drafts are contained in the Walinsky Papers, JFKL.

155 *The New Yorker*, 15 June 1968.

156 Schlesinger, *Robert Kennedy and His Times*, p. 934.

157 Victor S. Navasky, "The Haunting of Robert Kennedy," *New York Times* Magazine, 2 June 1968.

158 Interview, Oberdorfer.

159 Stein and Plimpton, *American Journey*, p. 248.

160 Ibid., p. 249.

161 Newfield, *Robert Kennedy*, p. 256.

162 See *Newsweek*, 20 May 1968, for coverage of this incident.

163 Schlesinger, *Robert Kennedy and His Times*, p. 953.

164 Interview, Sam Vagenas; Newfield, *Robert Kennedy*, p. 260.

165 Goodwin, *Remembering America*, p. 529.

166 Kennedy spent between $700,000 and $1 million in the Indiana primary.

167 Vanden Heuvel and Gwirtzman demonstrate that RFK may not have persuaded white ethnics in Lake County, *On His Own*, p. 349.

168 The Mankiewicz Papers at the JFKL contain the campaign response as well as the clippings regarding the flap.

169 Newfield, *Robert Kennedy*, p. 271.

170 Stein and Plimpton, *American Journey*, pp. 323–24.

171 See Robert F. Kennedy Chronology prepared by Frank Mankiewicz and contained in the Mankiewicz Papers, JFKL.

172 Stein and Plimpton, *American Journey*, p. 299.

173 *The New Republic*, 20 June 1968.

174 *Newsweek*, 17 June 1968.

175 Stein and Plimpton, *American Journey*, p. 293.

176 Scheim, *Contract on America*, p. 276.

177 Robert Blair Kaiser, *RFK Must Die! A History of the Robert Kennedy Assassination and Its Aftermath* (New York: Dutton, 1970), p. 469.

178 *Newsweek*, 17 June 1968.

179 Goodwin, *Remembering America*, p. 559.

180 Stein and Plimpton, *American Journey*, p. 334.

181 Scheim, *Contract on America*, p. 276. The *France-Soir* reporter on the scene described Cesar as drawing his weapon and firing it. *France-Soir*, 6 June 1968, pp. 1–2.

182 The reporter from *France-Soir*, 6 June 1968, indicated that Kennedy said twice, "J'ai mal" (I'm hurt). Charles Quinn reported Kennedy saying, "No, no, no," in Stein and Plimpton, *American Journey*, p. 337. Goodwin describes his final phrase, "Jack, Jack," in *Remembering America*, p. 558.

Index